STABILITY
AND
SOCIAL CHANGE

A VOLUME
IN HONOR OF

TALCOTT PARSONS

STABILITY
AND
SOCIAL CHANGE

EDITED BY

Bernard Barber
COLUMBIA UNIVERSITY

Alex Inkeles
STANFORD UNIVERSITY

LITTLE, BROWN AND COMPANY
Boston

CONTENTS

INTRODUCTION 1
Bernard Barber and Alex Inkeles

SOCIAL STRUCTURE

STABILITY, INSTABILITY, AND THE ANALYSIS
OF POLITICAL CORRUPTION 7
Neil J. Smelser

STABILITY AND CHANGE IN THE MEDICAL SYSTEM: MEDICINE IN
THE INDUSTRIAL SOCIETY 30
Mark G. Field

CONTINUITIES AND CHANGES IN SYSTEMS OF STRATIFICATION 61
S. N. Eisenstadt

AMERICAN SCHOOLING: PATTERNS AND PROCESSES
OF STABILITY AND CHANGE 82
Robert Dreeben

CULTURE

CHANGE AND STABILITY IN VALUES AND VALUE SYSTEMS 123
Robin M. Williams, Jr.

STABILITY AND CHANGE AND THE DUAL ROLE OF RELIGION   160
Thomas F. O'Dea

STABILITY AND CHANGE IN LEGAL SYSTEMS   187
Leon H. Mayhew

FROM PERIPHERY TO CENTER: THE CHANGING PLACE OF
INTELLECTUALS IN AMERICAN SOCIETY   211
Edward Shils

FUNCTION, VARIABILITY, AND CHANGE IN IDEOLOGICAL SYSTEMS   244
Bernard Barber

SOCIAL STRUCTURE, CULTURE, AND PERSONALITY

CONTINUITY AND CHANGE IN THE INTERACTION OF THE PERSONAL
AND THE SOCIOCULTURAL SYSTEMS   265
Alex Inkeles

DEVIANCE AND SOCIAL PROBLEMS

STABILITY AND CHANGE IN DEVIANCE   285
Albert K. Cohen

STABILITY AND CHANGE IN ETHNIC-GROUP RELATIONS   311
Harry M. Johnson

NATIONALISM AND NATIONAL SOCIETIES

AFTER THE REVOLUTION: THE FATE OF NATIONALISM
IN THE NEW STATES   357
Clifford Geertz

Continuity and Change in Japanese Society   377
Robert N. Bellah

METHODOLOGY

Research on Stability and Change in Social Systems   407
Matilda White Riley and Edward E. Nelson

The Contributors   451

STABILITY
AND
SOCIAL CHANGE

Bernard Barber and Alex Inkeles

INTRODUCTION

These essays were written to honor Talcott Parsons on his retirement from Harvard University, where he taught for more than forty years. In arranging this volume, the editors were anxious to avoid the miscellaneous feeling that usually characterizes a venture of this sort, believing that more honor would be done to Parsons, and more service to the field, by organizing a *systematic* work on *one* fundamental problem of sociological theory and research. We chose the problem of stability and change in social systems because it has been and continues to be at the center of sociological analysis. The contributors to this volume have much to offer on this vital but poorly understood issue. The theme is also appropriate in having been important to the work of Talcott Parsons.

Each potential contributor was asked to submit an essay on a topic in which he had long been interested and which had a definite place in our plan for systematic and comprehensive coverage of problems in social systems. In our letter of invitation we stressed that we sought for this volume "an integrated treatment of a great many aspects of stability and change in social systems." Further, we said, "Ideally, and we would like everyone to achieve this ideal, each chapter would be a broad, systematic discussion in that major aspect of social systems, or in that class of social systems, or individual social system, which the author has chosen as his special interest for this occasion." Finally, we asked potential contributors to "raise the most fundamental issues in their substantive areas" and to "relate their analysis to the results of research."

This volume, we feel, has in good measure achieved our goals. On the whole it is a systematic, comprehensive, and fairly well integrated analysis of the processes and problems of stability and change in social systems. Of course, shortcomings remain. For lack of space, or because some contributors did not feel they could do what we had in mind, we have had to leave a few gaps. For example, we would have liked something on group and organization structure, on the economy,

1

on kinship structure, and on science. These topics would have made our volume nearly exhaustive, but even without them we have a collection that is exceedingly comprehensive.

Though we cannot here review the theoretical and substantive richness of these essays, we will state — all too synoptically — the contributors' major understandings about stability and change in social systems.

In this volume social systems are construed as dynamic processes. If fully dynamic analysis were technically possible, that would be ideal. Since this is impossible now, recurrent structures or patterns in the process are taken as provisional points of reference for analysis of stability and change in these social systems. Both stability and change are inherently problematic, and neither can be analyzed except in relation to the other.

Three major types of structure or pattern in social systems are social structure, culture, and personality. Each has a variety of substructures that are the foci of the individual essays. Both the major types and their substructures are seen as complementary, interdependent parts of a dynamic system. As such, any structure or substructure can be taken either as an independent or dependent variable for analyzing stability and change. Change in one part of a social system causes pressures for change in another part. The responsive changes ramify in many directions throughout the system, including feedbacks to the starting point. None of this necessarily happens according to plan or prediction, though both are of increasing use in social systems. That is, change brings unanticipated consequences for other parts of a system and perhaps for the system as a whole.

The endless process of change is not smooth or costless. On the contrary, as Professor Smelser puts it in his essay, "The image of society that emerges from this perspective is one of continuously generated and regenerated tensions, strains, contradictions, and pressures to change." Social conflict and personal misery are inherent in social systems, as are social progress and the pleasure of personal achievement.

Finally, social systems are evolutionary systems. That is, sequences of changes can be thought of as "directional," as proceeding along specific scales or dimensions. In many of the essays in this volume social systems are viewed as evolving toward more differentiated, more generalized, and more integrated components. Evolution of this kind, however, like more limited sequences of change, is not all planned and smooth, but often unpredictable, involving the same strains, imbalances, and conflicts that all change does. Again, like all change, it is never automatic but always problematic.

We hope this general statement will be a helpful orientation to the essays and to the volume as a whole. In addition, in the headnotes for each of the essays we seek to highlight the issues, controversies, unsolved problems, and directions for advance that prevail in social system analysis. Finally, of course, we hope that this volume will do honor to Talcott Parsons and express our admiration and affection for him.

SOCIAL STRUCTURE

Using Parsons' conception of the generalized symbolic media of exchange, Professor Smelser proposes a new analytic definition of political corruption that can be used in any type of society. He treats corruption first as a dependent variable, showing how it is caused by unevenness in the rate of change of parts of even relatively stable, but especially of changing, societies. Then he treats it as an independent variable, showing how corruption affects both stability and instability in the social system. Also, Professor Smelser relates how corruption is only one of several functional alternatives for stabilizing and destabilizing or change-ful processes in social systems. Finally, he remarks the difference between short-term and long-run consequences of corruption.

Neil J. Smelser

STABILITY, INSTABILITY, AND
THE ANALYSIS OF POLITICAL CORRUPTION

THE LEAD-LAG PERSPECTIVE ON CHANGE

A fruitful way to regard the type of social change we call "development," "growth," or "modernization" is as a complicated network of leading and lagging sectors of change. From this perspective, development is, above all, uneven; the appearance of new structures and new groups in one sector of society sets up pressures to change in other sectors. Responsive changes in these other sectors, in turn, ramify in various directions — including feedbacks to the sector originally considered as the leader — and further multiply the pressures to change. The image of society that emerges from this perspective is one of continuously generated and regenerated tensions, strains, contradictions, and pressures to change.

Several ideas expressed in this essay developed from discussions with Mark Traugott, who was my research assistant in the summer of 1969. I should like to record my gratitude for his contributions.

To illustrate the lead-lag perspective let us suppose that the leading sector is the economic one — though often empirically it is not — and the society in question rapidly introduces an industrial system and a concomitant expansion of the market system. Such a change is likely to generate pressures in many directions. For example, it may place pressure on the family and educational systems to produce a higher — or at least different — quality of skills among potential recruits to the labor force. Or, again, the development of a regional or national labor market may threaten traditional sanction systems — based on ties of kinship or locality — by which individuals previously undertook their economic performances. Or, finally, introducing the industrial system may lead to the formation of new groupings based on position in the industrial structure — managers, workers, professionals such as engineers, for example — each of which develops expectations regarding its place in the society's status structure and its rights to political participation and influence.

To take another illustration, suppose the political sector is the leading one, and the crucial change is the introduction of a mass suffrage system — a change, incidentally, that has frequently closely followed political independence in many new nations. This kind of political change may raise concerns on the part of the political leaders about the qualifications of the electorate and their capacity to participate responsibly in the polity, and these concerns may generate pressures to upgrade the educational system, and, along with it, the political responsibility of the citizenry. Efforts to develop the educational system, however, may create further pressures to change, for one concomitant of increased education is a heightening of occupational expectations, and unless education is accompanied by a level of economic growth that can sustain a population with a higher skill level, the society is likely to be faced with diverse groups of overeducated, underemployed, and politically dissatisfied citizens.

In the lead-lag perspective the polity plays a most important and delicate role. Introducing new structural arrangements in any sector inevitably creates many structural bases for group formation and group conflict. At the very minimum, introducing a new structure — an industrial structure of production, for example — creates a group of those who are interested in pushing the change and a group whose economic basis may be threatened by the new structure. Even more, because the new industrial structure ramifies into other institutional sectors and initiates pressures for change, groups of pushers and resisters of change are likely to appear in these sectors as well. Structural change, in short, breeds an ever-shifting pattern of potential group interests and potential group conflicts. And it is the polity that inherits the assignment of attempting to come to terms in some way with this changing and unsettling pattern by using whatever means it has at its disposal, whether these be repression, accommodation, negotiation, or initiation of changes in the political structure itself.

From this general lead-lag perspective, analysis might proceed in many directions — toward studying institutional integration in a period of rapid change, toward studying the social bases of political protest, toward studying the evolution of new political systems, to name a few. In this essay, I intend to use this perspective to consider an old and somewhat intractable problem — political corruption. More particularly, I intend to try to bring some new understanding to bear on political corruption by considering it in the context of leads and lags in social change. Treating corruption as a *dependent* variable, I shall analyze it as a contrivance that flourishes particularly under conditions of unevenness and inequity in structuring social rewards — unevenness and inequity that arise typically but not, of course, always as a consequence of developmental leads and lags. Treating corruption as an *independent* variable, I shall consider it in terms of its implications for fostering political stability and instability.

In developing this argument, I have found two features of Talcott Parsons' theoretical formulations to be particularly illuminating which I shall use as the analysis proceeds. The first is his conception of the generalized symbolic media of interchange — wealth, power, influence, and value-commitments — as the major types of resources and rewards by which the various systems and subsystems of society are linked. In particular, I shall define corruption as a particular kind of "crossing-over" of economic and political rewards. In addition, I shall treat the shifting structure of these media as important conditions for the development of corruption and similar phenomena. The second of Parsons' ideas is the concept of structural differentiation, which is one main process by which leads and lags in developmental change are created, and also one main process by which the media of exchange come to be structured at higher levels of generalization.

The essay will touch four topics: (1) historical and methodological aspects of the study of corruption; (2) a definition of corruption in cultural and social-structural terms; (3) some conditions that are conducive to the development of corruption; (4) some consequences of corruption for the legitimacy and stability of a political regime.

THE STUDY OF CORRUPTION
AS A NATURAL PHENOMENON

The history of the study of corruption in American sociology and political science is a typical history of inquiry into an apparently ineradicable "deviant" phenomenon that excites widespread and continuous public outrage. An initial phase of inquiry — in the late nineteenth and early twentieth centuries — occurred when public concern with political corruption and "machine politics" was at a high pitch, and was dominated by a reformist spirit.[1] And although some early writers, notably Lincoln Steffens,[2] contributed some brilliant insights into the relationship between the structure of municipalities and the occurrence of corruption, the predominant "explanation" of corruption in this phase was essentially moral, tracing its cause to greed, ruthlessness, depravity, or some other undesirable feature of man's moral condition. Correspondingly, writers who opted for this explanation tended to think of moral or social control — to be achieved mainly through political reform — as the other main variable that might influence corrupt behavior.

A second phase of inquiry — it might be called the "functionalist" phase — marked an attempt to break away from this explanatory scheme based on immorality and its control. Moreover, this break moved in three different but related directions:

1. Corruption is a natural social phenomenon, and, as such, is subject to the same kinds of explanatory principles as "normal" social phenomena. Thus, in his now-classic work on the political machine, Robert K. Merton argued that the machine is one of those structures that "perform positive functions which are at the time not adequately fulfilled by other existing patterns and structures." [3]

2. In fulfilling these needs, moreover, corruption can and does have numerous consequences that are anything but evil — providing welfare services for disadvantaged citizens that otherwise would be without them; providing avenues of political and social mobility for underdog elements in the population; and providing a political accommodation among diverse groups that augments the stable functioning of the political system.[4]

3. Corruption, finally, can be understood as a manifestation not of unnatural or depraved motives, but of motives that are manifested in more acceptable walks of life. An example of this emphasis is found in Daniel Bell's essay, "Crime as an American Way of Life," which

[1] For a bibliography of early reformist efforts, as well as some early "apologies" for corruption, see Eric L. McKitrick, "The Study of Corruption," *Political Science Quarterly*, vol. 75 (December 1957), pp. 502–503.

[2] Lincoln Steffens, *The Shame of the Cities* (New York: Hill and Wang, 1968). Originally published in 1904.

[3] Robert K. Merton, *Social Theory and Social Structure* (1968 enlarged edition) (New York: The Free Press, 1968), p. 126.

[4] Ibid., pp. 126–136.

treats many criminal activities — including racketeering and corruption — as manifestations of the American desire for monetary success and social mobility.[5]

The functionalist treatments of corruption did not manifest the naive moralism of the preceding phase, but a new kind of moral stance — sometimes explicit and sometimes implicit — probably made its way into their analyses: a sense of moral superiority that arises when one assumes a new and more enlightened moral posture toward a phenomenon based on some new knowledge about it, which was regarded by one's predecessors in a naive moralistic way. Moreover, because the functionalist students' attitudes toward corruption were in some sense a reaction against the immediate past, and were in any case made more complicated by their own studies, the reformist thrust tended to be absent from their writings.

In the past decade or two corruption has been virtually unstudied by sociologists, but others — mainly political scientists and anthropologists — have carried on from the functionalist analyses, and have contributed several general statements on the causes and consequences of corruption in the political structure (particularly in the developing nations) and several case studies (also in the developing nations). Corruption has been treated, for example, as a mode of political integration in rapidly changing societies; [6] as a practice that may facilitate as well as impede economic and political development; [7] and as one among several alternative kinds of political influence.[8] One of my intentions in this essay is to attempt to extend these analyses by conceptual refinement and generalization of propositions.

Before proceeding, numerous features peculiar to corruption make its careful empirical study an especially difficult enterprise. I have already mentioned the tendency to react to it in moralistic terms. In one sense this is quite understandable, because corruption is often a phenomenon of immediate moral import in society; but, in addition, the tendency to respond moralistically is all too often an impediment to

[5] *Antioch Review*, vol. 13 (Summer 1956), pp. 131–154.

[6] M. McMullan, "A Theory of Corruption," *The Sociological Review*, vol. 9 (July 1961), pp. 181–201; Ronald Wraith and Edgar Simpkins, *Corruption in Developing Countries* (London: George Allen & Unwin, Ltd., 1963).

[7] See, for example, Nathaniel H. Leff, "Economic Development through Bureaucratic Corruption," *The American Behavioral Scientist*, vol. 7 (November 1964), pp. 8–14; David H. Bayley, "The Effects of Corruption in a Developing Nation," *The Western Political Quarterly*, vol. 19 (1966), pp. 719–732; J. S. Nye, "Corruption and Political Development," *American Political Science Review*, vol. 61 (1967), pp. 417–427.

[8] James C. Scott, "The Analysis of Corruption in Developing Nations," *Comparative Studies in Society and History*, vol. 11 (1968–1969), pp. 315–341.

dispassionate analysis of the phenomenon. A moralistic response tends to assign blame — and causes — without special attention to facts. Furthermore, data pertaining to corruption tend to be particularly inaccessible. For one thing, a given behavioral item — a public official receiving gifts from kinsmen, for example — may be defined as "corrupt" in one society but not in another. Hence it is not easy to develop standard comparative indices of corruption; the variable social and cultural contexts in which the behavior occurs must be taken into account, as well as the item of behavior itself. This fact creates enormous difficulties for the investigator interested in operationalizing the phenomenon for comparative study.[9] Another source of inaccessibility is that corruption, being widely regarded as reprehensible, is not often recorded; in fact, it is most often kept secret. And finally, the empirical study of corruption is made difficult because it is often a "hot" political subject, and the claims that groups make about the extent of corruption are likely to be overblown because the groups have an interest in discrediting the regime. As a result, the investigator is faced with the unenviable task of studying a type of behavior whose practitioners often have a vested interest in concealing it, and whose critics often have a vested interest in exaggerating it. These are perhaps some reasons why the systematic study of corruption has not advanced any further than it has.

CORRUPTION IN CULTURAL
AND SOCIAL-STRUCTURAL TERMS

Many social scientists' working definitions of corruption involve the distinction between public and private morality. Joseph Senturia defined political corruption simply as "the misuse of public power for private profit." [10] Wertheim identified the "common usage" of the term to refer to occasions on which "a public servant . . . accepts gifts bestowed by a private person with the object of inducing him to give special considerations to the interests of the donor." [11] And Nye defined corruption as "behavior which deviates from the formal duties of a public role because of private-regarding (personal, close family, pri-

[9] This problem of variability of sociocultural context as a source of difficulty in comparative analysis is not peculiar to the study of corruption. See Neil J. Smelser, "The Methodology of Comparative Analysis of Economic Activity," in *Essays in Sociological Explanation* (Englewood Cliffs, N.J.: Prentice-Hall, 1968), pp. 64–69. For a particularly incisive statement of the cultural variability of that behavior which might be called "corrupt," see W. F. Wertheim, "Sociological Aspects of Corruption in Southeast Asia," in *East-West Parallels* (The Hague: W. van Hoeve, Ltd, 1964), pp. 104–113.

[10] Joseph J. Senturia, "Corruption, Political," *Encyclopaedia of the Social Sciences* (New York: Macmillan, 1930), vol. 4, p. 448.

[11] Wertheim, "Sociological Aspects of Corruption," p. 105.

vate clique) pecuniary or status gains; or violates rules against the exercise of certain types of private-regarding influence." [12]

Such definitions, although unobjectionable as far as they go, do leave several questions unanswered: What is the formal status of the notion of "public"? Does it refer only to legal norms (as Nye's word "formal" implies), or does it refer to more general and less tangible cultural norms? [13] What is the formal status of the notion of "private"? Is it to be limited to personal pecuniary profit, or are other kinds of private gains to be included (as indicated in Nye's listing of "status gains" in addition to pecuniary gains)? Is there any common or universal definition of "private" and "public," or are these terms to be treated as culturally relative? [14] I should like to pose a definition of corruption that addresses these vexing questions.

A Definition Based on the Media of Exchange and Structural Differentiation

As the definitions above indicate, corruption is above all a matter of exchanging sanctions or rewards among two or more parties: as a prototypical example, the public official agrees not to enforce a law (a political sanction) if he receives a sufficiently generous bribe from a businessman (an economic sanction).

Taking this general feature of corruption as a starting point, I should like to propose a definition of corruption — and to set it off from related phenomena — by using the scheme of the generalized media as developed in the works of Talcott Parsons and his associates. [15] The generalized media are regarded by Parsons as the sanctions (or re-

[12] Nye, "Corruption and Political Development," p. 419.

[13] A discussion of this ambiguity is found in Scott, "The Analysis of Corruption in Developing Nations," pp. 317–321.

[14] Most investigators are wary of imposing any particular normative system — e.g., Western legality — as a universal standard for defining corruption. Even Senturia, whose definition appears to be close to an absolute and universal one, acknowledges that a corrupt act has to be judged by "the best opinion and political morality of the time." Senturia, "Corruption, Political," p. 449.

[15] Parsons has developed the conception of generalized resources and media in many different writings. See particularly: Economy and Society (with Neil J. Smelser) (Glencoe, Ill.: The Free Press, 1956), chs. 2 and 3; "On the Concept of Political Power," Proceedings of the American Philosophical Society, vol. 107, no. 3 (June 1963); "On the Concept of Influence," Public Opinion Quarterly, vol. 17 (Spring 1963); and "On the Concept of Value-Commitments," Sociological Inquiry, vol. 38 (Spring 1969), pp. 135–160. The articles on power and influence were reprinted in Talcott Parsons, Sociological Theory and Modern Society (New York: Free Press, 1967), pp. 297–382. Following references will be to this volume. I have developed these conceptions in a somewhat different direction in two of my own works. Social Change in The Industrial Revolution (Chicago: University of Chicago Press, 1959), especially chaps. 2, 3, and 8; and Theory of Collective Behavior (New York: The Free Press, 1963), chap. 2.

wards) that, along with other mechanisms, regulate and coordinate the activities of the various subsystems of a social system. The most familiar medium — wealth — is generated by the economy; is regarded, in keeping with economic tradition, as a measure of value and a medium of exchange; and, as such, is a vehicle for transacting economically valued commodities.[16] A second medium — power — is generated by the political system, and is defined as the "generalized capacity to secure the performances of binding obligations by units in a system of collective organization when the obligations are legitimized with reference to their bearing on collective goals and where in case of recalcitrance there is a presumption of enforcement by negative situational sanctions." [17] A third medium — influence — is generated by the integrative subsystem, rests on persuasion, and is best thought of as efforts by one actor to affect the behavior of another by appealing to norms that pertain to both as members of a common community.[18] And the final medium — value commitment — is generated in the latent pattern-maintenance and tension-management system; rests on duty (as contrasted with persuasion); and is a medium for "the activation of obligations, which are presumptively morally binding by virtue of [shared] values." [19] In their capacity as rewards and sanctions, these media may be conceived as "ways of getting things done" in the social system, and in the concrete structuring of social action they combine and recombine in numerous patterns.

For our purposes, it is important to underscore one particular feature of the media: *they may vary in their level of generalization.* In an economy based on barter, for example, wealth is at a low level of generalization, because it is no more general than the situational exchange of concrete commodities; in an economy based on money, wealth is more generalized, because it is a symbol of value for various commodities, and has value above and beyond specific situational transactions. Wealth is even more generalized in economies based on elaborate credit systems. One may also conceive of a "political barter" system — a system based on "log-rolling," for example — in which one political agent will perform a political action only if another political agent reciprocates with a corresponding political action. This is to be contrasted with a political system in which power is more generalized — for example, when political agents are given periodic authorization to exercise political power, as in an election, but are given some free-

16 See Parsons and Smelser, *Economy and Society*, pp. 139–143.
17 Parsons, "On the Concept of Political Power," p. 308.
18 Parsons, "On the Concept of Influence," especially pp. 366–371.
19 Parsons, "On the Concept of Value-Commitments," p. 143.

dom in exercising it in the intervening periods. And finally, value commitments may vary in their level of generality. If commitment to a religious value system implies detailed regulation of daily activities as a function of that commitment, it would be less generalized than a religious value system whose acceptance implies that the believer will conduct himself in a generally moral fashion.[20]

One of the chief social-structural concomitants of an increasing level of generalization of resources is a greater degree of structural differentiation in society.[21] The growth of a money economy from a barter economy involves the appearance of more complex systems of markets and more complex units involved in regulating and coordinating economic processes. The growth of a credit economy involves the rise of such new social units as banks, governmental credit agencies, collection agencies, as well as units to regulate these agencies. Likewise, the institutionalization of power on a more generalized basis typically involves the appearance of new political forms, such as legislatures, political parties, electoral systems, civil-service bureaucracies, and the like, all of which play a differentiated role in exercising more generalized power. In short, a high level of generalization of media and a high level of structural differentiation presuppose one another in a social system.

The generalization of media and structural differentiation are two major connotations of concepts like "development."[22] As these two kinds of phenomena emerge in a developing social system, moreover, social resources become more flexible and mobile — because they are generalized and freer from ascriptive and other situational links; resources also become more storable — again, because they are generalized, and less linked to situational exchanges; and, as a consequence, exchanges involving the media become more contingent. And finally,

[20] By this measure, classical Protestantism would be considered a more generalized value commitment than classic orthodox Judaism because of the greater contingency that obtains between commitment and the detailed regulation of the individual's situation. Durkheim contrasted Judaism and Protestantism in this way, though he did not use the language of the "generalized media" in doing so. See Emile Durkheim, *Suicide* (Glencoe, Ill.: The Free Press, 1951), pp. 158–160.

[21] On structural differentiation, see especially Parsons and Smelser, *Economy and Society*, chap. 5; Parsons, "Some Reflections on the Institutional Framework of Economic Development," and "Some Principal Characteristics of Industrial Societies," both in *Structure and Process in Modern Societies* (New York: The Free Press, 1960); "Some Considerations on the Theory of Social Change," *Rural Sociology*, vol. 26, no. 3 (1961), pp. 219–239; *Societies: Evolutionary and Comparative Perspectives* (Englewood Cliffs, N.J.: Prentice-Hall, 1966).

[22] Neil J. Smelser, "Toward a Theory of Modernization," in *Essays in Sociological Explanation*, pp. 129–137.

at the cultural level, an increase in generalizability of media and an increase in structural differentiation is also accompanied by the rise of a relatively autonomous "rationality" or "calculus" that is appropriate to the exchange of resources in the more differentiated sector of the system — a rationality relating to the exchange of economic resources, a rationality relating to the "public interest," i.e., to responsibility in the generation and exercise of power, and so on. A major part of the "rationality" governing the creation, acquisition, and use of the generalized resources is a normative framework that is formulated with diminished reference to ascriptive and situational bases of calculating action. Much of this normative framework, moreover, is found in the proliferation of formal law, another hallmark of "development." [23]

Given these observations, we may now present the minimum definitional requirements of the concept of corruption:

1. For corruption to exist, there must be a minimal level of structural differentiation of a political apparatus, and a minimum development of rationality — i.e., a normative framework — of the "public interest" that is distinguishable from the various "other" or "private" interests of the incumbent of a public role. This rationality has to do with political decision-making, the accommodation of conflicting political interests, and the administration of justice and equity in the system. Another way of saying the same thing is that power must be institutionalized in such a way as to be generalized *away* from ascriptive and situational considerations.

Wertheim made the kind of point I have in mind when he observed that

> what is nowadays meant by corruption . . . presupposes a social structure in which the separation between [public and private] account-keeping has either been carried through in actual fact, or else has been generally accepted by society as a criterion for proper conduct on the part of civil servants. Only then can the acceptance, or demanding, of gifts as a precondition for the bestowal of favours be regarded as

---

[23] Both Weber and Durkheim made this observation — though in different ways — in their discussions of the place of formal law in developing a rationalized, differentiated economy. Weber, for example, listed as one condition of maximum formal rationality of capital accounting "complete calculability of the functioning of public administration and the legal order and a reliable formal guarantee of all contracts by the political authority . . . formally rational administration and law." Max Weber, *The Theory of Social and Economic Organization*, trans. A. M. Henderson and Talcott Parsons (Glencoe, Ill.: The Free Press, 1947), p. 275. In *The Division of Labor in Society* (Glencoe, Ill.: The Free Press, 1949), Durkheim posited the proliferation of systems of restitutive law as the basis of integrating an increased division of labor.

"corruption" of the prevailing standards of morality. Therefore, a sociological analysis of corruption ought to be preceded by an historical treatment of the social awareness which brands certain types of conduct as corrupt.[24]

This kind of definitional requirement provides a basis for regarding the same action — e.g., receiving a gift from a kinsman — as corrupt in one society and not corrupt in another. We have, in short, made the definition of the phenomenon relative to the existence of a structurally differentiated and normatively regulated sector with a rationality of the public interest. We would expect, of course, that the cultural content and definition of the public interest would be highly variable, and the notion of the public should not be made coterminous with any particular sort of political system — e.g., democracy, socialism, communism — each of which has its own particular variant of the public interest.

2. The definition of corruption involves a "crossing-over" of economic and political sanctions. Corruption involves money payments (or gifts) made to public officials whose conduct is presumptively regulated by political norms, i.e., norms defined by the rationality of the polity or the public interest. In return for this money payment, the public official provides some political favor — an exemption from a political regulation, a charter to launch a business enterprise, and so on. Corruption, in short, involves trading economic for political rewards.

3. One further definitional stipulation is necessary: for an act to be described as corrupt, at least one crossing-over sanction must be at a low level of generalization, that is, situationally specific. Thus, for example, in one form of corruption — "conflict of interest" — the political agent takes a political action (or refuses to take action) that significantly affects his private economic welfare. The ungeneralized feature of the conflict-of-interest situation is the political act itself. In a second form of corruption — misappropriation — the ungeneralized aspect is the misuse of public funds for personal gains, a concrete political act. And in a third form of corruption — bribery — the political agent takes political action (or refuses to take it) in response to economic sanc-

---

[24] Wertheim, "Sociological Aspects of Corruption in Southeast Asia," p. 106. Wertheim goes on to discuss patrimonial-bureaucratic empires, which had no bureaucratic separation between private and public spheres, but which nevertheless generated accusations of corruption (Ibid., pp. 107–110). My own interpretation of Wertheim's observation is that these empires did in fact have normative expectations regarding the public responsibilities of the lords and princes, even though these were not codified into a system of public and private account-keeping.

tions. Again, the ungeneralized aspect is the specific political act, but in this case the immediate economic payment is ungeneralized as well.

Corruption, then, involves the immediate and situationally specific performance of a political act in exchange for an economic sanction. This definitional requirement is important if the phenomenon of corruption is to be set off analytically from other, related, but more generalized means of influencing political actions. The persuasive efforts of a faction, pressure group, or lobby — if it stops short of buying legislators' votes — differ from outright corruption, because there is a greater degree of contingency in the mode of political influence they exercise. Donating large campaign funds to a political party, in hopes that it will carry out policies congenial to the wishes of the donor, is also different from what we have defined as corruption, for this kind of political influence cannot absolutely guarantee a political act — the way corruption does — even though the politician may promise to deliver *if elected*. Although lobbying, campaign funding, and other forms of political influence may be considered as morally or politically reprehensible as corruption, it is necessary to find a basis of distinguishing among the several forms. It would seem that the level of generalization of the sanctions involved provides the key to this distinction.

Defined this way, corruption falls into a larger family of phenomena that involve a situationally specific crossing-over of different kinds of media. "Buying one's way into religious grace," for example, involves crossing over wealth and value commitments. Nepotism and favoritism involve distributing various rewards on the basis of some kind of particularistic or solidary relationship, which is an instance of "influence." A final example would be the case of providing political immunity (a political reward) because a person affirms his faith in a given religious position (a value commitment).

These situationally specific crossing-over types of relations may be expanded to include numerous "negative" examples as well, but I shall only mention them here and not analyze them further in this essay. One example would be to coerce a person politically to affirm a religious commitment. "Protection" and "extortion" are also examples, for they threaten that political (violent) sanctions will be applied unless economic payments are made. Another example is "moral blackmail," for example, forcing another person into taking a political action by threatening moral condemnation on personal grounds. And so is the "boycott," or using economic sanctions to secure political compliance in a conflict situation. These several types of situationally specific crossing-over phenomena vary in the degree to which they are held to be legitimate or illegitimate as means of controlling or influencing behavior.

THREE SETS OF CONDITIONS CONDUCIVE
TO THE DEVELOPMENT OF CORRUPTION
AS A POLITICAL FORM

Having defined corruption and set it in relation to several other similar phenomena, let us now turn to some social-structural conditions that are conducive to its appearance. In particular, we shall be discussing sets of conditions that are likely to result from the lead-lag phenomena so characteristic of rapid social development.

Competing Systems of Authority and
Political Influence in a Society

One of the most nearly universal features of political development is the tension that arises between national and local systems of political authority. As the term "nation-building" implies, political development involves the developing of a society-wide governing apparatus, legitimized by some religious, political, or nationalist values and ideology. One mission of national governments, moreover, is to mobilize citizens, in the name of the nation, to undertake the tasks necessary for development, whatever these may be. Invariably, however, this system of political authority proves difficult to institutionalize, because it is superimposed on an existing system or systems of authority, rooted in and legitimized by local, particularistic structures, such as kinship, community, caste, and tribe. The "leading" sector in this case is the authority system associated with the state apparatus, and the "lagging" sector is the traditional and localized authority systems.

Various students of political corruption have argued that corruption tends to flourish in the interstices of these competing systems of authority. McMullan, for example, has advanced the general principle that "the different levels of corruption in different countries depend on the extent to which government and society are homogeneous." [25] One argument he developed to illustrate this is that in some cases the demands placed on the public official to meet various family and tribal loyalties both obscure his loyalty to the nation and place financial pressures on him that will make him more likely to feather his financial nest by resorting to corrupt practices.[26]

[25] McMullan, "A Theory of Corruption," p. 185.

[26] Ibid., p. 186. A similar point is made by Wraith and Simpkins in connection with local government officials in Nigeria who regularly engage in corrupt actions, whereas officers of tribal unions do not do so in relation to their unions. Wraith and Simpkins draw the moral that "The Unions show that Nigerians are as capable as anybody of public as well as private integrity, provided that their deepest loyalties are engaged." It is the case, they argue, that loyalties to tribal unions are much stronger than that to the state. *Corruption in Developing Countries*, p. 50.

In addition to the fact that individuals with local, particularistic loyalties are not unwilling to buy off public officials, corruption, considered in the context of tension between two or more systems of political authority, may come to be structured as a kind of supplementary system of political accommodation or modus vivendi between the two competing systems. By an act of corruption the parties set up a new level of political coordination between themselves that is neither national-bureaucratic nor local-particularistic, but which acknowledges the existence of both systems of authority and the desirability of both to come to terms with one another. This character of much political corruption led McMullan to remark that it is something of an "emollient, softening conflict and reducing friction" and further to suggest, indeed, that "the greater the corruption the greater the harmony between corruptor and corruptee." [27]

In terms of the level of generalization of the media, the differentiation, universalization, and impersonality of state or bureaucratic authority involve a change in the level of generalization of power. Political sanctions are exercised — and expected to be followed — for generalized political loyalty to and support of a state apparatus, rather than for the claims that accrue because of common local residence or common kinship, tribal, or ethnic membership. Viewed from a social-psychological standpoint, institutionalizing a state apparatus simultaneously calls for a new kind of interpersonal trust in the system. A civil servant is to be trusted by the citizenry because of his presumed commitment to an occupational role that is implicated in the political-legal system. This depersonalization of the trust relationship is often unfamiliar to and unwelcomed by those whose trust is usually based on more immediate or particularistic relationships with others. The act of corruption can be regarded as an accommodation to the ambiguities that arise in the new, generalized relations between bureaucrat and clientele. Because the corrupt interchange is immediate and situational — a gift for a decision, a bribe for an act, a tip for an evasion, and so on — it brings the bureaucrat and client into a less contingent and less ambiguous relationship to one another. Corruption is a device that serves to concretize and reinfuse trust into the relationship between an impersonal authority system and its clients who may not understand or grant loyalty to that system.

Discrepancies in the Distribution of Rewards in the Stratification System

One way of characterizing a stratification system is to describe how the generalized media — wealth, power, influence (prestige), and so on

---

[27] Ibid., pp. 196–197.

— are distributed among the different positions and groupings in society.[28] Descriptions of these distributions would yield a map of the concentrations of wealth, power, legal immunity, prestige, and so on, in the society. Although the various distributions in any society are typically congruent with one another to some degree, there are invariably some actual as well as perceived discrepancies in the distributions. Some individuals and groups are — or feel themselves to be — higher on wealth than they are in power, higher in prestige than they are in wealth, and so on.[29] Furthermore, depending on the cultural values of the society in question, one or another of the types of rewards may be considered more desirable than the others.[30]

Given these considerations, we may adduce two closely related principles that will help us account for the mapping of corruption (as well as other "crossing-over" phenomena) in any society:

1. Corruption will flow toward the more valued reward. In a perceptive statement, Alexis de Tocqueville attempted to account for the different forms of corruption in countries with aristocratic and democratic traditions. "In aristocratic governments," he argued, "those who are placed at the head of affairs are rich men, who are desirous only of power. In democracies, statesmen are poor and have their fortunes to make. The consequence is that in aristocratic states the rulers are rarely accessible to corruption and have little craving for money, while the reverse is the case in democratic nations." Having observed this, he went on to argue that "the men who conduct an aristocracy sometimes endeavor to corrupt the people, [while] the heads of a democracy are themselves corrupt."[31] Put another way, Tocqueville was saying that in aristocracies power is more valued and men will expend their wealth to fortify it, whereas in democracies wealth is valued, and men will use political office to augment it. Whatever the merit of Tocqueville's generalization connecting democracy and wealth, and aristocracy and power, its logic certainly seems to throw light on the broad historical differences in the structure of corruption, for example,

[28] See Neil J. Smelser and Seymour Martin Lipset, "Social Structure, Mobility, and Development," in *Social Structure and Mobility in Economic Development,* ed. Smelser and Lipset (Chicago: Aldine, 1966), pp. 6–7.

[29] Max Weber, "Class, Status, and Party," in *From Max Weber: Essays in Sociology,* ed. H. H. Gerth and C. Wright Mills (New York: Oxford, 1958), pp. 180–195.

[30] For a discussion of the relationship between cultural value systems and the structure of stratification systems, see Talcott Parsons, "A Revised Analytical Approach to the Theory of Social Stratification," in *Class, Status, and Power: A Reader in Social Stratification,* ed. Reinhard Bendix and Seymour M. Lipset (New York: The Free Press, 1953), pp. 92–129.

[31] Alexis de Tocqueville, *Democracy in America* (New York: Vintage Books, 1945), vol. 1, pp. 233–234.

between the United States and England. Nineteenth-century corruption in Britain tended to be marked by the new wealthy classes buying their way into political and social positions, whereas the pattern in America has been predominantly public officials enriching themselves by granting political favors to wealthy individuals and groups who attempt to affect political regulations and decisions so that they can continue to augment their wealth. In both cases corruption is skewed in the direction of the more favored reward.[32]

2. According to the principle just adduced, the holders of less valued rewards will strive to obtain the more valued rewards by using the less valued ones. This principle may be generalized: in cases of incongruence of rewards, individuals and groups will "trade" — in part by corruption — in such a way as to move toward greater congruence. People will trade what they have (or feel they have) to obtain what they do not have (or feel they do not have). This principle, moreover, helps to reveal the structure of corruption in any society.

This principle is nowhere more clearly illustrated than in my study of Beachtown, a small New England coastal town in which the political control rested in the populous town area, whereas about 70 per cent of the township revenue was generated by a beach and recreation area that prospered because it catered to thousands of summer vacationers. The town area ranked high on political control (votes) and low on economic resources, whereas the beach area ranked low on political control and high on economic resources. In this setting a network of patronage and corruption grew up, with the political leaders of the city providing all sorts of jobs for townspeople that were financed, in effect, by beach interests, and the townspeople — through their elected officials — adopting a lenient attitude toward the business establishments on the beach. Viewed in terms of the media, the town traded political immunity for the beach area's money.[33]

Other investigators have noted the same tendency, sometimes involving many different social groups. From his study of local government in Nairobi, Werlin described the following pattern of political processes:

> African groups are ever ready to demonstrate, strike, and even to use violence, though their actions seldom take a highly organized form. European interest groups are said to use devious tactics to get their way, such as approaching African politicians through the diplomatic

[32] See Senturia, "Corruption, Political," p. 450; see also Peter Odegard, "Corruption, Political, United States," Encyclopaedia of the Social Sciences (New York: Macmillan, 1930), vol. 4, pp. 453–454.

[33] Neil J. Smelser, ed., Sociology (New York: Wiley, 1967), pp. 678–682.

corps. Asian groups are regularly accused of corrupt practices. Corruption and bribery are prevalent in underdeveloped countries, and are encouraged in Kenya by the division between African political control and Asian and European wealth.[34]

Greenstone noted a similar pattern in Kampala: "an anti-Asian political climate, a pro-African rhetoric with anti-imperialistic and racial slogans, and a series of side payments from those with money to those with various kinds of political influence." [35]

On the basis of his and Werlin's studies, Greenstone went on to observe that the situation of urban East Africa is not unlike the situation of American cities in the late nineteenth century. The political machine served as an intermediary in balancing political and economic resources. "The machine took bribes from businessmen and in exchange arranged [on behalf of immigrant groups] for favorable government policies," which took the form mainly of balancing party tickets ethnically, and taking favorable political positions toward countries from which the immigrants came.[36]

McMullan mentions a "typical pattern of corruption" in West Africa for the "ill-paid policeman to turn his power over wealthy illiterates into a supplement to his pay." [37] A further example is the would-be entrepreneur who bribes public officials to gain political immunity from the laws or regulations that might inhibit his business activities.[38] And finally, though at an entirely different level, the tendency for governments that are losing their legitimacy to resort to bribing or providing political immunity to groups is an example of a regime's efforts to shore up the resources it does not have (political legitimacy and support) by giving up the resources it still may command (wealth and discretionary law enforcement powers).[39]

Though discrepancies in the distributions of the generalized media are to some degree omnipresent in organized society, they are certainly

[34] Herbert H. Werlin, "The Nairobi City Council: A Study in Comparative Local Government," *Comparative Studies in Society and History*, vol. 8 (1965–1966), p. 192.

[35] J. David Greenstone, "Corruption and Self Interest in Kampala and Nairobi: A Comment on Local Politics in East Africa," *Comparative Studies in Society and History*, vol. 8 (1965–1966), p. 205.

[36] Ibid., pp. 206–207.

[37] McMullan, "A Theory of Corruption," p. 190.

[38] Leff stresses that this kind of corruption may have a facilitating effect on economic development, in that it frees resources for investment, and encourages competition and innovation in the economic sphere. "Economic Development through Bureaucratic Corruption," pp. 9–12.

[39] See the brief discussion of Rome in the fourth and fifth centuries in Smelser, *Essays in Sociological Explanation*, pp. 240–241.

likely to be extensive and extreme in those developing societies (including "advanced" societies undergoing rapid change) that are experiencing leads and lags in their various sectors. One concomitant of uneven social change is the formation of numerous groups — technologically obsolete groups, groups of new migrants, new entrepreneurial groups, new educated groups, etc. — who find themselves either acquiring or losing out on some social reward. Accordingly, corruption is one means for these groups either to spend what they have gained for what they do not yet have or to spend what they have not yet lost to protect or regain what they are losing.[40] Of course, not all situations of discrepancy among distributions of the media will lead to flourishing corruption. Corruption is not the only means by which these objectives may be attained. Therefore, it is necessary to consider the other means, to shed more understanding on the question of when corruption is likely to develop.

Corruption and the Availability of Other Channels of Exercising Political Influence

In his recent article, Scott argues that "corruption can often be more profitably seen as one of many processes of political influence rather than as simply the misuse of office in violation of community norms."[41] My view is that these two perspectives are not competitors in the race to explain corruption, but rather as complementary perspectives. Nevertheless, Scott's argument reminds us that corruption is one of a family of political processes, and that the structure of political opportunities conditions the degree to which corruption flourishes.

Two of the most pressing exigencies facing political leaders who are attempting to build the new nations are: (1) to gain a measure of legitimacy and support from the citizenry so that they may go about the business of governing; (2) to foster a variety of political avenues — interest groups, parties, consultative arrangements, etc. — so that the probabilities of long-term legitimacy and support may be increased.[42] Insofar as the regimes of the developing countries lag in these two regards, the probabilities of corruption developing increase.

---

[40] Zolberg notes that "what is usually called corruption . . . can be viewed, under certain circumstances, as a fairly rational distributive system which is based on other than rational-legal norms." Aristide R. Zolberg, *Creating Political Order: The Party-States of West Africa* (Chicago: Rand McNally, 1966), p. 160.

[41] Scott, "Analysis of Corruption in Developing Nations," pp. 324–325.

[42] This is not to say that all political leaders behave in such a way as to maximize these ends. In many cases leaders, uncertain of their legitimacy, attempt to silence politically interested groups, especially if they are in the opposition, thus perhaps diminishing the chances that they will enjoy legitimacy in the long run.

The regime that lacks legitimacy is in a poor position to control corruption for two reasons. First, lacking in legitimacy, it is not likely to command the loyalties of citizens, loyalties that serve as normative counterbalances to the attractions of corruption.[43] And second, also as a function of lacking legitimacy, the state will be less able to firmly enforce whatever laws or policies it may have against corrupt practices.[44]

We may agree with Scott about the second exigency that corruption is one of several means to attain political results, and, furthermore, it is likely to appear when other avenues are not available. In characterizing the arrangements of politico-economic exchange among Africans, Asians, and Europeans in Nairobi, Werlin noted that these arrangements existed "in the absence of competitive politics in Nairobi [which has a one-party system]," [45] suggesting, by that observation, that a competitive party system would be a functional alternative to corruption, subterranean influence through diplomatic channels, and street demonstrations. More generally, Leff has observed that:

> In most underdeveloped countries, interest groups are weak, and political parties rarely permit the participation of elements outside the contending cliques. Consequently, graft may be the only institution allowing other interests to achieve articulation and representation in the political process.[46]

And Huntington has argued that an increase in political awareness and participation in rapidly developing societies, combined with an inability of existing parties and other political institutions to absorb this increase, creates conditions that are ripe for the development of personal corruption.[47]

Yet it must not be thought that peaceful interest-articulation through parties, lobbies, interest groups, etc., is the only functional alternative to corruption. Political influence may be exercised through various kinds of noninstitutionalized political protest, such as mob actions and

[43] See above on legitimacy.

[44] Shils adds that other social controls may also be weak: "The inadequacy of the press as a standing enquiry into the probity of elected (and appointed) officials, which, in the more advanced states, is an intermittent safeguard against corruption, also serves to diminish inhibitions." Edward Shils, "Political Development in the New States," Comparative Studies in Society and History, vol. 2 (1959–1960), pp. 265–292.

[45] Werlin, "The Nairobi City Council," p. 192.

[46] Leff, "Economic Development through Bureaucratic Corruption," p. 9.

[47] Samuel P. Huntington, "Political Development and Political Decay," in Political Modernization: A Reader in Comparative Political Change, ed. Claude E. Welch, Jr. (Belmont, Calif.: Wadsworth, 1967), pp. 224–225.

revolutionary violence. If, however, this kind of protest is seen by groups as politically inadvisable or impossible, then the probabilities of their turning to corruption are greater. Scott observes that

> Where a minority is discriminated against and its political demands are regarded as illegitimate by the governing elite and the general population, its members may feel that open pressure group action would destroy what little political credit they enjoy. They may, therefore, turn to the corruption of politicians and/or bureaucrats to safeguard their interests and avoid damaging political attacks from more powerful groups.[48]

Or, more generally, when a ruling regime enjoys cooperative relations with (or is dominated by) a conservative military, it may be able effectively to repress political opposition, thus encouraging groups to seek other means of gaining political ends, including the means of corrupting political officials.

Corruption, then, emerges as a kind of half-way house between legitimized and regularized political channels of influence on the one hand, and the exercise of political influence by open challenges to the legitimacy of a regime. It implies a certain lack of loyalty to the regime and its laws and policies — because it involves an evasion of these — but at the same time it is an accommodation that implies a willingness to allow the regime to enjoy a continuing existence. Serving these and other functions, corruption itself may become institutionalized and quite widely accepted.

To conclude, I might suggest that the probabilities for the proliferation of corrupt practices are greatest when the following conditions combine:

1. when a political system has differentiated to the point where a normative framework concerning a distinctive "public interest" has evolved, *but*

2. when this differentiation is only partial, so that unambiguous standards of public probity have not supplanted traditional practices such as gift-giving;

3. when individuals and groups in societies experience real or imagined discrepancies in the distribution of social rewards;

4. when a political regime lacks the necessary legitimacy and support to enforce its own laws and policies, and

5. when institutionalized channels for interest-articulation are ill-developed, *but*

6. when the regime commands sufficient military force and other facilities to repress open political challenges to its legitimacy.

[48] Scott, p. 327.

SOME CONSEQUENCES OF CORRUPTION
FOR THE LEGITIMACY OF A REGIME

Up to this point I have been considering the legitimacy of a political regime by its status as an independent variable with reference to corruption. I have, for example, indicated that a regime with shaky legitimacy will be more likely to generate corruption, both because its administrative staff and citizenry, giving it limited legitimacy, are less inhibited in corrupting it, and because the regime itself, enjoying low legitimacy, is unlikely to be able to prevent corruption. To conclude, let us comment briefly on a few probable consequences for the legitimacy of a ruling regime, once it enters into corrupt relations with various individuals and groups.

The starting point for these observations is the point made at the end of the last section: corruption may be considered a functional alternative to other mechanisms of interest-articulation and to direct challenges to the legitimacy of the regime. Yet it is a functional alternative with peculiar characteristics. As we have seen, corruption involves a low level of generalization of the political and economic media: governments grant contracts or political immunity for specific and immediate money payments; or they secure immediate political cooperation of a political group by "buying it off." For this reason, corruption is a kind of political bartering system. It is to be contrasted with, for example, regular elections, in which political leaders are given generalized support, in the expectation that they will execute policies in the general interest of the electorate. It is even to be contrasted with pressure-group politics, in which trade unions, professional associations, business groups, and other interest groups permit the regime a margin of maneuverability, even though they may periodically press for specific laws, policies, and actions.

Corruption, then, may be thought of as a short-term functional substitute for other means of gaining the support and legitimacy of politically significant groups in the society. But because it is an immediate and situational type of exchange, it leaves the regime in a position of reduced flexibility and maneuverability. A corrupt regime is one that perforce ties up much of its political and economic capital in short-term exchanges that may accommodate or pacify individuals or groups. For this reason, the corrupt regime is less likely to be able to devote resources to pursue publicly espoused goals of development or civic improvement, on which its long-term support and legitimacy rest in part. Corruption may be regarded as a short-term means of shoring up political support and legitimacy, but its consequences for the maneuverability and effectiveness of a regime are such that it may lead to a vicious circle of declining legitimacy in the long run.

As we have seen, one condition that is conducive to the development of corruption is real or imagined inequities in the distribution of the generalized media among the individuals and groups in society. Yet as corruption develops, it is likely to aggravate those very conditions of inequity. When a regime enters into corrupt relations with a politically significant group, this is likely to become a source of relative deprivation and disgruntlement on the part of other, competing groups. The regime is likely, furthermore, to find itself subject to the same kind of demands from other groups in the name of equity. If the regime responds by attempting to pacify these other groups by corrupt practices or other forms of political barter, it may find itself increasingly hemmed in to a position of making moment-to-moment situational "deals" with various clamoring groups, and may find itself becoming increasingly inflexible and ineffective as a government.

If corruption becomes involved in the political process in this way, the regime is menaced by yet another possibility. Corruption has always been an inflammatory political symbol, mainly, I think, because it is — or is made to appear to be — a symbol of both a regime's loss of political integrity and its political impotence. The accusation that a regime is corrupt, even if the evidence for that accusation is relatively minor, may become an ideological rallying cry for political groups who may be dissatisfied with the regime on a variety of different grounds, and may be a main symbol around which an opposition movement crystallizes. If this occurs, the situation is ripe for toppling the regime by either constitutional or unconstitutional overthrow. But unless the new groups who come to power are able to legitimize themselves in such a way that gives them greater political maneuverability than their predecessors, they may find themselves tempted to engage in the same kind of political barter as their predecessors, and as vulnerable to political opposition in the name of corruption. If this is the case, the stage is set for the corruption-reform-corruption cycle,[49] in which the rascals are thrown out by citizens outraged by corruption, only to find the new leaders discovering rascality as a means of consolidating their political position, at least temporarily.

CONCLUSION

One conclusion that may be drawn from this essay is that corruption is a phenomenon with many facets and with consequences that ramify into many different sectors of society. Consider one type of corruption: bribery of a public official by businessmen to secure construction contracts. From an *economic* standpoint the consequences of these actions

---

[49] Lincoln Steffens described this cycle though he gave a different interpretation of it. *The Shame of the Cities,* pp. 195–214.

may be to break through the bureaucratic shackles of a regime and to facilitate some economic development that might otherwise have been inhibited; from an *integrative* standpoint the consequences may be to fashion a workable mode of interaction between the business and government communities; yet from the *political* standpoint the consequences might be to divide the business community internally (between those who benefit from the corruption and those who do not) and to create resentment of both business and government among other politically significant groups. With these diverse consequences, it becomes difficult and injudicious to venture any simple assessment or evaluation of political corruption.

In this essay I have been particularly concerned with the relations between social stability and instability on the one hand, and corruption on the other. In keeping with the conclusion just enunciated, it seems possible to identify several typical relations:

1. The genesis of corruption: irregularities in social change — leads and lags — appear to be among the major determinants of corruption because they occasion multiple actual and perceived discrepancies in distributing diverse social rewards, and encourage the "equalization" of these discrepancies by the situationally specific "crossing-over" of rewards. This generalization must be qualified, however, by the observation that conditions other than irregular social changes give rise to corruption, and that corruption is not the only response to shifting distributions of social rewards.

2. Corruption is likely to perform important stabilizing functions in society insofar as it constitutes a kind of informal cushion between its particularistic and universal sectors. It may also be regarded as a relatively stabilizing factor insofar as it is a functional alternative to forms of political expression and conflict — such as outright challenges to the legitimacy of the regime — that tend to be more immediately disruptive than corruption.

3. At the same time corruption may generate political instability. Because it is an immediate and situational — that is, ungeneralized — mode of political adaptation, it is likely to reduce the political maneuverability and effectiveness of a regime. Furthermore, because corruption itself tends to breed feelings of inequity in the political system, it often becomes the focus of political opposition to a regime, and the symbol around which different political groups mobilize to unseat the regime. In this way corruption may work as a viable adaptation of a shaky regime in the short run, but may generate consequences that erode these adaptations in the long run.

*Recognizing that the problems illness poses for any kind of per-
sonal and social stability are basic and universal, Professor Field
describes the types of medical system that are established in
primitive and contemporary industrial societies as a result of the
interaction between that system and the other subsystems of the
society. He traces the long-term evolution—partly successful,
partly not—of the medical system toward greater differentiation,
specialization, and need for integration. Concentrating on medicine in industrial society, he shows how the system is still in the
throes of evolution, with many system strains, imbalances, short-
ages, and conflicts. His detailed and concrete analysis has great
import for social policy in this field.*

Mark G. Field

STABILITY AND CHANGE
IN THE MEDICAL SYSTEM:
MEDICINE IN THE INDUSTRIAL SOCIETY

The proverbial Eastern wise man was once asked by his monarch what
was the most widespread occupation in the kingdom, and he answered
medicine. The king scoffed, so the wise man went and stood on the
steps of the palace with a bandage around his head, and moaned
loudly. Almost everyone who passed by sympathized and offered
"medical" advice: hot or cold baths, potions, fasting, praying, rest,
activity, and so on.

The king was convinced that medicine *was* the most common
occupation, perhaps because illness is one of mankind's universal
preoccupations. Pain and suffering, disability and death, the mysteries
of mental derangement, the agonies of many terminal diseases, the
tortures of incurable but not fatal illnesses — these are so intricately
woven into the total human condition that it may be fair to assume

that concern about health has been a feature of human culture almost from the beginning.

But if there is universality in the basic problem posed by illness to man and society, the response to it has exhibited an amazing range of cultural and social-organizational variability, and it is with the "medical" answer of modern society that this paper will deal. Although based primarily on the American case, this study has benefited from an examination of medicine in the Soviet Union and Western Europe. My hypothesis is that because certain quantitative forces and qualitative factors are present in industrial and urban society, a well-differentiated "medical system" emerges, and then undergoes a further process of internal differentiation. This process, in turn, affects the manner in which the medical system discharges its responsibilities toward patients and society, and thereby opens the way for further structural changes of a complex nature. My premise is that today's medical system is only the contemporary (and by no means definitive) form of an evolutionary process that parallels societal evolution.[1]

My approach is macrosociological, with the society (or nation-state) considered as the analysis unit, and structural-functional in that it seeks to locate the medical system in social space as part of the society for which it performs (or is expected to) functionally significant tasks (or considered as such). As an "open system," it must receive from the society certain generalized "inputs" or supports. These, in turn, are "problematic," not only because resources are always limited (with the one exception of culture, to which I shall return), but also because other systems must compete for these resources to perform their own functions. As we shall see, the changing nature of these inputs over time profoundly affects (indeed, often transforms) the medical system *and* its outputs (services).

In a paradigmatic way, I conceive of the medical system as consisting of at least three analytically separate components: (1) education and professional socialization, (2) research, and (3) services. I shall, in this paper, focus on services because they constitute, in the final analysis, what the medical system is all about. I see education and research as essentially "internal" processes that are the necessary underpinnings for services; services I see as transactions that move

<hr>

[1] On the concept of social evolution see Shmuel N. Eisenstadt, "Social Evolution," *International Encyclopedia of the Social Sciences* (New York: Macmillan and The Free Press, 1968), pp. 228–234; Talcott Parsons, "Evolutionary Universals in Society," *American Sociological Review*, 29:339–357 (1964); Shmuel N. Eisenstadt, "Social Change, Differentiation and Evolution," *American Sociological Review*, 29:375–386 (1964).

from the medical system and across its boundaries to recipients in the social system.

SOME "MEDICAL" NEEDS
OF THE SOCIAL SYSTEM

The concept of the social system implies a meaningful interrelationship among the different and functionally complementary parts of the system, so that change or disturbance in one part of the system is likely to affect the other parts and the system in general.[2] A social system may then be said to consist of a network of patterned and complementary social roles, organized within interdependent and interrelated institutional clusters in such a way that the institutionalized role (rather than the individual actor or member) is the basic constitutive element of social structure. Any individual actor, during his day or lifetime, thus fulfills various roles, and it is on the predictable performance of these roles that the social system's existence and its adaptation to and mastery of the environment depend, to a significant degree.[3]

The performance of social actors according to certain expectations is thus an important prerequisite for functioning social systems, and is in turn dependent on a series of mechanisms that must again be looked upon as problematic, such as socialization, institutionalization, and the control of deviant behavior. Through these mechanisms, society shapes the individual's ability to act and channels it along avenues consistent with the requirements of the social order. But capacity to act and indeed the very integrity and existence of the social system are also threatened, given the biological and psychological nature of the social actor, by the incapacity that results from illness, injury, and premature mortality. Ability to act, or the motivation to do so, may be vitiated by physical failure, the ultimate form of which is biological death, or by such emotional or psychological failure as mental illness or retardation, which causes erratic behavior or withdrawal from society, the ultimate form of which is social death as in severely psychotic or regressed patients. Indeed, health is a vital concern "because the capacity of the human individual to achieve is ultimately the most crucial social resource. Illness is . . . essentially a disturbance of this capacity to perform in socially valued tasks and

[2] For a thorough discussion of living systems see James G. Miller, "Living Systems: Basic Concepts," *Behavioral Science*, vol. 10, no. 3 (July 1965), p. 203, and "Living Systems: Structure and Process," and "Living Systems: Cross-Level Hypotheses," *Behavioral Science*, vol. 10, no. 4 (October 1965), pp. 337–411.

[3] Talcott Parsons, *The Social System* (Glencoe, Ill.: The Free Press, 1951).

roles."[4] The basic function, then, of medicine is to preserve (and even to enhance) the capacity of the individual to act when that capacity is threatened by illness and mortality.

From the viewpoint of society, and particularly of an "activistic" and highly complex industrial society, the preservation of mental and physical health, because of its potential effect on mental and physical capacity, has a significance that far transcends, but in no way excludes, the personal unhappiness that goes with illness, injury, mental incapacity, and death. The devastating impact of illness and premature mortality on the economy and eventually on the entire life of a society is well known and need not be detailed here.[5] One might add merely that the larger and the more internally complex, differentiated, and interdependent a social system becomes, the greater the potentially destructive impact of illness on that system. Furthermore, whereas in a primitive or peasant society the major health problem is the physical incapacitation of individuals as "hands," in a more advanced society, particularly one in which tasks are performed by mechanical and other nonhuman and nonanimal power, the increasingly important health problem is *personality* incapacitation through mental illness or emotional disturbance. Parsons also makes the conceptual distinction between the two and implies that there is a range roughly from the "purely somatic" to the "purely mental" that applies perhaps to all mammalian species. According to him, mental illness is best defined by role-performance, and somatic illness by task-performance. Both performances are institutionalized expectations in all societies.[6]

It may thus be conjectured that the saliency of mental illness may well increase with the differentiation and the complexity of a social system. This might explain why, for instance, mental illness at the present time is *considered* a more important problem in American than in Soviet society, although some evidence shows that in the two societies the incidence and prevalence rates of mental disorder (particularly the psychoses) are strikingly similar. American society underwent modernization considerably earlier than the USSR, where the

[4] Talcott Parsons, "Some Trends of Change in American Society: Their Bearing on Medical Education," in *Structure and Process in Modern Societies* (Glencoe, Ill.: The Free Press, 1960), p. 281.

[5] Brian Abel-Smith, for example, in a comparative study of health expenditures, has pointed to the vicious circle of poverty and ill health: "Countries had poor health because they were poor, and to some extent they were poor because they had poor health." *An International Study of Health Expenditures* (Geneva: World Health Organization, 1967), Public Health Papers, no. 32, p. 46.

[6] Talcott Parsons, "Definition of Health and Illness in the Light of American Values and Social Structure," in *Patients, Physicians and Illness*, ed. E. Gartly Jaco (Glencoe, Ill.: The Free Press, 1958), pp. 165–184.

major medical problems are still considered to be somatic, and where about half the population is still rural as against a much smaller proportion in the United States. As the Soviet Union (and other societies) catch up with the more industrial ones, the demands on the population will also change, and mental illness and personality disorganization will be recognized as having increased significance.[7]

Thus, because of the structural changes that have taken place in contemporary industrial society, it may well be that medical and psychological care will not be considered any more either a question of privilege or income, or even a question of "rights": in the modern society, it tends to become an aspect of social policy with fundamental "functional" implications and with increased claims on societal resources, human, material, and political.

To better conceptualize the nature and the functions of the contemporary medical system, I shall attempt to specify the sociocultural responses to illness by fairly universal mechanisms and roles intended to mitigate, neutralize, and, if possible, eliminate its impact on society and its members. By and large, four (and possibly more) analytically distinct such responses may be identified:

1. The *magical* response is an attempt to understand or affect the course of illness conceived as the result of the action of forces (deities or enemies, for example), which man tries to propitiate through certain actions, usually rituals. The magical response must be seen in the light of uncertain outcomes and man's desire to procure favorable ones. It often embodies an anthropomorphic perspective on causality (the "anger of the gods" must be placated somehow). It should be noted that this response tends to be action-oriented: ceremonial dances, sacrifices, and the wearing of amulets answer the need "to do something" about illness and uncertainty. "If you want the patient to recover, pray for him like you never prayed before" is a familiar verbal formula that epitomizes this response.

2. The *religious* response stems from man's attempt to get at the "meaning" of suffering and death with ultimate values. It attempts to reconcile man to the existence of phenomena that remain mysterious but which he must accept as the work of some higher providence whose designs he cannot plumb. The formula "the Lord giveth and the Lord taketh away, blessed be the name of the Lord" reflects this need; otherwise, the death of a loved child, for example, remains essentially meaningless. Why that child had to die can of course often

---

[7] Mark G. Field, "Soviet and American Approaches to Mental Illness: A Comparative Perspective," in *New Aspects of the Mental Health Services,* ed. Hugh Freeman and James Farndale (Oxford: Pergamon Press, 1967), pp. 294–333.

be given in clinical, biological, statistical, or "scientific" terms ("massive hemorrhage of the brain," "average yearly incidence"), but this is hardly likely to be a "meaningful" answer to bereaved parents. It must be noted that the religious answer, as defined here, is essentially passive, that is, oriented toward acceptance and resignation and that the "why" cannot satisfactorily be derived from a purely "scientific" or rational viewpoint.

3. The *compassionate/therapeutic* response stems from the need for comfort, sustenance, and "therapy" that the suffering, anxiety-ridden, frightened, and often psychologically disturbed or regressed patient (and frequently those near him) need during illness, suffering, or disability. It is the "virtue" or "love" that Paracelsus describes as one of the four pillars on which the healing art stands.[8] This response also must embody a fiduciary element; in other words, the patient, his relatives, and the society as a whole must trust the physician. When the latter uses the formula "Believe me, this is for your *own* good," he is (or should be) interpreted differently than if he were a salesman. Codes of ethics and institutionalized professional behavior are attempts to secure this confidence, which, because of the often intimate relationship between physician and patient, is critical for the effectiveness of the medical intervention. The compassionate/therapeutic response, at the same time, is intensely human and personal, because only another human being can provide it (it cannot, so far as I know, be automated).

4. The *technological* or *scientific* response is the application of "empirical" or "scientifically grounded" knowledge, techniques, and technology in a rational approach to alleviating or eliminating pathological states seen as the result of the action of "scientifically" identifiable and verifiable forces; it is, of course, what is often defined as "medical treatment" or "services," and is primarily an active, interventionist approach: stopping the bleeding, massaging the heart, giving an injection, or transplanting an organ. The usual verbal formula for this response is "the doctors are doing everything in their power to save the life (or limb) of the patient."

It may further be proposed that the "mix" between these four responses in any society heavily depends on its culture, structure, and general ethos. For example, a society that emphasizes mastery over nature, an activist orientation toward the problems it faces, and an involvement in the "world," such as Parsons suggests is the case of American society, will also be concerned with the health of its mem-

[8] The other three are philosophy, astronomy, and chemistry. Henry E. Sigerist, *The Great Doctors* (Garden City, N.Y.: Doubleday-Anchor, 1958), pp. 98–99.

bers.[9] And by the same token, the Soviet concern with the health and welfare of its citizens, which at first blush might seem incompatible with the usually accepted stereotype of totalitarianism, may be understood (in part, at least) by the dedication of the Soviet leadership to a program of rapid modernization that could hardly be carried out with a chronically sick and debilitated population plagued by low life expectancy.[10]

On the other hand, cultures and societies less concerned with mastering the world emphasize the more passive, the more "religious" reaction to illness, an acceptance of illness as the will of some greater power that can inflict and cure disease. As Sigerist writes, "At all times there have been persons who sought healing, even bodily healing, not from the physician but from the priest, who looked to religion for a cure." [11] One might further argue that this magical-religious approach, though undoubtedly soul-satisfying and fulfilling the needs for action and meaning, might not be as effective in reducing infant and child mortality as the scientific way; furthermore, one might propose that the magical and religious responses have become more the domain of religious specialists or philosophers, though not by any means exclusively. Indeed, even in a highly rational and scientific medical system, medical personnel must deal with uncertainty and with the problem of meaning and cannot dismiss these areas as irrelevant (the "optimistic bias" of the medical profession, for example, which is often without objective justification, may well be a magical response). But it might be said that in contemporary society the compassionate/therapeutic and the technical responses constitute the core responsibilities of the medical system. In earlier times such a differentiation between these four responses did not exist. This paper will therefore be concerned with the balance between the compassionate-therapeutic and technical responses in modern medicine, and with the possibility of a further differentiation between these two elements.

SOCIETAL RESPONSE TO ILLNESS: STRUCTURAL DIFFERENTIATION AND THE MEDICAL CARE SYSTEM

A retrospective look at societal and individual response to illness and premature mortality suggests that, in *very* primitive societies, this response was unspecific and undifferentiated, and so were the social

[9] Talcott Parsons, "Definition of Health and Illness in the Light of American Values and Social Structure."

[10] For a more detailed examination of these two aspects of Soviet society, see my *Soviet Socialized Medicine: An Introduction* (New York: The Free Press, 1967), chap. 1.

[11] Henry E. Sigerist, *The Great Doctors,* p. 7.

roles, collectivities, symbols, and facilities centered around morbidity and mortality. For example, on the origins of Greek medicine Sigerist comments that in the "early days it must have been primitive — a mishmash of religion, magic, and empirically acquired ideas and practices." [12] Early societies thus had no health "specialists," clinics, sanatoria, or hospitals any more than they had full-time teachers, agricultural experts, schools, factories, temples, parliaments, or large population centers. To the degree that "medical" functions were performed, we must assume they were performed by practically everybody (especially members of the family or kinship group) or not performed at all. It might be added, incidentally, that even today in our highly specialized and complex society, the family still retains some *residual* "medical" functions [13] such as the responsibility and care of sick children by the mother, who in the final analysis must decide whether or not to call for medical help. And, as the story at the beginning of this paper suggested, there is a little bit of the physician in each one of us, and even if we do not proffer medical advice, most of us are ever ready to counsel people that they "ought to see a doctor."

It can furthermore be surmised that fairly early in societal development specialized roles began to emerge around the health concern, and that the rise of medical or medico-religious specialists at such an early phase reflects the critical centrality of capacity, i.e., of the human ability to perform, and thus of health and illness. In the past, the "religious" and the "medical" concerns were often coterminous, as in classical Greek culture. Even today, anyone who has visited Lourdes, St. Anne de Beaupré, or other "miraculous" shrines can testify to the closeness of religion and medicine, and to the fact that in many past cultures the religious and the medical specialist were not yet differentiated from each other.[14]

The practice of medicine as a full-time, relatively specialized, and narrow occupation (whether by itself or in conjunction with religious, priestly, or perhaps other functions) and the rise of an individual specialist clearly identified as a "physician" mark the beginning of the structural differentiation of a medical role and of a medical culture

---

[12] Ibid., p. 10.

[13] Talcott Parsons and Renée Fox have demonstrated that "the modern American family cannot undertake *major* responsibility for the sick" (italics added). "Illness, Therapy and the Modern Urban American Family," in *Patients, Physicians, and Illness,* ed. E. Gartly Jaco (Glencoe, Ill.: The Free Press, 1958), pp. 234–243.

[14] Henry E. Sigerist, "The Social History of Medicine," *Western Journal of Surgery, Obstetrics and Gynecology,* 42:714–722 (October 1941); also in *Henry E. Sigerist on the History of Medicine* (New York: MD Publications, 1960), pp. 25–33. Also his *Civilization and Disease* (New York: Cornell University Press, 1945), particularly pp. 131–147.

from other, more diffuse, and less differentiated ascriptive matrices and lead to a series of important structural changes.

At the most obvious level, individuals must be recruited to work exclusively as physicians. These physicians must enjoy trust on the part of patient and society, and their activities must be considered legitimate (for example, cutting into patients' bodies). They are considered to have specialized knowledge or techniques that the rest of the population does not have and that they acquire from older physicians (usually through apprenticeship, and more recently through formal education and training). And finally, certain supports and resources must be placed at their disposal. These are of two most general types: political and economic. A political resource is the authority to make decisions (of a medical nature) that affect other members of the society, including auxiliary medical personnel; an example would be the right to issue "orders" or to dispose of a budget. Physicians also need economic supports and facilities to work as physicians. Among these are instrumentalities or "means of medical production," whether it be an aspirin, an operation theater, a specialized hospital, or the budget mentioned earlier. Without these, physicians are as useless as typists without typewriters, or electric typewriters during a power failure.

Furthermore, because the physician's occupation prevents him from directly providing for his own needs (raising his own food, building his own house, and so on), some arrangements must be made for the exchange of medical time for nonmedical time, first through a crude barter system in which the patient brings food, goods, or provides services to the physician, and eventually through a more sophisticated exchange, mediated in money terms (either fee-for-service or a form of third-party payment). In this exchange (Figure 1), the outflow of medical services and time to the patient is matched by a return flow to the physician, permitting him to purchase necessary goods and services for himself and his family. Therefore, although one might want to ask what should be the "proper" remuneration of physicians in contemporary society, one cannot question the need for this income or some equivalent, because the physician cannot feed his children or pay his rent solely from the dewy-eyed gratitude of his patients.

The evolution of "scientific" medicine in the nineteenth and twentieth centuries, the increase in scientific medical knowledge and the expansion of its applications, the development of new techniques and of biomedical technology have all led to increasingly complex and costly tools and facilities with which and in which the physician applies his skill to managing illness. The modern, heavily instrumented, and research-oriented university-affiliated teaching hospital is proto-

FIGURE 1

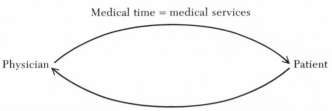

Medical time = medical services

Physician   Patient

Nonmedical time = nonmedical goods and services

typical of such facilities, and is indeed their most dramatic and sophisticated embodiment. The complexity of, as well as the sheer quantitative demand for, medical services increases at a faster rate than physicians can be trained to supply them: this then leads to a division of labor and the emergence of health workers who are neither physicians nor university-trained but who work within formal medical settings, usually under the direction of physicians, and who contribute to fashioning a medical care "product." The exact relationship of these new personnel to the physicians, whether they are treated as assistants, associates, collaborators, underlings, semiprofessionals, ancillaries, or auxiliaries, is irrelevant at this juncture, although in another context this is one of the major issues in the modern medical world. What matters here is that physicians in contemporary medicine now constitute but a small and decreasing proportion of those who are directly occupied in the medical system.

Without going into more detail, it may be said that contemporary society has a fully differentiated medical care system (or subsystem) that has boundaries (or boundedness), i.e., it can be identified, in the same way that the family, educational, economic, political, religious, and other systems can be identified and conceptualized. William Kissick points to the amazing diversity and complexity of that system, particularly in American society with its mixture of public, voluntary, and private agencies:

> [It is] represented by a multitude of resources, both human and material, and a myriad of services derived from these resources. It is composed of programs dealing with people and programs concerned with the facilities, programs related to services, research and educational activities. It requires the labors of physicians, dentists, nurses and other professional and technical health manpower, as well as clerical workers, janitors and so on. It encompasses hospitals, nursing homes, rehabilitation centers and health departments. It includes environmental control and biomedical research programs, the phar-

maceutical industry, hospital and medical insurance plans, large national voluntary health agencies, small areawide planning councils. It
is an interest of the federal, state and local governments and requires
the participation of uncounted individuals from all walks of life. . . .
[It] involves many secular endeavors—education, agriculture, commerce, recreation and conservation. . . . Finally it requires vast and
increasing expenditures.[15]

The expression medical or health care "system" is thus meant as
conceptual shorthand for the aggregate of efforts and resources, human, material, and political, that a society (taken as the unit of
analysis) sets aside for activities centered around health and illness.
The word "system" is not meant to imply that, in its internal structure
and functioning, it necessarily operates as an integrated system in the
usual sense. This certainly is not the case, particularly in the United
States, where medicine and medical care have sometimes been termed
a "non-system" because of their chaotic nature, lack of coordination
and planning, duplication, and gaps in services. Semantically it would
perhaps make better sense to talk of the medical "sector" or the medical "program(s)" of the society, though the first expression is too
passive in tone, and the second too dynamic. By "system" I shall continue to mean the aggregate of activities directed at prevention,
diagnostics, therapeutics, and rehabilitation — what Kerr L. White
defines as "the things done to and for all individuals who request or
require health services provided by doctors, nurses and dentists, and
the allied health professions." White sees no need to separate the
physical, emotional, and social components of illness, nor any need
to distinguish between the various sites of care or methods of payment.[16] As such the medical system provides, in its aggregate activities, a specialized service or output that is functionally important to
society and personally valuable to the individual. In turn that system,
because of its specialized activities, cannot be self-sufficient any more
than the physician in full-time practice, and it must receive several
types of resources from society that are conceptually analogous to
those mentioned earlier about the physician in solo practice. They are
called here *mandate-trust-legitimacy and information, knowledge, personnel,* and *instrumentalities.*[17]

[15] William L. Kissick, "Foreword" to "Dimensions and Determinants of Health
Policy," *The Milbank Memorial Fund Quarterly,* vol. 46, no. 1 (January 1968),
part 2, p. 7.

[16] Kerr L. White, "Organization and Delivery of Personal Health Services:
Public Policy Issues," *The Milbank Memorial Fund Quarterly,* vol. 46, no. 1
(January 1968), part 2, pp. 225–226.

[17] Michael Davis identifies the basic elements of medical services as (1) people,
(2) professionals, (3) facilities, (4) organization, and (5) finances. William Kissick
speaks of three *basic* resources: (1) health manpower, (2) facilities, including

Mandate-trust-legitimacy and information. To perform its functions the medical care system must enjoy trust in performing its mandate (providing medical or health services) and recognition that its activities are "legitimate." A "charter" must be granted by society specifying what the health system's obligations and privileges are. Society's trust is fundamentally important because of the "life and death" aspects of illness and the disastrous possibilities resulting from negligence or the exploitation of the patient. As White reminds us,[18] society symbolically enters into a contract with medicine. This fiduciary commitment often gives to health personnel (particularly professionals) the privilege of policing themselves and their activities and thus a relatively free hand in most professional matters.[19] This also requires mechanisms that articulate the medical system and the rest of society: among these is the need for communicating information from the society to the medical system (for example, what are the medical problems of the society in morbidity — quantitatively and qualitatively) and from the medical system to society (what are the requirements for manpower and financial support, for instance); this articulation also demands spokesmen acceptable to both, special boards and committees, and legal provisions (legislation pertaining to health). Finally, that mandate is usually (as seen earlier) both an expression of, and consistent with, the basic cultural values of the society.

Knowledge. A second indispensable resource of the medical system is a body of knowledge and techniques. This is a "cultural" resource and as such it can be transmitted and shared by medical personnel either orally through precepts (apprenticeship) or in the written form, or by an educational system (itself based on the general

---

equipment and supplies, and (3) biomedical knowledge of "state of the art." He sees organization and financing as intangible resources or mechanisms that serve to translate the three basic resources into health services. In William H. Kissick, "Health Manpower in Transition," *The Milbank Memorial Fund Quarterly,* vol. 46, no. 1 (January 1968), part 2, p. 53.

[18] White, "Organization and Delivery of Personal Health Services," p. 228.

[19] It might be argued that the question of the judgment or review of professional practices will, in the light of the development of hospital work and of instrumentation, increasingly become more "open" to outside scrutiny. The existence of tissue review committees and the computerization of hospital records thus permit a more "objective" review of the physician's work. The growth of malpractice suits may also be indicative of a trust erosion. In addition, the conflict between the experimenter's desire for knowledge and the human subject's desire to protect himself makes ethical review a necessity. On this subject, see the monograph by Bernard Barber, John Lally, Julia Makarushka, and Daniel Sullivan, *Experimenting with Humans: Problems and Processes of Social Control in the Bio-Medical Research Community* (New York: Russell Sage Foundation, forthcoming).

educational system of the society) in which formal and informal schooling, controlled by the medical system, is used. The knowledge resource is a nonfinite resource compared to the others mentioned here, because sharing, transmitting, and utilizing knowledge and techniques do not diminish their amount in a zero-sum sense. When a physician invents a new procedure to deal with a medical problem, this procedure can be applied by another physician or a million others without affecting that discovery.

But it should be noted that knowledge, and particularly its application, often does require substantial human and material investments and, as we shall see, in a field as labor-intensive as medicine it often increases the demands for personnel and funds rather than decreases them, as is usually the case in industry. In addition, important resources must be made available to the medical system in the search for knowledge through medical research; this research, in turn, heavily depends on the general state of science and technology in the larger social system and in the world in general. An example of this is the use of laser beams in some types of surgery. Two more points should be made: as medicine becomes more complex and organized, social-managerial research will take its place in medical research alongside the more traditional laboratory research to assist in organizing medical care and in its delivery. Also, because medical research is usually not classified, it is common for one medical system to apply the results of the research work of another.

Personnel. A contingent of specialized individuals whose central occupational concern is medical must be motivated, recruited, trained, socialized, and territorially allocated, and must apply the results of new research and the accumulated fund of knowledge, techniques, and technology to solving the society's health problems (prevention, diagnosis, clinical care, and rehabilitation), and must, in the aggregate, be involved in research, education, and services. As was pointed out, these individuals need not all be physicians (or even nurses), and their inclusion is predicated only on their formal contribution, direct or indirect, to some phase of the health system.

Instrumentalities. To fulfill their collective mandate, health personnel must have at their disposal the necessary political powers (i.e., the authority), the necessary capital goods (hospitals, clinics, instruments, drugs, and so on), and financial resources (budgets, salaries, and fees) without which they could not work as health personnel.

At the most general level, it is thus possible to conceive of the medical system as a *social mechanism for the conversion of generalized, nonmedical resources into medical outputs or services* ("services

FIGURE 2
Social system

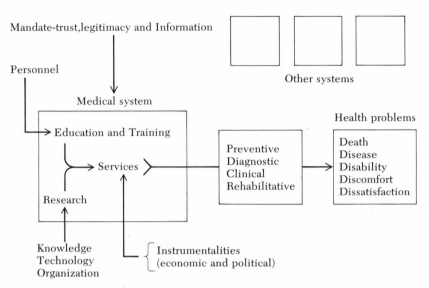

rendered by physicians, dentists, and other health professionals, plus all the goods and services consumed in connection with their work and under their direction" [20]). For example, choosing to channel human beings into the medical occupations and funds into building a hospital (rather than a school or a racetrack) eventually enables persons to perform complex abdominal surgery as against teaching English or racing horses. Schematically this can be represented as in Figure 2.

INTERNAL DIFFERENTIATION
OF KNOWLEDGE AND DEMAND

A closer look at the development of the medical system during the last hundred years, particularly in the West, will help us to identify salient features of that system in the modern world, and to suggest what lines of development are likely for the future. In most modern societies in the world today, and in the United States especially, the medical system has not only differentiated itself as a subsystem of the society — a phenomenon that took place most dramatically and irrevocably in the nineteenth century with the advent of "scientific" medicine

[20] V. R. Fuchs, "Basic Factors Influencing the Costs of Medical Care," *Report of the National Conference on Medical Costs* (Washington, D.C.: U.S. Government Printing Office, 1968), p. 17.

and industrialization — but presently *that subsystem is itself in a process of accelerated growth and internal differentiation and is moving from a relatively simple to a highly complex state.*

Two major (and to some degree interdependent) factors account for this process, in my opinion: the qualitative changes that result from new biomedical knowledge and its technological applications, and the quantitative changes that result from an increase of effective demand for medical and related services. These two factors correspond to two of the major inputs defined earlier: knowledge, and mandate-trust-legitimacy and information (the "mission" or "function" of the medical system). These two factors, in turn, affect the claims of the medical system for resources from the society by increasing the demand for manpower and for economic resources and political support (the other two inputs outlined earlier). Finally, this process of accelerated internal differentiation seems to have important implications for the nature and the quality (as well, of course, as the amount) of medical services the medical system is able to deliver to the society, which in the final analysis "pays" for these services from its personnel and political-financial resources.

According to Eisenstadt, differentiation is

> the ways through which the main social functions or the major institutional spheres of society become dissociated from one another, attached to special collectivities and roles, and organized into relatively specific and autonomous symbolic and organizational frameworks within the confines of the same institutional system. . . .
>
> Specialization is first manifest when each of the major institutional spheres, through the activities of people placed in strategic roles within it, develops its own organizational units and complexes and its specific criteria of action.[21]

The concept of complementarity of functions is important here as a criterion of differentiation. Otherwise, as Marsh points out, when "two or more structurally distinct roles or collectivities perform essentially the same function," the process is one of *segmentation*.[22]

It was suggested earlier that increases in knowledge and its technological application constitute important, largely primary variables. This is not to state that knowledge and technology are a kind of "demonic" force that operates independently of man's will and social decisions; but it is to convey the idea that once a discovery has been made, it exercises a strong pull on men and consequently on demands for applications. The insouciance of ignorance is thus replaced by the

21 Shmuel N. Eisenstadt, "Social Evolution," p. 229.
22 Robert Marsh, *Comparative Sociology* (New York: Harcourt, Brace and World, 1967).

guilt of potentiality. It is thus difficult, perhaps impossible, to go back to a situation in which it is as if the discovery had never been made in the first place. And it might be added that, because biomedical discoveries affect such fundamental aspects of man as his life and his health, pressures for them are bound to be powerful and have an emotional and universal appeal that may transcend traditional political and ideological differences. Good health care is, as Elling says, "an amazingly nonpartisan issue." [23] At the same time, the functional aspects of ill health, particularly when seen in an economic perspective — it is said that the common cold alone causes a loss of 100 million man days of production each year [24] — exercise their own pull for the application of medical measures.

The further implications of the large-scale application of biomedical technology are difficult to assess. On the one hand, just like any other invention or innovation, biomedical knowledge and technology may bring about a release or conservation of energy for the medical system and for society. For example, reducing certain types of diseases (poliomyelitis, measles, tuberculosis, or influenza-pneumonia) has dramatically reduced the demand for personnel and facilities to treat these conditions, and released them for possible other uses (mental illness and retardation, geriatric and degenerative diseases). Sometimes new technology permits a substantial saving in personnel and facility costs, and a higher level of accuracy. For instance, a portable electrocardiograph now being tested by the U.S. Public Health Service will enable *nurses* to take electrocardiograms routinely in patients' homes and have them immediately analyzed by a computer in Washington — all for one dollar per use, as against $10 to $15 at the doctor's office or in a hospital.[25]

On the other hand, *new knowledge and the introduction of new technology, rather than decreasing personnel needs and financial costs, often increase them drastically.* Thus, technology, in the medical area, contrary to the general experience in industry where it is labor-saving, often *increases* the demand for personnel, "because it keeps creating new things to do, instead of just new ways to do things." [26] As most

[23] Ray H. Elling, "The Shifting Power Structure in Health," *The Milbank Memorial Fund Quarterly*, vol. 46, no. 1 (January 1968), part 2, p. 133.

[24] *The New York Times*, October 27, 1966, p. 30, "Sabin Asks Coordinated Effort to Find Cold's Cause."

[25] S. Greenberg, "The Arrival of Electronic Medicine," *The Progressive*, 31 (June 1965), cited in Anne R. Somers, "Some Basic Determinants of Medical Care and Health Policy: An Overview of Trends and Issues," *The Milbank Memorial Fund Quarterly*, vol. 46, no. 1 (January 1968), part 2, p. 18.

[26] Report, *Secretary's Advisory Committee on Hospital Effectiveness* (Washington, D.C.: U.S. Government Printing Office, 1968), p. 6.

infectious diseases respond to medical treatment, individuals live longer and become candidates for a whole new range of illnesses (the so-called degenerative diseases) for which there is no known cure, and medical institutions for protracted care with personnel oriented to that kind of condition will be necessary. Medical technology thus does not necessarily reduce the need for personnel, but rather intensifies it as more people are needed to design, build, operate, and repair the new machinery. This is particularly true because medical care is, in essence, labor- rather than capital-intensive.

The complexity that results from the increasing internal differentiation of the medical system (both of roles and of the activities of collectivities such as hospitals, health centers, group practice, and so on) may be said to be "functional" or "beneficial" only to the degree that it improves the medical system's ability to fulfill its mandated task in an activistic society: to deliver an effective "product" that enables the society to cope with the problems of incapacity and disability presented by illness, injury, and premature mortality. It is difficult, and probably impossible, to make precise and categorical statements on the subject, because of the vagueness of the term "mandate," and the difficulty of setting up two control situations: one a relatively simple medical system, the other a relatively complex one. The question would then be posed: what would be the state of modern society, all things remaining relatively equal, if instead of having the kind of medical system it has today, it had a relatively simple one, consisting primarily of physicians trained for general and solo practice as they were a hundred years ago? I am not asking what would happen to contemporary society if, through some kind of strike, or disabling illness, or widespread catastrophe that would affect health personnel, the medical system simply ground to a halt and stopped functioning altogether. Such a question might be easier to answer, within gross limits, of course. But this is not the point. It is generally presumed that the internal differentiation and the increased sophistication of contemporary medical care permit the medical system to save more lives, to increase life expectancy, to reduce disability and suffering, to eliminate and mitigate many pathological conditions, and so on. But increased complexity, by itself, does not necessarily guarantee a better "output," if the increasingly narrow activities of the system's units are not, in one way or another, brought together into a comprehensive and well-ordered fashion, if they are not integrated into a real "system" of complementary parts.

It is my contention that a critical element in the medical system is (and will obviously continue to be) its organization — the integration of its differentiated elements — and the more complex that system is, the more strategic such organization becomes. In addition, the very process of differentiation and specialization contributes to a fragmentation of the medical services themselves and affects the compassionate/therapeutic component of medical care in an essentially negative way, as will be discussed. Before moving to a closer examination of these questions, it will be necessary to examine more fully what is actually happening within the medical system, and to document this process of differentiation.

Within medicine, as in many other areas, the most important factor is specialization or specialty practice. Specialization alters the professional and occupational roles in the medical system in both a vertical *and* a horizontal proliferation of specialized roles, thereby, as suggested earlier, making managing and integrating the activities and outputs of these roles more critical.

SPECIALIZATION, THE HEALTH PROFESSIONS, AND THE MEDICAL CARE SYSTEM

Specialization, whether professional, semiprofessional, or occupational, is one hallmark of contemporary, large-scale, industrial society, although the division of labor, the earliest phase of specialization, is probably as old as human society. In simpler societies it was based primarily on age and sex differences, and even until fairly recently occupational specialization was rudimentary compared to the proportions it has reached in the twentieth century. It is the result, principally, of the vast expansion of knowledge and its technological application. The fact that in the area of health care one must look at *at least* three major occupational groups already indicates a process of differentiation *within the medical area* and reflects the fact that the physician is no longer, by any means, the almost exclusive purveyor of medical care. Further differentiation through specialization *within* these groups also occurs, a process that is most marked among the physicians, but also increasingly visible among other groups.[27] The major groups follow.

Professionals. These professionals in medicine usually hold a doctorate from a university, and are usually physicians (M.D.'s and

[27] As Jones points out, there were, it is true, almost as many specialties among folk-practitioners of the eighteenth and nineteenth centuries as now exist among physicians: bone-setters, baruchers, wart-doctors, and others. What is new "is the refinement of knowledge and techniques underlying specialization and its growth within the control of a single profession." Louis C. Jones, "Practitioners of Folk Medicine," *Bulletin of the History of Medicine,* 23 (September–October 1949), pp. 480–493; and Eliot Freidson, "The Organization of Medical Practice," in *Handbook of Medical Sociology,* ed. Howard E. Freeman, Sol Levine, and Lee G. Reeder (Englewood Cliffs, N.J.: Prentice-Hall, 1963), pp. 299–319.

D.O.'s), dentists (D.M.D.'s and D.D.S.'s), or belong to some related group (optometrists, podiatrists, pharmacists, veterinarians).

From the 1930's to the 1960's, the change among practicing physicians has been dramatic: the percentage of general practitioners and specialists has almost reversed itself. In 1931 four-fifths of all American physicians were in general practice, and one-fifth in specialty practice; in 1966, about three-fourths of practicing physicians were in specialties, though it should be clear that those who declared themselves specialists and were reported in the figures were not necessarily all board certified.[28]

Past trends make it seem unlikely that the drift toward specialization will reverse itself or that the proportion of medical school graduates planning to go into general practice will increase. As Magraw points out, "This process (specialization and sub-specialization) is natural, irresistible and shows no sign of slackening. . . . Almost every defined medical specialty has one or several recognized sub-specialties requiring special knowledge, skills, and perspectives. These areas require a kind of expertness which necessarily precludes continuing general expertness in the parent area." And he adds that *"the specialization of the entire physician population within another 15 to 20 years, if not sooner, is likely."* [29]

The drawings in Figure 3 are an attempt, not to scale, to represent the past, present, and predicted trends in the balance between general practitioners and specialists in American medicine. The startling changes in proportion are clear.

Allied health professionals. These health professionals and allied, paramedical, semiprofessional, and technical personnel in health [30] are nurses, physical and occupational therapists, medical laboratory technicians, medical record librarians, dieticians, sanitarians, dental hygienists, associate degree or diploma nurses, X-ray and dental

[28] Thus 9,824 physicians in this country were listed in 1957 as certified by the American Board of Internal Medicine, or 53 per cent of the total number listed as full-time specialists in internal medicine. The number certified in surgery was 7,863; in pediatrics, 5,469; in psychiatry and neurology, 5,243; and in radiology, 4,559. These constituted, respectively, 57, 73, 64, and 96 per cent of all full-time specialists in each field.

[29] R. M. Magraw, *Ferment in Medicine* (Philadelphia: W. G. Saunders Company, 1966), pp. 145–149 (my emphasis).

[30] The lack of a universally accepted terminology for this and the next category of occupations reflects not only their recent appearance, but also, as will be pointed out later, a degree of ambivalence on the part of society and, particularly, of physicians. These categories as used here could be drawn differently, and regrouped.

FIGURE 3

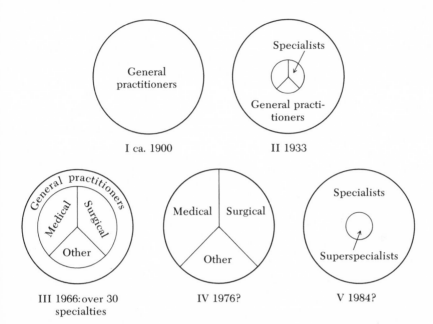

I ca. 1900   II 1933

III 1966: over 30   IV 1976?   V 1984?
specialties

laboratory technicians, and others. The great variety of occupations in this category may make it unjustified to lump them into a single category. But what is important is the growing diversity of jobs that individuals, other than those with advanced professional training, perform *within the context of health or medical services,* and technically (as well as legally) under the supervision and control of doctorate professionals.

Physicians today usually work not only with other physicians, but also with this increasingly large array of other health personnel. As the Health Manpower Commission reported, the volume of medical services provided under the direction of physicians has increased 81 per cent between 1955 and 1965 in the United States; this indicates how significant the "amplification" process is, because the increase in physicians has barely, if at all, kept up with the rise in the population. Thus, although the proportion of all types of physicians to constant population units in the United States has remained more or less constant (or has declined slightly), the number of other health personnel has tended to increase, and so has the diversity of new occupations, especially those resulting from the application of new technologies, such as "super-technicians for servicing artificial organs, nurse monitors for intensive care units, and systems analysts to bring modern management into medical care," [31] or nuclear medical technologists, radiological health technicians, and medical engineering technicians, hardly any of whom existed before World War Two.[32]

Thus, among allied health personnel, both a quantitative expansion and a constant process of internal differentiation are radically altering the nature of the medical team. In the United States at present, the so-called "health industry" is the third largest, in employed people, of seventy-one industries defined by the Bureau of the Census, with agriculture and construction ranking higher. In the so-called "health professions" — which include physicians (M.D.'s and D.O.'s), dentists, professional nurses, and other persons who are college-educated or professionally trained — from 1900 to 1960 the total number of such personnel has increased almost six-fold (5.78 times), while the number of physicians has not quite doubled (1.96 times). "Other health personnel" (all such personnel except for physicians) on the other hand have increased more than twelve times, with the most dramatic rise among professional nurses: in 1900 there were 640 professional nurses in the United States, and in 1960 there were over half a million (not all professionally active), an increase of almost 80,000 per cent (787.5 times). In these years, the proportion of physicians per 100 in all health professions has dropped by two-thirds (from 63 to 21). Whereas there was only about one professional nurse for 100 doctors in 1900, there were 208 in 1960.[33]

Other health occupations. Many occupations within the medical system are not specific to health, but are essential — for example, electricians, plumbers, and other hospital maintenance workers, physicians' secretaries, ambulance drivers, and so on. Of the 1960 estimated total of 2.5 million in the United States health services industries, 1.75 million belonged to what the census calls the health occupations (our first two categories here) and the rest (750,000) were in the supportive occupations not specific to health.[34]

There is reason to believe that the health services are now the

[31] D. D. Rutstein, *The Coming Revolution in Medicine* (Cambridge, Mass.: The MIT Press, 1967), p. 54.

[32] William F. Kissick, "Health Manpower in Transition," p. 58.

[33] The accuracy of the statistics given here could be challenged; furthermore, in many instances precise counts cannot be made, particularly if one takes into account variations in employment. But the general trend is unmistakable in most modern societies: the physicians who, in earlier times, constituted the majority of those in the medical area are now but a minority, though the leading or "managing" minority.

[34] M. Lerner and O. Anderson, *Health Progress in the United States, 1900–1960* (Chicago and London: University of Chicago Press, 1963), p. 221.

fastest-growing segment of the total American economy and will continue to be in the future.[35] From 1950 to 1960 the total U.S. civilian labor force rose 15 per cent, whereas health services personnel rose 54 per cent. Projections indicate that either health services or education will be the nation's largest consumer of manpower by 1970.[36]

STRUCTURAL CONCOMITANTS
OF DIFFERENTIATION AND EXPANSION

As seen earlier, two elements appear to be the critical forces causing structural changes in the medical system of contemporary industrial society, particularly American society. They have been identified as the increased application of biomedical knowledge and the surging demand for medical services. In addition to straining the society's manpower and financial resources, these two elements encourage the growth of specialization of professionals and health workers, and often lead them to assume administrative responsibilities. As someone said, nurses nowadays often see to it that nursing is done, rather than doing the nursing themselves. As a result, many in the medical care system cease being generalists and must curtail their direct contacts with patients.

In both cases, these professionals and allied health personnel have upgraded themselves or have been promoted to positions that, in a hierarchical scale, are superior to those they formerly occupied. As specialists or managers they usually acquire higher status, prestige, and increased financial rewards as their scope of concern is either narrowed and deepened (specialists), or is endowed with greater administrative responsibility (managers). Their upgrading or promotion is predicated on the assumption that their contribution in that new role will increase the effectiveness of the medical system. As a result, the health personnel hierarchy lengthens in the vertical dimension, as for example when the specialist and the superspecialist are added to the general practitioner, and it widens in the horizontal direction as more personnel are recruited into the medical system and as specialties are added at about the same level in the hierarchy to perform new and numerous tasks and to take care of an increasing number of patients.

If one attempts to visualize *all* those who, in a given society, are formally occupied in the medical system, a structure roughly resembling the usual social stratification pyramid might be drawn (see Figure 4). The dynamic nature of this structure is striking: where formerly

[35] Magraw, *Ferment in Medicine*, p. 166.
[36] Somers, "Some Basic Determinants of Medical Care and Health Policy," p. 20.

FIGURE 4

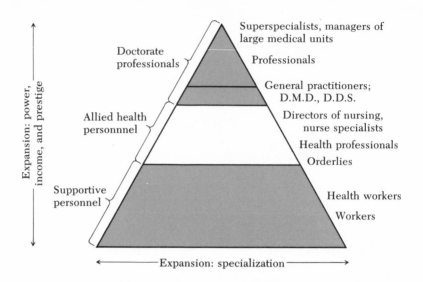

there were only physicians trained for general practice, there are now physicians in general practice, specialists, consultants, superspecialists, and physicians in administrative positions at different levels. Where formerly there were only general duty nurses, there is now a wide array of specialized registered nurses, and below them there are, as shall be noted in greater detail, several other "nursing" categories such as licensed practical nurses, nurses' aides, orderlies, and so on. Indeed, anyone who has been a patient in a hospital, particularly a teaching hospital, can testify to the bewildering variety and multiplicity of personnel (arrayed in different uniforms) who flash before his eyes.

DIFFERENTIATION AND DEPERSONALIZATION: TECHNOLOGY AND PATIENT ALIENATION

In the previous section, a process of upward mobility that results primarily from specialization and/or the assumption of managerial functions in medicine (and other fields) was mentioned. To state the medical situation simply: when a physician in general practice or a nurse in general nursing decides to *limit* his or her professional activities to a specialized condition or type of patient or to personnel management, society and the medical system have gained one specialist or manager where there was none before and lost one generalist where there *was* one before. Figure 5 shows the doctor-patient relationship before and after specialization.

The occurrence of "vacancies" in the system raises two important

FIGURE 5

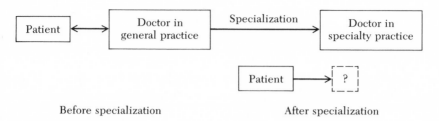

Before specialization   After specialization

questions: (1) Are the benefits of specialization great enough to out-weigh the losses incurred by vacating the generalist functions? (2) By what processes do these vacancies become filled, if at all? Let us briefly examine some major functions of generalized practice.

Access and primary diagnosis. One major characteristic of medical practice "in the community" was the continuous availability of the physician. Hanging the shingle was a symbolic act that signified that at this identifiable and known location, at almost any time, one could find a doctor, and medical ethics dictated that claims for primary medical care could not be turned down on any grounds. In this re-spect, even though in most instances the physician was in private practice as a member of a liberal ("free") profession, he was a "public servant" in the full sense. The "open door" also meant, in the simplest terms, that the patient could get into the medical system with the fewest barriers. He was thus "introduced" by his GP to the medical care system, however rudimentary it might have been. With the abso-lute and proportional decline of general practice in the community, particularly in the underprivileged neighborhoods, and the exodus of physicians to the suburbs, the potential patient has lost his important portal of entry into the medical system, although such functional sub-stitutes as the emergency rooms of hospitals have begun to develop. Moreover, even those physicians who are in general practice in the community often make themselves unavailable during evenings and weekends.

Allocation or triage. A further, analytically distinct aspect of the access and diagnosis problem in a complex medical system is the question of how, after preliminary diagnosis, doctors will allocate patients to the appropriate facilities and specialized personnel. This function is seen, perhaps in its sharpest form, under disaster condi-tions or on the battlefield, where the triage officer summarily decides where the victim must be sent next. The absence of such a role means that patients who need care are left to their own devices and may not get the right care at the right place at the right time. The allocative functions usually played by a general practitioner are thus a necessary complement to specialization in the sense that the GP (or triage officer) is assumed to have a fairly accurate cognitive map of the medical care environment, its resources, its strengths, and its gaps, and can thus refer patients to the appropriate personnel and facilities.

Comprehensiveness and continuity.   The general practitioner typically not only "cared for" an individual rather than a condition or an organ. He also cared for the patient's entire family by calling at the patient's home and by knowing other family members; in addition, through his familiarity with the community in which he lived and worked, the physician knew the social, economic, and psychological environment in which his patients lived and the kinds of pressures they were subject to. The increasingly "scientific" nature of medicine, with its search for the chemical or biological agent, has deflected the physician's attention away from the total social and psychological situation of the patient. In addition, changing the locus of medical care to the hospital presents the patient to the physician as an isolated specimen rather than one involved in multiple social relationships, some of which have a bearing on the illness. Finally, the closeness of the rapport between the general practitioner and his patient or patient's family permitted (in theory, at least) some continuity of care through the different and changing phases of illness, a continuity that often gets lost in the shuffle caused by specialization and by having the same patient treated by different personnel.

Orchestration and integration.   Insofar as the general practitioner considered the patient to be "his" patient — his *personal* medical responsibility — he could supervise the different and specialized medical services his patient received. The physician could call for this or that test or procedure, he could run interference for his patient through the medical maze, and in general he could be aware of his patient's medical progress, while at the same time keeping him informed and reassured. In this context, the hospital was the physician's own workshop, replacing either the patient's home or the physician's often ill-equipped office or private clinic. And if he used the services of a consultant, or later on of a specialist, he was still personally orchestrating the care of his patient. The disappearance of the generalist threatens this function, and failure to replace it by an appropriate functional substitute increases the possibility of error, duplication, and patient alienation.

Therapy.   These aspects of general medical practice suggest that specialization, with all the benefits it bestows at the technical level, often leads to the failure of the medical system to satisfy the patient's needs for reassurance, "love," and therapy. And as somatic illness is increasingly being conquered by specialized medical practice, the need for personality support, for establishing an intimate relationship with a professional in an impersonal society based on achievement and competition, is increasingly being neglected.

This is one reason why the decrease of general practitioners in the society has left the patient emotionally stranded, so to speak, and this may well account for the poor press the medical profession has received in recent years and the accusations levelled at it of coldness, indifference, and brusqueness. This also suggests that *the differentiation noted here should be accompanied not only by a process of integrating increasingly numerous and narrow specific outputs (as is the case in any complex organism), but should also be followed (at least in the area of medicine and medical care) by a parallel de-differentiation and generalization to provide the supportive, pastoral, and therapeutic aspects traditionally associated with medicine.* At the technical or instrumental level, increased differentiation increases the chance of technical errors through communications gaps, lack of discipline or control, and other problems that accompany an advanced division of labor. At the therapeutic level, the individual patient, particularly in the large, research-teaching center, must try to relate to many health personnel, he must undergo a large number of tests and procedures, and no one seems to know him personally. Caught in an impersonal medical technical juggernaut, surrounded by alien people, frightening machinery, pain, and the presence of death, his experience often assumes Kafka-esque proportions: the patient has become the victim of the "medicine of the absurd."

FILLING THE VACANCIES

The upgrading and promotion process that accompanies specialization and the assumption of managerial positions creates, as we have seen, "vacancies" in the medical system. In a typical bureaucracy with well-defined ranks and positions, such vacancies are usually filled by those below the vacated positions, usually through a seniority-merit basis, and an individual's "career" is typically a progression from rank to rank. The medical system, though it resembles a typical bureaucracy in some instances, in most does not. Because the professional and semiprofessional lines are well drawn and often jealously guarded, the movement of personnel from below into vacated positions does not take place so smoothly.

In nursing, for example, as the nurse assumes more managerial and advanced medical functions, her general nursing functions tend to be entrusted to licensed practical nurses; as the licensed practical nurse begins to assume nursing tasks, she delegates some of her original functions to nurses' aides; and as the system becomes desperate for personnel, it reaches into the community and attempts to enlist lay personnel. This amounts to a dual process of "downward transfer of functions" and a "de-skilling of jobs" to permit individuals with less formal training to assume at least some functions of those who upgrade themselves or are promoted.

This process becomes more complicated in the medical profession. For as general practice becomes vacated through specialization, no one with medical training stands below the general practitioner who might move upward to fill his role. Nurses, as a rule, do not become physicians, nor is it possible for a nurse to receive educational credits for her education against the requirements of medical training: she would have to start all over again. This incidentally is not true in the Soviet Union, where nurses and particularly *feldshers* (physicians' assistants) are encouraged to go to medical school and receive educational credits for their schooling and work experience. The absence of such a "career ladder" in the American medical system is an important impediment to filling vacancies. And yet, under the impact of the shortage of physicians and particularly of general practitioners, the same "downward transfer" of functions and "de-skilling" has also taken place to some extent. Nurses, for example, are now performing certain highly specialized "medical" functions that a few years ago only physicians would or could perform — functions that, at any rate, physicians would not have entrusted to nurses. Rutstein describes the advancement of nurses in administering needles as an example: in the 1930's, nurses could only inject a prescribed drug under the skin; they could not make a needle puncture. In the 1940's, some hospitals allowed them to draw blood *from* a vein (but not to inject medication). Now, in some hospitals, a small group of specially trained nurses gives all intravenous treatment, including drugs and transfusions; and technicians collect blood samples.[37]

As the nurse performs more complex tasks, with more responsibilities for the health and the lives of patients entrusted to her, and as she herself becomes more and more a specialist or administrator, then the original nursing duties, including the highly personal nurturing functions epitomized by the "guardian angel" or "mother surrogate" image, either do not get fulfilled or may be delegated, almost by default (as "menial" tasks), to less skilled personnel lower down in the hierarchy. These personnel move into the generalist slots vacated by nurses and

[37] Rutstein, *The Coming Revolution in Medicine*, pp. 69–70.

provide whatever "tender loving care" they can, as well as perform the more unappetizing tasks of emptying bedpans and changing sheets, which they will soon delegate to others below them.

In addition to this upgrading, general medical functions have been filled in other ways, at least in the American setting. Among professionals, "de-differentiation" occurs when specialists (particularly internists and pediatricians) assume the role of the generalist for their patients. Indeed, the role of the "specialist" in this context is unique and virtually unknown in other countries. He is perhaps best described as a "consultoid," because he is apt to have the training and the aspirations of a consultant but does the work of a generalist.[38] But not enough of them begin to fill the demand. In addition, foreign physicians and marginal medical roles (such as osteopaths) have been increasingly filling the role of general practitioner. Finally, as general practitioners have disappeared from many communities, collectivities such as hospitals play the role of general physician, available to all comers, on duty twenty-four hours a day, usually easily accessible, highly visible, and often better equipped than the physician in the community. Even our language reflects this shift. We formerly called a doctor when someone was sick, but now in an emergency we "rush him to the hospital." [39]

The emergence of specialists, considered to have more expert knowledge and therefore to occupy a position superior to the generalist, has left the latter often stranded in the role of the poor parent in the medical family despite the mystique that surrounds general practice. This negative judgment is often reinforced by studies that show that the level of medical sophistication in general practice is rather low.[40] In the United States, the stratification between the general practitioner and the specialist has been muted by the former's access to hospital facilities, but the gap between the two is much more marked in Great Britain, for example, where he is considered to have "fallen off the status ladder." [41]

In most countries where the general practitioners have lost prestige, professional bodies and practitioners concerned with general practice have risen to its defense and have proposed its revitalization, usually as a specialty commanding as much status as the other specialties, as

[38] White, "Organization and Delivery of Personal Health Services," p. 226.

[39] Magraw, *Ferment in Medicine*, p. 94.

[40] For example, Osler L. Peterson, Leon P. Andrews, Robert S. Spain, and Bernard G. Greenberg, "An Analytical Study of North Carolina General Practice, 1953–1954," *The Journal of Medical Education*, vol. 31 (December 1956), part 2.

[41] Lord Moran, cited by David Mechanic, "General Practice in England and Wales," *New England Journal of Medicine*, 279:680–689 (September 26, 1968).

in Denmark, for instance, where a physician can specialize in "General Medicine as a Specialty." [42]

One might well wonder, within the context of contemporary medical practice, whether training a "specialist in generalities" [43] is a realistic solution both to the shortage of general practitioners and their relatively low prestige, or whether a solution might not perhaps be found in a further differentiation between "technical" medicine (with its specialists and superspecialists) and general medicine (with its emphasis on the whole patient, particularly his psychological and emotional problems).

"VETERINARIANISM" IN MEDICINE: THERAPEUTIC POVERTY IN THE MIDST OF BIOMEDICAL ABUNDANCE

It has been argued that disorientation is the "price" the patient must pay for medical progress, life-saving techniques, and surgical wizardry. I would say, however, that the loss of the sustenance/therapeutic part of the medical role is the loss not of a peripheral but of a central aspect of medical care, an aspect that is of special importance in a society marked by activism and the mastery of nature, as we shall see.

It goes without saying that in an emergency situation when the individual's life hangs in the balance, the appropriate and life-saving scientific and technological intervention is preferred over the tender, sympathetic ministrations of health personnel who watch helplessly as the patient's life ebbs away. But in most instances the situation that faces the physician is not that dramatic, and the increasing inability of the medical system and the physician to provide for the sustenance of the patient impairs, in the final analysis, the effectiveness of the medical system. Indeed, it may be that the technical progress of medicine in the nineteenth and twentieth centuries has obscured one of its fundamental functions, which is perhaps best expressed by a motto carved on the lintel of the Hôtel-Dieu in Paris, one of the oldest hospitals in the world: "To cure seldom, to help sometimes, to comfort always." [44]

In a historical perspective, the function of the physician (and by extension the medical system as here defined) seems not to have changed

[42] World Health Organization, *World Health Statistics Annual 1963*, vol. 3 (Geneva, 1967).

[43] In 1966 the American Academy of General Practice announced a program and a campaign to make the family doctor a specialist, and in the spring of 1967 Governor Rockefeller of New York State signed a bill to establish a program to teach the general practice of medicine as a specialty in all state operated medical schools. *The New York Times*, March 27, 1969, p. 41.

[44] Cited by Robert Magraw in *Report of the National Conference on Medical Costs* (Washington, D.C.: U.S. Government Printing Office, 1968), p. 290.

appreciably over the centuries, and the demands that society and the individual patient make on the physician and the medical system have remained remarkably constant. The patient comes to the physician because he needs help, or better, because he needs care, in both senses — treatment and support (love). But the critical point is that progress in medical treatment has been accompanied by increased patient alienation of a special kind, compounded by the uncertainties and the anxieties that accompany illness and its association with disability, incapacity, and eventual death. As Malraux points out, a basic problem of modern civilization is that it is built around man as a physiological machine and not primarily as an individual person,[45] and in this context as an interesting (or uninteresting) medical case rather than a human being with his share of fears, anxieties, and emotions. It might be added that losing the sustenance function comes at a particularly critical phase in the evolution of society, because it is a society that has at its disposal very few readily available sources of intimate relationship of the expressive type outside the family. At the same time, this society becomes increasingly impersonal, competitive, achievement-oriented, and universalistic, and occupational success (the main criterion for achievement and recognition) increasingly depends on personality organization — that is, on psychological factors rather than physiological ones. And the physician, who traditionally was one major source of this expressive relationship, is becoming unwilling or unable to perform this function. To some degree, the psychiatrist plays this role, but in such small numbers that his impact, in the aggregate, on the emotional balance of a secular society, is extremely circumscribed.

It is possible to conceive (as suggested earlier) a further differentiation and even separation in the medical system. One kind of medicine would be propelled by specialization and fueled by biomedical knowledge and advances, and another kind of medicine would combine the supportive-therapeutic and other functions traditionally attached to general practice and the insights of psychiatry, and would effectively help the individual to "cope" with his adjustment problems and would direct him to somatic care when indicated. This would require the breaking of the unity of medical training, and educating two different (or even more) types of physicians. Although some would recoil at the idea of breaking this unity, the unitary concept of the "doctor" has already become more fiction than fact. When someone collapses at a gathering, as Elling remarks, it no longer makes sense to shout, "Is there a doctor in the house?" A range of specialists who really treat patients might answer the call, provided they are not afraid of mal-

[45] Henry Tanner, "Malraux Explains Some Changes in His Opinions," *The New York Times*, October 22, 1968, p. 41.

practice suits. But what about the other medical doctors: the administrator, the researcher, the "thing-oriented" specialist such as the radiologist, or the psychiatrist who for years has only *talked* to patients? Could they, Elling asks, do much more for the victim than a nurse or even the lay person trained in first aid? Thus, he says, "The physician is a myth, not only because doctors are trained in different types of programs but also because of differentiation within specialization." [46]

Thus the question that might be asked is whether the means of medical production (technology and hospitals) and the exchange of medical products (either on a fee-for-service or on a more "socialized" basis) have been so affected by new knowledge and the claims for its application that they have altered the doctor-patient relationship to the dysfunctional level, to the alienation of the individual and his physician from each other. These considerations of the paradoxical implications of the "industrialization" of medicine may serve as a partial explanation for the ferment in the relationship between the social and the medical systems, and for the dissatisfaction of both providers and recipients of care. This then opens the realistic future possibility of a further and formal differentiation between specialized medicine, whose practitioners would tend to speak a *universal* tongue of science and technology that is increasingly meaningless to the patient (except in the strictly technical sense), and a generalized and humane medicine (including psychiatry) whose practitioners would continue to deal meaningfully with patients in terms of their *particular* social and cultural background and their need for "care" in the dual sense of medical attention and of affection. This might go a long way toward counteracting the trend toward what has been termed in the Soviet Union "veterinarianism in medicine," [47] that is, treating man as an animal through an exclusively "natural-scientific" approach rather than as a sentient being with thoughts and emotions.

[46] Ray H. Elling, "The Shifting Power Structure in Health," pp. 119–143.

[47] "Vrach—eto myslitel'!" [The doctor—he is a thinker!], *Meditsinskaia Gazeta,* October 25, 1968, p. 3.

Social stratification is a stable and perduring subsystem in all social systems, Professor Eisenstadt holds, because such systems are not only differentiated but also make evaluations of their different roles, tasks, and rewards. Stratification changes as differentiation occurs along two dimensions: first, the specialization of roles; and, second, the separation of "the center" from "the periphery" of society. Professor Eisenstadt discusses what these two kinds of increasing differentiation mean for changes in strata formation, class consciousness, and class conflict.

S. N. Eisenstadt

CONTINUITIES AND CHANGES
IN SYSTEMS OF STRATIFICATION

Social differentiation and stratification are a basic yet distinct aspect of social organization, structure, and symbolism. The most important aspects of social structure that constitute the components of social stratification are, first, the fact that any social system is composed of interconnected roles, the incumbents of which are expected to perform different tasks. Second, the incumbents of these roles are usually allocated different rewards. Third, different individuals, categories, or groups of people in a society have differential access to such various positions or roles that are differentially evaluated. Fourth, the existence of such differential evaluation and of opportunities of access may possibly create, within any group or society, some type of hierarchy of roles or positions that may perhaps coalesce into some broader categories or into some groups or quasi-groups or both with some common identity and continuity, usually called strata or classes.[1]

[1] Talcott Parsons, "A Revised Analytical Approach to the Theory of Social Stratification," *Essays in Sociological Theory* (Glencoe, Ill.: The Free Press, 1954); Bernard Barber, *Social Stratification: A Comparative Analysis of Structure and Process* (New York: Harcourt, Brace & World, 1957); and Bernard Barber, "Social Stratification," in *International Encyclopedia of the Social Sciences* (New York: The Free Press and Macmillan, 1968).

But the process of stratification and strata formation does not constitute just an "objective" aspect of social structure and organization, which denotes the distribution of categories of people among different institutional spheres or about their control of different resources.

Beyond this stratification, the hierarchical ordering of social categories and groups is a basic component of self-identity and self-conception of people as members of societies, of the symbolism of social order, and of the way in which members of society tend to see their own place in the social and cultural order. But although social stratification in its organizational and symbolic aspects can be found in all societies, its concrete expression varies greatly among different societies. In this paper we shall attempt to analyze some similarities, differences, continuities, and changes in the nature of the stratification systems and strata formations in different societies — especially among primitive, "historical," and modern societies.[2]

SOURCES OF PRESTIGE

A very common designation or definition in sociological literature of such classes or strata has been by their differential control over, or possession of, the major types of resources and rewards that serve as the bases of any differential evaluation of positions — wealth, power, and prestige.[3] However, such a designation or definition of strata does not do full justice to the complexity and variety of the processes of strata formation in different types of societies. To approach this complexity, it is necessary to analyze, in somewhat greater detail, one major type of resources or rewards mentioned above, namely prestige.[4]

Of all the different rewards or resources, prestige seems on the one hand to be most "symbolic," most elusive, and least concrete. It does not seem to have those hard-core structural and organizational features that characterize money and commodities, power, coercion, and obedience. Its most obvious expressions are symbolic — such as esteem or deference given to people; conferral of medals or honorary titles; or keeping at certain distance from those who are attributed such prestige. Prestige seems also to be the most directly consummatory of all

[2] This analysis follows closely that presented in S. N. Eisenstadt, "Prestige, Participation and Strata Formation," in *Social Stratification* (Cambridge: Cambridge University Press, 1958), pp. 62–104, where a fuller theoretical discussion of many concepts mentioned here may be found.

[3] The problems of these definitions are discussed in Barber, *Social Stratification, op. cit.,* and M. Tumin, *Social Stratification: The Forms and Functions of Inequality* (Englewood Cliffs, N. J.: Prentice-Hall, 1967).

[4] S. N. Eisenstadt, "Prestige, Participation, and Strata Formation"; Edward Shils, "Deference," in *Social Stratification,* ed. J. A. Jackson, especially pp. 104–113.

the different rewards, i.e., it seems as if nothing can be done with it beyond merely enjoying the deference, reverence, or the special standing inherent in it.

And yet, on the other hand, in large parts of the sociological and historical literature on stratification, prestige manifested either in external status symbols, or in what is often called the "style of life" of different people and groups, is presented as constituting a basic *structural* component or aspect of stratification.

But the relations between these two aspects of prestige — the relatively consummatory symbolic one and its structural ramifications — have not been fully explicated in sociological literature. And yet a closer look at any group or society will show that within most and probably all groups or societies, at least those where such specific, distinct societal bases of prestige can be discerned, indicates at least some ways in which the symbolic and the structural aspects of prestige tend to become combined.

The first such base of prestige is the very membership in any collectivity (or subcollectivity), group, or society. Its second source is the ability to control the collectivity, represent it, and to define its goals and its central activities, or in other words to be in a sense in its "center." The third specific societal root or prestige base is the proximity to or participation in some broader sociocultural activity — cosmic or religious, scientific, etc. — considered relevant for defining a given collectivity or its members. Very often, those who seem to be closest to or who represent the essence of such order, tradition, or "mystery," who are knowledgeable about it, hold the most prestigeful roles.

These three sources of prestige have one common denominator — the quality of "participation": participation in a collectivity, in its center, or in some broader cultural order, even if the nature and quality of such participation may greatly differ with regard to each such "source."

But such participation is not only a base of prestige; it is one major aspect of prestige as a reward. The reward that is expressed by giving deference, by endowing somebody, whether an individual role or group, with prestige, is the recognition of his or its right to participate in any of these orders, or of his or its special contribution to them.

STRUCTURAL ASPECTS OF PRESTIGE

In this view prestige becomes less symbolic or "ephemeral" and more structural, more closely related to the use of other types of resources and to regulating differential access to positions. Allocating prestige and controlling access to participation in the "bases" of prestige become one major mechanism through which the different aspects of stratification previously outlined — the differential evaluation of positions, the uses of the rewards received for regulating access to positions and for symbolic consumption — become interconnected and become the starting points of the process of strata formation.

The most crucial of such structural aspects of prestige is, first, designating some *combination* of desiderata that is perceived by the members of such groups (or by people belonging to certain social categories), as well as by others, as being peculiarly bound to those who share certain types of personal and collective identities, i.e., some combination of personal qualities or attributes on the one hand, with differential participation in these collectivities, orders, and centers on the other. The first structural manifestation of such rights or claims to pursue certain goals by such differential participation is the upholding of different styles of life and the attempt to limit the participation of other groups in such styles of life.

The second structural aspect of prestige — most pertinent from the stratification viewpoint and most specifically articulated on the macrosocietal level — is the attempt to transmit the rights to such exclusive participation in different styles of life (and in the concomitant patterns of conversion of resources and of access to the various positions) to others who share, with the occupants of such positions, some primordial identity, the most important (but not the only) case of which is belonging to the same family.

STRATA FORMATION

The preceding analysis indicates why the usual starting point of defining strata or classes by their differential control over the basic economic and occupational, or "prestige," resources is at most only a convenient starting point for understanding processes of strata formation.

This analysis indicates that owning certain resources is not in itself the crux of strata formation. Rather the combination of *owning* resources with the *control* over the uses of such resources — over the conversion of such resources from one institutional sphere to another, from one group to another, from microsocial settings to the macrosocietal order, and of access to their respective positions, together with the stress on a common identity with some strong primordial components — that constitutes this crux of the process of strata formation.

But establishing such identities, and the concomitant regulation of desiderata, is not something "given" in any society; it is in itself part of a continuous process of social institutional interaction. As we shall see in greater detail, acquiring the rights to establish the criteria according to which different positions are evaluated and different styles of life are legitimized is crucial.

It is from such crystallization of differential evaluation criteria and status positions that some specific structural manifestations of stratification and status differences — such as segregating the lifestyles of different strata, the process of mobility between them, the steepness of the stratificational hierarchies, some type of status or stratum consciousness, as well as the degree and intensity of status conflict — develop in different societies.[5]

But although to some degree, each of these manifestations of status differences can be found in all societies, the degree to which they tend to occur varies greatly among different societies — just as does the degree to which strata formation becomes an autonomous dimension of social organization.

It is in the interplay between these two aspects of stratification — strata formation as an autonomous dimension of social organization on one hand and the concrete structural manifestations of status distance on the other — that some basic continuities, as well as differences, in the stratification system in various societies tend to become most clearly articulated.

STRATA FORMATION
IN PRIMITIVE SOCIETIES

Strata formation tends to become an autonomous aspect of social structure to the smallest extent in so-called primitive societies.

Although these societies comprise a very large variety of subtypes, on the whole they share some characteristics that have special importance for our analysis.[6] They are characterized, first, by a relatively low level of social differentiation and a relatively small degree of accumulating surplus of any kind, by a relatively high degree of structural equivalence of the different units composing them, and by a consequent relatively high degree of "mechanic" as against "organic" solidarity; second, by a very high degree of sociopolitical "embeddedment" in the cultural order; third, by a very small degree of distinction or differentiation between center and periphery in the "contents" side

[5] On these central aspects of stratification see among others Talcott Parsons, "A Revised Analytical Approach to the Theory of Social Stratification," *Sociological Theories;* Barber, *Social Stratification;* and Tumin, *Social Stratification.*

[6] On some aspects of primitive societies most relevant to our analysis see, for instance, M. Gluckman, *Politics, Law & Ritual in Tribal Society* (Oxford: Basic Blackwell, 1965); and S. N. Eisenstadt, "Introduction to the Section on Primitive Societies," *Political Sociology,* ed. S. N. Eisenstadt (New York: Basic Books, 1970).

of the cultural tradition; and, fourth, by the very strong emphasis on primordial relations and symbols.

In those societies, access to major positions is either distributed more or less equally or randomly among all members of a society, or the "rates" of such conversion in general and the rules of access to positions in particular are ascriptively fixed to such a degree that there is very little scope for different modes of conversion of various resources. Because of all these conditions in these societies we find social differentiation, but not social stratification or strata formation as an autonomous dimension of social organization. On the whole in these societies, there is a fixed conversion of resources into access to positions, and there develop but few possibilities of different ways to convert the resources or the rewards derived from one set of positions to others. Therefore, whatever social differentiation or differential evaluation of positions may develop in such societies, they do not give rise to a continuous, familial, and intragenerational struggle over the nature and scope of the linkages among the various components of stratification. Whatever such linkages develop, in these societies they are either relatively weak or entirely ascriptively fixed within territorial or kinship groups.

Hence the differential evaluation of positions is to a very large degree — although, of course, in varying degrees in different primitive societies — embedded within the more general system of social differentiation; also most manifestations of status distance and segregation are here embedded either in the ascriptive interrelations among territorial and kinship groups, or in personal, individual activities and positions, but not in the crystallization of society-wide groupings that cut across such ascriptive units and that tend to coalesce around some identities of their own. Hence strata formation does not tend to develop in these societies as a distinct, autonomous aspect of the social order.[7]

DISTINCTIVENESS OF CENTERS
IN STRATA FORMATION

Only insofar as some combination develops in any society of a relatively high level of differentiation, the disembeddedment of social structure and of cultural symbols from the more primordial bases — territorial and kinship — and of the distinctiveness of the centers from the periphery that the conditions arise also for the emergence of the

[7] On the distinction between "stratified" and "unstratified" primitive societies see: M. G. Smith, "Pre-industrial Stratificational Systems," *Social Structure and Mobility in Economic Development,* ed. N. J. Smelser and S. M. Lipset (Chicago: Aldine, 1966).

process of strata formation as a distinct, autonomous dimension of social organization.

The importance of a relatively high degree of technological development and of social differentiation as a basis for the emergence of a high degree of stratification has been often stressed in the literature and is by now almost self-evident; it might therefore be worthwhile to analyze here in somewhat greater detail the importance of the distinctiveness of centers in this process.[8] Such centers are one of the most important loci in which the rights to establish the criteria of evaluation of positions and control of conversion of resources tend to become vested.

In primitive societies, with their general characteristics of social differentiation and stratification, the problem of where the rights to establish the criteria according to which different positions are evaluated did not, on the whole, arise. These rights seem here to be embedded in the very process of interaction among the bases and territorial groups.

But this problem naturally arises in situations where the access to positions is not entirely random and/or the rates of conversion of rewards into resources are not fully fixed. Among the institutional settings in which such rights tend to become located, the most important, especially in macrosocietal settings, are the various social political and cultural centers.[9]

Although, needless to say, such centers are not the only mechanism through which such conversion is being effected, and many other mechanisms such as market or bargaining processes are also very important from this viewpoint, the centers play a crucial role in this process. The centers in this process have a special place because they combine, or may attempt to combine for stratificational purposes, the setting up of the basic symbols of personal, societal, and cultural identity; the control of participation in the various collectivities and sociocultural orders; and the setting up of societal goals and more "mundane" regulation of economic, legal, and other relations within a society. Hence such centers necessarily are crucial in the process of stratification in general, and in that of strata formation in particular.

[8] On the concept of center and its application in sociological analysis see Edward Shils, "Centre and Periphery," *The Logic of Personal Knowledge: Essays Presented to Michael Polanyi* (London: Routledge & Kegan Paul, 1961), pp. 117–31; Edward Shils, "Society and Societies," *American Sociology*, ed. Talcott Parsons (New York: Basic Books, 1968), pp. 286–305; and various introductions in *Political Sociology*, ed. S. N. Eisenstadt.

[9] For greater detail see S. N. Eisenstadt, *Prestige, Participation and Strata Formation.*

DETERMINANTS OF STRATIFICATION

In the following paragraphs we shall attempt to analyze the contribution to change in stratification systems of the two conditions just pointed out, i.e., the level of differentiation of the social structure in a society and the consequent variety of roles and positions; and the nature of the relations between the center and the periphery in a society.

These determinants can help in explaining the nature of stratification in different types of more differentiated societies (especially traditional-historical societies), both as they differ from those of primitive societies, as well as among themselves.

The first such obvious difference is how the level of social differentiation within them of the numbers of major institutional roles and positions that may serve as the starting points for strata formation varies.

From this viewpoint one may talk about a general "scale" of differentiation in which the primitive societies could rank lowest, the "traditional-historical" coming after them, and the modern societies on the most highly differentiated level.

Thus, for instance, compared with the relatively small number of specific occupational-economic roles in most primitive societies, in most patrimonial, feudal, or imperial societies, we find a much greater range of basic categories of institutional-occupational positions sharing some common life changes.[10] The most important of these are:

1. The peasantry, comprising the majority of the population.

2. Various upper- or middle-class urban economic or professional groups such as merchants, craftsmen (again possibly divided into big and small ones), and some professional groups such as lawyers, doctors, etc.

3. Lower urban groups composed of laborers, unskilled workers, etc.

4. Cultural or religious groups, especially priests and officials of organized religions or of more local cults.

5. The various administrative and political echelons, especially on the central but also on the local levels.

6. The upper groups or strata composed mostly of aristocratic lineages that control land and also to some extent central political and cultural resources.

7. The upper political elite, centered around the king or emperor, which may or may not have overlapped with some aristocratic and upper religious groups, and which by definition had the highest degree

[10] Ibid.; and S. N. Eisenstadt, *The Political Systems of Empires* (New York: The Free Press, 1969).

of control over the center or centers as they were established in these political systems.

Distinct from this structure, in modern societies we find much more complex social and economic differentiation and a much greater variety of occupational and economic categories and positions.

Although different occupations have been classified in a very great variety of ways in modern societies into broad class or status categories, some features common to most modern societies can be discovered.

Thus "upper" classes, sometimes divided into "upper-upper" and "lower-upper," would usually include:

Upper-upper: very highly qualified professionals, such as physicians, scientists, lawyers, college professors; high government officials, such as supreme court justices, diplomats, cabinet members; high business managers or owners, such as bankers, members of boards of directors of large corporations.

Lower-upper: some lower professionals, such as teachers, engineers, artists (writers, painters, musicians in symphony orchestras); medium-level administrative positions in government, business (accountants); owners of medium-sized businesses and enterprises.

The middle classes again usually are divided into two subcategories that include:

Upper-middle: other professionals, such as newspapermen, radio announcers, technicians, owners of small business; government officials such as welfare workers, other white-collar workers with similar positions.

Lower-middle: highly skilled manual workers, small business owners, routine white-collar workers, salesmen (usually identified with most of the working class).

The lower classes tend usually to be subdivided in the following ways:

Upper-lower: semiskilled manual workers, service workers, clerks.
Lower-lower: unskilled workers.[11]

[11] This categorization is based on the scale of occupational prestige found by the NORC study, published in *Class, Status and Power,* ed. R. Bendix and S. M. Lipset (Glencoe, Ill.: The Free Press, 1953), pp. 411–426; and also according to suggestions made by J. A. Kahl in *The American Class Structure* (New York: Rinehart, 1959), pp. 76–77; and W. A. Crockett, Jr., "The Achievement Motive and Differential Mobility in the U.S.," *American Sociological Review,* vol. 27, no. 2 (1963), esp. pp. 196–197.

These differences in the degree of social differentiation that can be found among primitive, "traditional," and modern societies are, however, only the starting points for the processes of strata formation within them.

CONDITIONS FOR STRATA FORMATION

Beyond these differences in the extent of social differentiation and occupational variability the processes of strata formation in these various societies are greatly influenced by their respective differences in the structure of their centers and in the relation between the centers and periphery that develop in historical (traditional) and modern societies.

Both "traditional-historical" and modern societies are distinct from primitive societies in that the newer societies have centers that are structurally and symbolically differentiated from the broader groups of the society. It is, as we have pointed out, the combination of the relatively high level of differentiation, the disembeddedment of social differentiation from ascriptive units, and the distinctiveness of the centers that create in both these societies, as distinct from primitive societies, the conditions for forming strata as autonomous dimensions of social organization.

But the structures of the centers, as well as their relations to the periphery, vary greatly between the traditional and modern societies, and these variations greatly influence the basic characteristics of strata formation within them.

The roots of the centers in traditional societies during strata formation within them are seen first in their traditions.[12] The crucial aspects of this traditionality seem to be the acceptance of tradition, of the givenness of some past event order or figure (whether real or imaginary) as the major focus of the collective identity of a society, and of the social and cultural order, as the ultimate legitimizer of change and as the delineator of the limits of innovation.

In these societies tradition served not only as a symbol of continuity, but as the delineator of the legitimate limits of creativity and innovation and as the major criterion of their legitimacy — even if in fact any such symbol of tradition might have been forged out as a great innovative creation that destroyed what till then was perceived as the major symbol of the legitimate past.

These connotations of traditionality were not, however, confined only to purely cultural or symbolic spheres; they had definite structural implications, the most important of which was that parts of the social

[12] For greater detail see Edward Shils, *Society and Societies;* and S. N. Eisenstadt, "Some Reflections on the Dynamics of Traditions," *Comparative Studies in Society and History*, vol. 11 (October 1969), pp. 451–475.

structure and some groups were — or attempted to become — designated as the legitimate upholders, guardians, or manifestations of those collective symbols as their legitimate bearers and interpreters, and hence also as the legitimizers of any innovation or change.

In the more differentiated traditional societies these functions became crystallized into the symbolic and institutional distinctiveness of the centers of the political and cultural orders, as separate from the periphery.

Concomitantly the center or centers always attempted to maintain a sharp structural and symbolic difference between the center and the periphery; the access of the periphery to the center was very limited, and the rules of such access were here, to a very large degree, controlled by the center.

These characteristics of traditionality and their implications for the relations between center and periphery within them had very important repercussions on the process of strata formation and of stratificational struggle in these societies.[13]

First, the tendency that developed in all these societies, albeit in different degrees, was to combine an expressly metaphysical or theological evaluation of different groups and roles with some legal or semilegal definition of the major positions and status.

Second, the center or centers of traditional societies, to a large degree, defined the hierarchy of the basic attributes that constituted the bases of prestige, their distribution among members of different subcollectivities, the specific goals and desiderata that were "tied" in with such attributes, and the differential rewards to which the holders of such attributes may have been entitled.

Third, and closely related, the centers attempted to regulate normatively the ascriptive linkages among the basic components of stratification. The major mechanisms through which such regulation was attempted were: (1) the ascriptive and/or legal limitation of the access to at least some of the most important institutional positions; (2) the regulation — through various sumptuary laws — of the symbolic use of resources by different groups; (3) the prescription in such ways of the styles of life appropriate for them; and (4) the upholding of various restrictions on the use of some resources and exchange activities — most clearly seen in the regulation of the output of guilds.

All these functions of the center were closely related to the facts that, first, in traditional societies, the participation in the total collectivity and in the center was largely mediated by participation in the respective subcollectivities and largely influenced by the degree to

---

[13] For greater detail see S. N. Eisenstadt, *Prestige, Participation and Strata Formation.*

which membership in any such subcollectivity entitled one to access to the center; and, second, that this in itself was to a very large degree regulated by the center.

At the same time, the prestige of these subcollectivities was at least partially legitimized by the center or centers, and such various sub-collectivities could therefore uphold their own exclusiveness with the help of some such, even if only partial, legitimation by the center or centers of the society.

The foci of the self-evaluation, status identity, and stratification struggle of most status groups or strata within traditional societies were greatly influenced by these characteristics of strata formation.

Insofar as we have adequate evidence, which by its very nature is more nearly adequate for the higher than for the lower strata, such status self-evaluation and identity were in these societies indeed often expressed in such metaphysical terms, by attributes legitimized in such ways by the center or centers and by proximity to the center and its major symbols.

Accordingly, many manifestations of status identity and distinctiveness — degree of segregation, mobility, or strata consciousness — tended, in such societies, to be described mostly by such metaphysical-religious terms, on one hand, and sought for legitimation by the centers, on the other.[14]

THE STRATIFICATIONAL STRUGGLE

These characteristics of strata formation in traditional societies in general, and of the place of centers in them in particular, have also greatly influenced the nature of the foci of stratificational struggle within them. As in any society, a very large part of the stratificational struggle consists, of course, of attempts by various groups to attain new rewards and resources, to improve their positions, or to improve their own life chances or those of their sons.

But insofar as the efforts of various groups also included attempts to legitimize such attainments for themselves or their families, the stratificational struggle was focused around the attempts to influence the center, or of some groups with access to it, to obtain from it one or several of the following benefits: first, prescribing the ascriptive access of members of different subcollectivities to the new higher position; second, legitimating the exclusive rights of access to such positions; third, legitimating the rights of various groups to be the bearers of certain (higher) social or cultural attributes or attaining an official revaluation of such attributes, thus also legitimating the rights of these groups to uphold various differential styles of life.

[14] For illustration see the materials in S. N. Eisenstadt, *The Political Systems of Empires,* esp. chaps. 5, 8.

It is true that many peripheral or marginal groups in these societies tended to give up any reference to the center and its symbols and to live in their own closed walls, or to be concerned only with the improvement of their immediate living conditions. But, insofar as they were oriented to some participation in the broader social or cultural order, they tended to uphold the center's right to a normative definition of the basic components of strata formation. This right was even very often upheld by those who did not accept the existing center and who attempted to change it, but without necessarily undermining these basic functions of the centers during strata formation.[15]

CHANGES IN THE STRUCTURES OF CENTERS

These characteristics of the center and of the relations between center and periphery have greatly changed with the shift to modernity. From its very beginning, modernity has been connected with a revolutionary concept and imagery. These revolutionary orientations, whatever their concrete contents, have tended toward a complete change of the nature and contents of the centers of the social and cultural order, of participation in them and of access to them, and of the relations between these centers and the periphery.[16]

In the contents of the centers, the major transformation concomitant with modernity has been the growing secularization of the centers and the "opening up" of their contents, i.e., the nonacceptance of the givenness of these, i.e., in the spread of the assumption that these contents can indeed be formulated anew.

The second major change in the structure of the centers in modern societies has been in the relation between the center or centers and the periphery (the broader social groups and strata). Modern social systems are characterized by the growing impingement of the periphery on the center and by the opening of the periphery's access to the center, by the permeation of the periphery by the center, and by the concomitant tendency to obliterate the differences between center and periphery, the membership in the collectivity emerging as an ascriptive title to participation in the center.[17]

This impingement on the center could be best seen in the political field. The broader groups and strata of society tend more and more to

15 Ibid., chap. 12.

16 See S. N. Eisenstadt, *Modernization, Protest and Change* (Englewood Cliffs, N.J.: Prentice-Hall, 1966), pp. 11–16; T. H. Marshall, *Citizenship and Social Class* (London: Cambridge University Press, 1950); E. Shils, "The Theory of Mass Society," *Diogenes*, vol. 39 (1963), pp. 45–66; and K. Mannheim, *Man and Society in an Age of Reconstruction* (London: Kegan Paul, 1935), esp. pp. 3–39, 79–108.

17 R. Bendix, *Nation-Building and Citizenship* (New York: Wiley, 1964), pp. 74–104; T. H. Marshall, *Citizenship and Social Class*.

impinge on the political centers, not only in making various concrete demands on it, but also by developing the aspirations to participate in the very crystallization of the center, its symbols and its institutional contours. The major social movements that have developed with the onset of modernization — be they national, social, or cultural — all manifest, in varying degrees and scope, this tendency.

Whatever the exact details of this drawing in of wide groups into the central institutional spheres of the society, they all epitomize the growth and concentration of the demand for equality. By virtue of the drawing in of various groups into the central institutions of the society, this demand has become not only an abstract ideal but also an overwhelming demand for growing concrete participation of all groups in all spheres of life.

In close relation to this a marked change has also developed in the nature of the bases or criteria of evaluating positions and of perceiving the social order. The religious-metaphysical bases of such evaluation that were, as we have seen, relatively predominant in traditional societies, now tended to be replaced by more secular bases in which the social order was perceived as an autonomous dimension of human existence.[18]

CHANGES IN STRATIFICATION COMPONENTS

It is out of the interrelations between the high level of differentiation, the changes in the relations between center and periphery, that some major characteristics of this process and of the stratification systems of modern societies have emerged.

A first, crucial aspect of strata formation in modern societies has been the weakening of the normative prescription of the linkages among the major components of stratification, i.e., among the differential participation in different collectivities and sociocultural orders; the definition of personal and collective identities in terms of some basic desiderata symbolized in different, distinct styles of life; and the differential control of resources and differential access to major institutional positions.

The most important manifestations of this weakening of such prescriptions has been the abolition — first gradual, then in later stages of modernization more far-reaching — of most legal limitations: first, access to political participation, i.e., citizenship; second, legal or normative-customary prescriptions of belonging to different strata and groups; and third, the various sumptuary laws that, as we have seen, attempted

---

[18] R. Dahrendorf, *Class and Class Conflict in Industrial Societies,* esp. chaps. 6–8; S. Ossowski, *Class Structure in the Social Consciousness* (London: Routledge & Kegan Paul, 1963), esp. p. 174.

to define legally the legitimate lifestyles of different groups in terms of their access to different desiderata and consumption patterns.[19]

Perhaps the most far-reaching change, and one that in a sense has been taken for granted in most of the literature and therefore has not been fully analyzed, has been the opening up, in principle, of all kinds of desiderata and goals to all members of the collectivity.

This opening up was evident first in the weakening or abolishment of the ritual, legal, or semi-legal normative designation of certain patterns of desiderata and of consumption as appropriate only to members of certain, ascriptively defined subcollectivities.

Similarly, most normative-ascriptive limitations on the access to resources and to positions — at least those limitations which were based on some type of formal hereditary transmission of the right to access — became weak and ultimately, with very few exceptions, were abolished.

Instead, access to economic, cultural, and political positions and, in principle, also to participation in different spheres of social life gradually and intermittently became open to all those who could qualify according to the requisite attributes. These attributes became more and more defined in universalistic terms and dissociated from membership in any subcollectivity based on some familial ties.

Similarly, most positions — and especially occupational and political ones — become accessible to all members of the collectivity, if they could qualify in some of these "objective" attributes.

Moreover, actual control over any of these resources or the occupation of any such position, did not become an automatic title to any specific differential standing in another institutional sphere, although it could, of course, serve as a very important resource base that could be used for obtaining such access.

Thus, one's place in the political or "social" sphere was not assured, as in many premodern societies, by one's economic or occupational standing or vice versa. Closely related to this, a great multiplicity of rankings of different positions also developed within and between different institutional spheres, much beyond any such heterogeneity that could be found in any traditional society.[20]

In reality, of course, this picture was very different. Strong tendencies to some coalescence among these different rankings always developed in all modern societies.

[19] T. H. Marshall, *Citizenship and Social Class;* W. G. Runciman, *Relative Deprivation and Social Justice* (London: Routledge & Kegan Paul, 1966).

[20] S. M. Lipset, "Social Class," *The International Encyclopedia of the Social Sciences* (New York: Macmillan, 1968); T. H. Marshall, *Citizenship and Social Class;* G. Lenski, *Power and Privilege* (New York: McGraw-Hill, 1966); W. G. Runciman, *Relative Deprivation and Social Justice,* esp. chaps. 2–6, 10, 11.

Similarly, many "older" groups (aristocratic, oligarchic, or even urban and rural strata) clung to the ideas that they and their children have the exclusive right of access to some positions, to some types of resources, and, especially, to desiderata and different styles of life. Many other new groups attempted to establish for themselves such claims — to social exclusiveness, to various types of "titles" — that would regulate, for their benefit, the access to desiderata and positions alike.

These attempts of "old" and "new" groups alike and their concomitant tendencies to maintain some status congruency constituted a basic part of the whole crystallization process of social strata in modern societies. But whatever the concrete outcome of these processes in different modern societies, in all of them, in contrast to traditional societies, these attempts could not have been fully legitimized by the center in either legal or ritual terms. On the contrary, the very structure and basic assumption of most modern centers have been opposed to such claims; hence such claims could enjoy only the very partial and informal legitimation of their respective groups.

Because of this in modern societies the center or centers could no longer be the sole focus or repository of the normative and organizational regulation of the relations between the various components of stratification.

The center became here less a legitimizer of different styles of life and differential ascriptive prestige and became much more a mechanism for redistributing resources.

THE CHANGING PLACE OF THE FAMILY

All the developments analyzed above have influenced many of the concrete ways in which the basic manifestations of strata or class organization, segregation, and identity in modern societies — as compared with traditional societies — have developed. They certainly did not abolish some basic manifestations of status difference and distance, although obviously they gave rise to many changes in their concrete structural expressions. But in some cases, when these expressions of status distance changed, these very changes tended sometimes to stress, often in rather paradoxical ways, the continuity with several of these manifestations in traditional societies.

One such paradoxical development can be found in the changing place of the family and of other primordially based groups during strata formation.

Although the basic characteristics of stratification in modern societies entailed a growing weakening of the ascriptive elements in stratification, especially the normative ascriptive definition of the linkages among different components of stratification, yet at the same time and in close relation with these, the importance of family or of other primordially or ascriptively based units in the crystallization of status and class orientations became greatly enhanced.

True enough, the importance of the family and kinship groups, as both controller of resources and the focus of transmission of titles and ascriptive access to positions, has been greatly weakened. At the same time, however, family and family-based groupings (kinship, neighborhood, etc.) not only continue to perform most vital functions in the patterning of the *actual* differential lifestyles of the major occupational categories, classes or, strata, but in many ways their importance in these respects has greatly increased.

It has been abundantly demonstrated in sociological literature that people belonging to these different occupations or status categories tend to differ in the patterns of their participation in different social, political, and cultural activities and organizations; in their patterns of consumption; in their time perspective; in how they perceive their own chances in the social order; in the major types of desiderata they emphasize and around which they tend to develop their distinct styles of life — be they security of jobs, high levels of consumption, and attainment of rewards, or the investment of resources in a future "career"; in their basic attitudes to their work, jobs, and careers; in their language usages, etc.[21]

Perhaps one of the most important aspects of socialization still largely influenced by family orientations has been specifying the limits of intermarriage and the choice of friendship patterns — in itself among the most important mechanisms in upholding these value orientations.[22]

These different patterns of social life, orientations, and motivations provide some of the most important mechanisms through which the members of different classes attain different life chances, or differential potentials of access to positions, which we have previously discussed. Thus the importance of family and kinship groups has become, in modern societies, even greater in upholding differential orientations to desiderata, of initial placement in the social order, and of initial access to differential rewards.

[21] See H. H. Hyman, "The Value Systems of Different Classes," in *Class, Status and Power*, pp. 488–99; R. Blauner, "Work Satisfaction and Industrial Trends in Modern Society," in *Class, Status and Power*, pp. 473–87; J. A. Kahl, *The American Class Structure*, pp. 108–19, chaps. 5, 7; L. Reissman, "Class, Leisure, and Social Participation," *American Sociological Review*, vol. 19, no. 1 (1954), pp. 76–84; K. Svalastoga, *Prestige, Class and Mobility* (Copenhagen, 1959), pp. 203–84; J. H. Goldthorpe, D. Lockwood, "Affluence and the British Class Structure," *Sociological Review*, vol. 11, no. 2 (1963), pp. 133–63.

[22] See, for instance, T. O. Laumann, *Prestige and Association in an Urban Community* (New York: Bobbs-Merrill, 1966), esp. chap. 5.

GROWTH OF CLASS CONSCIOUSNESS

The second aspect of strata formation in modern societies in which a rather paradoxical process of change from traditional societies can be discerned has been the growth of strata or class consciousness.

Despite — or because — that in modern societies social hierarchy was no longer fully articulated in religious and metaphysical terms that could serve as foci of group identity, strata or class consciousness tended to become an important, sometimes even basic component of the definition of the social order in a way which could never have developed in most traditional societies. The sole exception is the city-state of antiquity, which is the closest approximation to the modern situation.[23]

This rather paradoxical growth of "class" or "strata" consciousness, in such close connection with the weakening traditional ascriptive strata formation, has been rooted first in the fact that the conditions most conducive to developing countrywide strata consciousness — i.e., the possible autonomous access of the major groups to the basic social, political, and cultural centers — tended to become, because of the continuous impingement of the periphery and of the drawing in of various groups into the center, almost concomitant with modernity.[24]

Second, they were also reinforced by the growing secularization of the attributes by which such social order has been defined, on the one hand, along with the growing perception of the total social order and of one's standing within it in terms of such relations, on the other.

STRATIFICATION STRUGGLE
IN MODERN SOCIETIES

This very enhancement or identification of strata or class consciousness, connected as it was with the weakening normative-ascriptive aspects of stratification and the development of secular perception of the social order, gave rise, in modern societies, to several new aspects of identity and organization and converged most clearly in developing the specific characteristics of "stratificational" ("class") struggle in modern societies. Here, despite some continuities, the differences and changes from traditional societies stand out most clearly.

From these developments reference points emerged common to dif-

[23] See S. Ossowski, *Class Structure in the Social Consciousness*, and S. N. Eisenstadt, introduction to the section on "City States," in *Political Sociology*.

[24] See Edward Shils, *The Theory of Mass Society;* Talcott Parsons, *Structure and Process in Modern Societies* (New York: The Free Press, 1960), chaps. 4, 8; S. N. Eisenstadt, *Modernization, Process and Change*.

ferent groups and strata within the major social, cultural, and political spheres. These groups became, in many senses, mutual reference points of each other, in which they developed orientations to common norms and customs and compared each other in such common terms.

Because of this the perception of one's own standing in the social order tended, in the modern societies, to be described by one's *relative position* or placement within any of these spheres in relation to other groups. It tended to a very large degree to be based on the assumption of the possibility of equal and total participation in these orders — and not only by one's qualities of differentiation or participation in a culturally given prescribed order. Because of these factors different social groups and strata became increasingly aware of each other's standing in power, prestige, and wealth and began to compare their own and other groups' standings by relatively similar values and standards.[25]

As we have indicated, these had many repercussions on the specific characteristics of stratificational ("class") struggle in modern societies.

Thus a great part of the stratification struggle in modern — as in any other — society consisted on the one hand in attempts to directly better positions, acquire greater rewards, etc., and get access to better positions and better bargaining terms.

Similarly, a very large part of the stratificational struggle has consisted, as in other societies, of the attempts of various subcollectivities or elites of institutional spheres to claim that the attributes borne by them should become recognized as predominant in the society and that they should bear the highest rewards; and that they should become institutionalized as such by the center. But because of the major changes in the center structure in modern societies this was, as we have seen, no longer possible.

Hence, the focus of the stratificational struggle has shifted in modern societies from attempts to acquire the right to access to the center or of influence over it in order to prescribe the relations among the different components of stratification, to the acquisition, through domination of the center, of actual control of resources, to gain better bargaining or monopolizing positions in the various markets or with respect to the channels of access to positions. Although these in turn could help to keep up various informal lifestyles or patterns of exclusiveness that were, in a sense, contrary to the premises of the centers, they could no longer prescribe direct access to positions or to the center.[26]

[25] See especially W. G. Runciman, *Relative Deprivation and Social Justice.*
[26] See S. Ossowski, *Class Structure in the Social Consciousness.*

ORIENTATION TO CHANGE

This shift involved the development of modern societies and of new dimensions of stratificational struggle — namely, the growth of orientation to change in general and of the political dimension in particular as basic components of this struggle.

This development can be seen first in the fact that modern social and cultural orders were ushered in by revolutionary events within which the strong orientation was to change, and that a very large part of these changes indeed had to do with class or strata ideology and changing the contours of the system of stratification. The French Revolution, which emphasized the Third Estate, and the various revolutions in Europe in the nineteenth century up to the Russian Revolution, all illustrate this tendency.

But even beyond these "origins," a large part of "class" or "status" organization and consciousness has continuously involved, in modern societies, effecting changes in the social order, and large parts of the stratificational struggle are consciously and openly oriented to effecting changes in the stratification system — whether in the very principles of the system or in the relative standing of various groups.

Moreover, one major characteristic of these processes is that they tend usually to be openly, legitimately connected with political orientations and activities; one major expression of the attempts to effect different types of changes in the stratification system is manifested through open political processes, and many political activities in modern societies are oriented to class aims and symbols. Attaining the various stratificational aims, changes in the various stratification components, tended to become an explicit part of the political aims of various groups and strata.

Thus one major characteristic of modern strata formation is that classes are openly and legitimately connected with political orientations and activities. This does not mean, of course, that all political activity in modern societies has necessarily been an expression of class or strata interests or described as class or status ideology. It does mean, however, that class or stratum elements enter in a great variety of ways as components of modern political activities, and that conversely many types of participation in political activities and organizations constitute a very important component of strata formation in modern societies.[27]

[27] See T. M. Marshall, *Citizenship and Social Class;* R. Dahrendorf, *Class and Class Conflict in Industrial Societies* (Stanford: Stanford University Press, 1964); S. M. Lipset and S. Rokkan, eds., *Party Systems and Voter-Alignments: Cross-National Perspectives* (New York: The Free Press, 1967).

It is indeed here, as we have indicated, that some basic continuities and discontinuities between traditional and modern orders tend to converge, and we shall summarize them briefly. In the traditional societies the social order usually has been conceived as a derivative of the religious and metaphysical order; social hierarchy has been conceived as a derivative of such cosmic hierarchy; hence the bases of legitimation of social hierarchy were described mostly in such terms.

Therefore, although social forces and changes in stratificational positions in the modern order, as in any other society, caused many social conflicts, struggles, and changes, only rarely were the changes or conflicts, especially insofar as they were focussed on the central symbols of the society, conceived in purely social "class" ideas or symbols.

Only in modern societies (and to some degree in the city-states of antiquity) has social order been conceived in secular, autonomous terms, and therefore class symbolism also has become an autonomous dimension of the symbolic perception of social order, as well as a focus of conscious social change and social transformation.

Examining the closely connected patterns and processes of stability and change in the quantity and quality of American schooling, Professor Dreeben asks questions essential to all industrial societies. He asks what the educational system contributes to the other societal subsystems and to the society as a whole — not only the teaching of knowledge, it is clear, but the inculcation of values, such as universalism (in this country), and normative and emotional capacities for dealing with the authority systems required by modern occupational and political systems. Formal education also contributes to nationalism, to the sense of social citizenship, and to the maintenance of the cultural tradition. Thus, in a paradox that is only apparent, changes in the amounts of schooling in American society have probably contributed in some measure to its stability, though of course some of the cognitive, affective, and normative content of what is learned in school also stimulates social innovation and receptivity to social change. In sum, the connected processes of stability and change in the amounts and types of schooling in modern societies are far from simple or even clear to us as yet. Professor Dreeben raises some questions and opens some paths for further clarification of these issues.

Robert Dreeben

AMERICAN SCHOOLING:
PATTERNS AND PROCESSES
OF STABILITY AND CHANGE

Talcott Parsons has set the agenda for us all. His curiosity about Hobbes' problem of order has taken him through almost every field and path of sociology; fortunately that curiosity has been contagious.

I thank my colleagues C. Arnold Anderson, Charles E. Bidwell, and Jacob W. Getzels for their valuable comments.

82

Few have traveled the same distance; some, taking the same route, have seen different scenery; almost all have seen the initials on the trees indicating that he was there.

In the pages of this essay, though my approach is different than his, I address myself to questions that have concerned him, questions about education: more specifically, which aspects of American schooling have changed, which have remained the same, and how are the stable and changing aspects connected? To discover that what one has known all along to be true is at best but partially true (or possibly not true at all) is a most unsettling experience; but I have had that experience examining the well-known proposition that schooling becomes more prevalent as the economy and occupational structure of a society become more industrialized. Accordingly, an inquiry that began with changes in the occupational distribution and their relationship to the expansion of schooling led me far afield. The search for connections between the two forced me to consider changes in the structure of school organization, the growth of citizenship, and the social conditions under which individuals learn the principle of universalism and to act according to the demands of authority relationships prevalent in the public sectors of industrial society. The problem, then, is to discover how these elements are connected and how they change and remain constant relative to each other.

EDUCATIONAL AND OCCUPATIONAL CHANGE

At the risk of being called Philistine, I choose as my text not scripture or wise words but tables, and familiar ones at that. Consider first the changes in rates of American school attendance and completion from 1870 to 1960, as shown in Table 1. The second table contains information about the retentiveness of schools at critical junctures of the schooling process from 1924 to 1960.

The main trends over roughly the past century are unmistakable: increasing numbers of children attend school for increasingly large portions of the year. High school graduation dramatically has become more frequent as has enrollment in post-high school training institutions. Over the past 35 years or so, young people are increasingly more likely to remain in school, to graduate from high school, and to enter college. Almost the same proportion of the fifth-grade cohort graduated from high school in 1967 that survived the eighth grade in 1928. With certain exceptions, the likelihood of crossing the critical choice-points has remained stable. Except for the 1924–25 cohort, 90 per cent of those completing the eighth grade have entered high school; for all cohorts, the probability of an individual being graduated from high school, once having entered the twelfth grade, has

TABLE 1

Patterns of School Attendance, 1870–1960 [a,b]

Year	Percentage of population aged 5–17 enrolled in public day schools	Average days attended per pupil enrolled	High school grad-uates as percent-age of population aged 17	Percentage of population aged 18–21 enrolled in institutions of higher learning
1960	82.2	160.2	65.1	34.9
1950	81.6	157.9	59.0	29.9
1940	85.3	151.7	50.8	15.7
1930	81.3	143.0	29.0	12.4
1920	77.8	121.2	16.8	8.1
1910	73.5	113.0	8.8	5.1
1900	72.4	99.0	6.4	4.0
1890	68.6	86.3	3.5	3.0
1880	65.5	81.1	2.5	2.7
1870	57.0	78.4	2.0	1.7

[a]1870 to 1950 figures: U.S. Bureau of the Census, *Historical Statistics of the United States, Colonial Times to 1957* (Washington: U.S. Government Printing Office, 1960), Series H 225, 231, 233, 322, pp. 207, 210–211.
[b]1960 figures: U.S. Bureau of the Census, *Historical Statistics of the United States, Colonial Times to 1957; Continuation to 1962 and Revisions* (Washington: U.S. Government Printing Office, 1965), Series H 225, 231, 233, 322, p. 31.

TABLE 2

Estimated Retention Rates at Selected Grade Levels, 1924–1960

| Year entered fifth grade | Retention per 1000 pupils who entered fifth grade | | | | | |
	Enter eighth grade	Enter ninth grade	Enter twelfth grade	Graduate from H.S.	(Year)	Enter College
1959–60[a]	976	966	785	721	1967	400
1958–59[a]	960	940	782	717	1966	394
1954–55	948	915	684	642	1962	343
1950–51	921	886	632	582	1958	308
1944–45	858	848	549	522	1952	234
1940–41	836	781	507	481	1948	[b]
1934–36	842	803	512	467	1942	129
1930–31	824	770	463	417	1938	148
1924–25	741	612	544	302	1932	118
Per cent increase 1924–60	32	58	128	139		239

[a]Preliminary data.
[b]Rates not calculated because of influx of veterans.
Source: U.S. Department of Health, Education, and Welfare, *Digest of Educational Statistics* (Washington: U.S. Government Printing Office, 1968), table 8, p. 7.

been close to 90 per cent with no clear trend; and after World War II, the likelihood of a high school graduate to continue his schooling increased with time from roughly 45 to 55 per cent, although prior to the war fewer than 40 per cent made the transition. One can quibble about whether Americans are becoming better educated; without question more are spending a longer time in school. This banal generalization, however, raises many interpretive questions, one being major to this paper: *why the expansion of schooling?*

THE OCCUPATIONAL DEMAND ARGUMENT

Martin Trow's provocative thesis [1] that American education has undergone a double transformation asks two questions about expansion: what form has it taken, and why has it taken that form? Secondary schools, he maintains, originally elite preparatory institutions, later assumed the function of mass terminal education (the first transformation), and subsequently took on the task of mass preparation for higher education (the second transformation). If one assumes that high school graduation is a prerequisite for college entrance, the figures in the two right-hand columns of Table 1 support his contention: there is a small contingent of high school graduates and a slightly smaller one of college students (during the 1870 to 1910 period), suggesting that high schools served the preparatory interests of the few college entrants. (Without cross-tabulating high school graduates and college entrants, it is not possible to draw a tight connection between the two findings.) From 1920 on, both high school graduates and college students have rapidly increased — evidence consistent with the "second transformation" argument, though not providing definitive confirmation. Trow has clearly taken us beyond the crude notion of "expansion" by describing its pattern; data lend credence to his case.

The explanatory problem is more complex, and appropriately, Trow studies the connection between trends in schooling and the development of an industrial-commercial society. It is tempting to posit such a connection because it is easy to contend that changes in the pattern of schooling are consistent with changes in the composition of the labor force: that the expansion of the professions, the white collar salariat, and the tertiary sector of the economy all "require" an educated populace. Moreover, one can readily show that the higher the occupational level, the higher the median level of schooling associated with it. Plausible reasons account for this relationship; Trow refers to them as "the pull of the economy": changes in the technology and

[1] Martin Trow, "The Second Transformation of American Secondary Education," in *Class, Status, and Power,* ed. Reinhard Bendix and Seymour Lipset 2nd ed. (New York: The Free Press, 1966), pp. 437–449.

organization of work (particularly where writing and record-keeping are entailed) lead to changes in the occupational structure of the economy, which in turn lead to a diffusion of the belief that participation in the world of work requires acquiring skills learned in school — the occupational demand argument.

Sensible as this interpretation is, it leaves some questions open. To anticipate my story somewhat, by 1870 the United States was already a highly literate country; moreover, the expansion of schooling appeared to outrun the growth of those occupations for which schooling — particularly at the highest levels — seems to be prerequisite. There is reason to suspect, in other words, that the economic demand argument applies only partially, and that the expansion pattern in American education requires more elaborate explanation. (Trow, of course, did not neglect the ideology of equal opportunity, the prevalent desire for mobility, and the importance that Americans, since the beginning of their history, have attributed to education.)

Philip Foster, in his extraordinary historical study of Ghana,[2] shows that connections between economic and commercial development and education are subtle indeed, and that conclusions based on parallel sets of economic and educational indices linked only by plausible reasoning can be misleading. As one would expect, the elements of an urban economy with its characteristic occupational structure prevail in the coastal region of that country (rather than in the northern interior) with its centers of trade and government administration; moreover, the growth of Western (English) educational institutions was associated with the emergence of status distinctions more characteristic of a modern economy than of the lineage-based traditional economy of the hinterland with *its* status distinctions.

The economic development of the country, he argues, depends on job expansion in the modern sector of the economy; but when people observe that job opportunities are more realistically prevalent primarily in the governmental and commercial sectors, they will not opt for vocational training in the relatively small technical and blue-collar sectors, presumably crucial for economic development, because those parts of the economy are not large enough to employ them in sufficient numbers. Accordingly, those who seek schooling select the academic Western rather than the vocational variety because it is more likely to lead to employment, despite the country's "need" to expand its technical sector. It appears likely, then, that a balanced economy will support a variety of educational enterprises (academic and vocational),

[2] Philip Foster, *Education and Social Change in Ghana* (Chicago: University of Chicago Press, 1965); idem, "The Vocational School Fallacy in Development Planning," in *Education and Economic Development*, ed. C. Arnold Anderson and Mary Jean Bowman (Chicago: Aldine, 1965), pp. 142–166.

but that introducing vocational training in school settings will not develop the crucial technical sector of the economy. People, in other words, will prepare themselves for existing jobs, but educational institutions will not produce jobs. A major shortcoming of the British colonial government, Foster argues, was its failure to assure that substantial numbers of Africans were trained on the job in the artisan and technical sectors; and that establishing technical and vocational *schools* would be of little avail given the paucity of jobs to absorb their graduates.

Foster, like Trow, clearly deals with the relationship between occupation and education in both historical and ahistorical terms, but his argument, though similar in several respects, is more finely crafted. Both writers agree that if people see a realistic connection between school attendance and future employment, and they want to become employed, they will attend school. Accordingly, to the extent that employment opportunities expand, so will school attendance. But Foster cautions us, and in so doing sets limits on the occupational demand argument. When non-occupational inducements to attend school prevail, the distinct possibility is that schools will produce an educated contingent with skills and expectations inappropriate for working in the traditional sector of an economy, but appropriate for working in a modern sector that is too small to provide sufficient employment. The familiar outcome, occurring in Ghana and in other countries, is the emergence of a sizeable group whose reward for schooling is unemployment. Trow's argument, then, may hold only in modern nations and only when school attendance and employment are linked by realistic expectations.

The case for occupational demand is vulnerable at one more point at least. If the knowledge learned at school contributes to economic development via occupational employment, one should not necessarily conclude that only book-learning is relevant. C. Arnold Anderson reminds us that technical "know-how" makes a parallel contribution,[3] and know-how is more usually acquired through direct experience than from books. If true, the comparison between Ghana and the United States becomes most instructive. Foster claims that development in Ghana suffered because training opportunities in which able-bodied men could become artisans and semiskilled workers were absent. Although schools can impart some necessary modern work skills, apprenticeship and on-the-job training have usually proved more effective. The British, as a colonial power, brought with them the higher levels of a modern economy and academic schooling. Having

[3] C. Arnold Anderson, "The Impact of the Educational System on Technological Change and Modernization," in *Industrialization and Society*, ed. Bert F. Hoselitz and Wilbert Moore (The Hague: Mouton and Co., 1963), pp. 259–278.

neglected the blue-collar sector, they failed to create conditions (and jobs) to support vocational schooling, nor did they cultivate a class of artisans and semiskilled workers who could form a base from which an apprenticeship system could develop. The American experience differed markedly, as I shall show in more detail, but a tradition of artisanship, both in agriculture and manufacturing, has existed since the founding of the Colonies, a tradition that supported apprenticeship as a form of education. The occupational demand argument, as exemplified in Trow's work, should then be read in the light of a national experience in which the basic elements of a modern economy have existed at all levels for a long time and in which the educational component was and remains an institution of many parts, only one of which is formal schooling.

I am certain there is substantial truth in Trow's explanatory position and equally convinced that it does not contain the whole story — and Trow does not claim it does. It is difficult, however, to read Foster's and Anderson's work without wondering whether the growth of schooling and of educational institutions had substantial or modest effects on economic development in America, and if so, in what ways, how directly, and in combination with what other considerations; whether schooling made its main contributions to noneconomic areas; and whether, according to the logic of Mary Jean Bowman's argument,[4] the nature of industrial work activities had profound educative effects.

THE LITERACY ARGUMENT

It has long been suspected that schooling promotes literacy and that literacy contributes to industrial development. Though plausible, this reasoning lacks firm documentation. For somewhat over a century, if not longer, the United States has been a remarkably literate country. According to Carlo Cipolla's estimates,[5] adult illiteracy rates among American whites (ca. 1850) were about 10 to 15 per cent as compared to 45 to 50 per cent and 90 to 95 per cent in Europe and Russia, respectively. Moreover, the decline of American illiteracy (reported in the Census Bureau's *Historical Statistics* [6]), from that level to 2.5 per

[4] Mary Jean Bowman, "From Guilds to Infant Training Industries," in *Education and Economic Development*, ed. C. Arnold Anderson and Mary Jean Bowman (Chicago: Aldine, 1965), pp. 98–129.

[5] Carlo M. Cipolla, *Literacy and Development in the West* (Harmondsworth, England: Penguin Books, 1969).

[6] U.S. Bureau of the Census, *Historical Statistics of the United States, Colonial Times to 1957* (Washington, D.C.: U.S. Government Printing Office, 1960); idem, *Historical Statistics of the United States, Colonial Times to 1957; Continuation to 1962 and Revisions* (Washington, D.C.: U.S. Government Printing Office, 1965).

cent in 1952, is of some interest. These figures are interesting in light of a putative connection between schooling and literacy because the Census Bureau, for a somewhat later time (1870; see Table 1), reports day school attendance at a rate of 57 per cent among young people in the 5 to 17 age range. It is almost certain that less than 57 per cent of the whole population (as distinct from enrollees) had attended school, but exceedingly unlikely that the prevalent school attendance for the whole population was so low that nonattendance figures would even come close to those for illiteracy.

Apparently, a substantial portion of the American population was literate but unschooled during the late nineteenth-century period of expanding industrialization and urbanization. If true, this makes establishing the relationship between schooling and industrialization additionally problematic. Does schooling make the important contribution; if so, how does a population with substantial numbers of unschooled people become literate? Or is some combination of schooling, literacy, and other forces critical?

Although there are no ready answers, the work of Mary Jean Bowman and C. Arnold Anderson [7] sheds interesting light on these questions. In a tabulation showing the relationship between percentage of adult literacy and per capita gross national product (in ninety countries, 1950–1954), they find that all thirty-two countries with literacy rates below 40 per cent had per capita incomes under $300; five of the fifty-two countries with literacy rates below 70 per cent had per capita incomes of $300 or more (all with unusual characteristics associated with large income inequalities); thirty-two of the thirty-eight countries with literacy rates between 70 and 90 per cent had incomes of $300 or more; and only among the twenty-four countries with literacy rates between 90 and 99 per cent do a substantial number (twenty-one) have incomes of $500 or more. A positive trend in the relationship is discernible, but it must be put in context: the $500 income level is a low threshold; it is crossed in twenty-four countries, twenty-one of which have literacy rates of 90 per cent or higher; and in some, special economic resources (e.g., oil or mineral wealth) support an isolated industrial sector that can account for most high per capita income.

To sort out the contribution of literacy is risky; the Bowman-Anderson figures are only quasi-developmental because they rank countries according to literacy but do not trace the effects of increasing literacy within countries. Special economic circumstances, more-

[7] Mary Jean Bowman and C. Arnold Anderson, "Concerning the Role of Education in Development," in *Old Societies and New States*, ed. Clifford Geertz (New York: The Free Press, 1963), pp. 247–279.

over, also obscure the picture. It is reasonably safe to argue that the viability of highly industrialized societies (those with the largest per capita incomes) depends on nearly universal literacy; perhaps the *development* of modern industrialism (at least in the United States) does also, or so the 80 per cent American literacy rate in 1870 suggests.

How a population becomes literate is another question. Academically oriented schools undoubtedly contribute; and if Foster's observations in Ghana apply elsewhere, children attend such schools when a large enough modern sector *already exists* to employ their graduates. But the *creation* of that sector is perhaps the main goal of development. In this connection, Richard Storr's statement [8] is interesting, particularly after Foster's observations, that beginning in Colonial America and extending into the nineteenth century an apprenticeship system developed (notably in Massachusetts) in which masters, by contractual agreement and by law, were enjoined to train their charges in literacy as well as in their trade. At least in America, one can piece together some fragmentary evidence linking literacy to industrialization: the original settlement of the country by religiously bookish colonists, the early establishment of schools (though largely for noneconomic reasons) and their later proliferation, an apprenticeship system that encouraged literacy through occupational institutions, and a widely though not universally literate population already present at the start of industrialization.

Evidence that literacy constitutes the crucial link between educational expansion and economic development is at best fragmentary and probably only partially true. Literacy is undoubtedly related to school attendance, but people can become literate in other ways than by going to school. A defensible case can be made that a threshold of literacy — and a high one at that — must be reached if industrial expansion and occupational differentiation in the white-collar sector are to occur, and then only if a variety of other conditions, already mentioned, also prevail.

THE OCCUPATIONAL REQUIREMENT ARGUMENT

A further question arises about the connection between schooling and the economy. The growth of the professional and managerial sectors is too familiar to document here; it takes no great leap of imagination to connect this expansion with that of school attendance using the logic of "job requirements." Certain trends in the labor force composition from 1900 to 1960, however, must give us pause in

[8] Richard J. Storr, "The Growth of American Education," in *Education and Economic Development*, ed. C. Arnold Anderson and Mary Jean Bowman (Chicago: Aldine, 1965), pp. 130–141.

accepting this argument. Although occupational trends are usually tabulated according to gross classifications (such as that used by the Census), it remains to be seen whether particular occupations subsumed under broad categories follow the same trends, and if these changes appear consistent with the expansion of schooling and the widespread acquisition of diplomas. Accordingly, in Table 3, I present data indicating changes in the size of specific occupations as percentages of the labor force. The critical question is whether the character of the work in an occupation has undergone technological changes — changes in work activities for accomplishing occupational tasks — that plausibly require greater educational preparation. By necessity, without clear-cut criteria of technological change and corresponding educational attainments necessary for doing work, the answer must be somewhat speculative.

Consider several professions. Common sense tells us that pursuing these occupations requires mastering the skills (particularly symbolic ones) learned in school. But although there have been substantial increases in the rates of school attendance, especially in institutions of higher learning, greater than those of both the population and the labor force, the proportion of workers in several of these occupations (architecture, the clergy, law, and medicine) has remained almost constant over a sixty-year period relative to the size of the labor force. The expansion of other professions (accountancy, engineering, and nursing) is consistent both with the growth of formal schooling and with the fact that the technology underlying the practice of these occupations has advanced markedly. In cases where technological changes occur, particularly in occupations rooted in abstract principles, it is not surprising to find considerable reliance on high-level formal schooling.

Medicine and teaching represent interesting and contrasting cases. Medicine has undergone prodigious technological change since 1900, yet the proportion of doctors in the labor force has remained almost constant since 1920, suggesting that the occupation has not made a disproportionate numerical claim on the nation's educational resources. Teaching, however, the largest of the professions, has experienced at best minimal technological development since the turn of the century (perhaps over the last 2,500 years), yet increases in the amount of formal training obtained by teachers are easily documented. Moreover, the proportion and number of teachers in the labor force, as shown in Table 3, have increased, which accounts in part for the increased consumption of national educational resources.

The work of managers and officials is difficult to understand technologically and by its general underlying principles. Students of business

TABLE 3

Percentage Representation of Occupations in the Labor Force, 1900–1960 [a,b]

Occupation	1960	1950	1940	1930	1920	1910	1900
				Labor force (in thousands)			
	67,990	58,999	51,742	48,686	42,206	37,291	29,030
Professional, technical							
Accountants, auditors	.71	.67	.46	.39	.27	.10	.07
Architects	.04	.04	.04	.04	.04	.04	.03
Clergymen	.29	.29	.27	.30	.30	.30	c
Engineers	.81	.92	.56	.44	.31	.20	.13
Lawyers, judges	.31	.31	.36	.33	.31	.30	.38
Nurses	.93	.83	.72	.60	.30	.21	.04
Physicians, surgeons	.34	.33	.32	.32	.35	c	c
Teachers	2.25	1.94	2.09	2.14	1.79	1.59	1.51
Managers, officials, proprietors							
Construction, manufacture, transportation, telecommunications, wholesale trade	c	2.58	1.88	1.92	1.82	1.97	1.31
Retail trade	c	3.36	3.13	3.26	2.89	3.00	3.20
Banking, finance	c	.24	.24	.35	.28	.20	.27
Clerical							
All occupations	14.14	12.25	9.62	8.90	8.02	5.32	3.02
Sales							
All occupations	7.07	7.00	6.66	6.28	4.87	4.70	4.51
Craftsmen, foremen							
All occupations	13.59	14.15	11.98	12.82	12.98	11.57	10.54
Carpenters	1.35	1.72	1.50	1.88	2.09	2.18	2.06
Electricians	.52	.56	.42	.51	.42	.28	.17
Operatives							
All occupations	18.89	20.39	18.39	15.79	15.60	14.59	12.81

[a] 1960 figures: U.S. Bureau of the Census, Statistical Abstract of the United States: 1965 (Washington: U.S. Government Printing Office, 1965), table 316, pp. 230–235.
[b] 1900 to 1950 figures: U.S. Bureau of the Census Historical Statistics of the United States, Colonial Times to 1957 (Washington: U.S. Government Printing Office, 1960), Series D 125, 132, 136, 145, 157, 160, 161, 165, 171, 205–210, 220, 227, 248, 261, 267, 275, 338, pp. 75–76.
[c] Data are not reported when occupational classifications cannot be compared between decades and between the Historical Statistics and the Statistical Abstract.

and organizations have long tried to identify a cluster of skills and principles they can call peculiarly managerial and entrepreneurial, but without marked success. It is difficult, then, to ascertain whether and how these occupations have changed in what are supposedly the intrinsic tasks of the work. However, in the construction, manufacture, and telecommunications industries (wholesale trade is exceedingly problematic), there have been substantial changes in the prevailing technologies of production jobs to justify reliance on formal education in training managers. (Certainly some managerial and entrepreneurial skills are learned through experience on the job.) Accordingly, consistency is understandable between the growth of managerial occupations in these industries and that in schooling. Retail trade, banking, and finance have remained largely unchanged as components of the labor force.

Clerical, sales, craft (with the exception of carpenters), and semiskilled occupations have all increased in proportion. How much academic schooling beyond adequate literacy and numeracy obtainable in a secondary school represents relevant preparation in these occupations is moot. Many basic skills involved are acquired through experience and on-the-job training. The vast expansion of the clerical sector is clearly consistent with the growth of secondary schooling, but as far as actual job requirements (as distinct from general intellectual and social skills) are concerned, it is reasonable to ask how much formal schooling contributes to the job-related capacities of parts of the sales contingent, craftsmen, and operatives because much of their work can be learned on the job or in specific training programs.

The Census data speak only indirectly to the proposition that increases in the technological development and intellectual demandingness of occupations account for the expansion of schooling. Accountancy, engineering, nursing, and the managerial occupations fall within the scope of the generalization in that they have increased proportionally in size and have become more advanced technologically. Architecture, law, and medicine have developed technically and become more specialized, but have not increased proportionally; teaching has increased in size, but has remained technologically undeveloped. None of the last four occupations fits the generalization very well. The clerical occupations currently constitute a large segment of the labor force and have increased substantially since the turn of the century; they probably account for a good deal of the expansion in secondary schooling (though not in higher education). To the extent we can argue, then, that educational resources will be consumed by persons entering numerically expanding occupations in which work tasks have become more sophisticated, only a weak case can be made to support the contention that these occupational changes account for the expansion of schooling. But schooling has increased at a greater rate than growing occupations whose technological requirements are served by additional schooling. Accordingly, one must look for additional sources of demand for schooling.

Educational requirements for occupations are notoriously difficult to establish; by "requirements" I mean what people must know (or would be substantially better off if they did know) to do their work competently, not what credentials they must hold to gain employment. If for arguments, these requirements were used to establish a connection between educational and occupational expansion, at least presumptive evidence exists that many people acquire skills in lower and higher schools that will have little *direct* relevance to their future jobs. Certainly not all occupations in the Census classification of professional and managerial occupations "require" advanced schooling.

The problem of establishing connections between job requirements, expected educational attainments (credentials), and actual schooling has been stubbornly resistant to solution. R. S. Eckaus, in a critique of assumptions underlying "human capital" formulations,[9] has sought direct measures of occupational requirements that break the circularity of arguments based on correlations between schooling and income and between occupational level and schooling: the Specific Vocational Preparation (SVP) index, based on the duration of job training, and the General Educational Development (GED) index, based on expert judgments of the language, mathematical, and reasoning skills required to perform specific jobs. Although Eckaus rates occupations on each index and shows changes (1940 to 1950) in labor force distributions based on them, his use of the term "requirements" still, to some extent, confounds credentials with requirements. The SVP index explicitly refers to training expectations prevailing at a given time; hence, an increase in an occupation's SVP score can either mean that workers will have greater difficulty with the job if they lack additional training than if they have it, or that credential standards have been raised irrespective of changes in the work. Furthermore, it makes no distinction between formal schooling and apprenticeship, and ignores the contribution of on-the-job experience as distinct from both schooling and apprenticeship.

The GED index presents difficulties also, but of a different and perhaps more basic kind. Problems are inherent in relying on expert judgments to establish educational requirements for "average performance" on a job, especially because we do not know the extent to

[9] R. S. Eckaus, "Economic Criteria for Education and Training," *Review of Economics and Statistics*, vol. 46, no. 2 (1964), pp. 181–190.

which the three GED components can be substituted for each other. More important, the GED rating does not indicate what *range* of language, mathematical, and reasoning skills represents sufficient technical preparation. And the range question is the nub of the issue because we know that people with varying skills do perform the same work effectively; this and the fact that Eckaus and others seem impelled to translate GED scores into years of schooling create an uneasiness that actual job requirements and credentials have yet to be distinguished adequately. Eckaus, however, has clearly identified the issue and has moved us closer to this resolution.

The strongest case for linking job requirements and schooling can be made for occupations traditionally acknowledged as professions (as distinct from the broad Census classification of "professionals"). The numerically increasing *and* technologically advancing occupations constitute a small proportion of the labor force. Yet the expansion of th' American educational enterprise, particularly at the higher levels, and changes in the occupational system appear strangely out of line when viewed in juxtaposition; they raise the question of whether a vast credential-gathering apparatus has not evolved, an inflation in credentials with the demand factor as yet unidentified.

There is no question that the United States has a thoroughly schooled, if not necessarily highly "educated," population, as the figures in Table 4 testify. In addition, the post-World War Two period has witnessed an expansion of institutions of higher learning already in existence and an efflorescence of new institutions, primarily at the junior and community college levels. Americans are up to their necks

TABLE 4

Years of Schooling Completed Among Persons 25 Years of Age and Older, 1940–1960.

Years of school completed	Percentages		
	1940	1950	1960
8 years or less	59.6	46.9	39.6
1–3 years of high school	15.0	16.9	19.2
4 years of high school	14.1	20.2	24.6
1–3 years of college	5.4	7.2	8.8
4 years of college or more	4.6	6.0	7.7
Total	98.7[a]	97.2[a]	99.9

[a]Those failing to report years of schooling not included in the tabulation.
Source: U.S. Bureau of the Census, *Statistical Abstract of the United States: 1965,* (Washington: U.S. Government Printing Office, 1965), table 147, p. 112.

TABLE 5

Within- and Between-Occupational Changes Related to Schooling;
Employed White Males, 35 to 54 Years of Age, 1940 to 1960[a]

Years of school Completed	Within occupation changes (000)	Between occupation changes (000)
No years complete	−35	−36
1-4 years completed	−291	−161
5-8 years completed	−3549	−464
9-11 years completed	694	100
12 years completed	2363	51
13-15 years completed	505	90
16 or more years completed	314	420

[a]Selected from John K. Folger and Charles B. Nam, *Education of the American Population* (Washington: U.S. Bureau of the Census, U.S. Government Printing Office, 1967), table VI–4, p. 171.

in educational investments, both institutional and personal. Yet even a cursory examination of the Census listing of professional and managerial occupations, accompanied by a corresponding reading of the *Dictionary of Occupational Titles,* reveals many jobs whose holders can learn their work on the job or in specialized programs; many do even after college graduation.

Although, as noted earlier, establishing the relationship between amount of schooling and job requirements is difficult, John Folger and Charles Nam have marshalled evidence [10] that draws the connection tighter than I have. By analyzing Census data for the decades between 1940 and 1960, they have attempted to determine the extent to which changes in the level of schooling among employed white males aged 35 to 54 can be attributed to changes within occupations or to employment shifts between them. The former change would suggest that occupations at the same level "attract" increasingly more people with more schooling; the latter, that educational changes are associated with occupational ones. Their findings appear in Table 5. Clearly, change has occurred mainly within occupations; over these two decades, some jobs were being performed in 1960 by people with less schooling than those *in the same jobs* in 1940 (and others by people with more). If one assumes that actual work demands of similar level jobs have not changed radically, the latter finding suggests that

[10] John D. Folger and Charles B. Nam, *Education of the American Population* (Washington, D.C.: U.S. Bureau of the Census, U.S. Government Printing Office, 1967).

the job seeks the credential more than it does the skill, particularly among the high school graduates. (Folger and Nam are explicitly aware that the broad classification of occupations diminishes the interpretability of their results. They also observe, however, that between 1950 and 1960, the educational level of workers increased most in occupations that are stable or diminishing and in which the educational level in 1950 was less than 12 years — this strengthens their case.)

The most interesting exception to their generalization is that among college graduates there are greater shifts between than within occupations, suggesting that the better educated have sought work commensurate with their training. The largest *absolute* increase of highly educated workers was absorbed by the professions (although the proportional increase was small — 12 per cent — suggesting that the professions had all along attracted the highly schooled); the managerial sector absorbed the largest *proportional* increase (80 per cent; the absolute increase was more modest than that of the professional sector). These findings lend only conditional support to the argument that technical job requirements form the link between schooling and work; it seems to hold for the highest level, intellectually demanding, and technologically changing occupations.

In a provocative business and industrial study in which he marshalls the scarce and recalcitrant data on the relevance of educational attainment to job performance in blue-collar, white-collar, professional, and managerial occupations, Ivar Berg [11] finds that years of schooling completed by workers have little association (sometimes an inverse one) with performance ratings. The executives he interviewed seldom ascertained whether the quality of work was related to the amount of schooling workers obtained (though the appropriate data in some companies were available in personnel records), and frequently justified hiring college graduates (rather than those with less schooling) because completing college indicates perseverance — no matter what was studied there — and because college graduates possessed the "polish" that goes over well with clients. Berg's findings are heretical in the light of the conventional wisdom in that they question the connection between schooling and the job requirements prevailing in an industrial economy, all or most of whose professional, managerial, and technical workers, it would seem, should benefit in their work from having spent their youth in classrooms.

This excursion into problems of educational and occupational change brings us to an interpretive impasse. Justification is only partial

[11] Ivar E. Berg, *Certified to Work: The Great Training Robbery* (New York: Praeger, 1970).

for the proposition that increases over time in the extent of schooling vary directly with advances in the technical and intellectual demands of occupations characteristic of industrial societies like the United States, though the proposition does appear to hold among certain professional occupations. It seems implausible that simply the growth of a literate and schooled population can account for the rise of a modern occupational structure, but highly likely that the existence and continuation of modern societies depends on the availability of large numbers of people possessing literacy and numeracy.

The last century of American educational and occupational history literally provides no opportunity to consider the problem of social stability, which is not to say that, in the near or distant future, the indices of social change will not sit still for a while. Of course, one can claim that American society has been highly industrialized for some time — it is stable in that sense; but that is only a game of words. Whatever the empirical situation respecting stability or change, the critical question remains the nature of the connections between one institutional sector and another — in this discussion, between schooling and occupational life. By attempting to formulate these connections by three "arguments," I find myself forced outside any simple scheme that relates some particular change in the pattern of schooling with some corresponding change in the occupational realm for several reasons: some occupationally relevant capacities are learned outside schools; literacy, as one outcome of schooling, appears to be more a threshold phenomenon than a simple correlative one; the relationship between the amount of schooling and job performance seems hazy; for many occupations, the amount of schooling expected apparently exceeds the technological requirements of the work; and finally, school attendance rates surpass the growth of occupations for which schooling, particularly at the higher levels, appears appropriate. None of these contentions, of course, belies the importance of the complex and conditional connections between schooling and occupational life; they do, however, provide ample justification to consider the connections between schooling and other, non-occupational, institutional areas.

SOME NON-OCCUPATIONAL IMPLICATIONS OF SCHOOLING

By restricting the connection between educational and occupational change to rather narrow technological grounds, I have set up something of a straw man; however, it is useful to discover that a frequently enunciated and plausible contention has some loose pieces jangling. The original problem remains with us: why the diffusion and expansion of schooling in the United States? An interpretive impasse often signals a problem inappropriately defined, or at least partially so. The most vulnerable points in the occupational argument, it seems to me, are: (1) that the most significant outcomes of schooling are job-related skills; and (2) that attention is directed to the school-acquired skills presumably related to the work-performance side of occupational life without corresponding consideration of their relevance to other institutional realms. I question, however, only the general applicability of these points and do not repudiate them; basic literacy and numeracy, after all, are clearly required by all occupations from the level of operatives on up (as well as for some below that skill level), and graduate school is undoubtedly necessary for the most technically and intellectually demanding occupations. But one still finds such odd phenomena as individuals with high school diplomas having better employment prospects than those having completed eleven or twelve years of school who lack the diploma; and individuals with college diplomas who undertake job training (vocational) programs to prepare for the same work high school graduates are doing. In the latter case, just job experience or even seniority counts as much as credentials as far as working competently goes.

Give the demand, literacy, and requirement arguments their due (though we don't know precisely how much that is). There are, however, additional questions to address to the phenomenon of expanded schooling, although it is not yet possible to settle them convincingly. First, for example, whatever formal schooling may contribute to the performance of occupational pursuits, it may also provide various psychological capacities that individuals "require" in their daily activities as the clients (customers, patients, renters, litigants, depositors, passengers) of others in *their* occupational pursuits, as I have contended in an earlier publication,[12] because all adults are clients of many others. These client activities are so commonplace that we often forget that something must be learned to carry them out; and if I am not mistaken, Alex Inkeles [13] would readily include the psychological capacities to act appropriately as a client in his idea of "competence," as part of what it takes to participate as an adult in a modern industrial society. Moreover, there is reason to believe that the instructional lessons of school, the means of teaching literacy and numeracy, make some contribution to acquiring these skills, but the experience of schooling is far broader in its implications.

Second, the expansion of schooling can be interpreted as part of the

[12] Robert Dreeben, *On What Is Learned in School* (Reading, Mass.: Addison-Wesley, 1968).
[13] Alex Inkeles, "Social Structure and the Socialization of Competence," *Harvard Educational Review*, vol. 36, no. 3 (1966), pp. 265–283.

general development of citizenship in nation states, particularly in its "social" aspects, as T. H. Marshall [14] defined them. To attend school becomes a right, a sign that one has gained full participatory membership in a nation. Accordingly, we should construe school attendance, and increasingly attendance at institutions of higher learning, in the same way we understand universal suffrage (and the recent movement to lower the voting age to 18), and the right to a fair trial (and the recent movement to allow juvenile offenders to retain legal counsel), where both these contemporary movements represent attempts to extend the boundaries of citizenship.

Third, the diffusion of schooling can be understood as an aspect of American nationalism and the continuation of a cultural tradition. Much has been written in the educational literature and in the public prints about civics courses and inculcating patriotism; however, I am not concerned here about whether patriotism is the loftiest of virtues or the last refuge of scoundrels. The point is that national political stability — whatever value one places on that and its particular forms — depends to some extent on reasonably broad acceptance of certain premises for conduct; a national language; and mitigating deep social cleavages based on region, class, tribe, lineage, religion, race, and ethnicity. The Civil War and its legacy and the immigration experience have created severe strains on whatever forces support political and cultural unity in the United States. The racial backwash of the Civil War is very much with us; the problems that war created have not yielded readily to educational solutions. Though as Nathan Glazer and Daniel Moynihan [15] remind us, the pot of immigrants has far from completely melted, the strains of ethnic diversity have become less severe than those attributable to race; and although we cannot read *The Education of H*Y*M*A*N K*A*P*L*A*N* [16] as definitive history, we cannot ignore its message that the "American Night Preparatory School for Adults (English — Americanization — Civics — Preparation for Naturalization)" made its contribution to national unity by disseminating a common language as much as it contributed to literacy.

These three questions move us away from job-related skills as the primary outcome of schooling and lead to different concerns dealing more with the tacit curriculum of schools, their social organization, and the forms of social experience they provide for young people.

[14] T. H. Marshall, "Citizenship and Social Class," in *Class, Citizenship, and Social Development* (Garden City, N.Y.: Doubleday, 1964), pp. 65–122.

[15] Nathan Glazer and Daniel P. Moynihan, *Beyond the Melting Pot* (Cambridge, Mass.: MIT Press and Harvard University Press, 1963).

[16] Leonard Q. Ross [Leo Rosten], *The Education of H*Y*M*A*N K*A*P*L*A*N* (New York: Harcourt, Brace and Co., 1937).

The expansion of schooling is surely among the most dramatic secular trends of the past century of American history. However intricate its connections with changes in the occupational structure, it is nevertheless one of the main contributors to social stability. Shall we regard the idea that change can yield stability as a paradox? Not necessarily, if we consider the impact of schooling on the sentiments and capacities of men. That schooling can have homogenizing consequences is a defensible proposition though not a self-evident one; for insofar as it remains the prerogative of an elite and reinforces an accumulation of distinctive social identities based on primordial ties, it can contribute to the most virulent forms of social and political instability.

What sentiments and capacities are most germane for adopting patterns of conduct associated with clienthood in a modern industrial society, for becoming a citizen of a nation state, and for subordinating primordial ties to identify with a nation? And what aspects of the schooling process and the nature of schools appear most directly related to forming these sentiments and capacities? However much American institutions have changed, the facts remain that an aggregation of sovereign states was forged into a nation through adherence to a written constitution and through the decisions of a Federalist Supreme Court, that the Union prevailed — through war — over a deep regional schism, that immigrants were absorbed into a national entity, and that industrial and commercial institutions have characterized our economic life for a long time. My contention is that schooling has contributed to forming psychological competencies in individuals, which enables them to participate as adults in an industrial nation whose dominant political and economic institutions have not experienced *fundamental structural* change over the past century. The changes that have occurred, in other words, did so within the framework of prevailing structural arrangements. I turn, then, to a discussion of the emergence of modern schools and to the implications of schooling for the linkage between its psychological outcomes and the demands of modern industrial life.

CHANGES IN THE STRUCTURE OF SCHOOLS

Philippe Ariès [17] gives us a brilliant, meticulously drawn picture of medieval and post-medieval schools in Europe. He describes the early schools as lacking a gradation of subjects according to difficulty, an age dispersion of scholars in the same "class" so broad as to appear incredible by modern standards (as late as 1618, students aged 9 to 24 could be found in the same class — the precocious and the super-

[17] Philippe Ariès, *Centuries of Childhood*, trans. Robert Baldick (New York: Knopf, 1962).

annuated attended school together); the absence of any standard age for beginning school; the instruction of from several dozen to several hundred students by one teacher (sometimes with an assistant) in the same room; and the maintenance of control by corporal punishment (irrespective of age), humiliation, and reliance on informers. The idea of schooling as general preparation for an adult occupation was foreign to the medieval tradition; and schooling of this nature, largely consistent with training a clerical elite, endured for a long time.

During the period between the seventeenth and nineteenth centuries several changes in school organization accelerated, some of which had begun earlier. Children increasingly passed through an orderly sequence of classes and subjects, a temporal order was imposed on the various subject matters, promotion from class to class became more regular, a hierarchy of education institutions developed along with excluding both the precocious and the slow from the same class; in short, a growing recognition of the connection between age, ability, and school grade emerged, a connection later representing the underlying principle of modern graded schools. The medieval notion of childhood weakness, with its associated injunction to humiliate children, declined; in its place grew the idea that a sense of responsibility should be encouraged, that children should be prepared more generally for public adult life (conceived more broadly than preparation for the clergy) through gradual and careful training.

This truncated historical narrative will have to serve as an introduction to later developments on the early American educational scene. Bernard Bailyn [18] informs us that the seventeenth-century American family, holding a traditional obligation (of English origin) for cultural transmission, began to lose its efficacy in an environment where the press of unfamiliar and hostile conditions superseded those of tradition. Where, after all, were the supports for English tradition among a people, especially among the younger generation, who had elected to escape from England? These conditions and the growing expansion of new settlements in the wilderness made it increasingly difficult for families to meet old obligations of training their children in "learning and labor." According to Bailyn, Puritan families, with their strong commitment to literacy and Biblical learning and the fear that their children would become savages, established schools and assigned to them tasks of cultural transmission that previously came under family jurisdiction. The more vocational aspects of education became the responsibility of masters in an apprenticeship system, a quasi-familial setting without kinsmen. Unlike their English counterparts, masters in

[18] Bernard Bailyn, *Education in the Forming of American Society* (Chapel Hill: University of North Carolina Press, 1960).

colonial America were obliged to provide training in literacy (only reading at first, and in the early eighteenth century, writing and arithmetic as well) and in moral conduct.

As Bowman [19] indicates, schooling and apprenticeship developed at the same time; both entailed separating children from their families and to that extent laid the foundations for a public, nonfamilial sector of society. By contrast, during the early emergence of the factory system in England, apprenticeship required masters to assume more obligations of a familial nature than in the colonies; many children worked in factories apprenticed to their parents. At that time, education for English working-class children did not develop as independently of family life as it did in the colonies, nor did widespread schooling emerge to the same extent as a nonfamilial function.

The American reliance on schools was further strengthened by growing strains on apprentice training; masters found the obligation to foster moral values and literacy increasingly burdensome within the confines of an arrangement designed to create artisans and craftsmen who were in considerable demand in the labor market. The legal injunctions on masters (and the growing enforcement of them) to provide this additional, nonvocational instruction was perhaps a sign that this multifaceted form of apprenticeship was crumbling.[20] By this time, however, the seeds of important educational development had taken root. The colonists had brought with them *and sustained* a religiously inspired belief in the need for literacy; the circumstances of life and survival in bleak surroundings reinforced an existing commitment to train young people to do useful, economically productive work; schooling and apprenticeship provided institutional settings to meet both needs. As the prevailing apprenticeship system declined, a community-supported institution — the school — was available (though not flourishing because of scarce funds) to absorb its functions, to provide, in Bowman's words, for a "useful calling." With a school curriculum that afforded training in manipulating of symbols, preparation for a useful calling did not simply mean narrow vocationalism; accordingly, the outcome of schooling could be formulated as a generalized resource relevant to participation in a differentiating economy.

The experience of establishing schools in seventeenth- and eighteenth-century America, the problems of public finance, religious conflict, and the question of who should control have their legacies in our history to this day. Our system of schooling, however, assumed its basic outlines as the Common School emerged in the mid-nineteenth century. To speak of the "basic form" of American schooling perhaps

19 Bowman, "From Guilds to Infant Training Industries."
20 Storr, "The Growth of American Education."

conceals more than it illuminates. What aspects of the educational scene should occupy our attention: political ideologies, educational theories, building construction, foreign immigration, internal migration, changes in the composition of the labor force, methods of instruction, religious controversy, curriculum content; the variables or the constants?

One major impetus behind the movement for the Common School, according to Lawrence Cremin,[21] and perhaps the main one, was to provide children of diverse origins with those intellectual and moral virtues necessary for national citizenship and, in particular, to support the tenets of a republican government. The leaders of the movement, Horace Mann especially, espoused the need for the universality of this form of schooling and for its political and religious neutrality. It was, in short, an egalitarian movement; like all such movements, particularly in times of growing industrialization, of increasing foreign immigration with its attendant ethnic and religious cleavages, and, as in mid-nineteenth-century America, of regional conflict over the issue of slavery, it was bound to scrape on the reefs of deep-running social conflicts.

The educational issue at the time was how to create universal support for and participation in a national polity; although this explicit leveling principle was fully compatible with the tenets of the Judeo-Christian tradition in a predominantly Christian nation, the Common School struggle raged over issues imbedded in the conflicts between Protestants and Catholics, which were exacerbated by immigration, and between social classes (particularly with the substantial growth of the working class) rooted in a rapidly industrializing economy. The argument that the Bible (the Protestant Bible, that is) was the work of God while sectarianism was created by man cut no ice with those who did not accept the Protestant Bible. Furthermore, the well-to-do, able to provide an education for their own children and willing to lend philanthropic support to educate the indigent (an exercise in Christian charity), chafed at the idea of public taxation to finance schooling for everyone; nor did they relish the idea of sending their children to school with those of the poor.

The Common School movement, patriotic and nationalistic in character, non-sectarian in ideology (though in fact not quite so), has its parallel in the English Evangelicalism of the eighteenth century; to follow the argument of Reinhard Bendix,[22] both movements contributed to the social and political inclusion of potentially dissident

---

[21] Lawrence A. Cremin, *The American Common School* (New York: Bureau of Publications, Teachers College, 1951).

[22] Reinhard Bendix, *Work and Authority in Industry* (New York: Wiley, 1956).

groups in society. Essentially, the legitimate authority of the state over all citizens was at issue, and proponents of the movement were explicitly committed to the belief that schools attended by all children were more efficacious agents than the family and the church for promoting universal citizenship. The task was to be accomplished by instruction, particularly in how the system of government worked, in glorifying the nation, and of course in the basic skills represented by the three R's. The important goal of mixing diverse people was hardly lost on the Common School reformers; and with benefit of hindsight, the substance of the reformers' religious views was reasonably close to a "civil religion" as described by Robert Bellah,[23] a religion without sectarian content, though that was hardly acknowledged either by proponents or opponents of those views at the time.

Again, with benefit of hindsight, the equalitarian and nationalistic ideology of Common School reform appears somewhat premature; the problems of class and ethnic cleavage were relatively mild in the early nineteenth century compared to what they would become in the post-Civil War period of rapid industrialization and immigration. Perhaps the most important legacy of the movement, however, was the stabilization of a particular school organization, one that has remained predominant — though with certain modifications — to the present day: the graded school with self-contained classrooms. I would contend, moreover, that if the structural properties of a socializing agency, such as a school, remain the same (or nearly so), the experiences of children passing through it will be similar, and so will the psychological outcomes of those experiences.

STRUCTURAL CONSTANTS AND VARIATIONS IN SCHOOL ORGANIZATION

Arthur Stinchcombe [24] has argued the intriguing case that organizations established at one period in time differ in their social organization from those founded at other times; and once established, tend to retain their original structure. (I have oversimplified his contention somewhat, but not egregiously.) His case is basically technological: organizations take the form they do because the technology of production prevailing at a given time limits the forms of social organization consistent with the performance of work activities entailed in the technology; and unless there are technological innovations in some

[23] Robert N. Bellah, "Civil Religion in America," *Daedalus*, vol. 96, no. 1 (1967), pp. 1–21.

[24] Arthur L. Stinchcombe, "Social Structure and Organizations," in *Handbook of Organizations*, ed. James G. March (Chicago: Rand McNally, 1965), pp. 142–193.

area of production, the structure of organizations in that area will remain the same.

Does the argument apply to schools? With mild trepidation, Stinchcombe dates the origins of various industries; a reading of Ariès yields crazy-quilt trends — but trends nevertheless — in patterns of school organization. Accordingly, great caution is necessary when dating the "origins" of modern schools. Roughly between 1750 and 1850 in Europe and America, a diffusion of a type of school organization occurred consistent with the preparation of young people to enter the labor force, the explicit connection between age and capacity, and the separation of family life from life in the public institutions arena. During this century, in the latter part of which the American common school experienced notable development, age-graded schools emerged, with classrooms as their major structural units. Children left their homes to obtain instruction by a teacher and in the company of their age peers. Schooling, in other words, ceased to involve apprenticeship to a matter or deference to a tutor.

Stinchcombe looks to technological stability and change to account for constancy and variation in the structure of organizations, but one is hard-pressed to identify the technology of teaching. There is ample justification, however, to seek signs of stability and change in the ecological patterns of schools (and though Stinchcombe's formulation rests on technology, surely his work on craft and bureaucratic organization gives an equally prominent and convincing place to ecology). As the floorplans in the figure illustrate, certain critical ecological properties of schools have been petrified in their architecture; *the self-contained classroom has remained the basic instructional unit for more than 100 years*. Whatever the differences in size, location, building materials, and facilities, the more exotic design of the 1950's still contains rooms in which a batch of like-aged children receive instruction from a teacher in a space large enough to enclose them all; basically, only the spatial *arrangement* of classrooms has changed.

That the structural organization of classrooms had become fixed was perhaps the most important single educational development of the time. (To observe this element of constancy, however, is not to deny the occurrence of certain changes: the inclusion of more subject content in the curriculum, the increase in school attendance, the emergence of the track system, and the decline of the one-room schoolhouse. None of these, moreover, proved structurally conflicting with the self-contained classroom.) As to why this particular structural form has remained so stable, one can only speculate that none of the alternatives appeared viable: the medieval system had long ago vanished and in ways that led to the emergence of the modern class-

Architectural Designs for Schools

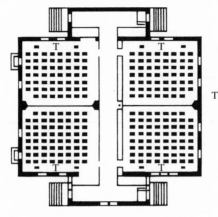

The Quincy School,
Boston, Massachusetts
1847–48

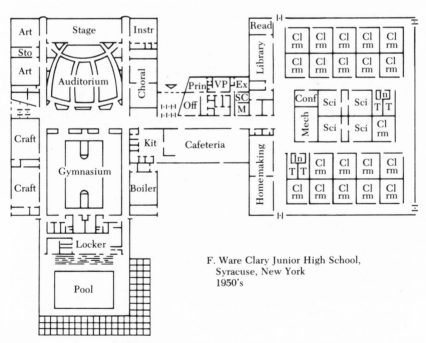

F. Ware Clary Junior High School,
Syracuse, New York
1950's

Source: The Cost of A Schoolhouse (New York: Educational Facilities Laboratories, 1960), pp. 22 and 65.

room; neither apprenticeship nor tutoring, both workable means of instruction in their own right, were consistent with instructing large numbers of children beginning to attend school. And the activities of teaching had not undergone any fundamental technological change — and haven't to this day — that might strain existing social arrangements to the point that new ones might appear. (Nothing happened to change teaching that was comparable to the introduction of the assembly line, for example, in certain types of manufacture.)

A school is basically a collection of classroom units, each containing anywhere from 10 to 60 pupils of about the same age, presided over by one teacher (a non-parental adult); it is a graded institution in that pupils enter it and pass through in age cohorts, completing in one year work whose difficulty is pitched roughly at a level commensurate with their age, before advancing to the next grade. Contemporary schools are distinguished according to level; although both elementary and secondary schools (as well as colleges) can be dated back to the earliest colonial years, high schools proliferated during the late nineteenth and early twentieth centuries. The recent research [25] on Massachusetts indicates an association between the increase in public high schools and the growth of manufacturing industry, urbanization, and a sufficiently substantial tax base.

By the late nineteenth and early twentieth centuries, the United States had become highly industrialized, which is reflected both in its occupational and economic institutions and in the character of its social classes. It had become increasingly urban — and would become more so — and its population had swelled not only in size but in diversity with the massive influx of immigrants from Europe. The magnitude and complexity of these changes are self-evident; according to the premise that changes in one part of a social system — a total society, in this case — produce changes in others, the fact remains that changes in the structure of the educational *system* were modest at best. Changes did occur, of course, and the connections between them and changes in other institutional areas are not difficult to trace. The decline of one-room rural schoolhouses could be expected to follow the migrating rural population to the cities and the massive settlement of immigrants in the great urban centers. That the demands of occupational life would include at least basic literacy and numeracy, and that employment opportunities would be available at all occupational levels, gave impetus both to the expansion of elementary and secondary schools and to school attendance. Moreover, the schools would also speed cultural assimilation for the foreign-born; at the

[25] Michael B. Katz, *The Irony of Early School Reform* (Cambridge: Harvard University Press, 1963).

least, new arrivals from overseas would have to master the language if later occupational opportunities were to materialize for them. With such a diverse and polyglot population, it is not surprising that the schools devised a mechanism to deal with enormous individual differences in the capacities of children: the track system.

It is not obvious, however, that changes in the economy and in the population would leave the organizational structure of schools (particularly classrooms) basically unchanged, but in fact these changes had little or no impact on the technology of instruction, the most likely source of change in school structure. The stability of these structural arrangements, moreover, supported the primary conditions both for the homogenizing effects of schooling (in that all children undergo educational experiences in the same kind of organization), and the creation of psychological capacities relevant to the demands of adult life in an industrial society. Of those capacities, the abilities to engage in non-familial types of authority relationships and to govern one's conduct by the norm of universalism are among the most important.

SCHOOL ORGANIZATION
AND PERSONALITY CHANGE

All societies must work out ways of dealing with the maturation of children. As Karl Mannheim said, getting older entails "fresh contacts," [26] changed relationships associated with leaving one group and entering a new one. But to formulate the question simply as "leaving" and "entering" is too general; we need to know what is problematic for individuals and their society when these events occur, and for this the ideas of Leonard Cain [27] help considerably. He reminds us that in absorbing successive generations into society, provisions must be made for (1) distinguishing age categories, (2) preparing individuals for later age statuses, (3) demarcating the boundaries between statuses and establishing means for crossing them, (4) determining which individuals belong in each category, and (5) setting standards of conduct appropriate for persons of different as well as of similar age. For my purposes the second is most pertinent. I view schooling as one societal mechanism for coping with the problem of generations and of age groups — in modern industrial societies with highly elaborated occupational systems, the question of how individuals become ex-

---

[26] Karl Mannheim, "The Problem of Generations," in *Class, Citizenship, and Social Development,* ed. Paul Kecskemeti (London: Routledge and Kegan Paul Ltd., 1952), pp. 276–322.

[27] Leonard D. Cain, "Life Course and Social Structure," in *Handbook of Modern Sociology,* ed. Robert E. L. Faris (Chicago: Rand McNally, 1964), pp. 272–309.

truded from their families of orientation and enter the public world in which they work and engage the services of others at work. Within this broad context, I concern myself with how schooling generates premises for conduct that predominates in adult public life; if the technological demands of employment do not readily account for the expanding school attendance (or do only in part), it is only natural to search for additional phenomena sufficiently widespread and plausibly related to schooling.

Both Inkeles [28] and Stinchcombe,[29] partly in reaction to the preoccupation of students of socialization with child-rearing practices, have argued persuasively that growing up should be formulated by what adult life holds in store as well by what parents do to and for their children. Schools provide experiences that allow children to pass through that phase of the life cycle bounded by immersion in the family of orientation at one end and participation in adult public life at the other. But what particular experiences does the school make available so that young people can learn to participate in a wide variety of relationships as adults, relationships of a strikingly different character than those prevailing within a family? (Note that schooling does not entail severing connections with one's family — most people are members of one or another kinship group throughout their lives — but rather provides opportunities to learn additional modes of conduct not readily acquired in a family setting.)

The assumption that parent-child relationships of authority are prototypical of all subsequent ones, though argued by some observers, seems gratuitous if not incorrect. Even if residues of early family life perdure, it is still necessary to look at the character of authority within the family *and* how children learn about the nature of authority in non-familial situations. Families are small solidary units held together by strong emotional bonds, close personal attachment, dependency, and expectations for mutual support; accordingly, one would expect that children in such a setting will learn that authority relationships are diffuse and personal in nature. The failure to obey or to accept responsibility becomes a matter in which affectional ties between people deeply involved in each other's lives become involved. This, clearly, is not the way the adult public world operates. But if the "prototype" assumption holds, and because a child usually spends at least the first five most malleable years within the household, why should not the familial type of authority become generalized and extend through time to other situations of authority?

One reason is that on entering school at about age six, children con-

[28] Inkeles, "Social Structure and the Socialization of Competence."
[29] Stinchcombe, "Social Structure and Organizations."

front vastly different social conditions in the classroom than they do at home, conditions that continue (with certain variations) for about twelve years. Consider, then, some social properties of elementary and secondary classrooms and their implications for learning principles of authority and of universalism.

1. Average classrooms contain about 30 pupils of very similar age; although it is a much larger unit than the family, the age dispersion of pupils is often less than that in two-child families and usually less than that in three-or-more-child families.

2. Customarily, one adult is in charge, not two.

3. Grading in schools means that a cohort of pupils completes the work of one grade, crosses a boundary into the following one, and in the process changes teachers. (Children do not change parents periodically.)

4. Teachers, by virtue of their position in the school hierarchy, assign tasks to pupils and evaluate them according to criteria of performance.

5. Because a classroom is an aggregation of like-aged children and teachers assign similar tasks to all, there is an important sense in which pupils are in the same boat — roughly equal in status, responsibilities, and opportunities — unlike the situation in the household where each child is a special case at least by virtue of his age, the clock by which we keep maturational time.

Although all these properties characterize both elementary and secondary schools, the latter have additional ones: (6) High schools are departmentalized; teachers instruct in one rather than in a whole range of subjects. They possess a *specific* competence. (7) Pupils, rather than spending most of their day with one teacher (as in elementary school) spend short periods with each of several teachers. Correlatively, each teacher confronts, on the average, about 160 pupils each day.

These properties of schools are so familiar they scarcely deserve mention — or so it would seem. In fact, when compared with family properties and viewed in the context of social demands characteristic of adult life, they have important implications for changes in premises for conduct. Consider the following. Because classrooms are much larger than families and all members (at least in principle) have roughly equal though lesser claims on the time and energy of a teacher than on parents, the school provides the first prolonged experience of *impersonality*, which increases as the pupil enters secondary school.

Yearly promotion not only means that pupils proceed to more advanced work but that they sever their association with last year's teacher and establish a relationship with a new one. Elementary school, in short, provides the first *systematic* lesson in forming and breaking transitory relationships with other persons; again, an experience uncharacteristic in families. Promotion, moreover, by its periodic occurrence provides children with opportunities to distinguish between persons and social positions. Every classroom has a teacher, but by changing classrooms pupils discover that the teacher is a different individual each time. True, families have their adult and sibling members; but because this membership does not regularly change, it is difficult for a child to settle the question of whether "mother" and "father," for example, represent distinct positions or whether "parent" is one position occupied by a male and female member; in fact, the question is not likely to arise.

In high school pupils can learn that authority can be based on *expertise.* The specific skill (based on subject matter mastery) of the teacher can be identified because all teachers are distinguished by different academic skills. In elementary schools, by contrast, each teacher possesses a mixture of subject skills and is also concerned, as Talcott Parsons commented,[30] with standards of good conduct — "deportment," as it used to be called — unlike the family where parental "skills" are at best amorphously defined and inextricably mixed with emotional expressiveness. What is more, the young person's passage through successive settings, each organized on different principles, provides opportunities to learn that different modes of conduct vary in appropriateness according to situation.

Classrooms are collective units, the conduct of whose members is mutually visible (and in that sense public). The members are like-aged children each of whom is assigned similar tasks by one teacher (and accordingly share common circumstances), which means that classrooms constitute social categories. The categorical reality of classrooms, delineated by the one-year tenure of pupils in them and the annual change of teachers (as well as by a certain social homogeneity), provides an opportunity for pupils to learn that whatever differences overtly distinguish them (their size, stature, intelligence, religion, ethnicity, and the like), their similarities take precedence within the classroom. Herein lies a social basis for learning the principle of universalism: that under certain specifiable social conditions, people with similar characteristics and in similar circumstances

[30] Talcott Parsons, "The School Class as a Social System: Some of Its Functions in American Society," *Harvard Educational Review,* vol. 29, no. 4 (1959), pp. 297–318.

shall be treated alike — categorically — irrespective of the other ways in which they differ.

Finally, with respect to superordination, the family provides no clear means for children to distinguish various bases of authority, because parenthood entails an undifferentiated mixture of personal dominance, specific competence, power based on age and generation, opportunities to exploit affection and dependency conditionally, and a broad range of circumstances in which the right and power to sanction can be exercised. The transition from family, to elementary, to secondary school, however, provides experiences from which children can learn to sort out these various dimensions of superordination and to identify the circumstances under which each is considered appropriate. At issue, moreover, are principles of legitimacy, the conditions under which children learn to acknowledge *the right* of adults to determine their conduct: which adults, under what circumstances, by what means, and in which areas of conduct. Schooling, insofar as it entails repeated and systematic variation of persons (teachers, pupils), situations (school grade, class size), and areas of conduct, provides a setting in which different types of subordination with their corresponding principles of legitimacy can be experienced.

The extraordinary expansion of schooling might well signify an inflation of credentials in occupations that have experienced little if any technological development. Evidence gathered by Berg and Lawrence Thomas [31] suggests that credentials may have greater influence in determining the level of entry into the labor force than performance on the job, and Census data suggest that occupations undergoing both numerical and technological growth do not employ enough people to account for the expansion of schooling (though they most probably account for some, and to that extent should not be ignored). Most occupations require a basic level of literacy and numeracy, and it is not implausible that this level can be acquired with eight years of schooling (perhaps with some beefing up of the elementary school curriculum). But the growth of professions and service occupations in the tertiary sector signifies that more and more people, *as clients*, seek the services of those engaged in these occupations, services that in most cases involve people in various types of relationships of authority (based on expertise, hierarchical position, seniority, tradition, or contractual arrangement), and require that they conduct themselves appropriately in situations where universalistic norms apply. Moreover, most people in the labor force (clerical workers, craftsmen and

[31] Berg, *Certified to Work;* Lawrence G. Thomas, *The Occupational Structure and Education* (Englewood Cliffs, N.J.: Prentice-Hall, 1956).

foremen, and operatives) are overwhelmingly engaged by means of hired employment in which the subordination side of authority is conspicuously evident. True, the skills required for employment in these sectors are frequently learned on the job; but if I read Robert Lane [32] correctly, the capacities for participating in relationships of authority are *also* learned through engagement in work activities with others.

Among the most frequent (if not always the most important) things that adults in modern industrial societies must master is getting along in situations entailing authority. It may seem absurd at first to think that anything much has to be learned to take a ride on a bus, take prescribed medication, follow a policeman's traffic signal, fill out an application for a job; in most cases, compliance is commonly taken for granted. The examples I have chosen are all commonplace, yet the principles of conduct underlying them are nothing of the sort. Each is predicated on the capacity of the subordinate to know what is appropriate in the situation, to know the boundaries of what the superior has a right to expect, to distinguish the person from the position he occupies, to accept the idea that anyone else *in the same circumstances* would (or should) be treated in the same way, to cope with the impersonality of a transitory situation and with the balance between impersonality and personal involvement when relationships are more enduring (as in the case of the law enforcement officials described by Peter Blau [33]). One need only read the poignant tale told by Elihu Katz and S. N. Eisenstadt [34] of the bus driver teaching the Israeli immigrant that the fare is not negotiable and the bus leaves according to schedule, not by the driver's whim and for his personal advantage, to appreciate what principles of conduct must be part of the psychological repertoire.

At least since the advent of the American common school (and whatever equivalents it has in other countries), predicated as it was on the recognized connection between age, capacity, and the graded difficulty of tasks, schools have been characterized by organizational properties that make experiences available from which young people can (not necessarily will) infer principles of authority and universalism that infuse so many situations in adult public life. Also, the pupil's classroom position is almost invariably that of a subordinate, which may account in part for the discomfiture that many Americans experi-

[32] Robert E. Lane, *Political Ideology* (New York: The Free Press, 1962).

[33] Peter M. Blau, *The Dynamics of Bureaucracy*, rev. ed. (Chicago: University of Chicago Press, 1963).

[34] Elihu Katz and S. N. Eisenstadt, "Some Sociological Observations on the Response of Israeli Organizations to New Immigrants," *Administrative Science Quarterly*, vol. 5, no. 1 (1960), pp. 113–133.

ence in positions of superordination. Nothing like the English pre-fectorial system has caught on in American public schools; but because schools in modern countries have much in common, and authority relations differ in certain respects from country to country, one should not attribute all variations in authority relations to schooling.

An institutional realm as central as education is likely to have impli-cations for other sectors of society than the economic. No surprise, then, that David Easton and Jack Dennis in a fascinating monograph on political socialization [35] find that children, as they proceed through school, begin to comprehend the institutional side of political life, while in the early elementary grades they view politics primarily in personal terms. This is clearly consistent with the contention that one outcome of schooling, particularly the capacity to distinguish persons from positions, is learning to engage in relationships entailing im-personality. But a nagging problem remains even if we accept the argument that the technological requirements of high-level occupa-tions account only in part for the expansion of schooling in America: the diffusion of schooling, measured in yearly increments, is not the same as the diffusion of credentials, measured in thresholds.

That more people attend school over an extended academic year for more years than was the case several decades or a century earlier is consistent with the expansion of national citizenship rights in vari-ous non-educational areas; although certain legal, residential, age, and nationality considerations define the boundaries of citizenship, holding diplomas of one degree or another does not. Accordingly, although the right to attend school can be viewed as a manifestation of citizenship, the same cannot be said for holding academic credentials: the latter, in other words, must be explained some other way — and herein lies the difficulty.

At best, I can offer speculative explanations. In a society character-ized by rites of passage of a most vestigial nature, high school and college diplomas and advanced degrees can be viewed in Arnold van Gennep's terms,[36] as indicating separation rites. Although the lines of separation are blurred, school degrees *roughly* identify the times at which young people reduce their dependency on the family and enter the labor force as more independent persons; the level of diploma represents a distributive indicator locating points at which individuals enter the labor market. Though plausible, this argument has two conspicuous weaknesses: separation from the family occurs

[35] David Easton and Jack Dennis, *Children in the Political System: Origins of Political Legitimacy* (New York: McGraw-Hill, 1969).

[36] Arnold van Gennep, *The Rites of Passage*, trans. Monika Vizedom and Gabrielle L. Caffee (Chicago: University of Chicago Press, 1960).

gradually (the punctuating function of credentials is then arbitrary as far as leaving the family is concerned), and possessing the diploma, as distinct from almost possessing it, provides little reliable evidence of job-related competence (at least not much beyond setting a threshold of literacy and numeracy at the high school level).

A defensible case can be made for the distributive function of credentials; the conventional wisdom of employers who use them as signs of perseverance may be correct (though we do not know). Employers do face the problem of selecting workers from a labor pool comprised of many individuals who cannot be readily distinguished by job-related competence. With some justification they can select on the assumption that the credential-holder has met certain minimum standards of performance on tasks known to the employer; they do not necessarily know whether the non-holder has missed by an inch or a mile. In an uncertain situation about competence, with pressure to decide, employers can reduce the size of the pool and the risk by applying a single standard across the board: the culturally prescribed criterion of universalism. At the same time, they can hedge by what the credential indicates about past school performance even though they cannot guarantee a good match between worker capacities and job demands or predict future promise with certainty. That must wait for indications of performance on the job. For the free professional, self-employed, the credential denotes "license" in the sense that Everett Hughes [37] uses the term: an indication of society's willingness to let some people do work that others are not allowed to do; and, of course, the professional's credential signifies successful performance at work, not just general academic competence. And as for entrepreneurs, the market speaks louder than the credential.

Finally, to the extent that the expansion of schooling constitutes an inflationary growth of credentialism, an explanation may lie in the propagation of universalism as an aspect of citizenship in a society lacking a traditional elite. If citizenship, particularly in the social realm (in Marshall's terms [38]), means the extension of welfare rights, and if schooling is included among those rights, then the principle of universalism means that whatever A is entitled to as a citizen, B is similarly entitled.

CONCLUDING OBSERVATIONS

Is education the great engine of social change, as those of the Progressive political persuasion maintained some years ago; or is it, to paraphrase William James, a great flywheel that keeps society running at

[37] Everett C. Hughes, "License and Mandate," in *Men and Their Work* (Glencoe, Ill.: The Free Press, 1958).
[38] Marshall, "Citizenship and Social Class."

a steady tempo? These are perennial questions, but they do not get us very far in understanding how education fits into the social order. Rather than take on the question of education in its entirety, I have attempted to interpret one of the most striking patterns of change in the past century of American history: the expansion of schooling. Does its growth in a national population contribute to change and stability, and if so, in what institutions? Or is it basically a response to events occurring in other institutions? I find at least two contentions persuasive. First, it is fruitless to ask whether schooling contributes to the change and stability of society in general; rather, one must identify specific institutions and specific psychological capacities before inquiring about what changes and what remains the same. Second, it is important to identify which society one is talking about; for in the American case, the expansion of schooling occurred in a nation with a cultural commitment to education, with existing economic institutions that "produced" outcomes similar to those of the schools, and where rapid industrial development proceeded with a highly literate population already present.

The challenge posed by the first three tables was to understand why American schooling has expanded in excess of occupational demands (with the latter construed in terms of occupational requirements). An answer, I believe, is that when a nation becomes increasingly industrial, more facets of it change than just the nature and distribution of occupations. Two changes are particularly important. First, with the creation of new occupations in the whitecollar sector, especially the professions, semiprofessions, and service occupations, a multiplicity of situations develop in which people become engaged as clients; just as schooling provides them with various skills that later have direct application to occupational pursuits, it also provides a range of psychological capacities that serve them both at work and in their encounters as clients. Literacy is a case in point. It is clearly an occupational requirement in most types of employment, but also a requirement for carrying out the mundane, inconspicuous, time-consuming activities that comprise our daily encounters as consumers, passengers, commuters, and the like, activities that are as much the stuff of modern society as going to work. Learning to accept the principle of universalism, moreover, has precisely the same logical status as literacy. Thus, if the occupational side of modern industrial development creates a demand for the outcomes of schooling, concomitant aspects of that same development provide an even greater demand for them.

Second, the growth of industrialism and the emergence of nation states, particularly in the West, have been accompanied by the extension of citizenship rights, among which is the right — more, the mandate — to attend school. Whether or not children enjoy it, schooling has become a compulsory good — like vaccination. Why schooling, along with the franchise, fair trial, property ownership, and the like, has become a right is beyond the scope of this discussion; the fact remains — it has. The citizenship argument, unlike the occupational demand argument, cannot be made on utilitarian and preparatory grounds. Schooling becomes part of the definition of citizenship — it is not a prerequisite for achieving it; accordingly, as the rights of citizenship diffuse, schooling diffuses with them.

Accounting for both the changes in and stability of school organization requires a different line of explanation: a technological one. For whatever the reasons schooling expanded with the advent of industrialism, it became clear that the medieval organization of schools became technologically unfeasible with rising enrollments. When schools became organizations for preparing children for a "useful calling," the classroom drama could not readily proceed with a motley cast of hundreds. A technology of instruction aimed at imparting specific capacities could not be maintained under such conditions, and the emerging labor markets in manufacture and commerce did create a demand for such capacities. The school characterized by age-graded, self-contained classrooms — the model of the common school — did provide an hospitable setting for such instruction; moreover, since the development of the common school, any innovations have yet to appear in instructional technology sufficient to change the character of school organization. The only changes have been those of rearrangement and accretion. The social organization of American schools, I submit, is likely to remain stable for some time; I see few if any pressures from non-educational institutions that will render the present structural arrangements untenable, and the impetus for technological innovations in instruction appears weak at best.

Have we reached a point in our history where the connections between educational and other institutions will remain stable, where there is a friendly matching between the human capacities that the schools supply and the social demands of other institutions — with a few delinquents here and some nasty incidents there? I doubt it. Certainly, the schools made significant contributions to the assimilation of European and Asian immigrants — the refugees of bitter revolutions and squalor abroad — during the nineteenth and early twentieth centuries; but they did not do it alone. Their record with the children of the Civil War — the American blacks — has been unimpressive. If I read contemporary history correctly, we now witness the demands of a domestic ethnic group, distinguished by color, for full membership as citizens, for equal access to all parts of the public domain. And if changes in schooling ensue as a result of this movement, I anticipate their occurrence more in the governance of school systems than in the social organization of schools.

We are also witnessing the emergence of disaffection among those who take the rights of citizenship for granted, the third and fourth generations of public school graduates. If universalism is the governing principle of national citizenship, perhaps this principle has its limits and limitations. For although universalism has been the common denominator of desired social values — equity, equality, universal participation — it also provides the underpinnings of uniformity, standardization, and the subordination of men's individuality and uniqueness to what makes them alike. Perhaps a reaction has begun to set in, especially among youth, to the conventional "goods" of an industrial society, manifest in questioning the value of a conventional occupational career, in choosing which particular wars are worth fighting, and in "doing one's own thing." How the reaction will affect the schools and other institutions in society remains to be seen. A reasonable case, I believe, can be made for the contention that the reaction too is in part an outcome of schooling.

CULTURE

Professor Williams has been one of the leading researchers and theorists in the field of values for almost twenty-five years. His work in general, and this essay in particular, demonstrate his highly successful blending of theoretical analysis and empirical synthesis and research. Professor Williams sees values as informational steering constituents of dynamic social systems. In addition to discussing the sources of stability and change in value systems themselves, he treats their consequences for change and stability in other subsystems of the social system. Professor Williams points to our lack of precise knowledge about, and need for "more accurate mapping of" the patterns of values in actual societies. Without such knowledge, neither social scientists nor policy makers can see the points of harmony, tension, and conflict between consensual and dissensual collectivities in a society. Professor Williams dismisses three charges often made against the conception of values that he holds: (1) that it asserts that behavior simply emanates from values; (2) that it requires an "oversocialized conception of man"; and, (3) that it is biased in favor of static conceptions of behavior and social systems.

Robin M. Williams, Jr.

CHANGE AND STABILITY
IN VALUES AND VALUE SYSTEMS

THE REDISCOVERY OF VALUES

At the high tide of atheoretical empiricism in the social sciences during the 1920's and 1930's in the United States, the use of the term "value" in any context other than that of technical economics was almost enough by itself to brand the user as "unscientific" or "soft." For surely "values" must belong to the repudiated world of religious, ethical, and generally humanistic discourse with which a real science could have nothing to do. Values were non-observable, intangible, subjective, immune to measurement; they simply had to be relegated to "medievalism" — presumably along with those pinheads so ambiguously populated by angelic hosts.

In this intellectual world of "hard data" — and of reflexes, instincts, economic interests, material factors, relations of production, geographic determinism, and the like — there appeared in the late 1930's a book with the outrageous title *The Structure of Social Action*. Readers — or scanners, for genuine readers at first were few — soon were confronted with a thesis that convinced some of the radically positivistic that their initial suspicions of heresy were not without foundation. The author immediately told them that the study dealt with a "voluntaristic theory of action," and the book insisted over and over again that *ends* (read "purposes," "goals," "ideas") were nonreducible in the conceptual scheme being developed. Action had an inherently "normative aspect." Although the term "voluntaristic" may have been an unfortunate choice, because of its inherited philosophical overtones, and gradually dropped out of later Parsonian formulations, the emphasis upon the partly autonomous normative components in the determination of social action has remained throughout the complex development of Parsons' contributions for more than three decades.[1]

The "normative components" legitimately may be defined in several, somewhat different ways. Essentially, however, normative "units" consist of *norms* (specific obligatory demands, claims, expectations, "rules") and of *values* (the criteria of desirability for conduct).

It has been consistently explicit in the several major Parsonian formulations that values are not concrete rules of conduct; nor have values ever been merged into the concept of "institution." Rather, institutions have been conceived either as complex sets of rules or as "value integrates";[2] in either formulation some consistent or systematic *combinations* of concrete criteria and objects of preference are implied. Parsonian theory has never fallen into the trap of confusing value *standards* with *objects of cathexis*, and values have not been assimilated to either existential beliefs or to concrete evaluations (such as ideologies). Beyond question, then, values for Parsons are defined by analytic constructs; they are not object-bound.

But if this conception is held, what can values possibly *be* — if, indeed, the existential verb here makes any sense? Can the social

[1] For a convenient brief summary and commentary on the main outlines of this development up to about 1960, see Max Black (ed.), *The Social Theories of Talcott Parsons* (New York: Prentice-Hall, 1961).

[2] T. Parsons, *The Social System* (Glencoe, Ill.: The Free Press, 1951), pp. 36–45.

actor "be committed to" or "come to internalize" a particular value? If so, values must be characterized by some quality of entitivity,[3] some boundedness or object-quality. And if a value may be likened in some way to an "object" (of regard, of affect, etc.), this conclusion would appear to rule out a sheerly nominal status, i.e., a concept of a value as *purely* a "tendency," "vector," or "principle" as inferred by an external observer. Otherwise values would be analogous to principles of syntax wholly unknown to the speakers of a language. In this event, the particular manifestations of correct or appropriate values would be positively regarded, to be sure, but one would be stretching the point to assert that the values themselves were objects of positive regard.

But is the implied problem really so difficult? Observation of processes of evaluation makes it quite clear that some values are, indeed, highly explicit, and appear to the social actor as phenomenal entities: the person can state the value, illustrate its application in making judgments, identify its boundaries, and the like. Other standards of desirability are not explicit; and social actors may even resist making them explicit. Nonetheless, some criteria of this kind can be inferred from selective behavior, and when such inference is presented to the behaving actor some individuals can recognize in their own conduct a value of which they previously had not been aware. In the enormously complex universe of value phenomena, values may be simultaneously components of psychological processes, social interaction, and cultural patterning and storage.[4]

Evidence that values do influence subsequent behavior is not available in the quantity and with the decisiveness we would prefer, but the total research-based data are nevertheless quite impressive. College students make occupational choices consistent with their values and change their occupational choices in directions consistent with their values as expressed at an earlier time.[5] Changes in vocational choices as recorded six years after a training program followed closely changes in broad types of values (as indexed by the Allport-

[3] Donald T. Campbell, "Common Fate, Similarity and Other Indices of the Status of Aggregates of Persons as Social Entities," in *Decisions, Values and Groups,* ed. Dorothy Willner (New York: Pergamon Press, 1960), p. 200.

[4] See the concise analysis by Ethel M. Albert, "Value Systems," *International Encyclopedia of the Social Sciences* (New York: Macmillan and Free Press, 1968), vol. 16, pp. 287–291.

[5] Rose K. Goldsen et al., *What College Students Think* (Princeton, N.J.: Van Nostrand, 1960), chap. 2; Morris Rosenberg, *Occupations and Values* (Glencoe, Ill.: The Free Press, 1957).

Vernon scale).[6] The rank-ordering of "salvation" in a set of twelve values is highly predictive of church attendance.[7]

DEVELOPMENT OF THE ESSENTIAL CONCEPTS

Data, concepts, and research methods for studying values have been drawn from several major fields — ranging across philosophy,[8] the social sciences,[9] cybernetics,[10] and several branches of the biological and physical sciences.[11] Certainly any review of the development of the main concepts of present interest — that is, values, beliefs, attitudes, norms, institutions, structure, system, change — would have to acknowledge the influence of Parsons' many contributions.[12] In his conception of values, Parsons has accepted Clyde Kluckhohn's definition, which in turn had been influenced by the earlier formulations of the Cornell Values Study Group [13] — formulations notable for their conspicuously interdisciplinary origins. The study of values cannot be confined to a single discipline or a narrow range of research methods.

[6] C. G. Kemp, "Changes in Values in Relation to Open-Closed Systems," in *The Open and Closed Mind*, ed. Milton Rokeach (New York: Basic Books, 1960), pp. 345–346.

[7] Milton Rokeach, *Beliefs, Attitudes and Values* (San Francisco: Josey-Bass, 1968), p. 169.

[8] Cf. Stephen C. Pepper, *The Sources of Value* (Berkeley and Los Angeles: University of California Press, 1958).

[9] See the review in the following publications by Robin M. Williams, Jr.: "Individual and Group Values," *The Annals of the American Academy of Political and Social Science*, vol. 371 (May 1967), pp. 20–37; "Recent Developments in Research on Social Institutions," *The Annals*, vol. 374 (November 1967), pp. 171–174; "The Concept of Values," *International Encyclopedia of the Social Sciences* (New York: Macmillan and Free Press, 1968), vol. 16, pp. 283–287; "The Concept of Norms," ibid., vol. 11, pp. 204–208.

[10] Norbert Wiener, *The Human Use of Human Beings* (Garden City, N.Y.: Anchor, 1954); Karl W. Deutsch, *The Nerves of Government* (New York: The Free Press, 1963).

[11] Walter Buckley, ed., *Modern Systems Research for the Behavioral Scientist: A Sourcebook* (Chicago, Aldine, 1968).

[12] To list the writings thus represented would approximate a complete bibliography of his works. Parsons himself has indicated as especially relevant to analyzing the place of values in social systems: Part II, "General Introduction," *Theories of Society* (New York: The Free Press, 1961); and, with Winston White, "The Link Between Character and Society," in *Social Structure and Personality* (New York: The Free Press, 1964). See the comment in "On the Concept of Value-Commitments," *Sociological Inquiry*, vol. 38, no. 2 (Spring 1968), p. 136.

[13] See Clyde Kluckhohn, "Values and Value-Orientations in the Theory of Action: An Exploration in Definition and Classification," in *Toward a General Theory of Action*, ed. T. Parsons and E. Shils (Cambridge, Mass.: Harvard University Press, 1951), p. 388, fn. 1.

Rokeach has made the case that the discovery of the relative ease with which "attitudes" could be measured and manipulated in the laboratory encouraged a concentration upon "problems of persuasion" rather than "problems of education and re-education." The apparent usefulness of studies or opinions and attitudes to the advertising industry, to government and political leaders, to various political propagandists, and to business management probably also contributed heavily to this emphasis. At any rate, the American psychological research of the last few decades apparently has emphasized short-term effects, group conformity, and techniques of presentation and persuasion, rather than the possible long-term effects of "socialization, educational innovation, psychotherapy, and culture change on values." [14] It is indeed very likely that a focus of attention upon quite short-range effects on relatively docile laboratory subjects would not supply a clear view of the long-range causal importance of pervasive values — which partly define the very limits of what is "possible" and "thinkable" in human conduct.

The dilemmas of defining value are many, but the most crucial in many ways is the choice between a broad and a narrow definition. Highly specific definitions fail to deal with important phenomena that we are forced to recognize as having value properties. Very broad definitions tend to equate "value" with preference, desire, liking, or satisfaction [15] — thus passing over the most distinctive feature of valuing, i.e., the partial autonomy of *criteria* of desirability from desire or wish.

The growing attention now given to values in research and theoretical formulations may help to reduce the confusion in thinking about human social behavior that often has resulted from the absence of a clear discrimination between *energy* and *information*.[16] Lacking an adequate conceptualization of values, some social thinkers have argued whether "ideas" are *stronger than* "material interests," or urged that "the sexual drive" is more powerful than moral norms, or elaborated many other pseudo-problems of this kind. Is a radar pulse stronger than a quart of gasoline? The question is manifestly absurd, unless further specified — and so are its psychological and social analogues. For ideas, moral norms, values, beliefs, and symbols repre-

[14] Rokeach, *Beliefs, Attitudes, and Values*, p. 159.

[15] Cf. Harold Fallding, "The Empirical Study of Values," *American Sociological Review*, vol. 30, no. 2 (April 1965), p. 224.

[16] Charles Ackerman and Talcott Parsons, "The Concept of 'Social System' as a Theoretical Device," in *Concepts, Theory, and Explanation in the Behavioral Sciences*, ed. Gordon J. Direngo (New York: Random House, 1966), p. 37 ff.

sent information, not energy. The energy of human action and the environmental energies that human action may release are controlled by information, by signals, by symbols.[17] The main *cultural* controls of action consist of (a) systems of knowledge and cognitive beliefs and (b) systems of values and norms.[18]

A value system is an organized set of preferential rules for making selections, resolving conflicts, and coping with needs for social and psychological defenses of the choices made or proposed. Values steer anticipatory and goal-oriented behavior; they also "justify" or "explain" past conduct. A "belief system" orients the actor to the putative realities of his existence. Definitions of reality are not wholly "arbitrary," but are open to wide variation, within which they are not rigidly restrained by environmental imperatives. Actual behavior selections result from concrete motivations in specific situations; both the motivations and the definitions of the situation are partly determined by the prior beliefs and values of the actor. A good illustration is the relatively well-studied area of occupational choices. Such choices have been shown to be constrained by awareness of actual personal and environmental conditions, by values, and by beliefs about opportunities for value realization. In American society, for example, there are widely shared and somewhat stereotypic beliefs concerning occupations and employing organizations. Some evidence indicates that the image of the job in the large corporation is of high pay, rapid advancement, and (somewhat less) a secure future, but of little initial responsibility or recognition and of little development of lasting friendships.[19] The preliminary testing on small samples so far reported show strongly patterned conceptions of the values prevailing in different organizations and occupations.

Valuations may refer to any existential objects, including ideas and symbols as such. Social structures and processes may be affected, of course, by differences in those values that are related to physical objects, cultural objects, personalities as biopsychic entities, and so on. However, special importance for social systems attaches to values that

[17] For a concise general statement see Geoffrey Vickers, *Value Systems and Social Process* (New York: Basic Books, 1968), chap. 7, "Aggregative Behavior," pp. 135–138.

[18] Parsons has given a very clear explication of "culture" as a set of informational controls in "An Approach to Psychological Theory in Terms of the Theory of Action," ed. Sigmund Koch, *Psychology: A Science* (New York: McGraw-Hill, 1959), vol. 3, pp. 612–711.

[19] Daniel N. Braunstein and George H. Haines, "Preference Scaling of Careers and Organizations," *Journal of Applied Psychology*, vol. 52, no. 5 (October 1968), pp. 380–385.

serve as criteria *for judging social systems themselves.* As Parsons recently stated:

> *The values which come to be constitutive of the structure of a societal system are,* then, the conceptions of the desirable *type of society* held by the members of the society of reference and applied to the particular society of which they are members. The same applies to other types of social systems.
>
> A value-*pattern* then defines a *direction* of choice, and consequent commitment to action.[20]

Values may be considered to constitute what Vickers calls "an appreciative system."[21] Such an affective-conceptual medium not only is essential to deal with the world, but actually constitutes the basis of any genuine society. Hence, such systems must change to cope with changing adaptative problems, yet at the same time they must retain some coherence, based on minimal consensus, or the social order will break down.[22] As components of the black box of the human social actor, values may be said to be complex precodings for behavioral choice — precodings that continually change in response to current inputs.

It is apparent that values are constituents of dynamic systems because of their *interconnectedness,* their *informational or directive effects,* and their capacity as *"carriers" of psychological energy.* By definition, values always involve a cultural content, a psychological investment, and the constraints and opportunities of a social system and of a biophysical environment. Changes in values are constrained and limited both by the "reality dimension" of all these interpenetrating systems and by the "internal" dimensions of consistency, congruence, or appropriateness among values and beliefs. When we can identify interconnected sets of values and beliefs that describe a preferred or "obligatory" state of a social system, we speak of an *ideology.* Actual concrete specifications of preferred conduct are *norms,* which in turn are referred to values for legitimation, for boundary setting, for redefinition, and for linkage to other norms. Eventually, we may confidently anticipate, closer analysis of symbolic and affective components

---

[20] Talcott Parsons, "On the Concept of Value-Commitments," *Sociological Inquiry,* vol. 38, no. 2 (Spring 1968), p. 136.

[21] *Value Systems and Social Process,* p. xii.

[22] From the standpoint of biological science, as well as social science: "In a world of flux, it is constancy, not change, that requires explanation; and the ecologist's world contains a number of patterns which preserve themselves over substantial periods of time with little apparent change," ibid., p. 35.

will identify more precisely defined units that themselves make up norms and values.

Because social action is almost always highly *specific*, value commitments can be effective only through remarkably precise interpretation and adaptation to enormously varied concrete situations. It follows that continuous fidelity to the essential meaning of evaluative standards *requires* a basic commitment by the social actor, most commonly a particular person who has internalized the value as a basic component of his personality as well as of his social status or social *persona*.[23]

Granting the inherent hazards of analogies in science, one can also recognize their evocative value. It has often been said that the social sciences are still searching for "fundamental units" of analysis. Perhaps it is not too far-fetched to suggest that the study of value-phenomena conceivably can provide several such units, in a manner somewhat parallel to the development of modern genetics. If ideologies are somewhat similar to chromosomes in complexity, organization, and functional modes, then norms might be compared to genes, and values to DNA/RNA — with still unidentified symbolic elements corresponding to the more specific biochemical bases of heredity. Whether these figures of speech are useful or not, there is at any rate a basic continuity between "the genetic component in the structure of organisms and the cultural component in the structure of action systems . . . value-patterns . . . [are] elements of the codes which 'program' the patterning of action."[24]

If these considerations are valid, a scientific approach to values must analyze the empirical weights of varying preferential precodings in relation to the immediate, fluid, ambiguous situations that typically are the settings for our behavior. There would seem to be no doubt that the value-space of human life necessarily becomes filled with standards relating to all the significant types of objects of experience. Values, accordingly, always are mapped on to the physical world, the human organism, other organisms, the biopsychic personality, social actors and relationships, cultural items, and cosmic or transcendental realms. The specifically *social* value orientations accordingly are embedded in a much larger setting of values and may be interdependent with any of these other orientations. In each main area of the total value-space, many different dimensions (modes) of valuing may be

---

[23] Parsons, "On the Concept of Value-Commitments," p. 144: "the primary sanctions that back value-commitments must be internal to the responsible unit."
[24] Ibid., p. 142.

developed. For the field of *social relations*, for example, the *criteria of desirability* may emphasize:

equality, or inequality
acceptance of authority, or rejection of authority ⎫ (collectivity
individual autonomy, or interdependence   ⎬ or self)
expressiveness, or restraint (affectivity/neutrality) ⎭
diffuseness, or specificity (diffuseness/specificity)
ascribed qualities, or excellence of performance (ascription/achieve-
    ment)
particularistic relationships, or categorical memberships
personalized, or universalistic standards
hostility, or affection, or indifference
dominance, or submission

There is evidence — which I find convincing — that a relatively few major value dimensions constitute the organizing principles for hundreds of specific beliefs and attitudes.[25] For example, Bales and Couch show that a very densely populated "value space" may be well represented in a certain kind of factor analysis by four orthogonal factors: (1) extent of acceptance of *authority;* (2) need-determined *expression* or value-determined restraint; (3) extent of acceptance of *equalitarianism;* (4) extent of acceptance of *individualism.*[26]

We know that values are learned. This means that they are developed through some experience — pain or pleasure, deprivation or gratification, goal-attainment or frustration or failure, social approval or disapproval, love or hate. Even very short-term experiences may appreciably influence evaluations and beliefs concerning both concrete objects and abstract concepts.[27] Repeated and pervasive experiences may be characteristic of large numbers of persons similarly situated in society; such experiences are described, discussed, and appraised. The communication of common appraisals may then build value standards widely accepted across many social and cultural boundaries.[28]

[25] Rokeach argues strongly for this conclusion in *Beliefs, Attitudes, and Values,* especially chaps. 1 and 7.

[26] Robert F. Bales and Arthur S. Couch, "The Value Profile: A Factor Analytic Study of Value Statements," *Sociological Inquiry,* vol. 39, no. 1 (Winter 1969), pp. 3–17.

[27] See the tantalizing experiments reported in Paul E. Breer and Edwin A. Locke, *Task Experience as a Source of Attitudes* (Homewood, Ill.: Dorsey, 1965).

[28] Alex Inkeles, "Industrial Man: The Relation of Status to Experience, Perception, and Value," *American Journal of Sociology,* vol. 66, no. 1 (July 1960), pp. 1–31. Cf. Herbert Hyman, "The Value-Systems of Different Classes: A Social Psychological Contribution to the Analysis of Stratification," in *Class, Status and*

APPLICATIONS: GENUINE PROBLEMS
AND PSEUDO-ISSUES

But it would be very remarkable indeed were values — which are *generalized* criteria of desirability — to prove to be highly predictive of concrete social behavior in all its precise responsiveness to the specificity of particular situations. If we could simply "deduce" such behavior by deontic logic from the a priori relevant values, it would follow that we would be dealing either with a world of "fanatics" and "psychotics" or else with a set of astonishingly simple and nonresistant situational realities. In a world of continually varying realistic exigencies and of multiple values, only a maniac or a saint will always act "consistently" in terms of a (1) simple, (2) prearranged, (3) hierarchy of (4) fixed desiderata.

In short, to pose various hypotheses which suppose that values under some conditions may influence behavior is not to make the absurd claim that all behavior merely expresses values and has no other determinants.[29] Any suggestion that Parsons' own view of the place of ideas and values in determining behavior (or, more narrowly, of social action) approaches such an emanationist position may simply be dismissed as grossly incorrect.

In fact, the Parsonian formulations have been used to develop important and challenging hypotheses concerning the interrelations among characteristics of values and value systems, of social systems, and of relationships of social systems to their environments. For instance, it has been proposed that at the level of institutionalized general value systems, social integration effected primarily through generalized values and norms requires both homogeneity of values and a unitary focus of decision-making. For example, there is this hypothesis:

> The more a social system relies on integration through the enforcement of system-wide values and norms, the more it is likely to be characterized by a greater homogeneity of values, and a more monolithic decision-making structure.[30]

Power, ed. Reinhard Bendix and Seymour Martin Lipset (New York: The Free Press, 1963); Melvin L. Kohn, *Class and Conformity: A Study of Values* (Homewood, Ill.: Dorsey, 1969); William Caudill and Harry A. Scarr, "Japanese Value-Orientations and Cultural Change," *Ethnology,* vol. 1, no. 1 (1962), pp. 53–91; Seymour Martin Lipset, *The First New Nation* (New York: Basic Books, 1963), esp. chaps. 6–8; Robin M. Williams, Jr., *American Society,* 3d ed. (New York: Knopf, 1970), chap. 11.

[29] Cf. the fuller statement in my "Individual and Group Values," *The Annals of the American Academy of Political and Social Science,* vol. 371.

[30] Terry N. Clark, "Stratification, Differentiation, and Integration," *Community Structure and Decision-Making: Comparative Analyses* (San Francisco: Chandler,

On the other hand, there are many indications that beyond some point of successively greater homogeneity of values, an inherent instability will develop in a social system. Study of the differentiating conditions for stable and unstable outcomes is just beginning but holds the possibility of very significant discoveries.

In much discussion and controversy concerning the part played by values in social structure and social change, the authentically important problems of analysis and explanation sometimes have been heavily obscured by an overlay of pseudo-issues and irrelevant political and epistemological assumptions. Let us attempt quickly to strip away two of these impediments. In the interest of brevity, we shall state these conclusions with minimum supporting evidence or argument:

Pseudo-issue 1: Are the concepts of values and value systems biased in favor of static, structural conceptions, as over against dynamic, processual emphases? The question may not actually be silly, but it hardly requires an extended answer. The answer is no, because nothing in the concepts favors one emphasis rather than the other.

Pseudo-issue 2: Does the study of values lead to an "over-socialized" conception of man [31] as a bloodless, over-intellectualized, rational actor? Answer: no; why should it? Values constitute one among many variables affecting conduct; their empirical importance is not predetermined by the act of studying them.

If basic moral-evaluative dimensions are caught up in the pattern-variables, as implicitly claimed by Parsons' description in *The Social System*, it should be possible to predict from known states of the pattern-variables to less known concrete social behavior. A hypothetical set of such predictions has been formulated by Works, and shown to be consistent with relevant data.[32] Thus it is predicted that the rank-order of tendencies on the part of whites to exclude black people from social relationships would be: highest in statuses or roles emphasizing particularism/qualities; lowest in those marked by universalism/performance; intermediate in the other two cases. Similarly, exclusion is predicted to be greatest when the orientations of diffuse-

---

1968), p. 40. The author adds: "The level of outputs is also likely to be higher than in a situation where there are greater differences in values between subsystems."

[31] Dennis H. Wrong, "The Over-Socialized Conception of Man in Modern Sociology," *American Sociological Review*, vol. 26, no. 2 (April 1961), pp. 183–193.

[32] Ernest Works, "The Pattern-Variables as a Framework for the Study of Negro-White Relations," *Pacific Sociological Review*, vol. 10, no. 1 (Spring 1967), pp. 25–32. We have omitted here a bibliography of some twenty studies that has operationalized one or more pattern variables.

ness/affectivity are dominant; least, when specificity/neutrality are expected and enjoined as appropriate for the white (black) actor who is taken as the point of reference.

The *anchoring effects* of value systems rarely can be seen by analyzing local cultures and social processes — for the local ecological, demographic, technological, and social-structural factors *already will have been "saturated" with numerous effects from prior social actions that have been partly determined by value components.* To detect these cumulative diffuse effects, comparative analyses are required. On the basis of a single society (or type of society) one may find that rules of kinship, marriage, and affinity seem rather clearly to derive from land tenure and property systems. Comparison of other societies may then show that similar effects can be correlated with equally stable and definite features of values as embodied in law and rules of morality.[33] Such affronts inflicted by data upon dogmatism are likely to occur whenever a respect for reality leads to careful investigation.

A recent study gives considerable support to the historical hypothesis that the antislavery movement's unity on behalf of black equality disintegrated in the 1870's, not merely because of the formal abolition of slavery, but because black equality was one among many values. Prior to 1860, other strongly held values of the antislavery proponents had not been in conflict with the preeminent position given to black equality; during the war and increasingly thereafter, other values came into opposition or contradiction. By 1877, many advocates of black equality were ready to acquiesce to the withdrawal of federal troops from the South — not merely "on grounds of expediency" but because *other* high-ranking values were at stake.[34]

The complexity of the value systems of a total society, to use a variation of a proverb, has to be explicated to be believed. The modes of variation that almost certainly are of great importance include at least the following:

1. *Centrality:* interconnections with other values: (a) within an individual; (b) across individuals
2. *Intensity:* rated strength of feeling; degree of affect aroused by violation or contravention

[33] As indicated, for example, in a comparison of north Ceylon and north Thailand; see Gehan Wijeyeswardene, "A Comparative Note on Ecology and Social Structure," *Man*, vol. 1, no. 1 (March 1966), pp. 95–101.

[34] See Sharon H. Carroll, "Elitism and Reform: Some Antislavery Opinion-Makers in the Era of Civil War and Reconstruction" (Ph.D. dissertation, Cornell University, 1969).

3. *Rigidity:* degree of resistance to efforts to change: (a) a particular value; (b) a set of values

4. *Explicitness:* frequency of statement; resistance to statement

5. *Pervasiveness:* frequency of manifestation across all collectivities and types of social activity

6. *Primitiveness:* degree to which values are taken for granted or are discussed, challenged, defended, and the like

7. *Stability:* persistence through time

8. *Agreement:* proportion of the population endorsing a value or set of values

9. *Consensus:* proportion of the population endorsing a value or set of values *and* aware of the endorsement of others

Surely, this list is not complete.

Particularly important among the structural characteristics of value systems that require penetrating empirical study are the clarity, stability, and firmness of both individual commitment and group consensus on the *rank-ordering of major values and of concrete behavioral choices oriented to those values.* It is certain that in at least some instances, two populations may have quite similar profiles or inventories of values but differ radically in relevant social behavior because of differences in consensus and commitment. For example, a study of American Indian teenagers has indicated that the dominant value orientations are similar among Arapaho, Shoshone, and white youths, and that structural obstacles to attaining success do not differ greatly between Arapaho and Shoshone. Yet Arapaho teenagers disproportionately manifest apathy, low aspirations, escapism, and self-other alienation. It appears that among the Arapaho there is *low agreement on ranking* of values, and lack of firm commitment to values based on the expectation of support and reward within peer groups.[35]

Value analysis in studies of social change can help to protect us from a mistaken readiness to attribute complex historical sequences to those simple and sovereign causes that always are so avidly seized upon by ideologues. Thus in the contemporary United States, the history of relationships of black and white people, which in the 1930's and 1940's was often so simply explained as "economic exploitation," is now even more simply explained as due to some ineffable amalgam called "white racism." Such vulgarizations are dangerous for social policy because detrimental to clear diagnosis and analysis. In contrast, a really sophisticated historical analysis clearly shows, for example,

---

[35] Stanton K. Tefft, "Anomy, Values and Culture Change among Teen-Age Indians: An Exploratory Study," *Sociology of Education,* vol. 40, no. 2 (Spring 1967), pp. 145–157.

that the American controversies over slavery remain inexplicable without reference to exceedingly complex and deep interrelations and incompatibilities of beliefs and values. As David Brion Davis says:

> Slavery, of course, was an economic institution closely tied to various social and political structures. . . . Yet the fact remains that it was a shift in value orientations that made possible the first organized protests against the institution . . . the very act of questioning brought deep conflicts to the surface and opened fissures in the prevailing ideologies . . . Abolitionism furnished a new basis for social organization and a new means for simplifying and socializing individual moral perceptions.[36]

As a final illustration of non-obvious implications of sociological analysis of values, we may note that opposition of interests and struggle among differently situated individuals and collectivities *within a continuing polity and societal system* actually can contribute to establishing and elaborating *generalized* values and symbols. For in such contentions, *each* party will appeal to values, presumably accepted by third parties, to legitimate its position and to attempt to recruit, support, or disarm potential opposition. If successive contests and conflicts then are successfully resolved *without repudiation of the values that legitimate the conflict-resolving process or mechanisms*, the more highly generalized values will come to be more and more regarded as axiomatic or unchallengeable. Although the specific social implications of the general value principle will be changed through successive occasions, all parties come to have a stake in maintaining the complex value referent as a resource for the future.[37]

THE EMPIRICAL SIGNIFICANCE OF VALUES: RESEARCH AND INTERPRETATION

Let us repeat for emphasis: values are not the same as behavior, nor even, as social conduct.[38] The importance of values in "predicting" or "explaining" behavior, therefore, has to be empirically ascertained, rather than decided a priori. The extent to which particular values

[36] David Brion Davis, "Some Recent Directions in American Cultural History," *American Historical Review*, vol. 73, no. 3 (February 1968), p. 706. For the relevant analysis in full, see *The Problem of Slavery in Western Culture* (Ithaca, N.Y.: Cornell University Press, 1966).

[37] For examples of the diversity of concrete meanings attached to the same generalized value (e.g., freedom, equality, democracy), see Frederick M. Wirt, "The Politics of Education," chap. 13 in *School Desegregation in the North: The Challenge and the Experience*, ed. T. B. Edwards and F. M. Wirt (San Francisco: Chandler, 1967), pp. 299–330.

[38] Cf. Ethel M. Albert, "Value Systems," p. 288. Contrast with Franz Adler, "The Value Concept in Sociology," *American Journal of Sociology*, vol. 62, no. 3 (November 1956), pp. 272–279.

will predict to particular kinds of conduct is affected by complex interactions among variables of at least the following kinds:

1. degree of psychological commitment of the actor to the value
2. knowledge or beliefs concerning consequences of action
3. context of interconnections with *other* values (number, rank in ordering of importance, compatibility, etc.)
4. consensus or dissensus among relevant social referents
5. social sanctions
6. time-perspective of the actor
7. attachment to a collectivity in which the value is shared
8. strength of non-value components of motivation

Many other relevant conditions undoubtedly enter into various kinds of behavior. The resulting complexity is evident, but does not preclude substantial progress in empirical research. At both the macro-level of total societies and the micro-level of individuals and small collectivities, existing studies offer a large amount of descriptive data, and a smaller but important set of causal or quasi-causal generalizations.

Leaving aside the more purely descriptive and methodological studies — which may be regarded as valuable preparatory mapping of the phenomena needing additional analysis — we find a fragmentary but highly suggestive accumulation of research findings. To state the case in minimal terms: there is now empirical evidence adequate to demonstrate that values are among the conditions associated with significant differences in the following kinds of attitudes or behavioral outcomes:

1. speed of recognition of words presented by a tachistoscope [39]
2. occupational-career choices [40] and occupations actually followed [41]
3. "cheating" on examinations [42]
4. political attitudes [43] and behavior [44]

[39] L. Postman, J. S. Bruner, and E. McGinnies, "Personal Values as Selective Factors in Perception," *Journal of Abnormal and Social Psychology*, vol. 43, no. 2 (April 1948), pp. 142–154.

[40] Rose K. Goldsen et al., *What College Students Think* (Princeton, N.J.: Van Nostrand, 1960), ch. 2; Morris Rosenberg, *Occupations and Values* (Glencoe, Ill.: The Free Press, 1957).

[41] E. K. Strong, *Vocational Interests 18 Years After College* (Minneapolis: University of Minnesota Press, 1955).

[42] Anne-Marie Dermine (Henshel), "The Relationship between Values and Behavior: An Experiment" (Ph.D. dissertation, Cornell University, 1969).

[43] M. Brewster Smith, "Personal Values as Determinants of a Political Attitude," *Journal of Psychology*, vol. 28, second half (October 1949), pp. 477–486; Rainer C. Baum, "Values and Democracy in Imperial Germany," *Sociological Inquiry*, vol. 38, no. 2 (Spring 1968), pp. 176–196; F. Wickert, "The Interrelationships of Some General and Specific Preferences," *Journal of Social Psychology*, vol. 11,

5. anti-Semitism [45]
6. juvenile delinquency [46]
7. choice of friends [47]
8. frequency of religious participation [48]

An inventory of hypotheses concerning values and empirical generalizations now available in the literature of the behavioral sciences
would be very lengthy, and a few instances will be enough to suggest
the range of interesting questions that already have received explicit
attention.

Values, our theoretical orientation would predict, should enter into
(affect) motivation in two main ways: first, by defining the *gratifications* that establish and reinforce motives; second, by defining the
sources of gratification. Conversely, a particular kind or type of motivation should affect behavior in different ways, depending upon the
presence and the particular content of relevant values.[49]

An analysis of the latter expectation is available for the case of the
relation between achievement motivation (n Achievement) and occupational preferences. In a study of 394 entering freshman males at five
two-year community centers of a state university, Lueptow found that
scores on the McClelland test of n Achievement were essentially unrelated to occupational preferences. Yet n Achievement is positively
related to a generalized goal of career accomplishment, whereas there
is (as expected) no relationship to "extrinsic" goals of status success,

second half (May 1940), pp. 275–302, and "A Test for Personal Goal-Values,"
ibid., pp. 259–274.

[44] Robert A. Levine, "The Internalization of Political Values in Stateless Societies," *Human Organization*, vol. 19, no. 2 (Summer 1960), pp. 51–58; Gabriel
A. Almond and Sidney Verba, *The Civic Culture* (Princeton, N.J.: Princeton University Press, 1963).

[45] R. I. Evans, "Personal Values as Factors in Anti-Semitism," *Journal of Abnormal and Social Psychology*, vol. 47, no. 4 (October 1952), pp. 749–756.

[46] Paul Lerman, "Individual Values, Peer Values, and Subcultural Delinquency,"
American Sociological Review, vol. 33, no. 2 (April 1968), pp. 219–235; John P.
Clark and Eugene P. Wenninger, "Goal Orientations and Illegal Behavior among
Juveniles," *Social Forces*, vol. 42, no. 1 (October 1963), pp. 49–59.

[47] R. P. Beech, "*Value Systems, Attitudes, and Interpersonal Attraction*" (Ph.D.
dissertation, Michigan State University, 1966); Robin M. Williams, Jr., "Friendship
and Social Values in a Suburban Community," *Pacific Sociological Review*, vol. 2,
no. 1 (Spring 1959), pp. 3–10.

[48] Milton Rokeach, "The Role of Values in Public Opinion Research," *The
Public Opinion Quarterly*, vol. 32 (Winter 1968–1969), pp. 555, 547–559.

[49] "It is not useful to speak of behavior as being determined by an internalized
rule like 'Be honest' or 'Don't cheat' if the rule does *not* predict the individual's
behavior and situational forces *do*." Lawrence Kohlberg, "Moral Development,"
International Encyclopedia of the Social Sciences (New York: Macmillan and Free
Press, 1968), vol. 10, p. 484.

security, or luxury. Therefore, "n Achievement appears to be related to 'career salience' but not to conscious intrinsic value-orientations." [50] In searching for mediating factors, the analysis shows that among the students having high college-qualification scores (suggesting of cognitive resources), high n Achievement is associated with preferences for occupations characterized primarily by satisfactions derived by task accomplishment rather than from extrinsic rewards. And, students with high achievement motivation tend to prefer occupations with primary intrinsic rewards only when their value orientations define the occupation as a locus for intrinsic satisfaction. When occupational roles are defined only by intrinsic gratifications, the tendency to choose intrinsic-satisfaction occupations is strong among high n Achievement students. Therefore, occupational choice appears to be affected by the motivational component only when a mediating value standard is present that identifies the occupation as an appropriate avenue for expressing and gratifying the need. The value orientation is essential, that is, in providing a basis for defining an appropriate goal-object.[51]

Although there are errors and inadequacies in some theories that have posited fixed development stages of value-orientations and moral judgments from early childhood to adulthood, evidence shows invariant sequences do exist. Piaget seems to have formulated cross-culturally valid principles in pointing to the tendencies in young children to judge acts as wrong if they are punished, to judge consequences without regard to intentions, and to make absolute and total judgments of right and wrong. On the other hand, there is not a universal age-graded trend from obedience-to-authority toward peer-oriented equalitarian moral judgments. However, convincing evidence exists that there is a culturally universal invariant sequence in moral (value) development; individuals or whole cultures may not move through all stages, but will follow the same order in whatever stages they do traverse, i.e.:[52]

I. *Pre-moral:*
   Stage 1.   Orientation to obedience and punishment
   Stage 2.   Naive instrumental hedonism
II. *Conventional conformity:*
   Stage 3.   Orientation to social approval; maintaining good relations with others; avoiding dislike

[50] Lloyd B. Lueptow, "Need for Achievement and Occupational Preferences: Some Operations with Value-Orientations as Intervening Variables in Need-Goal Relationships," *Sociometry*, vol. 31, no. 3 (September 1968), p. 307.
[51] Ibid., p. 311.
[52] Kohlberg, "Moral Development," p. 489.

Stage 4.   Authority-maintaining morality, e.g., conforming to avoid censure by legitimate authorities and consequent guilt

III. *Self-accepted principles:*

Stage 5.   Morality of contract, individual rights, democratically accepted law

Stage 6.   Individual principles of conscience

Concrete behavior rules may remain essentially unchanged throughout the individual's life-course even while the relation of the rules to the meta-order of values changes greatly. Such changes appear to follow a fixed sequence from (a) requirements based on power and external consequences, to (b) those based on exchange and gratifications, to (c) those based on maintaining legitimate expectations, to (d) those based on values, ideals or logical principles of social organization. Kohlberg maintains that the order is largely based upon necessary sequences of cognitive development:

> Concepts of legitimate expectations presuppose concepts of reciprocity and exchange, while general principles of social organization and justice presuppose concepts of legitimate expectations.[53]

But to know of values obviously is not the same as being committed to them. In the implementation of values, conversely, commitment alone does not automatically produce behavioral conformity. Only when norms or values are "activated" can they influence conduct, and activation requires some cognitive linkage between the normative component and other aspects of the behavior setting.[54]

Whenever social disapproval is expected to result from a value-conforming action, anticipated public disclosure of the action will reduce the rate of conforming responses.[55]

When behavior in accordance with a particular value is costly to the individual (by requiring sacrifices in other values or interests) and

[53] Ibid., p. 491.

[54] "A norm which is not activated is unlikely to have any significant impact on behavior *regardless of its content or of how strongly the person holds it.*" Shalom H. Schwartz, "Awareness of Consequences and the Influence of Moral Norms on Interpersonal Behavior," *Sociometry,* vol. 31, no. 4 (December 1968), p. 355. Schwartz presents data consistent with the interpretation that "awareness of consequences" activates norms — which then, and only then, influence action.

[55] Note the relevant evidence on "social constraint," showing that disclosing one's actions to others reduced "willingness to comply with the requested behavior": Lyle G. Warner and Melvin L. DeFleur, "Attitude as an Interactional Concept: Social Constraint and Social Distance as Intervening Variables Between Attitudes and Action," *American Sociological Review,* vol. 34, no. 2 (April 1969), p. 164.

especially when the individual cannot count on a compensatory future realization of the value, the sheer internalization of the value is not likely to be a sufficient condition for the requisite conforming behavior. As Firey has indicated in a study of conservation of natural resources, two other conditions appear to be necessary, namely, the institutionalization of sanctions and the linkage of conformity to the welfare of individuals and collectivities to which the social actor is strongly attached.[56]

The importance of this proposition for a theory of values has been somewhat neglected in much sociological and psychological literature — in which it appears to be assumed that values are not determinants of conduct unless they operate in an immediate, unmediated way directly through the motivation of the individual. The causal influence of values is much more complex than that, although we certainly must grant that under some conditions individuals do express their strongly internalized values, e.g., "follow the dictates of conscience," in the absence of either sanctions or social support. The more frequent pattern, however, is that specific norms that express the behavioral implications of a value become established and enforced through the actions of persons who reap advantages therefrom — or, at least, who do not incur excessive costs in so doing. Once the norms are effectively institutionalized, nearly everyone may conform because it is now "in his interest," even though few would have conformed without the super-added incentives of social sanctions and group attachments.

Both stability and change in values and value systems are affected by the *interaction* between the degree of consensus in the relevant social collectivity and the intrinsic characteristics of the values themselves. Thus, a hypothesis consistent with much evidence is that the more frequently a given value is opposed or challenged, the more elaborate (numerous, varied, and interrelated) will be the beliefs and symbols connected with the value.[57]

---

[56] "Conformity to values . . . requires an articulation of those values with social relationships in such a way that individuals find it socially expedient and psychologically satisfying to conform to them. Values which are not thus articulated with social relationships can have only an ideological status; they will not figure in overt behavior. Many future-referring values have just such an ideological status. In contemporary America, for instance, conservation values have something of this character." Walter Firey, "Conditions for the Realization of Values Remote in Time," in *Sociological Theory, Values, and Sociocultural Change: Essays in Honor of Pitirim A. Sorokin,* ed. Edward A. Tiryakian (New York: Free Press, 1963), p. 152.

[57] Cf. Rokeach, *Beliefs, Attitudes, and Values,* p. 21. Note the similarity to ideas developed by Karl Mannheim in *Ideology and Utopia* (New York: Harcourt, Brace, 1936).

Greatest change in a total matrix of values should be induced whenever two or more "central" and "terminal" values can be brought into relations of inconsistency or incongruity of some kind. Three main ways to bring such incongruity about are:

1. persons are induced to behave in a manner incompatible with their values;
2. persons are exposed to new information, including evaluations, from significant others that is inconsistent with one or more central values; and
3. persons are exposed to information about inconsistencies already present among their values.[58]

To test this last approach, Rokeach carried out the following experiment. Three groups (A, B, C) filled out questionnaires on equal rights for Negroes, equal rights for other groupings, and American policy in Viet Nam. A week later, all three groups ranked 12 terminal values. Two experimental groups (B and C) were given information designed to introduce dissonance concerning the rankings of *equality* and *freedom*.[59] Group A was a control group. Retests on values were administered to all groups at the end of three weeks and at the end of three months (see Table 1).

TABLE 1
Mean Changes in Rank-Order After Three Weeks

Group	Equality	Freedom
A	.79	−.47
B	1.47	.78
C	1.68	.70

In Group C, a division between those pro- and anti-civil rights demonstrations showed the results in Table 2.

Indications of the validity of the value indicators are (1) consistency of test results with other value-orientation measures, and (2) consistency of test results with known characteristics of samples of respondents. The relevant data appear in Table 3.[60]

The sheer correlation of values with beliefs, opinions, attitudes, and

[58] Rokeach, *Beliefs, Attitudes, and Values*, p. 167.

[59] Members of Group B were shown data interpreted to mean that the students "are more interested in their own freedom than they are in freedom for other people." Group C also was given this information, plus a discussion suggesting that those who are against civil rights care for their own freedom but not for that of others, whereas those favoring civil rights want freedom for themselves and other people as well. Rokeach, *Beliefs, Attitudes, and Values*, pp. 173–174.

[60] Data from ibid., pp. 169–170.

TABLE 2

	Equality	Freedom
Ranked *equality high*		
Pro-demonstrations	.36	.82
Anti-demonstrations	.00	.29
Ranked *equality low*		
Pro-demonstrations	3.16	.80
Anti-demonstrations	1.67	.49

TABLE 3

	Ranking (in set of 12) of Values of:	
	Equality	Freedom
Orientation to civil rights demonstrations		
Sympathetic and have participated	3	1
Sympathetic but have not participated	6	1
Unsympathetic	11	2
Special samples		
Policemen (50)	12	1
Unemployed whites (141)	9	3
Unemployed Negroes (28)	1	10
Calvinist College students (75)	9	9

other observed behavior shows only that there is a structure, a non-random patterning. To be able to infer causal sequences from values to other items we need some evidence that the value or value system was present prior to or simultaneously with the explicandum, that its presence is associated with a heightened frequency of the phenomena to be explained, and that there is a theoretically compelling connection. Varying degrees of "strong inference" are to be expected, of course. From analyzing much data, Melvin Kohn has developed a consistent and plausible pattern to support the belief that child-rearing practices derive in part from parental values, and that these parental values are substantially a joint result of social class and of class-linked characteristics of particular types of occupations.[61]

In a comprehensive analysis of data from a national survey, Kohn has found that "social class" is the most important variable accounting for differences in value patterns. Among the components of "class," education is the most important, followed by occupation; income adds little to the predictions of values from education and occupation. The relationships to values of these variables are continuous, linear, and additive. The study finds no evidence to support the supposition that

[61] Melvin L. Kohn, *Class and Conformity: A Study of Values.*

FIGURE 1

Hypothetical data

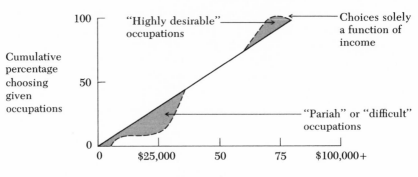

Expected income

disparities or "incongruities" between education, occupational level, and income have any important effect upon values and belief orientations.[62]

The relations between occupations and values have been explored in several other significant ways.

There are consistent and marked differences between educational and occupational levels of the American population in the criteria of desirability invoked in judging the "ideal" and "worst" features of occupations. Emphasized by persons of lower education and occupational position were: security, fringe benefits, physical conditions, and nature of supervision. Mentioned more frequently at the higher levels were: self-expression and development, creativity, active personal relationships, worthwhileness of the work, challenge, and opportunity for personal achievement.[63]

If nonmonetary values play no part at all in selecting an occupation, the proportion of persons freely choosing an occupation would, of course, be a direct linear function of anticipated earnings. However, if nonmonetary elements do enter into selections, the trade-off curve between income and other criteria of occupation desirability is not likely to be linear (see figure). Specifically, most individuals would likely reject some occupations even were the income extremely high (e.g., executioner, prostitute), because of social stigma, danger, disagreeableness, or moral repulsion. At the other extreme, some occupa-

[62] Ibid., chap. 8.

[63] The generalizations derive from a national sampling survey of more than 5,000 people: Franklin P. Kilpatrick, Milton C. Cummings, Jr., M. Kent Jennings, *Source Book of a Study of Occupational Values and the Image of the Federal Service* (Washington, D.C.: The Brookings Institution, 1964), pp. 82–83.

tions may be so desirable in prestige, freedom, pleasure, opportunity for creativity, and other non-monetary rewards that they frequently will be chosen even if low-paying. Over a wide intermediate zone, the nonincome rewards may be "psychologically equivalent," i.e., choice will be essentially responsive to expected income.[64]

A comparison of academicians and nonacademicians by major fields of specialization showed that even though persons in academic employment were *more* highly trained and worked as many hours as their nonacademic counterparts, they generally earned less. Persons who have foregone the higher incomes in business and industry to stay in academia emphasize "professional" values in their work; others emphasize "acquisitive" values; furthermore, there is a positive correlation between education level and professional values of originality, independence, freedom. Analysis of specific types of work activities shows that those of high academic emphasis are associated with low income. It is concluded that "nonmonetary values" do actually constitute a trade-off with money income for the choice between academic and nonacademic employment.[65]

Hardly more than a beginning has been made as yet in the systematic empirical study of the causes and consequences of differing kinds and degrees of *value consensus* in carefully specified settings.[66]

[64] *Within* certain just-noticeable differences in income, decisions presumably will be made on non-monetary grounds. See Daniel N. Braunstein and George H. Haines, "Preference Scaling of Careers and Organization," *Journal of Applied Psychology*, vol. 52, no. 5 (1968), p. 381.

[65] John F. Marsh, Jr., and Frank P. Stafford, "The Effect of Values on Pecuniary Behavior,". *American Sociological Review*, vol. 32, no. 5 (October 1967), pp. 740–754. Their main finding (p. 740) is that "employed professional and technical workers forego monetary returns relative to their non-academic, private industry, government and self-employed counterparts."

[66] For a sense of the various approaches and methods used in the relevant research one might review the following: Florence R. Kluckhohn and Fred R. Strotdbeck, *Variations in Value Orientations* (Evanston, Ill.: Row and Peterson, 1961); Herbert Hyman, "The Value-Systems of Different Classes: A Social Psychological Contribution to the Analysis of Stratification," in *Class, Status and Power*, pp. 426–441; M. B. Smith, "Personal Values in the Study of Lives," in *The Study of Lives: Essays on Personality in Honor of Henry A. Murray*, ed. Robert W. White (New York: Atherton, 1963); Paul Hollander, "Models of Behavior in Stalinist Literature; A Case Study of Totalitarian Values and Controls," *American Sociological Review*, vol. 31, no. 3 (June 1966), pp. 352–365; W. F. Dukes, "Psychological Study of Values," *Psychological Bulletin*, vol. 52, no. 1 (January 1955), pp. 24–50; William Caudill and Harry A. Starr, "Japanese Value-Orientations and Cultural Change," pp. 53–91; Roy E. Carter, Jr., "An Experiment in Value Measurement," *American Sociological Review*, vol. 21, no. 2 (April 1956), pp. 156–163; T. S. Langer, "A Test of Intergroup Prejudice Which Takes Account of Individual and Group Differences in Values," *Journal of Abnormal and Social Psychology*, vol. 48, no. 4 (October 1953), pp. 548–554; Charles W.

Yet the information already derived from the limited research available illuminates many "classical" problems and raises important new questions. The following illustrates significant findings and hypotheses:

> Among American college students (a sample of 5,422 persons at 99 colleges and universities), the likelihood that an individual will violate a norm of behavior: (a) is lower in a context of group disapproval, independent of the person's own approval or disapproval; (b) the seeming effect is greatest for individuals who do not disapprove and least for those who disapprove strongly; (c) the putative contextual effect does not appear, on the average, until the proportion strongly disapproving reaches a level between 40 and 60 per cent; (d) the "group deterrent" seems to have a main effect upon persons who themselves disapprove of the deviant behavior at the level of 20–39 per cent strongly disapproving, but the most pronounced drop in nonconformity among individuals who do *not* personally disapprove does not appear until as many as 80 per cent of their fellows strongly disapprove.[67]

Thus, the individual behavioral correlates of consensus seem to depend upon both the intensity of the individual's own rejection of disapproved conduct and the extent of consensus in the local social environment.

It is reasonable to accept the three major assumptions concerning beliefs (and, in our terms, values) suggested by Rokeach: (1) different values have differing degrees of importance to any given individual; (2) resistance to change is greatest for beliefs and values that are most important ("central"); (3) if a particular value or belief is changed, the more central it is, the more numerous will be changes in other beliefs and values.[68] Our general assumption for present purposes is that *differences* or *similarities* in the more important values and beliefs will have greatest effects upon relationships between individuals or collectivities of different ethnic categories.

Thus, it becomes necessary to specify not only what is meant by "similarity and difference," but also "importance" or "centrality."

Rokeach defines "importance" of a given belief solely as connectedness or functional communication with other beliefs: the more "con-

---

Morris, *Varieties of Human Values*, (Chicago: University of Chicago Press, 1956); L. V. Jones and Charles W. Morris, "Relations of Temperament to the Choice of Values," *Journal of Abnormal and Social Psychology*, vol. 53, no. 3 (November 1956), pp. 345–349; David Horton Smith and Alex Inkeles, "The OM Scale: A Comparative Socio-Psychological Measure of Individual Modernity," *Sociometry*, vol. 29, no. 4 (December 1966), pp. 353–377.

[67] William J. Bowers, "Normative Constraints on Deviant Behavior in the College Context," *Sociometry*, vol. 31, no. 4 (December 1968), pp. 370–385.

[68] Rokeach, *Beliefs, Attitudes, and Values*, p. 3.

nections" with other items, the more important. It is then proposed that connectedness will be greater for those beliefs (values) which:

1. concern one's own existence and identity, rather than those who are less directly relevant to this matter;
2. are shared with other persons, rather than not shared;
3. have been learned by some kind of "direct encounter with the object of belief," rather than being derived from other persons;
4. are not considered to refer to arbitrary "matters of taste." [69]

Notice particularly that these criteria do not refer to *intensity* of conviction. For example, people may feel intensely about some "matter of taste" — but if their orientation changes, few other beliefs are affected. In such an instance, the belief would be rated as relatively unimportant, no matter how strong the affective component; likewise, beliefs of the same intensity may vary greatly in connectedness. Beliefs (values) may be classified from highest connectedness to lowest, as follows:

1. primitive beliefs, with complete consensus: completely unchallenged assumptions
2. primitive beliefs, with zero consensus: unchallenged idiosyncratic convictions
3. authority beliefs: what persons and groups are to be believed and trusted, or to be followed as models and guides
4. derived beliefs: beliefs which are accepted because of the authority from which they are considered to originate
5. inconsequential beliefs: those derived from direct experience, but not closely connected with other beliefs

This classification does not seem to allow for the existence of nonprimitive beliefs and values that involve (1) some direct experience, (2) substantial but not complete consensus, and (3) many connections — e.g., empirical knowledge, scientific knowledge of human biology, psychology, sociology, and the like. Nevertheless, the ordering proposed is plausibly based and potentially very useful; it deserves careful empirical study.

Thus, as applied to intergroup relations, the classification implies that differences in beliefs and values between members of two social categories or collectivities are most likely to have important effects when they concern "primitive beliefs" or "authority beliefs." It is not immediately obvious, however, whether one should expect greatest effects from differences in primitive beliefs or in authority beliefs. That primitive beliefs are assumed to have greatest connectedness suggests greatest effects in this case. But disagreement at that level may be dismissed as incomprehensible and not open to discussion, whereas differences as to acceptable authorities are eminently arguable and

[69] Ibid., p. 5.

therefore hold the possibility of great threat to a whole system of beliefs and values. This reasoning then further suggests that derived beliefs, being easily invoked in communication and likely to be open to disagreement, may in some case be even more likely to elicit conflict. Tendencies in this direction would be accentuated if each of the communicating parties, knowing the derived character of the other's position, regards the other as possibly open to persuasion. Thus, Protestants and Catholics might not discuss such a primitive belief as "death is inevitable," or the authority belief that the Pope is infallible in statements on faith and morals (tacitly "agreeing to disagree"), but still enter into highly consequential controversy on questions of derived beliefs about birth control or censorship.

Using the criterion of interconnectedness to test the centrality or importance of a belief to an individual, we might order values from more important to less important *in a social system* according to the number of interconnections with other values.[70] In the case of centrality in a social system, however, the connectedness must be manifested in communication among units of the system and not simply within the personalities of individuals.

A great variety of empirical indicators of connectedness no doubt could be developed, and in advance of systematic evidence it would not be possible to guess which might be most adequate for particular research purposes. A very simple and obvious approach would be to secure ratings and ranking of interconnections from samples of individuals located within the major statuses, social categories, and collectivities of the system. Averages of such estimates for each value in each sample could then be compared, and summary scores computed. An indirect method of arriving at actual *communicative* connections among values would be to chart flows of interaction among major statuses, social categories, and collectivities, having derived independent measures of the values held in each. Various indexes could be devised from these data, for example: (a) among adult males, the proportion of whites committed to the value "equality" who are communicating with blacks holding the same or a different value; or, (b) an index of dissimilarity among collectivities derived from the proportion who would have to change value positions to equate the value distributions.

RESEARCH POSSIBILITIES:
VALUE STABILITY AND CHANGE

The generic ingredients for successful research on stability and change in values and on the sources and consequences of value differences — within and between social systems — presumably are the same as those

70 Ibid., pp. 4–13.

needed for advances in explaining any other aspect of human social behavior. The requisites include: conceptualization of units and variables, and relationships among them; hypotheses; research techniques and methods; study designs; and substantial accumulation of knowledge in the special field of inquiry.

For the study of values we have an exceedingly rich conceptual apparatus, much refined and clarified in recent years in terms close to the requirements of research operations. Many dimensions of value phenomena have been identified and related to other determinants of social behavior. A large array of research instruments has been developed to index values, e.g., the Allport-Vernon Values Test,[71] the tests devised by Woodruff and Divesta,[72] scales and other indicators developed in studies previously cited in this chapter, including Goldsen et al., Wickert, Lerman, Clark and Wenninger, Rokeach, F. Kluckhohn and Strodtbeck,[73] Caudill and Scarr, Dermine, Inkeles, Kohn, Almond and Verba, Bales and Couch, and others.

The development of reliable and valid techniques for indexing values is of the highest importance because the availability of research techniques strongly influences the development of basic substantive theory.

A brief and easily answered Value Survey has been developed by Rokeach that lists 18 terminal values ("preferred end-states of existence") and 18 instrumental values ("preferred modes of behavior"); respondents rank the items in each list by importance as guiding principles for daily life. Utilized in a national area-probability sample of adults, the survey showed substantial differences among adherents of Catholic, Protestant, and Jewish faiths and non-believers; likewise, major differences in values were associated with both perceived importance of religion and with frequency of church attendance.[74] This research instrument permits investigation of change and stability in the rank-ordering of values. For example, it is intuitively appealing to suppose that the likelihood of change is lowest for values ranked at the top or the bottom of an individual value hierarchy. This supposition has been supported by test-retest comparisons with the Value

[71] Gordon W. Allport, P. E. Vernon, and Gardner Lindzey, A Study of Values (Boston: Houghton Mifflin, 1960).

[72] A. D. Woodruff and F. J. Divesta, "The Relationship between Values, Concepts, and Attitudes," Educational and Psychological Measurement, vol. 8 (1948), pp. 645–649.

[73] See also: Fred L. Strodtbeck: "Family Integration, Values, and Achievement," in Education, Economy, and Society, ed. A. H. Halsey et al. (New York: The Free Press, 1964), pp. 315–347.

[74] Milton Rokeach, "Value Systems and Religion," Part I of the H. Paul Douglass Annual Lecture to the Religious Research Association, June 19, 1969 (to be published in Review of Religious Research), pp. 1–21 and tables.

Survey: [75] the relationship between change and rank-ordering is clearly U-shaped.

The initial learnings of values, as the main lines of Parsons' analyses show, are mediated through early diffuse *identifications* with particular persons: the "incorporation" or "inculcation" first takes place in strongly affective experiences, in a context and through relationships that are perceptually and cognitively quite complex. Presumably the reinforcements of value models are intermittent and often constituted by conditional rewards of approval and affection. We would expect those value patterns that are established first in the developmental processes to be *virtues,* rather than either *rules* or *abstract criteria* or principles of judgment; they are based upon emulation of models or upon idiosyncratic generalizations made by the individual under the partial direction of those two influences.

Rokeach has posited and has developed data consistent with the following order of resistance to change, from most to least, in "beliefs": [76]

1. primitive consensual beliefs;
2. primitive non-consensual beliefs;
3. "authority beliefs";
4. "derived beliefs"; and
5. "inconsequential beliefs."

For present purposes, we may read "value" for "belief," reserving the possibility that beliefs which are *both* existential and evaluative will be more resistant to change than beliefs which are primarily existential.[77] (Beliefs about the existence of the cosmos and of the self have special features that cannot be discussed at this point.)

Clearly predictions of any changes resulting from incompatibilities, dissonance, or incongruities will depend upon some estimate of the *relative* weights of *relevant* differences in (a) cognitive beliefs, (b) values, (c) positive or negative cathexis of persons, (d) positive or negative evaluation of reference individuals or groups, (e) instrumental interests. Thus a very strong value congruity might determine friendship even when many cognitive beliefs are dissonant, or a strong cathexis may override sharp differences in instrumental interests. Furthermore, predictions depend also upon whether differences and similarities operate as all-or-none factors, or in additive, multiplicative, or some other manner. For example, the degree of liking be-

[75] C. C. Hollen, *The Stability of Values and Value Systems* (M.A. thesis, Michigan State University, 1966). Cited by Milton Rokeach, "The Measurement of Values and Value Systems," pre-publication paper, 1969, p. 11.

[76] Rokeach, *Beliefs, Attitudes, and Values,* pp. 40–53.

[77] Gratton Kemp, "Changes in Values in Relation to Open-Closed Systems," in *The Open and Closed Mind,* ed. Milton Rokeach (New York: Basic Books, 1960), pp. 335–346.

tween two individuals might vary as a function of additive (net) similarity of values — or, on the contrary, it might follow an all-or-none or "step-function" principle such that a slight positive or negative balance induces either strong liking or strong disliking.

The information now available to us suggests that the values most resistant to change have the following properties: (1) they involve psychologically primitive beliefs for a high proportion of social actors, and (2) they are highly interconnected with other values for a high proportion of the individuals who endorse them; in the social system, they are (3) high in centrality, (4) pervasive, and supported by (5) strong sanctions and (6) high consensus; (7) supporters of the values hold positions of high prestige and authority; in the cultural system, the most resistant values are (8) congruent with many other values and beliefs, and (9) are symbolized in many different ways. Values having these characteristics will be strongly sanctioned and actively defended and promoted.[78]

It has been suggested that three procedures characterize the advocacy of values.[79] A person seeking to induce another to accept a new value (which may make it essential to renounce an old one) or to modify a value position may attempt:

1. to define a problematic situation, event, object, or relationship as being within some category to which the value advocated already attaches, e.g., a "crime" is redefined as "illness" or as a "cry for help," thus invoking values of humanitarianism, compassion, social effectiveness, and the like
2. to increase the salience, preference-rank, affective intensity, or other aspect of the importance of the new value or the new application of an already established value
3. to create a new value, to elaborate it, and to establish it in a set of relationships to other values, beliefs, and knowledge

Clearly the question of sources of stability and change in values as components of actual social relationships requires answers that go beyond the properties of values as components of individual personalities. Conditions in the personality system of the individual affecting receptivity to change operate in *interaction* with factors in the social system that facilitate or retard change.[80] In the simplest case, the de-

[78] Additional characteristics will undoubtedly be developed eventually.

[79] Vickers, *Value Systems and Social Process*, pp. 121–125.

[80] For example: "Statistical analyses show a highly significant interaction between receptivity in the personality system and receptivity in the social system. In the social system having a low value for innovativeness, the correlation between scores on the Dogmatism Scale and adoption rate is —.40; in the social system having a high value for innovativeness, the correlation is —.09." Rokeach, *Beliefs, Attitudes, and Values*, pp. 145–146.

gree of receptivity to change is an additive, linear function of an individual's favorability to a given change and the average receptivity of other persons in his immediate social milieu; in other instances, accelerating or diminishing rates may give curves of various shapes.

Values that at the same time are isolated or compartmentalized within the individual's psychological system and are held by persons scattered more or less randomly across the units of a social system should be most accessible to change through mass communication. Induced changes in such values, however, would be expected to have minimal structural consequences in the social system.

Prediction of short-run social changes from knowledge of values will require more accurate mapping than now exists of patterns of values and beliefs on to specific statuses and collectivities.[81] Only then is there a realistic possibility of estimating points of tension and the magnitude of consensual and dissenting collectivities.[82]

A differentiated society necessarily has a complex set of specifications of its main values; [83] furthermore, rapid social change continually brings unpredicted effects. Complex specificity together with unanticipated changes necessarily generate numerous new problematic relations between the generalized value system and the "operating" values and norms applicable to specific practical situations. The tendencies then arise, on the one hand, toward alienated criticism of alleged hypocrisy and cynicism, and, on the other, of absolutistic or fundamentalistic reassertion of the generalized values and of their *identification* with the concrete values to which the advocates are committed. If these tendencies are empirically important, as they seem to be, the stability of complex societies may depend strongly

[81] Cf. Marie Augusta Neal, *Values and Interests in Social Change* (Englewood Cliffs, N.J.: Prentice-Hall, 1965).

[82] Specific examples of such mapping of values on social formations include: Herbert Hyman, "The Value Systems of Different Classes: A Social Psychological Contribution to the Analysis of Stratification," in Reinhard Bendix and Seymour Martin Lipset (eds.), *Class, Status and Power* (Glencoe, Ill.: The Free Press, 1953); William H. Sewell, Archie O. Haller, and Murray A. Straus, "Social Status and Educational and Occupational Aspiration," *American Sociological Review*, vol. 22, no. 1 (February 1957), pp. 67–73; Bernard C. Rosen, "Race, Ethnicity, and the Achievement Syndrome," *American Sociological Review*, vol. 24, no. 1 (February 1959), pp. 47–60; Richard E. DuWors, "Persistence and Change in Local Values of Two New England Communities," *Rural Sociology*, vol. 17, no. 3 (September 1952), pp. 207–217; Hyman Rodman, "The Lower-Class Value Stretch," *Social Forces*, vol. 42, no. 2 (December 1963), pp. 205–215.

[83] Parsons has consistently held that "it is essential to think in terms of value-*systems*: complex action systems cannot be 'governed' by a single undifferentiated value, nor by discrete, unrelated, particular values. . . ." "On the Concept of Value-Commitments," p. 147.

upon (a) continuous and rapid respecification of generalized values, (b) ability to create frequently new generalized values, and (c) insulation of absolutistic reactions in non-political modes.

A whole set of crucial empirical problems, which urgently need concentrated research attention, center upon the effects of high levels of value generalization in structurally complex social systems. High levels of structural differentiation, if successfully stabilized, produce *generalized and explicit* values. The more pronounced the process of generalization, the greater will be the number of different types of specific value content and of levels of concreteness or generality that must be legitimized by reference to the master generalized values. But the larger the number and the more diverse the connections between concrete, particular values and generalized standards, the more points there are at which value absolutism may challenge the legitimacy of existing implementation or expression of the generalized values. In one direction, "fundamentalistic revolts" emerge that define existing social arrangements as "hypocritical" or "decadent" and call for a return to absolute and concrete commitments. In another direction, the legitimacy of the prevailing value-system as a whole is challenged in the name of a revolutionary change. The third possibility is the integrative process of institutionalizing new generalized values that resolve the primary oppositions and conflicts. The crucial empirical problems are to specify the combinations of conditions that determine the relative importance [84] of the three main outcomes, i.e., fundamentalistic regression, schismatic revolutionary outcomes, or institutionalization of new integrative value generalizations.[85]

Social stratification systems, insofar as they are systems of *ranking* rather than merely factual orders of distribution of scarce values, involve consensus on value; and changes in such consensus will lead to changes in the structure of the system.[86] Only if we were confronted with a distributive order based on sheer power and power

[84] It is not known how the importance of values and beliefs to individuals as indicated by (1) their *long-term rankings*, expressed in many situations, will relate to (2) "importance" (causal weight) in a particular situation in which *salience and immediate urgency* are evoked for values "normally" low in ranking.

[85] Parsons, "On the Concept of Value-Commitments," p. 159.

[86] "The concept of stratification presupposes, explicitly or implicitly, a wide consensus on the criteria and expressions of rank in a society, among people who comprise a rank continuum. . . . It also implies a wide consensus on values, attitudes, motives and goals." Gerald D. Berreman, "Stratification, Pluralism and Interaction: A Comparative Analysis of Caste," in *Caste and Race: Comparative Approaches*, ed. Anthony de Reuck and Julie Knight (London: Churchill, 1968), p. 52.

alone would we reach the limiting case in which value consensus approaches zero. Although there are plural societies held together primarily by imposed power and economic interdependence, the accompaniment always is discontinuity in ranking. In highly developed caste systems, each ranked grouping has a distinctive subculture within some overarching commonality of beliefs and values. Any *sectioning* of a society by limits upon social interaction results, in the long run, in the growth of cultural differences. When the closure of interaction runs along lines of social stratification, the growth of such cultural divergence always contains potentialities for social change.

If there are marked divergencies and incompatibilities of values and beliefs concerning criteria of distribution and ranking, as among the main strata of an inequalitarian system, any marked change in economic position or political power among the strata or ranked groupings will produce conflict and widespread challenges to the authority of the upper strata.[87]

No firm, empirically based theory appears to be available as yet that would permit us to predict *in general* that values change "more slowly than" norms or social structures. However, most analysts of social values seem to agree that the values which *legitimate and provide generalized direction* for *particular* institutions generally change only after the structure or the functioning of the institutions has changed. Although this proposition is highly general (and not tested by systematic attempts to falsify it in a series of concrete instances), it certainly can be illustrated in enough cases to indicate that the sequence does frequently occur.[88]

It is likely that a very frequent form of important long-term change in value patterns is the case in which conviction and commitment gradually are withdrawn from an institutionalized complex of specific beliefs, values, and symbols (incorporated in an unified set of practices and social relationships). Eventually, in such instances, individuals no longer engage in the practices and social relationships, and no longer assent to the explicit beliefs and values. Nevertheless,

[87] Ibid., p. 54.

[88] Note this comment on late twentieth-century trends in the United States: "Finally, there is the growing disjunction between the 'culture' and the 'social structure' . . . the culture becomes more hedonistic, permissive, expressive, distrustful of authority and of the purposive, delayed-gratification of a bourgeois achievement-oriented technological world. This tension between the 'technocratic' and the 'apocalyptic' modes, particularly among the intellectuals, may be one of the great ruptures in moral temper, especially in the universities." Daniel Bell, "The Year 2000 — The Trajectory of an Idea," *Daedalus* (Summer 1967), p. 645.

even individuals who have thus withdrawn from the specific content will, if originally socialized in the institutional complex, retain a set of implicit and unacknowledged beliefs and values consonant with its major "premises." For example, individuals who were socialized in family and religious groups to render thanks to benevolent deities may be expected to retain, often after they have rejected the tradition, a value-belief system in which the universe is believed to be orderly and is evaluated as "good"; such persons may continue to react to success, achievement, and enjoyment as "gifts" and to express "gratitude" for good things and for the avoidance of disaster. In short, they still "thank God" long after specific myths and symbols of traditional religion have been avowedly discarded.

Because moral values — by definition — stand near the top of the hierarchy of "cybernetic" cultural controls and because their "control" operates only through internalization and the commitment of the individual personality, innovations of moral values as such or major changes in their social applications have quite special characteristics. For one thing, change at this level will involve especially strong psychological tensions and ambivalence. Advocates of change are likely to retain some attachments to the older values they are striving to displace; in reaction, they are likely to exaggerate the "absoluteness" of the change. In the same way, defenders of the threatened values are likely to emphasize the threat as total. These psychological processes are stimulated and then accentuated by social processes of polarization. Were only these components operative, moral value innovation always would result either in severe social conflict,[89] or in quick extinction of the incipient change. The severe conflict would ensue when there is substantial, even if latent, continuity between the new and the old value positions, and when both are held by many strongly committed and socially powerful members of the society. Quick extinction, on the other hand, would result if there were essentially *no* continuity between new and old values, so that the innovators initially *must* constitute a very small and highly aberrant, repulsive, and dangerous element of the collectivity.[90]

When controlled and moderated within an integrated pluralistic system of other values, the theme of instrumental activism may serve, as it were, many expressive and socially integrative values. At

---

[89] As Albert Camus has said, "pure and unadulterated virtue is homicidal." *The Rebel: An Essay on Man in Revolt* (New York: Vintage, 1958), p. 297.

[90] "If the first flashes of a charismatic movement immediately polarized the attitudes of individuals at the commitment level, the result would almost certainly be quick suppression of the movement." Parsons, "On the Concept of Value-Commitments," p. 157.

an extreme, however, "instrumental activism" becomes an intense central preoccupation, largely divorced from control by other values, and changes qualitatively into a *different* world view. As an overriding ultimate, a transformation occurs: the theme becomes one of *acquisition* and *omnipotence*. In terms of acquisition, it becomes a final goal to have all we want, whatever we want, whenever we want. And:

> Existentially, we may describe it as never accepting the fact that we must die and that we have only what we have, right here and right now. It is not only that we want, we want supremely and absolutely. There is always something out there to reach for with the promise that this time it will be what we really wanted. . . . We believe it and make ourselves miserable in the impossible quest for fulfillment.[91]

A shift among intellectuals in their evaluation of values in our society seems particularly marked in the area of work and achievement. Increasingly common is the acceptance of the rather sweeping diagnosis of "alienation," alleged to derive from loss of control and initiative by workers over their work and conditions of life. It is frequently held that in an economy of extreme interdependence, large organizations, specialization, and automation, an ethic of cooperation rather than competitive striving must be developed.[92]

Social movements that stress value absolutism counter to some aspects of the established system tend to generate processes of social de-differentiation. Given a commitment to a highly rigid set of values, the range of social statuses and activities that are clearly legitimate tends to narrow; at the same time, the value absolutism eventually favors centralized leadership and control. The commitment to the value innovation tends to displace or reduce other value commitments and to preempt a large proportion of resources (time, energy, money, skills, "social credit") of the members or adherents. If the struggle is very intense, the members may repudiate family obligations and normal work, and may reject orderly procedures, rational processes, search for empirical knowledge, long-term prudence, and so on. A single-valued "ethic of sentiment" tends to take precedence over a multi-valued "ethic of consequences." [93]

---

[91] Philip Brogadir in "Discussions," *Proceedings,* Second Annual New Congress for Mental Health, *New York State Journal of Medicine,* vol. 67, no. 14 (July 15, 1967), p. 1996.

[92] Cf. Aaron Levenstein, "Technological Change, Work, and Human Values," *Social Science,* vol. 42, no. 2 (April 1967), pp. 67–79.

[93] Parsons, "On the Concept of Value-Commitments," p. 157.

SOME POSSIBILITIES AND PROSPECTS:
IMPLICATIONS FOR SOCIAL
SCIENCE AND SOCIETY

It is a clear implication of functional theory of social systems that the more highly differentiated societies necessarily will have the most advanced separation of cultural from social systems, and of the specific norms from the more generalized sets of values. Both these developments themselves directly imply enhanced variety and lability in particular social structures — hence, greater flexibility and change, especially in adaptive and goal-attainment activities. Particularly in such societies, the character and extent of value-consensus is highly problematic. In terms of the stability of authority and of stratification, it may turn out that the most crucial kind of consensus is not awareness of agreement on values but a consensus of knowledge and belief, e.g., what power exists, how it is exercised, who controls what, what the authority-holders are doing and why, how they will react to challenges, and the like.[94] In the broadest sense, this is a cognitive-conceptual consensus, and it need not involve high agreement of evaluations.

In very complex societies that are also undergoing incessant and rapid changes, persons with very simple value commitments are highly vulnerable to loss of integrity. They are likely to see the choices in such undifferentiated terms that the *generalized* commitment tends to be experienced as a choice between *cynicism and amoral opportunism* or *fanaticism* — or, as often happens, frequent oscillation or compartmentalization.

Any value orientation accepted as one among many values in a culture will if pressed to extreme limits, disregarding other values, produce unexpected and undesired implications and consequences.

Example 1

Who does not want freedom?

Who does not believe in some aspects of equality of human rights?

But, what happens if we demand instant and total freedom or instant and total equality? Total freedom is chaos, and the end result always is a dictatorial order. Total substantive equality requires a tight system of social control.

Example 2

Strongly oriented as it is to social mobility, activity, individual achievement, and the future, American society could not fail to place

94 See Berreman, "Stratification, Pluralism and Interaction," p. 55.

a high value on youth as a life stage and upon young people as "the hope of the future." A society that has so greatly emphasized progress and has developed a cultlike stress upon being up-to-date provides a setting especially favorable to efforts by young people to intimidate their elders by defining the beliefs, values, goals, and norms of the latter as anachronisms, grotesque survivals of an outmoded past.

Within recurring situations in societies of a particular kind — e.g., agricultural-feudal versus urban-industrial-democratic — particular value orientations, repeatedly experienced and reformulated by many persons over extended periods, eventually will become intellectualized as components of a comprehensive world view. Linked with numerous other existential and evaluative conceptions, a given subset of value orientations may so monopolize attention and legitimacy as to constitute the very *context* (or framework) *within which* more particular ideologies and major societal and political issues are defined, discussed, and fought over. A crucial contemporary case seems to be the axiomatic quality of the value orientations of "equality" and "freedom" — in contrast to classical conceptions of order and hierarchy.

Most "ancient" and "medieval" political orders developed from a long background of violence and misery; were maintained with violence, although internal misery may have been alleviated for considerable periods; and disintegrated with great violence and misery. In preindustrial societies, most men perforce saw the world as one of limited resources, unavoidable scarcity, inevitable hardship. For many men for most of recorded history, even minimal safety of life and limb depended upon authoritative protection by the strong, and even minimal subsistence depended upon an enforced order. From countless experiences with scarcity, violence, and acute social dependence, such hierarchic evaluative world views evolved as the medieval Christian doctrines or the developed Hindu views of caste.

What appears to be distinctive about the modern outlook is the spread over a great deal of both the Eastern and Western world of a completely antithetic value-belief system that: (1) *rejects the postulate of scarcity;* (2) *devalues the idea of social order,* both in the sense of discounting the empirical difficulty of maintaining or rebuilding the institutions of order, and in the sense of depreciating the *desirability* of order; (3) *posits the unconditional desirability of freedom;* and (4) *posits the unconditional desirability of equality,* in contrast to hierarchy. No more explosive combination perhaps has thus far confronted political man in complex large-scale societies.

The flavor of this outlook has been vividly caught in Irving Kristol's description:

It is a distinguishing characteristic of the modern age that "equality" should be not merely an abstract ideal but also a politically aggressive idea. It is generally accepted — it is, indeed, one of the most deeply rooted conventions of contemporary political thought — that the existence of inequality is a legitimate provocation to social criticism. Every inequality is on the defensive, must prove itself against the imputation of injustice and unnaturalness. And where such proof is established, it never asserts itself beyond the point where inequality is to be tolerated because it is, under particular conditions, inescapable. That inequality may be per se desirable is a thought utterly repugnant to the modern sensibility.[95]

To the extent that equality is thus stressed, the great and growing inequalities among different parts of the world and the great difficulty of eradicating some conspicuous inequalities within our own national society generate severe tensions, oppositions, and conflicts.

An essential immediate problem in the highly dynamic industrialized societies of the late twentieth century is to *guide* or *channel* their enormous physical and social energies:

> The idea that liberty means freedom from limitation rather than freedom to choose our limitations is a particularly dangerous delusion for the overcrowded inhabitants of a rather small planet.[96]

The complex high-energy society is intricate, and its survival in anything like the form of a pluralistic liberal democracy is very much open to question. Clashes of values resonate with great speed and force in a permeable social structure, suffused with mass communication. High and increasing demands are made upon existing social arrangements. The growth of the public sector increasingly makes societal allocations a highly visible *political* process. Changes in group structures, especially in family and peer groups, appear to increase the demand for "instant salvation" through the total restructuring of societies.[97] It remains to be seen what the actual consequences will be in a world of explosive population growth, great interdependence, much political instability, and incessant change. Greater understanding of the place of values in social systems surely warrants some sociological effort in the years just ahead.

[95] Irving Kristol, "Equality as an Ideal," *International Encyclopedia of the Social Sciences* (New York: Macmillan and Free Press, 1968), vol. 5, p. 110.

[96] Vickers, *Value Systems and Social Process*, p. 21.

[97] "Unless a community is presumed to be suicidal it will give greater priority to its continued existence than to the form of that existence." Richard Shelly Hartigan, "Urban Riots, Guerilla Wars, and 'Just War' Ethics," in *The Religious Situation: 1968*, ed. Donald R. Cutler (Boston: Beacon Press, 1968), p. 457.

This paper's title itself points to the dual role of religion with respect to stability and change in social systems. Professor O'Dea shows why religion can be both a conservative and a revolutionary force in social systems, depending in part upon its own character at a given time and upon the character of its conditioning institutional and motivational situation. He explores how "dynamic" religion, which is likely to cause social change, tends to be transformed into "static" religion, which inhibits it. For illustrative purposes, he pays special attention to the contemporary traditional societies of South Asia, which on the whole have had conservative religions up to now. He explores whether and how the religions of these societies might become more "dynamic."

Thomas F. O'Dea

STABILITY AND CHANGE AND
THE DUAL ROLE OF RELIGION

THE DUAL SOCIOLOGICAL
SIGNIFICANCE OF RELIGION

The relation of religion to society is complex; its consequences in social life manifold. In this essay we shall focus our attention on one aspect of this complicated phenomenon, the relationship of religion to social stability and change. Religion has been an important conservative force in human society. By relating man to a Beyond, a Beyond that is responded to as sacred and ultimate, religion has provided men with a feeling of belonging, a mode of relationship, and a sense of direction, which they could experience as possessing an ultimate ontological grounding whatever the mythic or rational languages that might have been used to express it. It provides a basic relation to *what is* and *what is there* for groups of men that is seen as right and proper, and indeed availing unto salvation, the world

160

being what it is.[1] In traditional societies, such a religious world view and the ritualistic expressions in which it was continually reasserted became the object of general consensus. Part of the ontological explanation these views and expressions provided also justified the society's norms and institutions. The society's basic allocation processes and their consequences — the differential allocation of functions, facilities, and rewards — were given a sacral reinforcement. Religion thus became a preserver of society, and its cultic rites and liturgies "the means by which the social group reaffirms itself periodically." [2]

This conservative role, this "Durkheimian function" of religion has been very evident in history, but it has not been the only one. Max Weber, who was by no means unaware of the conservative aspects of the phenomenon, saw as well the dynamic and even revolutionary implications possible to religion. Man's reaching out for a relationship to a Beyond, man's sensitivity to aspects of his experience that "transcended experience" in its routine everyday quality, need not simply reflect back in the sacralization of his social and cultural creations but may indeed have quite the opposite significance.

Weber saw charisma and the kind of authority based upon it as sacred and in important respects therefore religious. It was "specifically outside the realm of everyday routine and the profane sphere." [3] He saw religious charisma as an important breakthrough phenomenon that was dynamic and even revolutionary in its consequences. Its purest form he found exemplified in the Hebrew prophets whom he saw raising Israel to a more transcendent comprehension of its historical predicament and a more universal grasp of the ethical implications of its experience. Israelite religion despite its preservation of a folk form does indeed offer us "the picture of a self-universalizing religion,"

---

[1] For example, see Mircea Eliade, *The Sacred and the Profane*, tr. Willard R. Trask (New York: Harper Torchbooks, 1961); and G. van der Leeuw, *Religion in Essence and Manifestation*, tr. J. E. Turner, ed. Hans H. Penner (New York and Evanston: Harper Torchbooks, 1963).

[2] Emile Durkheim, *The Elementary Forms of the Religious Life*, tr. Joseph Ward Swain (Glencoe, Ill.: The Free Press, 1954), p. 387.

[3] Max Weber, *The Theory of Social and Economic Organization*, tr. A. M. Henderson and Talcott Parsons (New York: Oxford University Press, 1947), p. 361. On Weber's idea of charisma as not only *extraordinary* but also *sacred* see Talcott Parsons, *The Structure of Social Action* (Glencoe, Ill.: The Free Press, 1949), ch. 17, pp. 640 ff. Three characteristics which Weber attributes to charisma throughout his work are *unusualness, spontaneity,* and *creativity* — the characteristics that Western theology attributes to God. See Thomas F. O'Dea, *The Sociology of Religion* (Englewood Cliffs, N.J.: Prentice-Hall, 1966), pp. 23–24. It is also interesting to note that Robert Lowie, following the precedent of R. R. Marett, uses the term *extraordinary* to designate the *sacred*. See Robert Lowie, *Primitive Religion* (New York: Boni and Liveright, 1924), pp. xv ff. and 338 ff.

a process begun "through the agency of the great prophets." [4] Usually the Hebrew prophet

> spoke on his own, i.e., under the influence of spontaneous inspiration to the public in the marketplace or to the elders at the city gate . . . his oracles highlighted obscure fates of the future like lightning out of somber clouds. Such prophecy was authoritarian in character and averse to all orderly procedure . . . the prophet was a private citizen.

The prophet claimed to speak for God and to voice his uncompromising demands upon the covenant people. "Indeed, unconfined by priestly or status conventions and quite untempered by any self control, be it ascetic or contemplative, the prophet discharges his flowing passion and experiences all the abysses of the human heart." Yet this is not a "personal" in the sense of private assertion. In this emotional ecstasy a new universal vision takes form. "And yet, despite all these human frailties, characteristic of these titans of the holy curse, it is not their private motives but the cause of Yahwe, of the wrathful God that reigns supreme over the uproar." [5]

Thus religion can show itself a mighty element breaking through the cake of custom to proclaim new demands that upset the status quo and challenge accepted notions of propriety. Prophetic proclamation contributed further to the dissolution of myth and the development of a transcendent ethic that was not to be identified with any society or any existing social institution. Commenting on this the Frankforts speak of the "abysmal difference between the Hebrew and the normal Near Eastern viewpoints" concerning the social order. They note that for the Bible "God created the existing social order; but, quite characteristically, this order did not derive any sacredness, any value, from its divine origin." [6]

Weber saw religious beliefs as constituting answers to significant existential problems that arise in human experience. Such systems of belief, as Parsons put it, come to possess a degree of "independent causal significance" in conditioning human action.

> Weber attempted to show that problems of this nature, concerning the discrepancy between normal human interest and expectations in any situation or society and what actually happens are inherent in the

[4] Gustav Mensching, "Folk and Universal Religion," in *Religion, Culture and Society*, ed. Louis Schneider (New York: Wiley, 1964), p. 256, translated by the editor from Gustav Mensching, *Die Religion* (Stuttgart: Curt E. Schwab, 1959).

[5] Max Weber, *Ancient Judaism*, tr. Hans H. Gerth and Don Martindale (Glencoe, Ill.: The Free Press, 1952), pp. 271, 273.

[6] Henri Frankfort, Mrs. Henri Frankfort, Johan A. Wilson, and Thorkild Jacobsen, *Before Philosophy* (Hamondsworth, England: Penguin Books, 1949), p. 243. The authors are commenting on I Samuel 2:2–8.

nature of human existence. They always pose problems of the order which on the most generalized line have come to be known as the problem of evil, of the meaning of suffering, and the like.[7]

Different religious systems of thought gave different answers, which provided the basic ingredients of modal definitions of the human situation in various cultures.

But the implications of Weber's work go beyond this. Religious systems of thought may not only explain, justify, and thereby sacralize the situation as understood in a given culture or civilization, they may break through to new insights that lead to new ideational formulations. Hence religion may provide not simply a posture of relationship to what already is but a sense of direction with respect to what yet may be, a sense of orientation to the future; its emphasis may be dynamic rather than static. Moreover, we are dealing here not simply with the conception of the role of ideas in history but with the reciprocal influences on and partial determination of ideas by situations, including socially structured situations.

To use one of Weber's examples, the fact of being "threatened by enslavement" by an "external political power" and with "enslavement or proletarization" by "domestic forces" conditioned the most unusual phenomenon of a peasantry becoming a "carrier of religion" in ancient Israel.[8] Their situation "conditioned" but did not "determine" their religious outlook. Human creativity in a situation, influenced and constrained by that situation, is recognized by Weber. Later phenomenological formulations of how men constitute society in their activities and interactions in the contexts of situations are anticipated and implied in Weber's work.[9] There is no question of any "uniform determinism of religion by situational factors." [10]

Religious ideas arise out of situationally conditioned experience and once they are the object of consensus and are institutionalized in a society they become significant to that society's definition of its situation and of itself and thereby influence decision and action in significant ways. Moreover, religious ideas are also indicators of motivational factors and, because they and their implications are taught in a variety of learning situations, factors themselves influencing motiva-

[7] Talcott Parsons, "The Theoretical Development of the Sociology of Religion," in *Essays in Sociological Theory*, rev. ed. (Glencoe, Ill.: The Free Press, 1954), p. 208 and *passim*.

[8] Max Weber, *The Sociology of Religion*, tr. Ephraim Fischoff (Boston: Beacon Press, 1963), p. 80. See also note 5 above.

[9] See for example Schütz's defense of Weber in Alfred Schütz, "Concept and Theory Formation in the Social Sciences," *Journal of Philosophy*, vol. 51, no. 9 (April 1954).

[10] Max Weber, op. cit., pp. 95–96.

tion. They become, through this kind of socially structured setting, canalizers of motivation.[11] To state briefly the upshot of this tradition of analysis, religion may be said to be both a *noetic integrator* and a *canalizer of motives.*

Almost two decades ago Julian Huxley suggested that man's role in nature is to become the "agent of evolution" to direct its further progress, or, to use his words, to conduct "that process to still further heights." Huxley declared that to perform this task man must have solid knowledge and in addition an evocative and unifying idea — what he called a "noetic integrator."

> Gods have been extremely potent noetic integrators in the last few millennia of human history; but it is becoming clear that *God*, like all other concepts involving the animistic projection of man's mental and spiritual attributes to non-human nature, is ceasing to have interpretive value and needs replacing by some non-animistic construction, such as the concept of a self-transforming and self-transcending reality.[12]

Huxley's brand of death of God theology aside, the significance of the noetic integrator as perceived by him sums up an important insight of the sociological tradition of the study of religion.

As a noetic integrator and a canalizer of motivation providing basic orientation to men, religion may be either a conservative or a revolutionary force. It may, in Bergson's terms, be either "static" or "dynamic" religion.[13] In static religion, in religion as a conservative force, the tendency is for religion not only to sacralize the status quo but to become compromised with it in a variety of ways and to develop defensive and often rigidly defensive positions in relation to whatever is seen as threatening or challenging it. In dynamic religion, in religion that proclaims new insights, a kind of openness is involved and a reaching out toward new formations of social institutions and new formulations of religious ideas. Dynamic religion "sustains man by the very movement it imparts to him putting him again in the stream of the creative impetus. . . ."[14] Both static and dynamic religion involve what we have called mixed motivation. Religious insights and idea-

---

[11] See for example Robert N. Bellah, "The Sociology of Religion," *International Encyclopedia of the Social Sciences* (New York: Macmillan, 1968), vol. 13, pp. 406–413.

[12] Quoted from Thomas F. O'Dea, "The Secularization of Culture," *The Commonweal*, vol. 64, no. 3 (April 20, 1956), p. 69.

[13] Henri Bergson, *The Two Sources of Morality and Religion* (Garden City, N.Y.: Doubleday Anchor Book, 1954), chaps. 2 and 3, tr. R. Ashley Audra, Cloudesley Brereton, and W. Horsfall Carter.

[14] Ibid., p. 179.

tional formulations appeal to a variety of human motivations that they canalize behind their own ideas and implications.

Established religion, however — religion that is institutionalized and tending to become static — finds itself in a dilemma about such mixed motivation. "The stable structure which thus develops becomes capable of eliciting a wide range of individual motives and of focussing diverse motivations behind the goals" of the religion, a process that "can, and often does, result in a subtle transformation of the goals and values themselves." [15] Mixed motivation may so transform religious values and aspirations that their chief function in a given situation becomes one of buttressing the existing social forms and the particular allocations of power, functions, facilities, and rewards that they entail. Dynamic religion, on the other hand, tends to mobilize diverse motivations but to place them more genuinely at the service of religious values. To summarize at the risk of simplification, static religion tends to reduce religion to the conservative function, the "Durkheimian function," to make religion a defender of things as they are — a process in which the religious element itself becomes distorted to play a role not intrinsic to its own essential character. Dynamic religion on the other hand offers the occasion for newness and constituting new modes of relationship and new definitions of the situation. In time, of course, dynamic religion tends to become transformed into static religion. Indeed, static religion is always part of the background of dynamic religion.

RELIGION IN CONTEMPORARY TRADITIONAL SOCIETIES — SOUTH ASIA

In his monumental study of South Asia, Gunnar Myrdal asks that religion in that region "be studied for what it really is: a ritualized and stratified complex of highly emotional beliefs and valuations that give the sanction of sacredness, taboo, and immutability to inherited institutional arrangements, modes of living, and attitudes." As such, "religion usually acts as a tremendous force for social inertia," and Myrdal states that he "knows of no instance in present-day South Asia where religion has produced social change." Moreover, such popular religion, "religion as it exists among the people," Myrdal finds to be

[15] Thomas F. O'Dea, The Sociology of Religion (Englewood Cliffs, N.J.: Prentice-Hall, 1966), p. 91. See also Thomas F. O'Dea, "Five Dilemmas in the Institutionalization of Religion," Journal for the Scientific Study of Religion, vol. 1, no. 1 (October 1961), pp. 30–39; and "Sociological Dilemmas: Five Paradoxes of Institutionalization," in Sociological Theory, Values and Sociocultural Change, ed. Edward A. Tiryakian (New York: The Free Press, 1963), pp. 71–78. For a background article see Talcott Parsons, "The Motivation of Economic Activities," Essays in Sociological Theory. See footnote 45 below.

"irrational." He states: "In particular, social and economic stratification is accorded the sanction of religion. The attitudes, institutions, and modes of living and working that make up and are reflected in this stratification do constitute very real inhibitions and obstacles" to social change and economic development.[16]

One is reminded of Weber's statement many decades before that the "popular religions of Asia" presented men with a world which "remained a great enchanted garden" in which salvation can be found only "through ritualistic, idolatrous, or sacramental procedures." [17] Myrdal says, "An important problem for research is whether, to what extent, and how fast, secularization is diminishing the force of this source of social inertia and irrationality. . . ." [18] In this Eastern situation, Myrdal distinguishes between "religion in its more lofty meaning" and popular religion. The former or "higher religion" he sees as characterized by a "flexibility and ambivalence" that makes it "not necessarily inimical" to social change. Yet it is clear that the impulse to change in South Asia comes not from religion — though "higher religion" may be used to support it and probably does undergird its sense of rightness and direction for modernizing intellectuals — but from what Myrdal calls "modernization ideals," which constitute the real substantive core of their orientation for the elites and which are derived from the West.[19] Moreover, religion "as a social fact cannot be identified with, and has, indeed, very little relation to, religion on the 'higher' level which a number of present-day 'social reformers' in India want to preserve."

Myrdal's conclusion is that secularizing the folk religion is a necessary precondition of development. He sees this not to be in conflict with "religion on the 'higher' level," but as requiring "the eradication of the ballast of irrational beliefs and related valuations." He says, "But as religion is part and parcel of the whole complex of people's beliefs and valuations, their modes of living and working, and their institutions, it needs to be reformed in order to break down inhibitions

[16] Gunnar Myrdal, *Asian Drama: An Inquiry into the Poverty of Nations,* vol. 1 (New York: Pantheon, 1968), pp. 103, 104, 105.

[17] Max Weber, *The Sociology of Religion,* tr. Ephraim Fischoff (Boston: Beacon Press, 1963), pp. 269–270.

[18] Myrdal, *Asian Drama,* p. 105.

[19] Ibid., p. 78. On modernization ideals see pp. 54–57 and *passim.* Myrdal gives them as rationality, development and planning for development, rise of productivity, increased levels of living, social and economic equalization, changes in attitudes and institutions that would bring about a united and integrated national community characterized by considerable equality, social and geographical mobility, attitudes toward work that support productivity, improvement of health conditions, and democracy.

and obstacles to development." And he quotes K. M. Pannikar, "The fight against customs leads directly to the reform of religion." [20] Pannikar sees religion as related to what he calls "traditionalism," the breakdown of which he sees as necessary to the development of "liberal political institutions." [21] One is reminded of Nehru's statement: "The spectacle of what is called religion, in India and elsewhere, has filled me with horror, and I have frequently condemned it and wished to make a clean sweep of it. Almost always it seems to stand for blind belief and reaction, dogma and bigotry, superstition and exploitation, and the preservation of vested interests." [22]

Myrdal finds it doubtful that change can successfully be brought about in South Asia "without a deliberate reformation of popular religion that would drive out superstitious beliefs and elevate in their place the cherished rites, philosophical thoughts, and general moral precepts accepted by most of the intellectuals." But he also suspects that "they may be no basis for a reformation of religion," and notes that "there are now very few organized attempts at religious reformation in any South Asian country" in contrast to an earlier situation in India where "from the beginning of the nineteenth century a series of religious reformers tried to modernize Hinduism," reformers who "were under obvious Western influence." [23] The last and most spectacular figure was Mohandas K. Gandhi, who combined religious and nationalist impulses, a Mahatma, a great souled one, who aspired to spiritual renewal as part of emerging national independence. But Gandhi's spiritual message has been constrained within existing Indian attitudes and institutions and it is at best latent. What India has done with it is perhaps best symbolized by the fact that the frail remains of this nonviolent man were borne to cremation on a gun carriage! It is significant in our context that we speak of reforming institutionalized religion to remove rigidities and obstacles that inhibit change, and not

[20] Ibid., p. 107, pp. 105–106.
[21] K. M. Pannikar, *Afro-Asian States and Their Problems* (London: Allen and Unwin, Ltd., 1959), p. 94.
[22] Jawaharlal Nehru, *Toward Freedom* (New York: John Day, 1942), p. 240. Nehru was most exceptional in Indian life in publicly admitting agnosticism, and he wrote in 1964 stating that he did not want religious rites performed for him after his death, a wish that was ignored. See *Indian and Foreign Review* (June 15, 1964), p. 4. Cited from Myrdal, *Asian Drama*, p. 108. Yet Nehru was in certain respects of a religious cast of mind and temperament, which is to be seen in his attraction to Gandhi and his recognition that, "Science does not tell us much, or for the matter of that, anything, about the purpose of life," and that "There have been great mystics, attractive figures, who cannot easily be disposed of as self-deluded fools." Nehru, *The Discovery of India* (New York: John Day, 1964), pp. 14–15.
[23] Myrdal, *Asian Drama*, pp. 106, 108, and 109.

of how to achieve religious insights and initiatives that could provide noetic and motivational support for change. Religion in these countries has obviously lost initiative and the noetic and motivational resources for confronting contemporary conditions are sought elsewhere. Religion as a social fact has become "static religion."

THE PLACE OF RELIGION
IN THE SOCIAL SYSTEM

Myrdal defines a "social system" as consisting "of a great number of *conditions* that are causally interrelated, in that a change in one will cause changes in the others." He assumes *"unidirectional causal relationships* between the various conditions: a change in one condition will be assumed to tend to change the others in the same direction." He later points out that there are "exceptions to this general rule, when *the secondary changes instead move the system in the direction opposite to that of the policy-induced primary change."* He conceptualizes six categories of such conditions from "the 'economic' angle," which corresponds to the focus of his study. These six broad categories are:

1. output and incomes
2. conditions of production
3. levels of living
4. attitudes toward life and work
5. institutions
6. policies

The conditions in the first three categories represent broadly what is usually referred to as "economic factors," whereas categories 4 and 5 represent the "non-economic" ones; category 6 is a mixture and is usually considered to belong to the "economic factors" when the policies aim at inducing changes in conditions 1–3, but not otherwise. Often only categories 1 and 2 are considered in "economic" analysis. In the social system there is, however, no up and down, no primary and secondary, and economic conditions do not have precedence over the others. The demonstration and analysis of the interdependence pervading the system could just as well have been made from another angle, and the conditions classified in different categories and in a different order. Such classification would have covered the same social reality and would have had the same analytical content.

Myrdal finds that

> many economic models and the major part of the work on planning for development in South Asia are based on certain assumptions usually left implicit, or abstract and unclear. The three main ones are:
>
> (a) That analyses can be safely concentrated on the interaction of the

conditions in categories 1–3 and on those policies in 6 that are directed at inducing changes in conditions 1–3. Frequently even category 3 is left out of account.

(b) That the chain of causation between the conditions considered is not impeded by attitudes and institutions.

(c) That the conditions under 4 and 5 (attitudes and institutions) are highly responsive to change in 1–3 or even 1 and 2. [24]

The key significance of attitudes and institutions is emphasized by Myrdal. He also points out that they change slowly and are often highly resistant to any tendencies to change induced by developments in the "economic" sectors. He argues that they must be studied and understood and that unless policy is developed to change them development will remain problematical. It is necessary to see the total picture of the real social system. Economic problems must be placed in "their wider setting." They must be seen in an approach that is "broadly 'institutional.'" Moreover, he calls "for greatly intensified research efforts along these lines." He even speaks of the necessity of developing a "sociology of knowledge" to study the sources of biases towards economic primacy and easy progress on the part of Western social scientists engaged in planning in the region.[25]

What Myrdal calls attitudes and institutions (categories 4 and 5) include religion as a central and massive component of the social realities that they designate. His pleas for an institutional perspective repeat in our time the emphasis of Weber, introduced to America a generation ago by Parsons and a few others. Weber wrote in his criticism of those who gave dominance or primacy to such "economic" or "material" factors that it was not his aim "to substitute for a one-sided materialistic an equally one-sided spiritualistic causal interpretation of culture and history. Each is equally possible, but each, if it does not serve as the preparation, but as the conclusion of an investigation, accomplishes equally little in the interest of historical truth." [26] The time has come to place the study of religion within its own many-sided cultural and social context. Indeed economic problems must be seen "in their wider setting," but it is equally important that the scholarly study of religion see religion too in such a broader social and cultural framework — see it as a central part of the attitudes and institutions of the total society.

Parsons has conceptualized a social system also as an interdepen-

---

[24] Ibid., vol. 3, pp. 1859–1860, 1877, 1863–64.

[25] Ibid., vol. 1, pp. 7, 27.

[26] Max Weber, *The Protestant Ethic and the Spirit of Capitalism*, tr. Talcott Parsons (New York and London: Scribner and Sons, Allen and Unwin, 1930), p. 183.

dent differentiated whole in terms of his definition of "action" and its attendant conditions. Action is categorized by two phases, *adaptation*, that is, manipulating means and conditions to achieve an end, and *goal attainment*, a final or consummatory phase; the latter is categorized by the social structure that provides the context for action, *integration*, and the interior human dispositions that provide the support for action in the personality structures of individuals, *latent pattern maintenance and tension management*.[27] These four phases characterize action and its situation and as such are present as dimensions or aspects of all social systems. The differential importance of each will vary in different social systems. Clearly the two dimensions A and G in Parsons' scheme are more or less identical with Myrdal's categories 1 to 3. But this is true only if we assume that the action by which the social system becomes structured during its emergence is action concerned with adaptation to or mastery over its environment as a source of the necessities of survival and sustenance — in short, work. That is to say, if action is understood as what has been called rational adaptive action. In other situations and in other social systems nonadaptive activities and expressive response may indeed constitute central human purposes. Where is religion in this? We noted that popular religion in South Asia was a very important part of Myrdal's categories 4 and 5. If we apply Parsons' scheme to these same societies it is also obviously to be found as significant in the *integration* and *latent pattern maintenance and tension management* categories. Clearly we are dealing with religion in its conservative role, its Durkheimian function, static religion. As a noetic integrator and canalizer of motivation, religion here is concerned with maintaining things as they are and not with the forward thrust of action. Yet forward action, indeed even so-called rational adaptive action, must have goals of more than mere practical significance, must have justification in terms of a larger view of man. Where are such goals and such justifications for new kinds of action to be found in societies such as those we have been considering? Myrdal points to the necessity for policy-making to take up the problem of changing attitudes and institutions and points to the lack of significant internal reform of religion in the region. He sees the surrogate role of noetic integrator and canalizer of motives being performed by the "modernization ideals," but finds that this is done badly because of the lack of "rootedness" of these ideals in the society and

[27] See, for example, "A Revised Analytical Approach to the Theory of Social Stratification," in Talcott Parsons, *Essays in Sociological Theory*, rev. ed. (Glencoe, Ill.: The Free Press, 1954), pp. 386–439; and Talcott Parsons, *Societies: Evolutionary and Comparative Perspectives* (Englewood Cliffs, N.J.: Prentice-Hall, 1966).

culture. Religion, however, remains conservative and often a barrier to achieving these ideals. How does religion come to perform this static role? How does it develop this Durkheimian function? How does it become residual and resistant to the initiation of adaptive action in terms of new ideals — action that would change the society? How does religion get caught in the complex web of mixed motivations that characterize such a function? How can it develop a relationship to creativity and initiative and be brought to perform a dynamic role? We cannot really answer these questions. In fact, before they can be answered satisfactorily there will have to take place the development of more adequate theory — a systematic categorization of the characteristics and conditions of static religion — and carrying out much more research on the popular religion of traditional societies. In fact, as Myrdal states emphatically, we know very little about the life conditions of the common people of South Asia. That includes their religious condition as well.[28] We are concerned here with an attempt to sketch tentatively some of those theoretical elements and to gain some perspective on the kind of research needed. Such considerations suggest a further question: In what sense would it be significant for religion to become dynamic in South Asia and the Third World that is attempting to develop?

SOME STRATEGIC CHARACTERISTICS OF DYNAMIC RELIGION AND RELIGION SURROGATES

We have already noted that with the passage of time the tendency is for dynamic religion to become transformed into static religion. That is to say, dynamic religion in its most obvious and frequent manifestation is *preinstitutionalized* religion, and the chief tendency of religious development is toward institutionalization and therefore toward performing the conservative role. In the process of institutionalization precedents become normative and thereby pattern behavior. Such patterning narrows the range of possible behavior and tends to rule out any marked novelty. It is a process that goes from spontaneity of activity to stability of performance. Seen from this view, dynamic religion would be religion largely at the beginning of the process of institutionalization. For static religion to become dynamic then would require that men learn how to carry out a "deinstitutionalization" process — a "moulting" process for society. It would require that religions

[28] Cf. Oscar Lewis, *Village Life in Northern India* (New York: Vintage, 1965), pp. 249–259. See also S. C. Dube, *Indian Village* (Ithaca, N.Y.: Cornell University Press, 1955); L. S. S. O'Malley, *Popular Hinduism* (Cambridge University Press, 1935).

in some way institutionalize self-reformulation as a self-conscious never-ending process, which would be more intensely pursued at some times, but always present to some extent. The problems involved in learning how to do this in a reasonably orderly manner and without a radical loss of substance would be very great and we understand little that would be involved.

This continual process of reformulation, in addition to the grave danger of losing the substance of the religious tradition, would tend to founder on two other phenomena. First, it will threaten the psychological security of many for whom the older formulations provide orientation, meaning, and justification. Second, it will confront the fabric of mixed motivations characteristic of institutionalized conditions and thereby threaten important vested interests and even basic self-definition or identity for many. In much of South Asia such institutionalized self-reformulation is made additionally complex and more difficult because of the insignificance or absence of such large specifically religious organization as the church in Christianity, or a conception of the universal brotherhood of the believers, such as the *umma* in Islam.

A second source of the distinction between static and dynamic religion is in the ideas of a religious tradition. Some ideas bear a greater affinity with and are more likely to become the occasion for breakthrough than are others. Here a tremendous amount of research is necessary. Moreover, some ideas have a dynamic character — they proclaim a dynamism that cannot be altogether neutralized by becoming institutionalized.

It is recognized by various scholars and social scientists that Western society is unique in that it and it alone produced a rationally oriented nontraditional economic order on a grand scale, science and scientifically based technology as central to its methods of work, a marked secularization of thought, and a dynamic adaptive society in which tradition plays a relatively minor part, and that today the rest of the world borrows, adapts, and assimilates the various elements of these Western developments, at times in the forms of their Marxist reworking and reinterpretation. A main thrust of Weber's work was that religion was a central and significant factor in making these developments possible, that the basic structure of the Western cultural mentality found its formulation and later its sustenance in Biblical religion, and that the deep complex of ideas and feelings about what man is and what he ought to be doing as it is found in Biblical religion remained basically undisturbed and more or less the same throughout all changes in beliefs, forms, and emphases, at least until the nineteenth century.

Here we are concerned with the possible dynamic elements and implications of a religious tradition. In Western tradition, some have received considerable scholarly attention and we have already alluded to several. Prophetic and Messianic breakthrough, an increasing heightening of transcendence and a concomitant universalism, and a tendency toward demythologization are perhaps central. They result in separating the sacred from society, in granting primacy to the individual who is more and more directly related to God. This last characteristic remains the case despite the undoubted importance of the community (Israel or the Church) as a covenant community and therefore the institutional context of the individualized relationship. The Bible, and consequently Biblical religion, was erected upon experiences that were understood as "the mighty acts of God," establishing a covenant people first in the Old and then in the New Testament. The Bible and Biblical religion pass on what were experiences of breakthrough. They involved for the believer the reality of history and of a goal to be realized within history — or even one might say a goal to realize history. The emphasis on the individual, which is at the same time a heightened emphasis upon individual inwardness, is brought into the most intimate relationship with the external reality of history. Thus the reality of man's situation in the world is seen as most closely related to his relation to a Beyond. With the failure of the Second Coming to take place in the early Church this historical emphasis tended to recede into the background.[29] It did not, however, disappear. That it remained real can be seen in the millenarism of the Middle Ages and the period of the Reformation and beyond even to the renewal effort of our own day.

Despite the great importance of contemplation and mysticism, and of sacramentalism, in the Western tradition, the involvement of men in historical reality was a most significant consequence of Biblical religion. Other influences were undoubtedly important in strengthening these precipitates of Western religious experience. The most important are probably Hellenic rationality and Roman law, although such situational exigencies as the barbarian invasions and the break-up of long-standing social and political institutions that the men of the ancient world thought of as eternal must have had deep effects. The result was that Western man was called forth from and driven out of the "great enchanted garden" of folk religion. He was led not simply to the path of contemplation, which is always the path of the few (though very significant for the continued vitality of all religion), but also into a confrontation of history. This came at first in apocalyptic

29 See for example Martin Werner, *The Formation of Christian Dogma,* tr. S. G. F. Brandon (Boston: Beacon Press, 1957).

forms, as in the Joachimite enthusiasm, but also in terms of a growing political realism as in Dante's *De Monarchia*.

IMPORTED DYNAMIC IDEALS AND INDIGENOUS STATIC RELIGION

Judaic religion discovered (or invented) apocalypticism, which Christianity took over. Thus did Western religion prepare for Western man's later increasingly self-conscious adventure in "making history." The forms involved are varied and the line of evolution at times involuted. From Joachim's "age of monks" to the "Fifth Monarchy Men" of Cromwell's New Model Army, on to Hegel's conception of history as a series of breakthroughs to greater freedom and rationality and Marx's secular apocalypse of the proletarian revolution, these and other notions of man's self-realization in history presented varied meaningful modes of historical participation to men in the West. In secularized form they continued to bear a marked structural resemblance to their religious form and to provide an orienting and unifying idea to social movements and institutions — to act as noetic integrators and canalizers of motivations. The most important of these Western religion surrogates in the last two centuries have been liberalism, nationalism, and socialism. The modernization ideals that Myrdal found among the governing and influential elites of South Asia bear a close structural and historical relationship to these precipitates of Western history.

> Even before independence, the modernization ideals were prominent in the programs of the liberation movements. Later they were often inscribed in the new constitutions. They now appear as the declared main goals in the development plans with which all the countries of the region are equipped and in the introduction to reports by public commissions and committees considering questions of major reform. The programs and general pronouncement of the various political parties regularly adhere to them, or at least avoid contradicting them. They are reiterated in speeches, in leading articles in the press, and in the textbooks for schools and universities. . . . This official creed of the South Asian countries is composed mainly of the ideals long cherished in the Western world as the heritage of the Enlightenment and more recently realized to a large extent in the "created harmony" of the welfare state. . . . The modernization ideals are mainly the ideology of the politically alert, articulate, and active part of the population — particularly the intellectual elite. . . . The modernization ideals are all, in a sense, alien to the region, since they stem from foreign influences.[30]

[30] Myrdal, *Asian Drama*, pp. 54–55; 73.

These Western-derived ideals provide the noetic integrator and canalizer of motives for the strategic elites in these countries. Robert K. Lamb has written, "When elites come to power in periods of crisis, they do so in part by their ability to rally the community around a drive for new goals and by their skill in propounding a new value system acceptable to a majority of the community." [31] Can the elites in South Asia do this? They are in a sense part of more conservative social classes and groupings and are not able by their modernization ideals alone to move such groups against what they perceive to be their own interests. Moreover, they are understandably reluctant to use harsh measures should they be required to do so. One result is that these nations are ruled by what Myrdal calls "soft states, both in that policies decided upon are often not enforced, if they are enacted at all, and in that the authorities, even when framing policies, are reluctant to place obligations on the people." In this situation developed a "dichotomy between ideals and reality, and even between enacted legislation and implementation. . . . There is an unwillingness among the rulers to impose obligations on the governed and a corresponding unwillingness on their part to obey rules laid down by democratic procedures." Consequently, "the belief that ideals are important but that their realization must await a change of heart became the basis for rationalizing the discrepancy between precept and practice," and this despite the fact that the "modernization ideals were, and still are, proclaimed as sort of a state religion." In this situation the elites do not rally the community around new goals and do not successfully propagate new values among the population. Rather they become bogged down in the complex web of mixed motivation and the vested interests they support that sustain the status quo and impede change. [32]

Behind this lack of social and political leverage of the new elites lies a fundamental fact — the superficiality of the new modernization ideals, their lack of rootedness in the indigenous culture, their distance from the attitudes and habits of mind of the masses of the population. In the history of the West, Christianity converted the lower middle classes of the ancient cities and then became the outlook of elites and later the established religion of the Empire. In the West, state sovereignty developed slowly over a long period and with many conflicts as did consciousness of national identity. In the West, secu-

---

[31] Robert K. Lamb, "Political Elites and the Process of Economic Development," *The Progress of Underdeveloped Areas,* ed. Bert F. Hoselitz (Chicago: University of Chicago Press, 1952), p. 34.

[32] Myrdal, *Asian Drama,* vol. 1, pp. 66, 276, 277. On corruption and mixed motivation see *Asian Drama,* vol. 2, pp. 950, 952.

larization began over two millennia ago and was reinstated in the High Middle Ages as a significant development in Western culture. In the West, the secular ideologies bore a structural resemblance to the older religious belief systems and grew out of their secularization and demythologization. Hence such ideas had time to penetrate into the deeper layers of the Western mentality and to affect the shaping and forming of Western needs and motivations. The derived and borrowed spiritual basis for modernization in the East occupies a much less favorable position. There the this-worldly turning and secularization characteristic of the Enlightenment has affected only narrow circles of people and then often not in any impressive depth. The new ideals imported from the West lack profound rooting in the cultural and social make-up of the region — sociological and cultural rooting among the people and even psychological rooting of great depth among members of the elites themselves.

In these countries, traditional popular religion appears largely as an obstacle to economic and social development, sophisticated higher religion as neutral but confined to small educated circles and devoid of genuine initiative as a noetic integrator and canalizer of motives necessary to exert powerful leverage for change. It should also be noted that this inherent weakness of the modernization ideals is no longer compensated for by the prestige and moral ascendency of the West from which they were borrowed. The fact that the West itself is experiencing a time of deep and anguished reconsideration of values, goals, and meaning and faces profound problems of social and political reorganization is not lost upon the East nor upon the Third World generally.

An Indonesian student of this situation has also noted

> that the developmental process itself is not a self-justifying proposition. The possibility of raising living standards and attaining greater material wealth may, in many cultures, not be sufficient enticement to make mobilization of the motivational forces in the traditional sectors of society very effective.[33]

To the problem of religion sanctifying custom and retarding change, Soedjatmoko adds that of the "progressive breakdown of traditional social structures, with their established customs, and the difficulty of relating to emerging new ones," which has had the effect of leaving "many in our traditional societies with great uncertainty and anxiety, leading in some cases to a genuine *crisis of identity.*" He sees an in-

---

[33] Soedjatmoko, "Cultural Motivations to Progress," *Religion and Progress in Modern Asia*, ed. Robert N. Bellah (New York and London: The Free Press and Collier-Macmillan Ltd., 1965), p. 2.

adequacy of nationalism alone to become the noetic integrator and canalizer of motivations and speaks of "the challenge to religion." "The limited capacity of secular ideologies to mobilize motivational forces in the traditional sectors of our society is conditioned by the inseparable connection of cultural values and attitudes in our societies with the complex of religious beliefs." He does not see the realistic possibility in Indonesia and the other countries of South Asia of effecting a "dispersal of charisma" from traditional areas of life to the economic sector, as Edward Shils suggested a decade ago.[34] "When everything has been said and done, it is only a new religious impulse from within the religion concerned that can give the process of reorientation and redirection a new and real vitality." To this statement Soedjatmoko adds "that we can only hope for this response, we certainly cannot wait for it," and states that it is "incumbent upon modernizers to try, as much as possible, to establish more effective communication with the traditional and religious sectors. . . ."[35] Moreover, he also points out that the West no longer provides an evocative symbol, as we have already noted: "The problem is compounded by the fact that the modern world — rent as it is by schisms and itself in obvious crisis — into which these traditional societies are moving does not present a particularly attractive model of any obvious superiority to the traditional purposes of life and society."[36]

This consideration of the character of dynamic religion and the indifferent record of religion surrogates to provide a substitute for it in South Asia suggests an answer to the final question previously raised: In what sense would it be significant for religion to become dynamic in South Asia and the Third World which is attempting to develop? Quite simply it may be said that such a change may be strategic to successful development in the region. But there is a more profound answer. The possibility of these countries maintaining a continuity of identity throughout the development process would involve not simply reducing the conservative role and inhibiting consequences of their religions, but reformulating their content in such a manner that indigenous ideals and implications of the native past can be brought into relationship with the evolution of new ideas, values, and institutions. To speak of a culture maintaining a continuity of identity is to speak of preventing a serious development of anomie with its baneful social and psychological consequences (and their political implications). It is

[34] Edward Shils, "The Concentration and Dispersion of Charisma, Their Bearing on Economic Policy in an Underdeveloped Country," *World Politics*, vol. 11, no. 1 (October 1958), p. 12.
[35] Soedjatmoko, "Cultural Motivations to Progress," pp. 6 and 8.
[36] Ibid., pp. 2–3.

also to speak of building new societies in which emerge meaningful tasks and goals for those involved both with respect to contemporary problems and past values, distilling from the two authentic meaningful orientation to the future. As Soedjatmoko notes: "if the traditional religions find it within themselves to respond positively and constructively to the new challenges," then indeed they "might even help to inculcate into the modernization process values that might help in shaping a uniquely new society." Moreover, although advocating that the elites "take more seriously" the religious elements of their societies and urging them to "heightened self-awareness in relation to the many ways in which their nations' pasts continue to impinge upon their dreams of the future" to "increase their effectiveness as modernizers," he recognizes the limited results to be expected from such policy. "The mobilization of the motivational forces embedded in the cultural and religious subsoil is open to deliberate manipulation only to a degree. It is only fully possible when activated from the inside, from the wellspring of religious life itself." [37] What is suggested is that genuine development in these countries would appear to involve a renewed development of religion as central and strategic to the entire venture. The alternative may well be failure with whatever enormous repercussions that would entail for the region and for the world, or the organized and deliberate attempts by powerful minorities using force as well as propaganda forcibly to uproot the old culture and to promote "great cultural revolutions." Myrdal urges new states in the area to move vigorously in all sectors of the social system including those of "attitudes" and "institutions." He finds that in India, for example, the notions of "voluntariness" and "democratic planning" are utilized to cover up a fundamental reluctance to make use of strong policies throughout the society in support of development and its requirements in terms of obligations. "The real and very serious dilemma covered up by this verbal fuzziness about the ideal of voluntariness is that *there is little hope in South Asia for rapid development without greater social discipline.*" This will require that "regulations" be backed up "with compulsion." He concludes that "it is beyond doubt that *rapid development will be exceedingly difficult to engender without an increase in social discipline in all strata and even in the villages.*" [38] What is needed, Myrdal is convinced, is a frontal attack on all major problems simultaneously, which means that so-called economic planning be accompanied by even broader plans to alter radically attitudes and institutions. He finds the supposition that "sufficiently strong and rapid" attempts to induce "indirectly" changes in attitudes and institu-

[37] Ibid., pp. 10, 9, 7.
[38] Myrdal, *Asian Drama*, vol. 2, p. 895, 899. Italics in original.

tions will work to be "glaringly untrue." He suggests that *a large and rapid change of attitudes is not more difficult than a series of small and gradual changes.*" But he also concedes that:

> it is admittedly very difficult to carry out reforms that offend against established institutions and attitudes, especially since those in power, responsible for reforms, often share these attitudes and have a stake in preserving the institutions through which they are molded. . . . To a varying extent this is as true, or almost as true, of the dictatorships in the region as it is of those governments that come to power through elections.[39]

But the prospects of breaking down the barriers to development in the South Asian countries would be quite different if in a country like India, for example, the government were really determined to change the prevailing attitudes and institutions and had the courage to take the necessary steps and accept their consequences. These would include the effective abolition of caste, prescribed by the constitution, and measures, accepted in principle, that would increase mobility and equality, such as effective land reform and tenancy legislation; a rational policy for husbandry, even if it required the killing of many half-starved cows; eradication of corruption at all levels; enforcement of tax laws; effective taxation on income from land; a forceful attack on the problem of the "educated unemployed" and their refusal to do manual work—in general, enactment and enforcement, not only of fiscal, but also all other obligations on people that are required for development. It would mean mobilizing the underutilized agricultural labor for permanent improvements in agricultural production and creation of social capital; a large-scale and effectively carried on campaign to spread birth control; and so on.[40]

Myrdal points to the "Gandhian ideology" as an indigenous influence that would support such a policy and states that similar ideas are to be found in the other countries. The Gandhian ideology that embraced the idea of profound spiritual renewal and moral transformation of the individual and society has mostly become honored in the breach, though honored in the breach indeed it is. Many observers

---

[39] Ibid., vol. 3, p. 1910. It is not of course true of the Communist dictatorships. For an account of basic strategy based upon the Chinese experience of aggressively combatting traditional religion, Buddhism, Taoism, Islam and Christianity, see Li Wei-han, *The Catholic Church and Cuba — Program in Action* (Peking, China: Foreign Languages Press, 1959). For a brief account of the Chinese attack in several stages and a discussion of Maoism (a term not used in China) as a religion surrogate, see Donald E. MacInnis, "Maoism and Religion in China Today," in *The Religious Situation 1969*, ed. Donald R. Cutler (Boston: Beacon Press, 1969).

[40] Myrdal, *Asian Drama*, vol. 3, pp. 1909–1910.

have noted the irony of this situation as India prepares to celebrate the hundredth anniversary of the Mahatma's birth. The basic problems remain and remain no nearer solution. How can such a general social transformation necessary for the economic and political development for which the elites aspire and which sheer survival would indicate as crucial be possible without an indigenous widespread change in what Soedjatmoko called the "religious subsoil" of these cultures? And how is this possible without a revival of what we have called dynamic religion in the region?

THE PROBLEM FOR THEORY AND RESEARCH

Let us repeat here the questions raised in the section about religion in the social system. How does religion come to perform this static role? How does it develop this Durkheimian function? How does it become residual and resistant to the initiative of adaptive action in terms of new ideals — action that would change the society? How does religion get caught in the complex web of mixed motivations characteristic of such a function? How can it develop a relationship of creativity and initiative and be brought to perform a dynamic role? [41] At that point it was suggested that before such questions could be answered there will have to be a considerable development of theory and much more research concerning the conditions and characteristics of religion as it really exists in traditional societies. The problem of developing such theory and research is indeed the problem for the sociology of religion at the present time.

It is important to be clear about one elementary matter at this point. One cannot plan or manipulate people into a religious renewal through using social science. I agree with Jaspers that "Planning is possible in the realm of the mechanical and rational, not in that of the living and of spiritual reason," and that "The boundary of all planning and fabrication is set where man must give himself freely to his opportunities. Here what he can achieve is essentially incalculable; when purposefully willed it is spoiled or destroyed." [42] Then what can study and research do? First, they can clarify problems, and clarifying problems remains a condition of all intelligent response. Such clarification can contribute to policy formation not in the sense

[41] The crisis of Western religion and indeed of Western ideology is such that no one can see the ultimate issue of present attempts at reformulation in the West. See the present writer's two attempts to analyze and suggest a modest prognosis of this situation in Thomas F. O'Dea, *The Catholic Crisis* (Boston: Beacon Press, 1968); and *Alienation, Atheism and the Religious Crisis* (New York: Sheed and Ward, Inc., 1969).

[42] Karl Jaspers, *The Origin and Goal of History*, tr. Michael Bullock (New Haven and London: Yale University Press, 1953), pp. 184, 186.

of making possible total and draconian measures presumptuously considered assured of success, but by making it possible to design partial plans and to understand the risks involved in planning and the probable consequences of profound but partial efforts. Moreover, study and research can deepen our intellectual grasp on the specifics of the human condition in these societies so different from our own, thereby enhancing our authentic knowledge of human problems generally. Such nonmanipulative knowledge can increase our own self-understanding and our concomitant understanding of the human situation, and thereby increase our freedom and intellectual mobility when confronted with difficult problems of social situations. Such a contribution would be most significant to the developing elites in these countries. Moreover, it is quite possible that such clarification of problems and such a contribution to developing wisdom in human matters might prepare the ground for the kind of renewal and reformulation the situation would appear to demand. Though indeed the spirit bloweth where it listeth, such preparation might not be without creative significance.

For theory, first it is necessary, as we have said above, to see religion in its total social setting. It is also necessary to understand its content both on the "higher" and on the popular levels and the relationship between the two. At the present time those concerned with seeing religion in its total setting show little interest in deeply understanding the content of religious traditions or the intrinsic meanings of religious beliefs, whereas those immersed in studying content, especially perhaps in the study of Eastern religions, pay too little attention to the general social setting and indeed to the content of popular religion. First, it is necessary to develop a working relationship between sociologists and anthropologists on one hand and those engaged in the substantive study of Eastern religion on the other. But this working relationship must go farther than it has and become the study of religion qua religion seen at the same time in its total societal setting and in terms of its manifold manifest and latent social and psychological functions. Religion must be studied in its specific situation and such study must be genuinely interdisciplinary. The challenge for theory is to develop adequate categories for this study of religion that will do justice both to inner content and the situation, and to the relations between the two.

We know, for example, something about the typical conditions attendant upon what we called dynamic religion. They are *mutatis mutandis* quite similar to those presented by Troeltsch in his discussion of the socioreligious struggles of the eleventh-century Lombard towns and those of Norman Cohn in his study of medieval millenarism. Cohn suggests the decisive factors conducive to the rise of millenarian movements in a basically three-part hypothesis. It is first necessary that there be present in the culture or the traditional world-view ideas "which include a promise of a future world of bliss." The presence of such ideas "provides the indispensable basis for a millennian faith." It is also necessary that there be some "frustration or anxiety or humiliation which is unaccustomed and which cannot be tackled either by taking thought or by any institutionalized routine." Millenarism becomes possible when a certain kind of situation is shared by numerous people and when there are ideas around to enter into the definition of the situation and direct hopes of a millenarian direction. To these two Cohn adds a third — the presence of a prophet or we might say of creative religious leadership: "It is the prophet who carries out this adaptation of traditional lore and who becomes the bearer of the resulting ideology." If the prophet "possesses a suitable personality and is able to convey an impression of absolute conviction," he is likely to become in the properly conducive situation the leader of a millenarian movement. The situation provides the "opportunity" for the prophet or for creative religious leadership; the latter provide the creative reformulation of the religious content.[43]

In Troeltsch's treatment of the Gregorian agitation in the eleventh century Lombard cities, we also observe a situation of widespread social and religious discontent among the lower classes, many of whose members were recently mobile, having come into the towns from the rural areas, and who resented being closed out from any satisfying participation in the city and the hierarchical, clerically dominated church. They resented the upper classes who ruled them and the church that expected them to be mute and passive but that taxed them. The ideas of the early church, its equality, voluntary poverty, and congregationalism, were known and proved attractive. In this situation with these ideas about, Gregory VII initiated the so-called Hildebrandine reform. He set out on his widespread and vigorous attack upon corruption in the church, thereby providing the catalyst for the discontented populace. As a result "the laity rose in passionate struggles against the married clergy, with their simony," causing a turmoil and confusion unprecedented in the religious life of Italy. Thus the opportunity was created for the heretical Cathari sect to get its start, with a partly new, partly old set of religious ideas embodied

[43] Norman Cohn, "Medieval Millenarism: Its Bearing on the Comparative Study of Millenarian Movements," from *Comparative Studies in Society and History*, Supplement II, 1962. Quoted from *Religion, Culture and Society*, ed. Louis Schneider (New York: Wiley, 1964), p. 177. See also Norman Cohn, *The Pursuit of the Millennium* (New York: Harper Torchbooks, 1961).

in sectarian lay religious groups, which was to rival the church for many decades.[44]

In dynamic religion an "idea" and a "situation" are brought together by "creative leadership." What can we say about the situation that characterizes static religion? In this case, the ideas of the religious tradition have been adapted to and compromised with a justification of the existing social situation. Its notions of the sacred and its call to a relation with it have become attached to established relationships and statuses confirming and sacralizing them. Such an adaptation is usually characterized by a complex development of mixed motivation in which intrinsically religious feelings and motives — feelings and motives concerned with relationship to the sacred realm — are brought together and entwined with motives and feelings concerned with position and stake in society — with the enhancement or defense of interests. It is also often a situation in which those who escape from this sociopsychological web take the path of individual contemplation or the cloistered life of the esoteric religious community, which have a negligible feedback upon the larger society. It may often be a situation in which the self-conscious, thought-out, and "purified" religion of the elite has little communication and little structured relationship with the popular religion — in which "higher religion," to use Myrdal's term, is not structurally integrated with popular religion and has little impact upon it except to confirm it as it is in an indirect way.

Obviously we need to know much more about popular traditional religion and its situation. The conditions conducive to static religion need to be much more thoroughly understood, especially the precise ways and the secular processes in which it coalesces with vested interests in society and with the closely related development of mixed motivation in the individual. If that were understood, questions such as the following could be asked, not simply from the view of policy manipulation, but as part of scholarly discussion between students and others interested both within and without these religious traditions. How can the situation of static religion be modified toward dynamic religion? What elements present in the situation and in the content of a static religion have to be developed or counteracted to move it toward a dynamic condition?

The first theoretical component for the kind of study and research we have proposed is that of locating religion in its situation — understanding the content of the religious tradition within its situation. But what aspects of the situation or what condition of the situation ought to be sought out as most helpful in this kind of study? Here we sug-

[44] Ernst Troeltsch, The Social Teaching of the Christian Churches, vol. 1, tr. Olive Wyon (New York and London: Macmillan; Allen and Unwin, 1931), p. 351.

gest that an important problem in the situation provides the most useful focus. The response of a group or a community to an event that challenges established interests and values offers to the student a view of the situation most susceptible to diagnosis and analysis in depth. In aligning the components of the community when faced with such a challenge event, effective values and interests are revealed; how the people involved see them, defend them, or enhance them becomes apparent.[45] In such a setting it becomes possible to raise questions about the meaning of religious convictions and their function — their implication in the interconnectedness of the specific social situation — which allow us to observe "religion as a social fact." To the ideas of the content of religion in a situation we add then another theoretical category, the *challenge event* and the consequent alignment of the social components of the situation in relation to its catalytic effects. This will enable us to distinguish a further analytical element — the specific groups and alliances that emerge and their various lines of *combination* and *conflict*. We may represent what we have been saying in the following paradigm.

Content of the
religious tradition

in a $\longrightarrow$ in
relation $\longrightarrow$ Challenge
to   event

Situation

The reference presented schematically in the figure offers us a fundamental context for analyzing religion "as a social fact." What is suggested now is that this situational frame of reference be "crosscut," so to speak, by a vertical set of concepts that distinguish important levels of analysis for studying human behavior. Men act in situations and they are related to and respond to situations on numerous levels. Interests and values both influence behavior and they become interrelated in complex ways. Moreover, the exact location of the individual in his situation — his status and role, for example, — also becomes a

[45] For an example of simple but analytically effective challenge events and the way they distinguished two communities, see Evon Z. Vogt and Thomas F. O'Dea, "A Comparative Study of Values in Social Action in Two Southwestern Communities," *American Sociological Review* (December 1953), pp. 645–654. Republished in Thomas F. O'Dea, *Sociology and the Study of Religion* (New York: Basic Books, 1969). With respect to mixed motivations see the article "Five Dilemmas in the Institutionalization of Religion," *Journal for the Scientific Study of Religion,* vol. 1, no. 1 (October 1961), pp. 30–39, republished in the same volume. See also footnote 15.

significant focal point as does the position of the group or institution of which the status and role are a part in the larger social system. It must not be forgot that man is also a biological organism, inheriting the raw material of his needs, interests, aspirations, and values from his ancestors. He is moreover affected by ideas that we have already designated as important among our analytical elements. These foci of analysis, which provide a structure by which we may look at the elements presented in the figure, are interpenetrating levels of analysis in terms of which it is important to observe the behavior of man. They are not mutually exclusive categories. Rather they involve each other in definite ways and it is possible to arrange them in a hierarchical order. Man is an *organism* and this enters into and influences his action, but he does not act simply as an organism. He develops and organizes in his learning experiences from infancy on a personality or self-system that canalizes the energies of the organism in social directions and gives them social and cultural meaning. Man acts as a *self*. But the self is not isolated; it is not a "situationless" entity. Rather it develops in and under the influence of situations and exists in relation to situations. Men are members of social groups and act in that context. Man also acts in a *role*. The role is part of a structure, part of a network, of an organized matrix of other roles related systematically together. Moreover, the *institution, organization,* or *group* of which the role is a part represents an adaptation to an environment in terms of human needs and aspirations as specifically developed in a situation. It also represents a complex of ideas and values brought over into the present from earlier experiences of the group by ancestors no longer living. Men, acting as biological organisms that have developed selves in learning which occurred in social situations, act in roles that are located in larger human groupings which came into existence around specific tasks or in pursuit of specific aspirations, and which give concrete form to certain *ideas*. They also act in relation to the *ideas* themselves that canalize motivations and integrate definitions of the situation of action and not only in terms of how these ideas are made specific within the total "organism-self-role-institution-idea" complex, but in and of themselves. We can present this complex schematically.

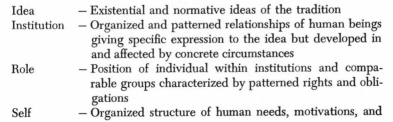

Idea	— Existential and normative ideas of the tradition
Institution	— Organized and patterned relationships of human beings giving specific expression to the idea but developed in and affected by concrete circumstances
Role	— Position of individual within institutions and comparable groups characterized by patterned rights and obligations
Self	— Organized structure of human needs, motivations, and

Organism   propensities to response developed by learning in social
                 situations on the basis of human heredity
                 — Biological subsoil upon which human action rests, whose
                 energies are canalized and given meaning by the four
                 upper levels and whose inherent tendencies influence
                 that meaning and provide its basis

It is suggested that a further theory development to meet the kind of problem presented in this article must be carried out along the two lines schematically presented in the figure and in this list. There must be a more precise and more sensitive delineation of the elements of the total setting — the content of the religious tradition, the structure of the situation, and both in relation to a challenge event. Human response and action in the total setting so delineated must be analyzed within the hierarchical paradigm presented in the schematic list. Obviously this schema must itself be explored further for its significance. It imposes little on the thought of the investigator and leaves its interconnections to be discovered empirically.

We have tried to present here a merely suggestive adumbration of the direction in which theoretical development needs to go to handle adequately our problem. One of the most regrettable conditions characteristic of sociology as a discipline is the separation that usually prevails between truly sophisticated theory and research. It is my conviction that the theoretical development sketched here can be carried out only in close relation to research focussed upon the kinds of problems with which this paper has dealt in its substantive sections. The frame of reference presented gives important leads about what significant questions we should ask and in what kind of situation we should ask them in designing research on these matters. It is proposed as a step toward acquiring a more complete and a more differentiated picture of the religious situation in traditional cultures and its relationship to the total societal situation. Such a research program can only be carried out, as we stated at the outset, by developing a working relationship between social scientists and those scholars engaged in the substantive study of religion. It is suggested that developing the kind of reference proposed here would provide a common intellectual ground that has not existed in such efforts in the past. By viewing religion as a noetic integrator and a canalizer of motivations within a frame of reference that is adequate to handling the several aspects and levels of reality involved, we can move toward answering the questions raised here and develop a more adequate knowledge of dynamic and static religion. Only in this way can scholarship and social science contribute to the solution of problems characteristic of our contemporary crisis.

*As we have seen, the relations among subsectors of social systems
are vital in analyzing stability and change in those systems. Both
stability and change require an "openness" to pressure of the
subsectors on one another. In this essay, Professor Mayhew raises
the theoretical question of whether the subsectors might not be
sufficiently "open" in this way and gives a tentative answer in
his description of the relations between the legal system on the
one hand and various other systems, such as solidary family, religious, ethnic, and police groups on the other. He feels that "the
legal apparatus is not sufficiently articulated with the operative
units of society," which thus become effective "obstacles to
change, rooted as they are in networks of particularistic ties and
well-protected interests." His question and his answer suggest
fundamental problems for sociological theory, for the possibility
of integration in American society, and, of course, for social
policy.*

Leon H. Mayhew

STABILITY AND CHANGE
IN LEGAL SYSTEMS

INTRODUCTION

The current challenge to legal order in America also challenges some
of our concepts of stability and change in social systems. Some versions of functional theory tell us to look for mechanisms that support
and reaffirm the underlying structure of social systems even as other
elements are undergoing adaptive change. These mechanisms can
only operate in well-ordered, well-organized systems. The theory of
the social system posits just such a system. It depicts a systematically
organized society with closely integrated subsystems that respond to
each other's requirements. It proposes a society with great capacity
for social control; the activities of individuals, groups, and other

components can be matched to the requirements of the larger system. When we look at actual empirical societies we observe less integrated entities. As sectors of society become differentiated from one another they often become insulated from one another and develop the capacity to resist social control. Law, considered as a differentiated institution, is often presumed to have the specialized function of providing the high-level ordering and control mechanism posited by the theory of the social system. Law is supposed to provide for responsive change with a basic framework of constitutional order. But a differentiated legal system may lack sufficient articulation with the other differentiated systems of society and so lack the capacity to exercise successful social control. There is considerable evidence that this is true in America today.

PARSONS' CONTRIBUTION

During the last thirty years Talcott Parsons has devoted a large portion of his intellectual energies to the problem of stability and change. He has sought to develop a grand conceptual scheme in which stability and change are not mere opposites but related and integral elements of ongoing social life. In this enterprise of theory construction two themes have been especially prominent: First, in the theme of change *of* social systems, Parsons has stressed evolutionary ideas, calling our attention to the enormous functional capacity of modern forms of social organization. Second, in the theme of change *within* social systems, the central concept has been a hierarchy of control, the idea that social structure consists of hierarchically arranged layers of order wherein changes in lower levels are controlled by stable layers of order at higher levels.[1]

In this era of violent confrontation, of far-reaching revolutionary demands and pervasive discontent, the concept of a hierarchy of control is put to a severe test. For those who have thought or hoped that order and progress can be wedded in the rule of law these are particularly trying times and, for this reason, the question of the applicability and validity of the hierarchy of control to the American legal system is of compelling interest.

This essay discusses three contemporary pressures on the American legal system — the demands for equality for minority groups, the demand for legal representation for the poor, and the demand for police control. These demands provide a convenient and appropriate vehicle

[1] Talcott Parsons, "An Outline of the Social System," in *Theories of Society,* ed. Parsons et al. (New York: The Free Press, 1961). Pp. 30–79 contain an account of the hierarchy of control and of the problem of depicting and explaining change.

for considering the more general problem of the adequacy of using a hierarchy of control as a strategy for studying social change.

THE HIERARCHY OF CONTROL:
FIRST PHASE

As one examines Parsons' various statements on change and the social system some movement can be detected toward an account of social order that relies less on the concept of a perfectly integrated social system. In earlier statements the model of the social system appears to posit rather complete consensus among all participants. Recently, as Parsons has confronted more macrosociological and evolutionary problems, consensus within populations has become more problematic.

In the earlier phase the hierarchy of control was presumed to consist in a set of layers of consensus on normative order. The content of the highest layers, concepts of *meaning* and *social value,* are the most abstract and the most resistant to change. At the next level down, *norms* are more specific than values. Norms define standards not for the whole society but for institutional sectors. Their content is derived from higher level values by a process of *specification* of the implications of social values for the realistic problems of order present in the various sectors of society. Hence, norms are more changeable than values; they reflect more closely the changing exigencies of life. And so on down the hierarchy of control: collectivities (more specifically, collective goals and the normative patterns within organization) are yet more specific, changeable, and responsive to realistic exigency. Finally, roles (the normative expectations governing the conduct of concrete actors) most accurately reflect the changing pressures of day-to-day existence. And yet, roles and collectivities, like the more general norms above them, have a component that is derived from the normative content of layers of consensus higher in the hierarchy.

The scheme envisages a dual concept of causation: Down the hierarchy, flows *control,* the specification of normative content downward, labelled control because the downward flow of normative content serves to stabilize the system and to limit the forms and processes of change within broad but definable limits; *conditioning* flows upward and is so called to connote the responsiveness of the normative order to the realistic conditions of social life, the pressures, demands, and "structured strains" endemic in any group.

The interaction between the two types of process is called *institutionalization.*[2] As social systems respond to problems and disturbances, the downward flow of normative implications establishes a network of

[2] For a summary of the theory of institutionalization see Leon Mayhew *Law and Equal Opportunity* (Cambridge: Harvard University Press, 1968), pp. 1–31.

normative order. As a normative order comes to capture and control the interests and resistances of concrete persons and groups, a set of normatively defined social institutions emerges that regulates, integrates, and stabilizes collective enterprise. Hence, the process of social change over time can be viewed as the progressive establishment of social values in organized social life.[3] Values are seen as having always been present but over time may progressively permeate lower levels of order.

THE HIERARCHY OF CONTROL: AN APPRECIATION

Before turning to the second phase of thought on the hierarchy of control, it would be well to comment on the reasonableness of the first scheme. To some this image of society seems absurd. It is seen as grossly idealistic, as reifying ideas and abstractions, and as endowing norms and values with the capacity to act by "responding," "establishing themselves," etc. In my view such phrases result from mere ellipses of speech and no reification is either intended or necessary. It is entirely possible to state the ideas in a purely nominalistic and naturalistic fashion. The concepts are not necessarily either true or useful but they are eminently plausible. The theory merely supposes that when actors face problems of resolving conflict or of constructing and ordering cooperative activity they do not face these problems *de novo*, as if they had no prior common meeting ground. Rather, they draw upon shared meanings and values as a resource for meeting common problems. The downward flow of values through the hierarchy of control is a by-product of this concrete, motivated search for common premises for use as resources in constructing institutional arrangements. I would suppose that it is more unreasonable to assume that actors ignore what fixed investments in common frames of reference and commitments are available. Nor is there any reason to suppose that this scheme necessarily represents actors as mere automatons, over-socialized men whose conduct only expresses social norms built into their personalities. On the contrary, the theory specifically posits that the normative is only one component of action and that social arrangements also reflect interests and other realistic exigencies.

Moreover, Parsons' position is grounded on a powerful premise in philosophy of science. He believes that to study variability and change we must first discover or posit stable reference points. With Durkheim, he believes that "to think conceptually is not merely to

[3] Talcott Parsons, *The Structure of Social Action* (New York: McGraw-Hill, 1937), p. 732.

isolate and group together the common character of a certain number of objects; it is to subsume the variable under the permanent. . . ." [4] This conception of science has a very long history. Parsons is following one aspect of the Greek tradition, the tradition of the early Ionian cosmologists who sought for the permanence that lies behind changing appearance and found it in the "justice" that is imminent in the moral order. The theory of the permanence of justice extended even to the natural world; witness the famous aphorism of Anaxinander: "It is necessary that things should pass away into that from which they are born. For things must pay one another the penalty and compensation for their injustice according to the ordinance of time." [5] Heraclitus, who is often cited as the author of the theory of ceaseless flux, did indeed say "You cannot step twice into the same river; for fresh waters are ever flowing in upon you." [6] But he shared the central concern of his fellow philosophers. Ceaseless flux makes stability problematic; again the concept of justice is the key to understanding permanence. We are often regaled with Heraclitus on rivers but are less often treated to his commentary on the sun: "The sun will not overstep his measures; if he does, the Erinyes, the handmaids of Justice will find him out." [7] Even more interesting in connection with the hierarchy of control is his definition of wisdom: "Wisdom is . . . to know the thought by which all things are steered through all things." [8]

Now the concept that justice is the law of nature has obviously been quite forgotten as a theory in natural science, or at least transformed into the various laws of equilibrium and conservation. But Parsons is not ready to give up the Greek tradition and its analogues in modern Western thought in the realm of the social. Although he would view the moral order as historically and culturally relative and not as a natural object, he does propose that the ultimate postulates of the normative order are the most stable reference points for social structure and that any science of change must find such anchors. If we insist that at every level of human conduct is a continuous reconstruction of objects and transvaluation of values, then there is no sociology, there is only history. It may well be that it is an error to

---

[4] Emile Durkheim, *Les formes élémentaires de la vie religeuse* (Paris: Alcan, 1915), pp. 626–627.

[5] Quoted in Werner Jaeger, *Paideia: The Ideals of Greek Culture* (New York: Oxford University Press, 1965), vol. 1, p. 159.

[6] John Burnet, *Early Greek Philosophy* (Cleveland, Ohio: World Publishing, 1957), p. 136.

[7] Ibid., p. 135.

[8] Ibid., p. 134.

suppose that values and ultimate concepts of meaning are empirically the most stable elements of society, but the general idea that change occurs within stable concepts is not to be dismissed lightly in favor of the notion that everything is always changing.[9] Nor can we easily banish the idea that the stable elements in the social realm are historically relative principles governing social relations rather than laws describing man as a natural or physical object.[10] Moreover, if definitions of ultimate reality and value come to be rather deeply ingrained in human personality, then it is not altogether ridiculous to suppose that the basic structural reference points are what he says they are.

The notion of a hierarchy of control must also be appreciated as a rather clever device for retaining the concept of equilibrium as a way to explain permanence without at the same time committing analysis to a static theory of homeostasis. If disturbance is equilibrated by changes at lower levels that draw upon and reaffirms higher levels, then stability and change have been brought into the same theory.

THE HIERARCHY OF CONTROL: SECOND PHASE

Enough has been said to suggest that Parsons' theory of the hierarchy of control is not arbitrary and naive but is grounded on quite sophisticated and humanistic postulates about the nature of science and man and is constructed in profound appreciation of the technical problems involved in forming conceptions of stability and change. More seriously questionable is the assumption that large populations in fact share the same ultimate premises of meaning and value. Because concrete societies are formed by the conglomeration of diverse peoples, through conquest, migration, the importation of labor forces, the extension of the reach of urban centers of influence, and so forth, the assumption of consensus on a high order of cultural premises appears far fetched.[11] But it is precisely on this point that Parsons' evolutionary theory seems to hedge a bit. It is possible to see in Parsons' recent statements on evolution a concept of society as something

[9] Parsons is quite explicit about the heuristic character and necessity of his key assumptions about stability and change. See the statement on page 70 of "An Outline of the Social System."

[10] For a good statement on the error of regarding man as merely a natural object and the relation of this problem to the Eleatic tradition, see Ernst Cassirer, An Essay on Man (New Haven: Yale University Press, 1944), ch. 10.

[11] See Leon Mayhew, Society: Institutions and Activities (Chicago: Scott, Foresman, 1970) for an extended critique of the concept of society as a social system and a statement of the structural importance of the conglomeration of societal populations.

other than an integrated social system.[12] Consensus on basic values does not extend to the entire societal population; it is located in an elite. In archaic and "historic" societies elite values fail to penetrate the society. The process of modernization is a process of progressive *penetration* of the values of elites into the total society or, alternatively stated, a progressive *inclusion* of the population in the institutional order.

New dimensions are added to the concept of the hierarchy of control once one drops the assumption that an entire society shares values and instead limits consensus to an elite. The theory continues to posit a society facing problems of coordination and conflict. Its members draw upon a store of cultural symbols and values in the search for solutions and, if solutions are successful, they become institutionalized. This process of institutionalization leads to a downward penetration of cultural values into the norms and institutions of the society. But the relevant values are elite values; [13] they are the values of the most dominant segment of the society. Values are borne primarily by groups in a position to guide social change so as to maintain the supremacy of their own values and their own established position within the institutional order. When integrative problems and conflicts challenge the position of an elite, the elite seeks to maintain the social order by extending the established institutional apparatus and the elite values on which it is founded. Perhaps this account prods the theory a bit beyond the boundaries that Parsons would maintain, but something approaching this general line of argument is necessarily involved in any attempt to render naturalistically his recent statements on elites, inclusion, and cultural penetration as elements in the process of institutionalization. At this point it is necessary to insist that contemporary American society is considerably less "modern" than the sociological stereotype of modernity. American society has by no means achieved the full inclusion of all citizens in the life of society. It is possible that in this instance the "elite" includes the majority of the population, but there are several groups

---

[12] This statement and the following account of institutionalization as the extension and penetration of elite values are an interpretation of several recent works of Parsons: "Some Considerations on the Theory of Social Change," *Rural Sociology*, vol. 26 (1961), pp. 219–231; *Societies: Comparative and Evolutionary Perspectives* (Englewood Cliffs, N.J.: Prentice-Hall, 1966); "Evolutionary Universals in Society" in *Sociological Theory and Modern Society* (New York: The Free Press, 1967), pp. 490–520; "Full Citizenship for the American Negro" in *Sociological Theory and Modern Society*, pp. 422–465.

[13] The reader should remember that elite values are not necessarily elitist values; they are the values avowed by an elite, not the valuation of elite systems or social exclusiveness.

whose partial exclusion is becoming increasingly problematic — especially minority groups and the poor. The pains and problems, indeed the bitter and violent conflicts, that accompany attempts to include these groups in the American social structure form a structural backdrop for any consideration of concrete strains on the American legal system within the framework of the theory of institutionalization and the hierarchy of control.

LAW AND THE HIERARCHY OF CONTROL

In a general way the theory of the hierarchy of control adequately represents the legal response to problems of inclusion. Many modern legal reforms can be described as contributions to civic incorporation; legal systems include by bringing all citizens within the same legally guaranteed normative order so that everyone is, to use the common phrase, equal before the law. Civic incorporation can be described as legal in the generic sense; it is not a response limited to the American legal system or to the peculiar problems faced in the United States. Nevertheless, the universalism implied by the process of civil incorporation dovetails with the strong strain of universalism in the American value tradition. Hence, in implementing programs of civil incorporation higher level values are being reaffirmed. The theory of the hierarchy of normative control posits exactly this affirmation of values.

A great deal of evidence shows that the makers and interpreters of American law have responded to the pressures of inclusion by strengthening the guarantees of membership and by making explicit the equal rights of all participants in society. The legal response to contemporary demands has been to reaffirm the institutional order and its moral postulates by extending to a greater range of participants the rights, protections, benefits, and opportunities offered by the legal order, which is precisely the mechanism of change postulated by the hierarchy of control. But before illustrating this idea in more concrete detail, a preliminary account of the potentially vitiating weakness of civic incorporation as a means of inclusion would be helpful.

FORMAL AND SUBSTANTIVE JUSTICE

The success of legal responses to social problems depends on whether they result in substantive change in the society or merely extend formal rights.[14] Pressing demands for inclusion are often met by extending legally guaranteed opportunities. But legally guaranteed

[14] Max Weber's distinction between formal and substantive rationality is in *Max Weber on Law in Economy and Society*, trans. Max Rheinstein and Edward Shils (Cambridge: Harvard University Press, 1954), especially the discussions on pp. 188–191, 224–255.

opportunities may or may not result in changes in the real structure of social participation and, in the last analysis, inclusion means the substantive participation of a group in the full panoply of roles and institutional arrangements of society; it means, for example, not merely the formal right to vote but substantive power, not mere legal guarantees of the right to work but actual participation in the full range of economic roles, and so forth.

The legal response is formal in one of two senses. Either it redefines the normative order itself or it creates new procedural opportunities within the legal apparatus. The former may be termed the *extension of formal rights* and is illustrated by the pronouncement by the Supreme Court that defendants accused of serious crimes have the right to professional representation. The latter may be termed the *extension of formal facilities* and is illustrated by the establishment of a system of public defenders who provide the required professional representation. Neither extension guarantees substantive improvement in the position of excluded groups. Both are changes within the boundaries of the legal system that may or may not change the status of citizens within other social systems. The possible ineffectiveness of the formal granting of rights is obvious and well documented. The merest reminder of the historic ineffectiveness of the Civil Rights Act of 1865 is enough to lay that point to rest. But even extending facilities need not produce substantive change because the effective grant of procedural opportunities may not provide any leverage over the established order. Staying with our example of professional representation, to increase the procedural fairness of criminal trials does not affect the forces that draw some groups into the more criminal activity and imputations of criminal activity than others.

Indeed, the more insistent and rapid the process of inclusion, the less auspicious any attempt to solve problems by extending formal rights and facilities within the legal system. To operate within the legal system is to offer opportunities on terms dictated by the policies and rules of the established order. But when groups come to demand *immediate* inclusion on a "piece of the action right now," "can't wait," "you change, not me" basis, they are asking for inclusion *on their own terms*. They are demanding not the extension of elite values but the recognition of their own values, and conflict becomes clearly manifest at a very high level within the hierarchy of control.

The foregoing analysis implies that fruitful discussion of the applicability of the hierarchy of control to law and social change requires understanding of the relation of the legal system to the other institutional orders within society. The following analysis of concrete demands on the legal system assumes that the capacity of legal change to cope with social change depends on the institutional connections between the legal system and other social spheres.

THE LAW OF CIVIL RIGHTS

The history of civil rights laws provides the clearest example of the themes of this paper. There has been an independent response within the legal system to the pressures of inclusion, a response that clearly reaffirms the higher order values of the elite within American society. But the response has been inadequate to the immensity of the structural problems involved. The famous school desegregation opinion of 1954 and its subsequent extension to other institutions occurred within the legal system, bypassing the political apparatus. The highest court in the land established that, as a matter of law, no one can, within the entire realm of state action, exclude anyone from any opportunity by race.[15] This declaration clearly reaffirms the values of universalistic treatment and equal opportunity. The decision had an immediate impact in decreasing deliberate segregation, particularly in some border states, but, as is well known, in most of the South change has ranged from slow to non-existent.

In the United States, as in most Western nations, the institutional organization of education reflects the inherent tension between the political and the solidary sectors of society. State-organized education systems presume to intrude upon the traditional socialization of the young by solidary groups — familial, religious, and ethnic. In the United States these problems were resolved by creating a dual system of public and proprietary schools operating with a high level of local control. The articulation of national legal authority and locally controlled education is not close. Without close links between national and local levels of educational policy it is difficult for changes in policy in the national legal system to actually control problems at lower levels in the hierarchy. In accordance with the theory of the hierarchy of control, normative reorganization occurs but, because of the structural isolation of the legal system, alterations in higher level norms are ineffective.

The crucial consequence of local control has been the institution of the neighborhood school. The neighborhood school links the structure of participation in education to a wide variety of solidary and particularistic influences. In consequence, even apart from problems of outright resistance to the orders of the court, American education is permeated by patterns of de facto segregation. Deeply embedded patterns of de facto limitations on educational opportunity can frus-

[15] See *Brown v Board of Education*, 347 U.S. 483 (1954) and the series of cases extending this case to areas outside of education.

trate the aspirations of those who would include minority groups merely by maintaining strict adherence to universalistic standards. Now the demand is insistent for affirmative action to reorganize education on a color-conscious basis. This movement can either take the form of demands for bussing programs to produce desegregated enrollments or, in an even more ironic reversal of color-blind values, programs designed to reassert ethnic identity, as illustrated by the various black studies and Chicano studies programs now being demanded (and granted) in American colleges and universities. The militant black leader now asserts that to be treated universalistically is to be denied identity and, more crucially, to be denied any realistic opportunity to develop a power base from which to capture "a piece of the action." [16]

Demands of this sort greatly strain the legal system because they challenge current legal versions of the response to problems of inclusion. When Antioch College is warned that its black studies program violates federal civil rights law because it constitutes a form of segregation we have certainly seen a full circle of ideological movement. Specifications of the legal meaning of equal opportunity, painfully institutionalized after many years of battle, increase the inclusion of minority groups in American life, but despite (or perhaps because of) partial success, more equal treatment is now damned as a subtle form of racism. The legal order is in a bind; what is required to deliver on its implied promises contradicts its historic means and justifications.[17]

The problem is not limited to education. Indeed, it is inaccurate to date the beginning of the legal response to problems of inclusion from the desegregation opinion of 1954. The legal response in the twentieth century reaches back to the original FEPC movement and to the creation by executive order of the first Federal Fair Employment Practices Committee in 1941.[18] In the FEPC movement we see both the extension of formal rights *and the extension of formal facilities*. The administrative law of civil rights not only purports to guarantee equal treatment to all groups but also creates specialized legal agencies charged with implementing this goal and with actively protecting citizens whose rights have been denied. The history of the administra-

[16] The classic manifesto of this position is Stokely Carmichael and Charles V. Hamilton, *Black Power* (New York: Random House, 1967).

[17] For a set of interesting attacks on the problem of reconciling color-conscious programs with legal standards see Robert L. Carter et al., *Equality* (New York: Random House, 1965).

[18] Executive Order No. 8802, Federal Register, Vol. 41 (Washington, D.C.: U.S. Government Printing Office, June 25, 1941); Lewis Ruchames, *Race, Jobs and Politics* (New York: Columbia University Press, 1953); Frederich Kesselman, *The Social Politics of FEPC* (Chapel Hill: University of North Carolina Press, 1948).

tive civil rights law parallels — in fact includes — the history of the controversy over school desegregation.

The original FEPC failed to achieve congressional support and was disbanded after World War Two. Almost immediately several Northeastern states established FEP commissions, modeled upon the defunct federal committee, but with more effective powers. In the subsequent twenty-five years many states and local communities followed suit.[19] The legal powers of these commissions have been progressively strengthened and their jurisdiction expanded to cover discrimination in public accommodations, education, and housing as well as employment, and the Civil Rights Act of 1964 established such a commission at the federal level. The value of equal opportunity has now been specified, embodied, and elaborated throughout our legal order at every level — in federal law, in federal administrative regulations, in the laws of thirty-seven states and scores of local communities, and in hundreds of organizational constitutions and labor contracts.

Despite the breadth of this legal attack agreement is fairly wide that the administrative law of civil rights has been, at best, only moderately effective, and that the basic weakness of administrative technique has been reliance on the complaints of aggrieved individuals.[20] Individual complaints fail to provide legal agencies with jurisdiction over broad patterns of exclusion, let alone leverage over the structural forces that create and sustain unequal patterns of participation in community life. Established mechanisms for recruiting a labor force, the application of elite standards to peripheral groups, and, more generally, all the forces of inertia that reproduce today the structures of yesterday, do not respond to mere increases in our willingness to treat people universalistically.

The original commissions against discrimination, after surveying the political climate, adopted relatively conservative policies. Even when new forces in the political community promised support for more militant postures and programs, most old-line state commissions remained locked into the political roles that they had made for themselves. The more recently established local commissions, such as the agencies in Pittsburgh, Philadelphia, and New York City, have grown up in the political vacuum created by the relative immobility of the state commissions. Their aggressive activity has been highly praised

[19] Joseph Parker Witherspoon, *Administrative Implementation of Civil Rights Law* (Austin: University of Texas Press, 1968).

[20] Ibid., pp. 158–161. See also Leon Mayhew, *Law and Equal Opportunity*, pp. 152–198; Philadelphia Commission Against Discrimination, *Annual Report* (1962); Minnesota Commission Against Discrimination, *1959 Annual Report* (1960); New York State Commission for Human Rights, *Annual Report* (1965); Henry Stetler, *Minority Group Integration by Labor and Management* (Hartford: Connecticut Commission of Civil Rights, 1953).

but, to my knowledge, their efforts have not been subjected to a searching audit. At any rate, the more they engage in affirmative action to change the structure of participation, the more exquisite become the unsolved tensions between color-blind and color-conscious policies.

The FEPC movement represents a legal reaffirmation of a strand in the American value tradition: the values of equal opportunity and color-blind universalism. The movement aspired to incorporate all through the extension of values, an idea very much in line with the concept of the hierarchy of control. But the capacity of the legal system to change the society through alterations in the order of legal norms is limited. In a sense the legal system is too isolated; it is capable of thoroughgoing reorganization of the logical structure of its own norms, but it is not closely responsive to the pressures and obstacles in the social orders that it purports to regulate. It is well integrated with the elite structures that it serves to stabilize, but too insulated from the daily realities of discrimination in all its forms to cope with its own failures. In consequence breakdown is incipient in the hierarchy of control and fundamental social conflict.

The foregoing argument goes beyond the commonplace observation that changes in law do not always produce changes in behavior. The argument involves an assertion about the social system; the parts of the system are not sufficiently integrated for normative reorganizations within the legal sector to alter the structure of other constituent systems. It is not just that citizens resist legal changes; rather, the structural conditions of effective legal control do not exist. Hence, when new legal standards are enunciated, the values of the system are reaffirmed and its promises made more visible and specific, but tangible changes are not forthcoming. When the legal attack upon the problem fails, the next round of demands challenges the legal system itself. Moreover, the legal system now has less flexibility of response because in elaborating an involved system of rules and agencies against discrimination commitments to given ideas about the meaning of equal opportunity become entrenched. According to this argument, failure is not rooted in motivated resistance to new norms, but in a system incapable of the smooth feedback and control contemplated by the theory of the hierarchy of control.

LEGAL SERVICES

One important form of inclusion in society is enjoyment of the benefits, rights, and protections granted by its normative order. This implies participation in the institutional machinery within which these rights are interpreted and implemented. Given the complexity of this apparatus and the importance of links to persons who have the technical capacity and the informal power to use legal machinery effectively, access to professional legal representation is an important dimension of social inclusion.

We now possess considerable evidence that access to legal representation is stratified. The poor do not have equal opportunity to present their grievances to effective tribunals or to protect themselves from arbitrary and illegal action.[21] There has been a substantial legal response to this problem. At the level of the formal extension of rights, the Supreme Court has made some notable contributions to extending access to counsel. On the criminal side, this has involved affirming the right to state-appointed counsel to indigent defendants and appellants.[22] In civil practice the court has struck down attempts to prevent new forms of professional practice designed to increase access to counsel.[23] At the level of formal extension of facilities, the right-to-counsel cases have stimulated the development and reform of systems of appointed counsel and public defense and, in the civil arena, several programs designed to extend legal services have been established.

The movement to extend legal services is not a recent development. The legal aid movement began before the turn of the century and, though this movement never met the full demand for legal services, it did provide some aid and expanded considerably during the 1940's and 50's. The legal aid movement was conceived around the idea of supplying advice and representation to the indigent through a community law office staffed primarily by volunteers but with some full-time staff. At a national level the movement was organized and sustained by the National Legal Aid and Defender System. By 1965 nearly 250 legal aid societies provided services in over 400,000 cases. In addition, over 150 defender organizations provided assistance in some 200,000 criminal cases. Even 600,000 cases a year did not, in the eyes of the professionals involved, meet the real demand for professional services.[24]

The most important recent program to increase legal aid was estab-

[21] Jerome E. Carlin, Jan Howard, and Sheldon Messinger, "Civil Justice and the Poor," *Law and Society Review*, vol. 1 (November 1966), pp. 9–89.

[22] *Gideon v Wainwright*, 372 U.S. 335 (1963); *Douglas v California*, 372 U.S. 353 (1963).

[23] *NAACP v Button*, 371 U.S. 415 (1963); *Brotherhood of Railroad Trainmen v. Virginia*, 777 U.S. 1 (1964); *United Mine Workers of America v. Illinois State Bar Association*, 88 S.Ct. U.S. 353 (1967). On these cases see Murray L. Schwartz "Changing Patterns of Legal Services" in *Law in a Changing America*, ed. Geoffrey Hazard (Englewood Cliffs, N.J.: Prentice-Hall, 1968), pp. 109–124.

[24] See A. Kenneth Pye, "The Role of Legal Services in the Anti-Poverty Program," *Law and Contemporary Problems* (Winter 1966), pp. 211–249.

lished under Title II-A of the Economic Opportunities Act of 1964,[25] which, in effect, provided for substantial economic support for local legal aid programs under the sponsorship of bar associations and neighborhood legal service centers and under the direction of the United States Office of Economic Opportunity. Some observers hoped that the latter program form could be more effective for it permits the representative agency to operate without the constraining hand of bar associations, tied as they are to local politics and to traditional conceptions of the role of the attorney.[26]

Again we can see the hierarchy of control in operation. Programs of legal assistance seek to increase the inclusion of the poor into the society by reaffirming the value of the rule of law and by seeking to incorporate all citizens within the legal orbit. This affirmation is endorsed even by the American Bar Association, which has followed the trend and proposed new canons of responsibility designed to increase commitment to the right to professional representation.[27] But this sort of affirmation has only limited capacity to produce structural rearrangements that change the terms of participation in the society or alter the balance of power.

The limitations in the policy of seeking civic inclusion by extending legal services are manifest in what appears to be the cycle of disillusionment among professional participants in legal service programs. Initial idealism founders when the young attorney discovers the triviality of many complaints brought to him, when he tires of coming out a loser, when his clients do not share his own idealism, and when their complaints are ill-founded both factually and legally. He learns that well-founded and strategic complaints (that promise potential leverage on society for the disadvantaged as a class) are rare. He learns to prize these complaints, to divert resources to them, and to emulate his higher status colleagues' taste for the "big case," for the appellate work wherein big issues are decided. But when decisions in big cases, even favorable decisions, fail to provide any but the most marginal tangible advantages, to alter incrementally the moral order but not to produce noticeable structural effects, he turns his attention to advocating grass-roots political organization — bloc clubs, cooperatives, and various self-help projects.

That there was a store of idealism to be disillusioned is itself mute testimony to a general failure to appreciate that the legal system is primarily organized around stabilizing and protecting economic relationships. The social organization of property entails a substantial

25 78 Stat. 508, 42 U.S.C. Art. 2701-981 (1964).
26 Carlin et al., "Civil Justice and the Poor."
27 *The New York Times,* January 25, 1969.

legalization of relationships and produces a pattern of recurrent contacts between citizens and attorneys.[28] To argue that extending legal services to the poor will implement their rights and improve their status is to suppose that there is a significant set of latent offensive and defensive opportunities in the legal order. The legal representatives of the poor need only mobilize the legal order. For the most part such opportunities do not exist.

The cycle of disillusionment is analogous to the progressive recognition of the substantive failure of the commissions against discrimination. The latent assumption in the program of laws against discrimination was that a reservoir of individual experiences of discrimination could be used to obtain jurisdiction over the perpetrators of discriminatory acts. It was hoped that aggrieved individuals would present useful complaints to civil rights agencies and that the agencies could use these complaints as a means for eliminating discrimination policies. Such hopes were ill conceived. Most individual complaints were directed against firms that already employed substantial numbers of minority group members and involved relatively low status positions already available to minority groups.[29] This should not be seen as a surprising fact because complaint patterns reflect not patterns of aspirations but the established structure of participation. Complaints reflect the daily life experiences of complainants, and these in turn are shaped by the structural and organizational forces that bring citizens into contact with organizations and opportunities. Citizens bring complaints against organizations where they are already employed, or where they think they might become employed, organizations that are already the most deeply involved in providing opportunities.

Comparable limitations shape the entire array of potential complaints against the established order. The average citizen does not carry around a set of grievances with strategic potential. It would seem that on the whole black citizens have more to complain about in regard to the structure of the society than white citizens. We could also expect that, given the relative poverty of the black group, legal services would be harder to obtain among potential black litigants. And yet a survey undertaken by the present author and Albert J. Reiss, Jr., in Detroit immediately before the 1967 riots showed that as many white as Negro citizens reported inability or unwillingness to consult an attorney about legal matters. In response to the query "Have you ever wanted to go to a lawyer but didn't for some reason?"

---

[28] Leon Mayhew and Albert J. Reiss, "The Social Organization of Legal Contacts," *American Sociological Review*, vol. 34 (June 1969), pp. 309–318.

[29] See footnote 20.

17 per cent of Negro and 19 per cent of whites answered "Yes." In regard to the respondents' most serious problems with neighbors, landlords, public officials, discrimination, and merchants in equal proportion, 6 per cent of both whites and non-whites reported wanting but failing to see a lawyer. Only more intensive analysis could provide precise information on patterns of relative need, but these figures suggest an absence of close correspondence between structural exclusion and the pattern of demands for legal representation within the legal arena. Rather, there is an array of personal disputes and grievances, desires for immediate and utilitarian improvements of personal problems, and uncertain, vague malaise.

This is not to argue that it is unnecessary to provide legal services or to belittle the real grievances of citizens. It is only to say that merely blanket increases in representation by reaffirming formal rights fail to provide control of the political structure at crucial leverage points. What is required is careful selection of issues and vigorous application of power at strategic pressure points. Change in general norms by no means guarantees the requisite level of precise specification of goals and targets. In Parsonian theory such specification occurs within the political system. Political specification can be observed in the political activities of those who implement civil rights laws and legal service programs. The leaders of these agencies attempt to seek out strategic targets, to enter the political arena, and to make law effective by selective applications of legal power. Such officials are by no means impotent but their capacity is problematic, which is precisely the vitiating paradox of the theory of hierarchy. Legal authority is effective only when it enters into a political arena and, once embroiled in the realm of politics, its capacity cannot be taken for granted. Normative reorganization may or may not produce structural change. There is a necessary intermediate condition: close articulation of normative change and effective power.

In a sense this articulation exists in the American legal system. There is a hierarchy of courts, and lower courts are responsive to the decisions of higher courts. Operative courts are reasonably responsive to the actions of the legislature and, in specific cases, the executive faithfully carries out the commands of courts. But the articulation of power and norms in the daily operations of the courts does not guarantee articulation in a larger sense; the hierarchy of control presumes that the whole complex of operative legal decisions is both responsive to the demands of citizens and controls the power centers in society.

The experience of the legal aid movement shows that such articulation is difficult to achieve. It is clear that most problems perceived by citizens as legal matters do not particularly relate to the pressing collective demands for civic and social inclusion. In recent years the legal aid movement has been closely tied to the war on poverty, but legal aid has not proven to be a very potent weapon. Those who wish it were more potent complain of the public demands for more "service"; this complaint can only be understood as a complaint against the *political* irrelevance of the typical request for legal services.

What were once thought to be answers to what I have called the problem of articulation have not proven adequate. Separating legal aid from professional associations, placing the aid office in the neighborhood, and putting representatives of the poor in positions of authority in the aid office only increase the demand for services. And, to repeat again the central message of this section, the performance of requested services does not attack fundamental problems of effective inclusion in the civic order. Only when aid officials enter into the political process, seeking appropriate targets and working for focussed aims, are the crucial problems brought under frontal attack.

CONTROL OF THE POLICE

The problem of police control is an excellent example of the foregoing point. Would improving legal services to the citizen prevent the abuse of police authority? That there are a set of formal legal restrictions on the authority of the police does not demonstrate that access to professional representation will, in fact, permit the citizen to mobilize these formal norms on his own behalf. It is extraordinarily naive to suppose that extending legal services to a poor man will provide him opportunities foreclosed to his well-heeled fellow citizen. Constitutional law severely limits the legal power of the police to subject person and premises to search. Suppose a citizen is harassed by the police by illegal searches of automobile, residence, and person. Courts will exclude evidence obtained in this way but a trial may not be at issue. What realistic opportunities does he have to obtain redress or to prevent future harassment by legal action? There is some question as to whether it could be prevented by a command decision in the police force itself, let alone by an impotent appeal to legal theory in a courtroom. Again formal rights, and even formal facilities, do not guarantee real leverage on the social order. The actual organization of authority and participation presents a more crucial set of problems.

Although the tensions between minority groups and the police have been simmering for a long time the general problem of police control catapulted to national attention with the ghetto riots, such books as *The Algiers Motel Incident,*[30] and especially with the disturbances at

[30] John Hersey, *The Algiers Motel Incident* (New York: Knopf, 1960).

the 1968 Democratic National Convention. Police conduct in Chicago at this time and its portrayal in the national media have probably brought the police legitimacy to an unprecedented low.[31]

Police legitimacy is a crucial postulate of the theory of the stable social system as outlined in Parsons' works. According to Parsons, all normative orders rest, in the last analysis, on sanctions — on the use of physical force. If public authority within a social system cannot invoke the use of force to support the normative order without undermining its own legitimacy, the system is unstable. This is precisely the problem now faced by university administrators confronted by illegal and disruptive protest. There is often little, or only moderate support for protest actions, but, given the low legitimacy, indeed hatred, of the police on college campuses, when administrators call the police, sympathies swing. Moreover, college authorities are quite incapable of controlling police methods, and when police come on swinging clubs, dragging people by the feet or hair, and even, in a recent instance, using shotguns quite indiscriminately, the backlash from bringing police on campus is magnified. Student radicals are aware of this and in some circles deliberate provocation of police officers has become a "rational" form of political activity.

The corrective response within the legal system to the problem of police controls has been less sweeping than the response to the problems of discrimination and legal representation. Results have been even less impressive. Despite the well-known flood of due process decisions from the Warren Court little has been done to enforce the rights of citizens vis-à-vis police on a routine basis. As previously noted, the appellate system works through a flow of trials; and routine police work, as well as such not-so-routine activities as riot control, do not directly involve the courts.

The variety of forms of police organization and control makes it difficult to generalize adequately, but it is probably fair to say that formal guarantees of protection from the police have little chance of implementation within current procedures. Apart from the fact that reliance on individual complaints is an ineffective way of attacking *patterns* of abuse, the protective devices and the political power of the police is overpowering in most individual instances. Legal responses that rely upon specification and elaboration of the official limits on police activity, though they may decrease the policeman's sense of official support for his work, do not alter the day-to-day pressures and constraints on police conduct.

[31] James McEvoy and Abraham Miller, "San Francisco State: On Strike . . . Shut It Down," in *Black Power and Student Rebellion*, eds. McEvoy and Miller (Belmont, Calif.: Wadsworth Publishing, 1969), pp. 12–31.

The Civilian Review Board movement, an approach to adding formal facilities to formal rights, has a long history and an inauspicious record. Boards have been established in a half dozen cities, have been destroyed by the political action of police groups in some cities, and have been ineffective in others.[32]

One emergent radical demand calls for vesting complete control of policing in the neighborhood community. It has been argued that even were this extreme proposal implemented the results would be disappointing because the strains involved are embedded in the nature of the policing functions, not in police mentality.[33] Be that as it may, the demand for exclusive local control of policing is very radical. Because of the intimate connection between force and normative order such a demand implies a level of pluralism in the social order not contemplated in previous definitions of the value of pluralism. To demand an absolutely independent police force for a subterritory within a system is, in effect, to demand the dissolution of the system. In Parsonian terms, the sovereignty of the system is destroyed when its jurisdiction is broken.[34] Were the proposals for independent policing implemented the resulting social structure could not be interpreted as a new manifestation of operations within a hierarchy of control; the change is too fundamental. Consequently current demands for independent policing are *problems for* the hierarchy of control, not examples of its successful operation.

The response on the police side has also created problems for the hierarchy of control. Convinced that they do not receive sufficient social support for their duties on the front lines in the battle against crime and disorder, frightened by political and racial unrest, and bewildered by a line of hostile court decisions, the police have dug in. A new element has been added to the protective organization that insulates police from community control. To such traditional devices as benevolent associations, in-group loyalty codes, and the like, a new and more active political program has been added — a growing alliance of the police and right-wing organizations and movements.

Police are overrepresented in the John Birch Society, conservative law enforcement officials are prominent in national police associations, and high-level officials have participated in various right-wing affairs.

[32] Aryeh Neier, "Civilian Review Boards — Another View," *Criminal Law Bulletin*, vol. 2 (October 1966), pp. 10–18.

[33] James Q. Wilson, "Dilemmas of Police Administration," *Public Administration Review*, vol. 28 (September–October 1968), pp. 407–417.

[34] Talcott Parsons, "Problems of International Community," in *International Politics and Foreign Policy*, ed. James Rosenau (New York: The Free Press, 1961), pp. 120–129.

Police support for conservative and self-interested movements is not limited to a general ideological affinity for appropriate causes. Active lobbying and other direct political methods are used.[35] The theory of the hierarchy of control (and its associated concept of political sovereignty) contemplates an agency of force that is neutral and bureaucratic in the Weberian sense. The increasing politicization of the police runs counter to the stabilizing process of a hierarchy of control. Rather than integrating a disturbed system it contributes to further polarization.

SUMMARY

In a general way the concept of a hierarchy of control depicts the process of challenge and response in the American legal system, even in the case of the severe problems of inclusion currently wracking American society. On the other hand, recent events suggest that contemporary legal change in American does not quite comply with all of the assumptions and images of the hierarchy of control. It is true that there have been attempts within the legal system to reassert value premises by extending rights and facilities. The prime value has been universalism. This is as might be expected, for universalism is intimately associated with the concept of the rule of law; the process of civic incorporation is a process of including all of a population within a universalistic normative order. However, extending formal rights and facilities has not always produced real change in the structure and terms of participation. The legal apparatus is not sufficiently articulated with the operative units of society. The implicit theories of society embodied in legal reforms do not square with the real character of the obstacles to change, rooted as they are in networks of particularistic ties and well-protected interests.

One way to summarize this point is to refer to Neil Smelser's description of social movements as "short-circuits" of the hierarchy of control.[36] The participants in social movements demand change at a high structural level, without reference to the realistic problems of securing facilities and reorganizing the lower levels of order. It would appear that "social movements" can occur *within* established hierarchies, in the sense that official responses to disturbance and attempted reconciliations within established political and legal struc-

[35] See Jerome H. Skolnick, *The Politics of Protest* (New York: Ballantine Books, 1969), pp. 268–292 (Staff Report of the Task Force on Violent Aspects of Protest and Confrontation of the National Commission on the Causes and Prevention of Violence).

[36] Neil J. Smelser, *Theory of Collective Behavior* (New York: The Free Press, 1963).

tures can be similarly detached from the real exigencies of implementation. "Short circuiting" within established hierarchies violates the assumptions of the hierarchical model; as I understand it the theory of the hierarchy of control posits the gradual movement of problems upward in the hierarchy as they became progressively solved and a high capacity within established higher levels to control activity at lower levels. Instead we see uncoordinated and ineffective solutions proposed at various levels in the system. Intermediate levels are by-passed and changes at high system levels take place that cannot be implemented at lower levels. Many proposed solutions even ignore the highest levels of values that, according to the theory, are the ultimate "thermostats" in the system.

Of course it is possible to find or create abstractions that will comprehend both the order of the past and the demands of the present. Indeed, both the authors of demands and those who are forced to accept demands will, to persuade and justify, do just that! This is more a testimony to human ingenuity than a demonstration that yet a higher level of structural order was really "there" all the time. I see no alternative to concluding that conflict has reached the level of values themselves and that we are witnessing a search for new definitions of legitimacy.

THE FLAW IN THE THEORY:
AN INTERPRETATION

How did the theory go wrong? At what point in developing the technical apparatus of action theory were the blind spots built into the scheme? It will not do to merely parrot the current popular phrases: "System theory cannot deal with process; Parsons cannot deal with change; structural-functional thought is inherently conservative." Such facile commentary is a substitute for the difficult analytical investigation that must precede the development of an adequate theory of society.

The flaw can be more specifically located; it flows from ambiguities and tensions in Parsons' treatment of the relations between the sub-sectors of society. Parsons posits two main types of relations between social realms. One is the hierarchy of control. The other is the process of differentiation with its concomitant forms of reintegration.[37] The first type assumes, as we have noted, a hierarchical relationship between institutions. Law, as the main arena for the elaboration and interpretation of a society's normative order, is located very high in

---

[37] Talcott Parsons, "Some Considerations on the Theory of Social Change." See also Leon Mayhew, "Action Theory and Action Research," *Social Problems*, vol. 15 (Spring 1968), pp. 420–432.

the control hierarchy. Problems in the political and economic realms are referred upward to the legal system for appropriate normative solution.

Differentiation, on the other hand, presents more horizontal forms of relations between institutions. When what was once unified becomes separate because of differentiation, the reintegration of the separated units becomes problematic. The crucial form of reintegration is exchange, and in this Parsons follows a very long line of theorists of the division of labor. Functionally specialized realms exchange mutually beneficial resources. Here the imagery is not of vertical hierarchy but of horizontal exchange between independent systems. One form of interinstitutional relation posits control and the other admits independence.

The latter theory provides a more realistic picture of the place of the legal system in a differentiated social order. In a specialized legal system the legal process revolves around constructing and elaborating legal rules. These rules and their lines of development may or may not reflect all the exigencies of the upward pressure exerted by concrete integrative difficulties. To such extent the legal process is autonomous. Its participants work out legal problems as technical exercises within a normative tradition. There are points of contact with the real world; financial and political support is exchanged for useful authoritative pronouncements. But the legal system, like the other institutional spheres that it purports to regulate, has its own constraints and rules, its own history, and its own politics.

The differentiation of semiautonomous social realms is particularly important in the light of my earlier comment that the capacity of legal change to cope with social change depends on the institutional connections between the legal system and other social spheres. The logic of the hierarchy of control presupposes that in integrated social systems appropriate connections exist. The logic of differentiation suggests that they may not. We need more adequate theories of the forms of non-integration.

As a differentiated school system develops, or a specialized legal profession or police force, various insulating and protecting devices emerge. The differentiated spheres come to meet the larger society only at certain fixed points and through limited exchanges. Differentiation involves "truces" or rules of the game, and such rules themselves become a part of the legal order. They are reflected in the rights of the participants in separate spheres vis-à-vis one another. These rights in turn limit the capacity of the legal system to produce change without upsetting a complex of legal order deeply embedded in the fundamental structure.

To return to an earlier example, consider the specialized school system. The independent authority of the school system vis-a-vis the representatives of solidary groups was purchased by limiting central political control over compulsory education. The stable differentiation of home and school was not achieved by making one dominant and the other subordinate, but by an institutionalized standoff. Each institution has power within its own realm. The law must either respect the terms of the compromise or fundamentally alter the underlying legal arrangement of the system. The legal system cannot merely pass messages down a hierarchy of control with law at the top, schools in the middle, and solidary groups at the bottom. Rather all three are autonomous but interrelated institutions. The legal sector cannot change the other sectors of society without itself profoundly changing. This would not be the change through reaffirmation supposed by the theory of the hierarchy of control.

A modern society is highly differentiated and specialized. It is composed of numerous autonomous institutional spheres and organization centers, loosely bound by dependence in the larger society, but free within those limits to develop along independent lines. In the United States the coherence of the social order relies on manifold interdependencies of various interests, on the delicate balancing of conflicting demands, and on historic compromises. These compromises define both the spheres of autonomy of various groups and interests and, conversely, the limits of their insulation from external demands. At the same time the society is wracked by severe conflicts over the inclusion of depressed groups. No single institution (or type of ordering mechanism) is in a position of superordinate control. The legal system cannot, by fine adjustments of rules and procedures, equilibrate the severe disturbances of contemporary life.

Professor Shils analyzes some of the changing and stable elements in the values and situation of the American culture-bearing elites. Throughout our history, until about the time of the Depression, these intellectual elites were at "the periphery" of the society, alienated from and without direct influence over the political and other executive elites. Beginning in the Depression and culminating in the postwar period, there was a great movement of the intellectuals to "the center" of the society, that is, into intellectual executive roles or into close and continuing advisory relationships with the executive elites in government, business, and elsewhere. Recently, however, persisting elements of the older intellectual traditions have reasserted themselves and have created deep alienation of the intellectuals from those at the center of the society. Professor Shils raises some fundamental questions about the effects of this alienation of the intellectuals on the legitimacy of the political elites and on the stability of the American societal system.

Edward Shils

FROM PERIPHERY TO CENTER:
THE CHANGING PLACE OF INTELLECTUALS
IN AMERICAN SOCIETY

The primary intellectual roles are constituted by: (1) creating patterns of symbols of general significance through the action of the imagination and the exercise of observational and rational powers and their precipitation into works; (2) cultivating the stocks of intellectual works; and (3) transmitting, through interpretation, the traditions of intellectual works to those who have not yet experienced them. The secondary role is the performance of intellectual-practical (or intellectual-executive) actions in which intellectual works are intimately involved.

211

Each of these two roles, the primary and the secondary ones, has a culture that may, for analytical purposes, be distinguished into a *substantive culture*, which consists of beliefs, categories of perception, and rules referring to the performance of the role, and a *penumbral culture*, which asserts beliefs about the value and dignity of the role and the works produced in it, and about the actual and proper relationship of the performers of intellectual roles and those who perform other roles in society.

Those who perform intellectual roles constitute the intellectual classes. The intellectual classes differ from society to society in composition and structure. They differ, for example, in numbers or size; they differ in their distribution over the various types of intellectual roles, and in the genres of works that they produce. They differ in their creative powers and in their knowledge of and attachment to the stocks and traditions of works; in their degree of internal differentiation and specialization. They differ, too, in the magnitude of their performance of secondary intellectual-executive roles in their respective societies, in the degree of integration with other elites of their society, and in their influence on these elites and therewith on the working of their societies. The intellectual classes also differ in their penumbral culture, i.e., in their beliefs about intellectual actions and intellectual roles and about the proper place of intellectual actions and intellectuals in society.

Intellectuals exercise influence on their societies, i.e., on the predominantly nonintellectual institutions and elites of their own societies, through the works produced in their primary and the actions performed in their secondary roles. Their influence is a function of the attitudes of the nonintellectual elites — political, economic, military — toward intellectual works, intellectual institutions, and intellectuals; it is also a function of the establishment by the nonintellectual elites of secondary, intellectual-executive roles in the executive subsystems of society. The changes in the secondary roles of intellectuals in the United States and in their penumbral culture constitute the theme of what follows.

In most societies, prior to the present century, intellectuals exercised such influence as they did mainly through creating patterns of belief that permeated the outlook of the nonintellectual elites, usually very slowly and with long delay. They were enabled to do this by serving as tutors, courtiers, or advisors, and by their contribution to the creation of the intellectual ambience in which rulers moved. By preaching and exemplifying of religious beliefs and precepts, they also influenced the mass of the population more directly. When they performed intellectual-executive roles as civil servants or as ecclesiastical administrators, they acted in accordance with a code that was part of their secondary penumbral traditions. Insofar as authority could be said to govern the working of their respective societies, they shared in this control. They were very seldom actually rulers, because ruling and the process of preparation for accession to ruling do not combine easily with the performance of the primary intellectual actions.

The penumbral culture of intellectuals in the West, particularly in modern times, has included a marked distrust, and even abhorrence, of the nonintellectual elites in politics and in the economy. Institutions, established traditions, incumbents of positions of authority, and intellectuals who have accepted these have been severely criticized and rejected. This particular secondary penumbral tradition has varied among western societies and in different epochs of each of these societies. Present-day American society is an instance of a society in which the intellectuals — literary, humanistic, and academic — for a century were alienated in sentiment and imagery from the nonintellectual elites, both national and local. They shared only slightly in the exercise of authority in American society that developed with minimal participation by its contemporary intellectuals. This condition changed in the second third of the twentieth century. The society became an increasingly "intellectual-based" and "knowledge-based" society. Education became an object of universal aspiration as a means to a better life and a higher social status. American society became a national society in which the distance between center and periphery was diminished through the formation of a common national identity, common foci of attention, and a common constellation of values. These major changes were accompanied by major changes in the structure and culture of the intellectual classes. Intellectual institutions proliferated and the numbers of intellectuals grew correspondingly. As the number and proportion of intellectual-executive roles increased, the outlook of sectors of the nonintellectual elites absorbed many elements of the intellectuals' ethos.

The incorporation of intellectuals into the exercise of authority and influence in a society has usually been accompanied by their attachment to the central value system. The confluence of these two processes of incorporation into the central institutional system, and of attachment to the central value system, strengthened the former and secured internal peace. Naturally, it could not protect that society from all the vicissitudes of uncontrollable ecological and demographic changes, from the emergence of new centers of power outside itself and the inevitable ravages that are consequent on the limits of foresight, neglect, pride, rigidity of judgment, and the "inadaptedness" of conduct. In the United States, however, the confluence, after first producing such an effect for a third of a century, has now generated in the past half-decade a regressive effect. Because of their expanded numbers, their more frequent incumbency of authoritative roles, and the great permeation of their ethos resultant from the increased prominence and predominance of intellectual institutions, the developmental and integrative processes of American society have been obstructed. Authority has been weakened; the center of society has been placed in a moral shadow.

AMERICAN INTELLECTUAL DISSATISFACTION

From the time of the Jacksonian Revolution until the administration of Franklin Roosevelt, intellectuals — particularly literary and humanistic intellectuals — in the United States found much to distress them in the actions and culture of the ruling groups of their society. The long persistent, indeed, still lingeringly persistent, preoccupation of American intellectuals with Europe was part of an attachment to a culture in which they thought intellectuals "counted." The preoccupation with Europe was dominated by the fact that Europe was, in literature, in science, in scholarship, and in art, the very center of creativity. They were also awed, though sometimes resentfully, by European power. These features of cultural creativity and military and economic power of the European metropolis were very influential in the formation of the American intellectuals' image of Europe. They should not, however, obscure the utopian function of Europe for American intellectuals. Europe was, for American intellectuals, a place where intellectuals "counted," where intellectuals were respected and taken seriously by those strata of society that exercised power.

Looking around at their own situations, what did they find? Public life was a shambles, corruption rampant: mammon enthroned and the muses rusticated, unregarded, disrespected, sometimes even, in spectacular cases, persecuted. The fate of *Leaves of Grass*, of Dreiser's early novels, the scandal of Maxim Gorki's "wife," the trial of Art Young, Max Eastman, and the editors of *The Masses* stood out as characteristic episodes.

American politicians appeared to their fellow countrymen to be very different from European politicians. Edmund Wilson epitomized a view that had been widely held when he wrote: "Our society has finally produced in its specialized professional politicians one of the most useless and obnoxious groups which has perhaps ever disgraced human history — a group that seems unique among the governing classes in having managed to be corrupt, uncultivated and incompetent all at once. . . ." [1]

The businessmen were of a piece. Among literary men, especially those who made the running from the Civil War onward, businessmen had a very bad press. There were very few like Dreiser who admired power so much that a figure like Cowperwood, the hero of *The Financier*, could be made acceptable by sheer force of character. The army offered no respectable career; the church was hopeless; the Roman Catholic hierarchy the epitome of benightedness; and the Protestants, ranging from the despicable stuffiness and sycophancy of the Episcopalians and the Presbyterians in the presence of the mighty, to the innumerable sects of ranters and Bible-pounders who had fallen out of the bottom of the Baptists and Methodists, were no better. The civil service had never been an object of aspiration to American intellectuals: [2] here and there one of them was ingloriously employed in it, Melville as a minor official in the customs service, Whitman a clerk in the attorney-general's office, some sound scientists in the Department of Agriculture.

The society at large appalled them. For the most part, American scholarly and literary intellectuals lived in a world they never made and for which they took no responsibility. But they were not immune to the claims of the primordial ties. They suffered from their membership in a society to which they were bound by an unexpungible identity and which at the same time revolted them. They were perverted patriots tied to a country from which they could not release themselves and which they could not love. The self-exiled Americans in Paris lived among other Americans. Few were able to denationalize themselves even by long residence abroad.

EXCLUSION FROM THE CENTER

American intellectuals were pained by their membership in a society whose rulers seemed to have no need for them. This was partly a misunderstanding. They could not have come into existence in the United States had the government and the society been totally anti-intellectual. Universities were maintained with increasing munificence after about 1880, periodicals with quite large audiences and of a re-

[1] "An Appeal to Progressives," *The New Republic* (Jan. 14, 1931), reprinted in *The Shores of Light: A Literary Chronicle of the Twenties and Thirties* (London: W. H. Allen, 1952), p. 529.

[2] One major public action of American intellectuals between the Civil War and the Spanish-American War was the campaign to reform the civil service. This would have entailed replacing the power that politicians exercised in the form of patronage by appointments on the basis of educational qualifications and performance in examinations.

spectable intellectual level existed, giving intellectuals, literary men, and publicists places to publish their shorter and some of their longer works. Some publishing firms produced their works and sold them to an American audience. The federal government, despite the anti-intellectualism of many politicians, probably employed more intellectuals than most European governments. Many intellectuals were hidden away in the Surgeon-General's Office, in the Geodetic Survey, in the Bureau of Indian Affairs, in the Patent Office, and later in the Department of Agriculture, which in time became a leading intellectual institution in agricultural economics and statistics. They were, however, obscure and they did not move in the circles of the powerful. They worked peacefully and quietly and they were unknown to the great world. They were specialists and the literary and humanistic intellectuals had little sense of affinity with them. The country was huge and there were many colleges and universities; the literary and humanistic intellectuals did not usually pass through the same institutions as the scientific civil service.

It was from the great world that all the intellectuals felt excluded. It was in the great world — the center of society where it appeared that decisions were made and where the regalia reposed — that the intellectuals felt the cold wind of indifference and perhaps contempt.

And they were largely correct in this.

The political elite felt no need for the support or the collaboration of the literary and humanistic intellectuals and it did not seek their company. For the most part, the political elite in the United States had come up through long service in the political machines, where in the rough and tumble of the ill-educated, they had learned the arts of compromise and combination and even more unsavory things. The American political elite was largely the product of a populistic polity and had not, by origin or by association, acquired the refinements of European political elites drawn from the aristocracy and gentry and the professional classes.[3]

Nor did the big businessmen think they needed university graduates, even scientists, in their firms. Only the chemical industry employed university graduates in large numbers; the chemists were kept in research and in production but they rose in management only after they had lightened their burden of scientific curiosity. Agriculture too

[3] American intellectuals, particularly the humanistic intellectuals and some of the nonbohemian literary men, had for a long time believed in the superiority of the genteel and the well-born. This lasted until well into the 1920's and it faded only with the great depression. This naturally nurtured a prejudice against the uncouth politicians in his "long-johns": his galluses, his string necktie and his chewing tobacco. Long after the respect for gentility has disappeared and the backwoodsman among legislators has become rare, the stereotype persists.

used students in the state agricultural research stations. They had a significant part in the advance of American agriculture and they were respected by farmers. The agricultural scientists were, however, specialists. They were local and not national notables, and they regarded themselves as scientists, not as part of a larger class of intellectuals. Iron and steel, coal mining, and the railways on the other hand — the great industries of the industrial expansion of the half century between the Civil War and World War One were the industries in which the great free-booting capitalists operated — had no use for intellectuals. The technological and managerial innovations that gave these industries their central place in the American economy and that enabled the American economy to come to the forefront of the world, arose from within the industries themselves. They were not the products of research done by university-trained scientists and engineers. The great capitalists who patronized art patronized either long-dead painters or society painters, disesteemed by the intellectuals who regarded themselves as custodians of the more advanced "European" culture. They had nothing to do with literary men or even scholars.

Banking progressed without economists; the federal government likewise eschewed the knowledge and wisdom of economists although Wisconsin and a few other progressive states drew on what knowledge they possessed. Such social work as there was, was done by local politicians and by amateurs of the prosperous classes, some of whom had strong personalities and outstanding intelligences and became important humanitarian reformers. Only in the press, in the churches, and in the reformist politics of certain states among the central institutions did a certain kind of intellectual hold his own.

In the press, where the reportorial function was regarded as proper training for a young man aspiring to become a naturalistic novelist, a certain robust class of intellectuals was to be found. The interchange between the press and the literary and the humanistic intellectuals between 1890 and 1910 was more pronounced, above all in the muckraking era, than that between the intellectuals and any other sector of the elite. In fact it was through the press that American intellectuals reentered the center of society — but they did so as an active counter-elite, depicting the depredations of corrupting plutocrats and corrupt politicians. Some stayed on to play a part in the reform politics of Theodore Roosevelt and Woodrow Wilson. By the 1920's much of this participation had disappeared and it was recalled by the generation of intellectuals that came to prominence after World War One as a failure.

At the periphery of the Protestant churches, a certain kind of active, social-reforming, Christian intellectual was to be found, but on the whole literary and humanistic intellectuals had no affectionate connections with these circles. Theologians and ecclesiastical dignitaries, insofar as they had intellectual roles, were regarded as alien to the valid intellectual tradition. Those who had close connections with the plutocracy and the leading politicians were regarded by literary and humanistic intellectuals as traitors to the true cause of the intellect.

Thus, American society, although it was nurturing a vigorous and creative body of intellectuals of many diverse interests and talents, could scarcely be said to have been structurally dependent on their cooperation, and insofar as it actually was dependent, in agriculture, in the chemical industry, and in the scientific civil service, these functions were invisible to those parts of the intellectual classes — the literary and humanistic intellectuals — that designated themselves as "the intellectuals" and who had grievances against American society for its neglect of intellectual things. Through much of this period, many of the most accomplished literary and humanistic intellectuals were hostile towards the other sectors of the elite. They censured the indifference of these other sectors towards intellectual things and, by implication, towards intellectuals. They thought that a good society, quite apart from any merits it might have in the relations between rulers and ruled or among fellow citizens or in the conduct of parents and children or in the accomplishments of the practitioners of crafts and professions, must, in justice, accord a high status to intellectuals in the circle of rulers. As a result, many intellectuals lived in an "inner exile," and some lived in actual, voluntary exile.

Politicians and businessmen were well aware of this mainly silent, but sometimes harshly expressed hostility. They paid the intellectuals back in their own coin. They despised them as effete and unmanly, as Anglophile and snobbish. When American universities began to bestir themselves intellectually from the 1890's onward until the 1930's, academics, mainly in the social sciences, were sporadically harassed, threatened, and dismissed from their posts for criticizing existing economic and political institutions and those who exercised authority in them.[4]

Yet American society prospered, this withdrawal of intellectuals notwithstanding. It was a rough and in many respects a callow society, but it performed great things. It settled the open country, coped powerfully with nature, and drew great rewards; it attracted vast populations from among the wretched of the earth and assimilated them to a new way of life that prized individual exertion and accomplishment. Its conflicts — except for the Civil War — were not often deep or long-

[4] See Edward Shils, "Limitations on the Freedom of Research and Teaching in the Social Sciences," *The Annals of the American Academy of Political and Social Science*, vol. 200 (Nov. 1938), pp. 144–164.

lasting, although they were frequently violent. Government, despite a long period of pervasive corruption, was brought into increasing responsiveness to popular desires. A common culture was formed out of heterogeneous elements; an inclusive educational system was developed that not only diffused the common culture but also provided the early stages of what later became a prodigious scientific and scholarly creativity.

All this was accomplished with a relatively marginal participation of the highly educated or intellectually most creative. The growth of the powers of the federal government owed most to the exertions of very strong personalities among legislators, mainly Midwestern and Northwestern populists — usually men of no great culture but intelligent and of strong character.

Business entrepreneurs, farmers, professional politicians, journalists, amateur social workers and religious and social reformers, labor leaders, civil servants, school administrators, and judges were the main architects of the growth of American society. The growth of American society was its transformation into an urban and industrial society, liberal and democratic generally in its political institutions, and increasingly drawing its heterogeneous, newly entered, ethnic segments into a national society and a common culture. Only the rural Negroes in the South as a relatively massive minority and a few small pockets of Indians in their reservations were omitted from this contraction of the space between center and periphery. The leading agents of this transformation included only a few intellectuals in crucial and prominent roles. Men like Theodore Roosevelt and Woodrow Wilson, Herbert Croly and Louis Brandeis, John Dewey and Alfred Mahan were very influential in guiding the policies and providing the ideas that led American society into its new form, but they did not affect the image of the anti-intellectual character of American society that dominated the thought of American literary and humanistic intellectuals.[5]

INTELLECTUAL REINCORPORATION
INTO THE CENTER

The coming and conduct of World War Two greatly widened and complicated the reincorporation of the intellectuals into the center of American society, which had begun in the Progressive era. The curve that had swung upward in the period of the new liberalism relapsed, following World War One, into a trough as deep as any in the nineteenth century. Then, in the 1930's at a time when the great depression was

[5] The persistence of this view is manifested in Professor Richard Hofstadter's *Anti-Intellectualism in American Life*. Despite Professor Hofstadter's thorough scholarly mastery of the facts, his important book permits it to be believed that the anti-intellectual Yahoos have had the upper hand at all times.

transforming American society in so many significant respects, the intellectuals reentered the center. The damage to the puritan ethos that had previously been unchallenged, in principle, except for a very small number of reformers and bohemians; the assimilation of Jews into the center; and rising expectations concerning the creative capacities of governmental action were among the major effects of the great depression. All these involved the intellectuals, touched on their interests, gave them new opportunities to assert themselves.

Ordinarily, a crisis like the great depression disintegrates a society and discredits its elite. In part this is what happened in the United States. The business elite was discredited and so was the incumbent Republican administration. The clergy, associated with the reigning economic and political elites, saw their authority diminished at the top, although at the level of parish and congregation, their devotion and solicitude was acknowledged. The decentralized character of Protestant ecclesiastical organization in the United States helped to save the status of the religious elite. Municipal and state political elites on the other hand would have suffered a further diminution of their already not very high prestige had the new national administration under Franklin Roosevelt not acceded to power. As a result of Roosevelt's indomitable personality in the face of every vicissitude and every failure, and the appearance and, to some extent, the reality of effective action by his administration, the legitimacy of the authority of the state governments was saved — undeservedly.

But the chief beneficiary among the elites of the policies of the Roosevelt administration were the central political elites themselves and the intellectuals. The numerous reforms instituted by or credited to the federal government — first, and most symbolically, the National Recovery Act itself, the reforms in agriculture that halted and reversed the course of the disasters suffered by the entire rural population, the enactment and implementation of the new social security arrangements, the guarantee of bank deposits, the encouragement and protection given to trade unions of semiskilled workers, the various public work schemes, and salvaging youth through the Civilian Conservation Corps and the National Youth Administration — all contributed to the restabilization of American society in a new structure after the disaggregation that had been going on since the end of 1929.

The great expansion of governmental activities permitted and necessitated a very large-scale recruitment of new civil servants from outside the existing cadres. In a very short time and in a way they did not expect or demand, the aspirations of the civil service reformers of the last quarter of the nineteenth century were brought into reality. The British and German practice of recruiting the administrative elite from the universities — so much admired for so many years by American intellectuals with civic concerns — was given an approximate American counterpart.

The "brain trust" of the presidential campaign of 1932, which drew primarily on Columbia University social scientists, foreshadowed the role that intellectuals were to play throughout the remainder of the Roosevelt administration. From the very beginning of his term, academic intellectuals, primarily professors from the law faculties of the major universities, as well as economists and political scientists, were called to the highest offices in practically every new administrative agency. Professors and historians were sent abroad as ambassadors; the National Planning Board, although its chairman was the president's uncle, was replete with academics. The National Academy of Sciences began to move into the role from which it has never since receded. There had never been anything like it in the history of American universities, never anything like it in the history of the American intellectual classes since the formation of the republic and the drafting and promulgation of the Constitution.

Some of these intellectuals were given major administrative responsibilities; on the whole however, they did not become administrators. Many who were appointed as legal counsel to departments and agencies were assigned the tasks of devising substantive policies to be espoused by the president and to be enacted into legislation by Congress. Even when they had administrative posts, their tasks were to think about policy on behalf of the president. They formed an extended, informal personal cabinet around the president, superseding the actual cabinet.

The outbreak of the war in Europe was followed by a gradual movement toward American participation. Lend-lease legislation brought in more academic lawyers and some economists. American entry into the war produced a vast proliferation of new organizations. The greatest of these was the Manhattan Project, which drew scientists of many sorts and of the highest quality into government service on a scale never undertaken before in any country or in any epoch. There were many other major scientific projects. Other new organizations that drew on intellectuals to fill their ranks were the Office of Strategic Services, the War Production Board, the Board of Economic Warfare, the Office of Price Administration, and the Office of War Information. Older departments expanded their activities; the Department of State, the Department of Justice, and others added new functions, provided places for intellectuals: university teachers of law, economics, history, geography, and even political science and sociology. Anthropologists and linguists, even teachers of French, German, and English literature and practically every other discipline of the human sciences served in minor policy-making, and in important intelligence and administrative capacities in civilian and military organizations. The physical and biological scientists were absorbed to a probably greater extent — there were more of them and there was more precedent and basis for their services. Mathematicians and statisticians were heavily drawn upon. For the most part, these academics were glad of the holiday from teaching and they enjoyed the excitement of proximity to great events and to great authority, as well as the occasional exercise of power on their own.

The combination of opportunities to carry on work that continued their peace-time activities with immeasurably greater resources and in contexts that excited by their proximity to power, together with their affirmation of the general purpose of the war, brought American intellectuals into solidarity with the political and even the business and military elites of the country. Many who had been fellow travellers of the Communist Party in the 1930's rallied to the government after the period of embarrassment that lasted from the signing of the Ribbentrop-Molotov agreement in September 1939 to the German invasion of Russia in June 1941. It is true that those with firm Stalinist attachments gave only a conditional affirmation to the government, but they too shared — even if only superficially and hypocritically — in the general consensus of the intellectuals. In contrast with World War One, when many Americans had expressed reservations about America's engagement in the war, there were few pacifists or isolationists or conscientious objectors.

When World War Two ended, the unanimity of intellectuals was broken by the reemergence of the Stalinists and their fellow-travellers maneuvering for protective cover behind Henry Wallace and by small circles of Trotskyites and miscellaneous non-Stalinists. Still there remained a very comprehensive consensus. Most leading intellectuals in the natural and social sciences and the humanities who had been in government and military service returned to academic life, but they did not give up their sense of being at the center. Many retained an active relationship with the government, either with the Department of Defense or with other governmental or quasi-governmental bodies that wished to retain the connection with intellectuals formed during the war with such happy results. New research institutions were established, living mainly from government research contracts, and some were able to attract natural and social scientists of a very high quality. This too maintained a sense of affinity with the center.

The end of the war saw the emergence into public light of a new phenomenon in the United States: pressure groups of scientists seeking to influence governmental policy through public agitation, representations to legislators, and to the highest levels of executive branch. The Szilard-Einstein letter to President Roosevelt was the first step in this process. The atomic scientists' movement — of which *The Bulletin of Atomic Scientists* and the Pugwash meetings are monuments — was a remarkable expression of civility in a sector of the American intellectual classes that had never concerned itself much with politics.

The expanding universities greatly increased the opportunities for teaching and research appointments, and salaries increased. There were more graduate students to work with and libraries improved. For many university teachers, especially those who had completed their studies early in the great depression, and who, despite the niggardliness of those times, had survived, the situation seemed beyond the dreams of avarice. Carrying out scientific and scholarly research did not seem incompatible with serving the government; there seemed to be an identity of interests. Its goodwill toward intellectuals — despit McCarthyism — appeared to be self-evident. Through an elaborate system of federal government support, scientists at their universities did research in which the military was sufficiently interested to provide financial support — although it should be emphasized that much of this research had only the most tenuous connections with military practice. The profusion of opportunities and resources turned many heads and bred a state of mind in which all things seemed possible because the reign of scarcity appeared to have ended.

Industry and commerce had learned from the wartime experience of the government and from the conduct of the war and they too sought the services of the intellectuals — mainly chemists, physicists, mathematicians, statisticians, and economists. The tremendous expansion of television and advertising absorbed many literary and artistic intellectuals or provided supplementary income for them. The affluence of the country enabled literary men to benefit from the prodigality of private foundations, grants for young established writers became common, and the shift of emphasis at the undergraduate level of the universities to expression rather than learning and to "presentness" rather than "pastness," gave literary men an entrée to the universities and to jobs therein that had been previously unknown.

American intellectuals were now honored in their own country. Even literary intellectuals who had not enjoyed the enormous prosperity of the academic intellectuals felt their tradition of alienation being eroded.[6] Some tried to remind themselves that it was not their

[6] The two symposia conducted by *The Partisan Review* expressed what was happening among the chief heirs of the tradition of alienation among literary and humanistic intellectuals. See Newton Arvin et al., *America and the Intellectuals* (New York: PR series no. 4, 1953), originally published as "Our Country and Our Culture" (*Partisan Review*, 1952). See also James Agee et al., *Religion and the Intellectuals* (New York: PR series no. 3, 1950).

calling to affirm their principles embodied in the practices of their society. Others were well aware of the dilemma created by their new functions and of the larger intellectual consensus and the demands of the traditions in which they had grown up. The general revulsion against Stalinism as practiced in the Soviet Union and the "people's democracies" and by the Communist Party of the United States made it easier for intellectuals who had in the past been uncompromisingly anticapitalist to reconcile themselves to post-war America.

By the end of the 1940's, America had become the center of the world. The increasing number of American academic and literary intellectuals who went abroad — thanks to the largesse of their government and the private philanthropic foundations — were made aware of this. The bitterness of the anti-Americanism among foreign intellectuals only testified to their preoccupation with America. American intellectuals were even less able to resist the attractive power of the centrality of the United States. From the condition of being peripheral in a society that they believed was culturally provincial, American intellectuals came to see themselves as effective members of the center of an intellectual metropolis. Their earlier feelings of provinciality had not been experienced as a happy condition. They embraced with enthusiasm the escape from peripherality in a province to centrality in a metropolis.

At the root of this affirmation was the reality of a strong state. Although the dominant, most visible tradition of American intellectuals of almost all kinds has been distrust toward the regnant political and economic powers, it has — at least since the 1880's — been associated also with a tradition that asserts that the ills of society can be cured by a strong and virtuous authority. Long before American intellectuals became socialists, Stalinists, Trotskyists, or whatever, they believed that "the state should do it." When the idea of planning, very simplistically conceived, came upon the scene, it was seized upon as the right solution.

POSTWAR GOVERNMENT-INTELLECTUAL COLLABORATION

Education has always been regarded as a good thing in America. The state universities and the land grant colleges as well as the universality of public education without fees and the late school leaving age were evidence of this. Science, too, had been spoken of in terms of awe and in anticipation of benefits. But pure science, abstract thought, and the life of letters tended to be treated with levity and disparagement. In the period after World War Two, higher education, scientific, technological, and to a lesser extent, humanistic research and belles lettres, were all elevated. In this period what had been esteemed became more esteemed; what had been disparaged was treated more seriously. The munificent support by government and business alike of higher education and research in private and state universities bespoke the widespread conviction of the nonintellectual elites of the value, practical and glorious, of the intellectuals. The intellectuals were of the same view. It appeared as if an old dream had come true.

Through the length and breadth of the academic and nonacademic intellectual classes, particularly in the natural and social sciences, this self-serving view was espoused. Grants and subsidies for study and research were available and even those who were in principle opposed to the government and "the system" were able to avail themselves of such benefits and were eager to do so.

There was little dissent by the intellectuals from the obligation laid upon the universities to educate and train persons who could fill all the various roles in the higher level of government and business administration and technology thought to be needed for further developing the American economy. It was taken for granted by the critics of the "organization man" no less than by others that the universities should do this and that the government and businessmen should provide the money for it. The doctrine of the "multiversity" was only a precipitation of what was already general policy and belief.

Multiversal training had in fact been done by American universities in earlier decades, but it was done on a much grander scale in the two decades immediately following the Second World War. Those responsible for the institutions were delighted to have their services so tangibly appreciated. University teachers were equally pleased: the expansion provided more students to train in research and for teaching careers. Expansion also contributed to approximation towards the ideal of equal access to higher education, thus meeting one standing grievance of the populistic and radical wing of the alienated intellectuals against the universities — that they were for the offspring of the rich.

Many new roles opened to intellectuals that had scarcely existed before the war: scientists were in the Department of Defense and in the Office of Science and Technology; [7] economists joined the Council of Economic Advisors, a scientist was chief scientific advisor to the president, the entire apparatus of the National Science Foundation were scientists. In the Policy Planning Board of the Department of State, academics and historians and political scientists served together with such distinguished professional diplomat-intellectuals as George

---

[7] The agitational, critical role of the scientists in the first years following the war shrivelled as scientists became advisors, members of grant-awarding panels, etc. The high point was reached when the American section of Pugwash was nearly assimilated into the disarmament agency.

Kennan and, at a somewhat lower level of the intellectual hierarchy, Paul Nitze, Charles Bohlen, and Louis Halle; in the Department of Defense, which became more science-based than any other part of the government or part of any government, a series of eminent scientists occupied the office of Assistant Secretary with responsibility for guiding the immense research activity of the armed services; an academic economist became the dominant spirit in the reorganization of the procurement policy of the Department of Defense. Private organizations like the Rand Corporation performed research on contract for the Air Force on matters at the very center of military policy. There were many roles filled by intellectuals in the two decades after 1945 which had not even existed previously.

Old roles became more influential. In the Federal Reserve System, which had become more important than ever before in maintaining the economy in its state of stability *and* growth, academically trained economists retaining intimate relations with the academic economic professions were more numerous, more prominent, and more influential than previously. Professors of law outside the government played an important part in selecting their best students to serve as clerks to Supreme Court Justices. Congressional committees invited intellectuals to testify before them with greater frequency than before, and several staff directors of certain important committees such as the Senate Foreign Affairs Committee have been intellectuals of reasonable stature — an unprecedented development. High officials turned repeatedly and frequently to the universities for assistance, enlightenment, counsel, guidance, and personnel. This structure of collaboration between the government and the intellectuals was the achievement of Democratic administrations — and the intellectuals had always had, at least since the Wilson administration, a penchant towards the Democratic Party as the relatively antiplutocratic party and the party of the ethnic outcasts and therefore the party closer to an alienated outlook. The practice was not, however, notably reduced by the Republican administration of President Eisenhower.[8]

The Kennedy administration continued the collaboration begun under President Roosevelt in a more spectacular way and reached out more energetically towards the literary and artistic intellectuals as well.[9]

---

[8] The great weapon in the verbal armory of the New Left, the term "industrial-military complex," was given to the nation as a parting gift by President Eisenhower, but he in his turn had it entrusted to him by one of his court intellectuals.

[9] Despite the elevation of Robert Frost to the equivalent of poet laureate, no literary intellectuals attained the intimate and influential position that had been held by Robert Sherwood in his relations with President Roosevelt.

With varying external fortunes, the Johnson and the Nixon administrations continued the dependence. Although the alienation in sentiment of American intellectuals in the two latter administrations has been in many respects more vehement and acrimonious than it has been since the 1920's and perhaps than it has ever been before, Patrick Moynihan and Henry Kissinger, President Nixon's two chief advisors — both with cabinet rank — in domestic and foreign affairs are among the most distinguished intellectuals in the country. Professor Milton Friedman's ideas probably have more direct influence in the Nixon administration than any economist has had in any major country since John Maynard Keynes in Great Britain and the United States.

So much for the incorporation of the intellectuals into roles of authority and influence in American society. Let us look now at some of the social consequences of this great change in the prestige and power of intellectual roles in American society.

SOCIAL CONSEQUENCES OF THE CHANGING INTELLECTUAL ROLE

All consequences of the enlarged and more central roles filled by intellectuals in every sphere of the life of American society in the twenty years following the end of World War Two cannot be traced here. It was certainly large, very ramified and very pervasive; the United States became to an unprecedented extent an "intellectual-based" country. It was a major change for a society formerly described by intellectuals as more uncongenial to the life of the spirit than any great society known in history.

Let us take the major changes and attempt to estimate the part intellectuals played in them. First, the changes: the relatively easy transition from war to peace, the demobilization, then the continuing growth and stability of the economy; then the remarkable integration of American society — twenty years of internal peace, of moderating political conflict, of strikes without violence; the continuous improvement in the condition of the Negro; after the end of McCarthyism and of the persecution of the shrivelled remnant of the Communist Party, a greatly broadened tolerance of political dissent, a greater freedom of individual action, particularly in the private sphere, the further attenuation of puritanism; a reduction in ethnic hostility except in the Southern states,[10] a reduction in the traditional animosity among Roman Catholics, Protestants, and Jews.

[10] The "backlash" among whites has amounted to very little outside the South. The growth of anti-white sentiment among Negroes is largely a phenomenon of the last half decade following the period to which I refer.

To some extent, these accomplishments were the fruit of older ideas from the Keynesian economists of the 1930's, the liberal ideas of equal justice before the law and of equality of opportunity, the idea of the moral equality of all human beings drawn from certain strands of protestant Christianity and from the Enlightenment. The main general feature of all these changes was the narrowing of the distance between center and periphery by reducing the moral ascendancy of the center. In large measure, this was made possible by the extraordinary productivity of American agriculture and industry, that was in some considerable measure the result of the work of the agriculture research stations connected with the land grant colleges, and of the scientific and technological research in chemistry, metallurgy, food processing, electronics, industrial management, etc. The affluence of American society helped to change the self-image of the mass of the population in the working classes and the lower middle classes by permitting their standard of living to improve, by permitting them to receive more education and to live in a more "appropriate" style, which was adapted from the middle class. The development of mass communications technology contributed to the creation of a single national society with a common focus of attention and, to some extent, a common culture.[11]

The economic growth and stability of the period undoubtedly owed something not only to the scientific and technological research to which I have already referred, but to the vigorous empirical research and elaborate theoretical analyses of economists inside the government and outside it. The improvement in the condition of the Negroes — much of which was a function of their urbanization and "Northernization" in connection with growing employment opportunities in industry — was certainly affected by the change in opinion to which judicial decisions and a more humane public opinion contributed; these in turn were affected by the research done by sociologists on the situation of the Negro, — which was epitomized and summarized just at the end of World War Two by Gunnar Myrdal's American Dilemma.

The attenuation of puritanism had been moving apace with the urbanization of American society but its models and legitimators who had fought for it for a long time were literary and humanistic intellectuals. If the whole country has been turned into a macrocosm of what

[11] The "intellectualization" of the mass media was evinced in the weekly periodicals of mass circulation. The Saturday Evening Post and Collier's among the deceased, and Life and Time among the still surviving, all became more and more "intellectual" in their most recent phase. Works of great art and superior literature and culture became a large part of their stock in trade. Even the ocean of triviality and meretriciousness that constitutes much of this common culture is the product of intellectuals — many of them intellectuals manqués who resent their self-exclusion from intellectual grace.

used to be found only in Greenwich Village and among the bohemians of Chicago and San Francisco, the model provided by one sector of the intellectuals has certainly played a part. To this should be added the shattering blow given to puritanism by the "pill," which was the product of elaborate research by biochemists and physiologists.

The general culture of impulse owes much of course to the weakness of authority in the family and in society. This certainly cannot be accounted for without reference to the long intellectual tradition of the restriction of the legitimacy of authority from the seventeenth century onward. The popularization of psychoanalysis through Margaret Mead, Erich Fromm, Karen Horney, and many others less gifted, the research of Arnold Gesell and the educational doctrine of John Dewey, all led to Dr. Spock's famous handbook of child rearing. It is not by accident that humanitarian and liberal attitudes toward children and their rights began and is still most widespread in families in which the parents are more highly educated. Assertions about the power and influence of intellectuals should not disregard this.

ALIENATION AMONG AMERICAN INTELLECTUALS

The affirmation of American society and culture and participation in its direction and orientation at the center and in numerous sub-centers did not absorb all American intellectuals; nor was the affirmation unqualified in those who were engaged in it. Alongside of and intertwined with the acts of affirmation in practice and in statement was a continuous denial.

This denial had an illustrious and honorable line of direct descent from the aesthetic alienation of Edgar Allan Poe and Henry James, the moral alienation of Herman Melville and Theodore Dreiser, the patrician alienation of Henry Adams, the bohemian alienation of Floyd Dell and Art Young, and the Marxian alienation of Scott Nearing, Upton Sinclair, and Norman Thomas. In the 1920's these different currents of alienation crossed each other with partial fusions. H. L. Mencken, Ernest Hemingway, Sherwood Anderson, John Dos Passos, Edmund Wilson, and many others continued this line through the 1920's and into the 1930's.

The Communist Party and its agents who conducted *The New Masses* attempted to amalgamate these various kinds of alienation and to exploit them by giving them the status that Dante gave to Virgil, namely, that of annunciations of the comprehensive alienation of Marxism-Leninism. They were, however, hampered by their guilefulness and their need for political purposes to appear to be something that they were not. *The Partisan Review*, following its removal shortly after its birth from the control of the fellow travellers and agents of the Communist Party, was a more genuine heir and representative of some diverse traditions of the alienated American intellectuals.

The Communists lost their hegemony during the war. Having renounced their identity in the larger cause of the Soviet alliance with the Western powers, they could not recover significantly after the alliance ended. In publishing and literary circles they were shunned after the war. Their friends took cover. But although the Communists and their friends hid or changed their external guise, a more honest alienation was expressed in *The Partisan Review* and in *Politics*. *The Partisan Review* became the organ of a miscellaneous bundle of alienations and it could not withstand the delights of being at the center. Its Trotskyist anti-Stalinism tended to fade into American anti-Communism. Alienation and reluctant affirmation mingled in its pages. *Politics,* on the other hand, was for the pure in heart; in a more humorless and a more self-righteous way, it continued in the traditions of *The Masses* and *The Liberator*.

The main criticism of American society by the alienated intellectuals of the late 1940's and most of the 1950's — the critique of mass culture — was found in *Politics*. The self-destructive tendencies of capitalism and the baseness of the politicians yielded their place of honor in the alienated intellectuals' image of American society to the vulgarity of American culture and to the damage that this mass culture did to the high culture. This critique, which had a multiple ancestry in patrician disdain, aesthetic revulsion, puritanical disapprobation, and a highbrow Marxism, did not have a wide adherence. Literary publicists and a handful of sociologists under the influence of German *Edelmarxismus* were its chief carriers. It was probably shared in a fairly inert manner by the academic humanists whose preconceptions were directed by the older tradition of aesthetic alienation and the abhorrence of the genteel classes for money-grubbing and the baser pleasures.

The critique of mass society and of mass culture did not have a long life. Many of its proponents, eager to swim in a new, more turbulent stream, jettisoned it for something stronger and more fashionable.[12]

POST-1965 INTELLECTUAL ALIENATION

Since the mid-1960's a pronounced change in the relations of American intellectuals to the center of their society has occurred. This change set in shortly after President Lyndon Johnson acceded to

[12] One could not go on inveighing against "mass culture" while praising a new radicalism which includes hipsterism, the Beatles, pot and acid rock, and being covered with buttons like a "Pearly."

power. The first triumphs of the Negro civil rights movement had raised hopes and then led to frustrations. The "poor" were discovered — not the working classes who remained written off as the brutish enjoyers of mass culture and who were now regarded as gross, unthinking supports of the existing order — but the lumpenproletariat who have never enjoyed such a good press as in the past five years. The flowery rhetoric and ill-natured bearing of President Johnson reawakened the dormant animosities of the American intellectuals towards the plebeian professional politician. The failure of the military leadership of the country to bring the war in Vietnam to a successful conclusion broke the attachment to authority that had grown up among American intellectuals when American power appeared supreme in the world.

The affirmative attitude that had been so common before Johnson's election was not solely a product of the perception in American society of values — moral, aesthetic, and political — that were part of the intellectuals' internal traditions. It had also been the result of their attraction to strong and effective power, which has always been characteristic of intellectuals. At a time when America was only a province of the great European world and when the political and economic elites were indifferent and even sometimes hostile toward literary and humanistic intellectuals, American intellectuals saw no merit in those who ruled American society. When, however, they were taken to the bosom of those who exercised power and when those leaders seemed to be the most powerful elite the world had known, American intellectuals found much to be pleased with in their situation and in the situation of their country. Once the power began to falter, however, to be not merely unsuccessful in action but perplexed and lacking in decisiveness and self-confidence, numerous intellectuals — literary, publicistic, scientific, and humanistic — decided that the American political elites were no longer worthy of their affection. No condemnation could be strong enough. It was not simply the older accusations of vulgarity and venality and indifference to "life's finer things." The accusations were more bitter. The accusation of "genocide" became the coin of the intellectuals' realm — "genocide" at home and abroad. In its more extreme forms, in the view of Noam Chomsky for example, any performance of a governmental service was culpable.

What was striking about the hyperbolically acrimonious criticism of the post-1965 alienation was its relationship to the older traditions of intellectual alienation. The first initiators of the new alienation had been either socialists of the tradition who had abstained from the incorporation into and from affirmation of the center — *Dissent* and Michael Harrington, or Stalinoids like Paul Sweezy, the late Leo

Huberman, and I. F. Stone, who had survived the hard times of the late 1940's and the 1950's and 1960's. The new alienation, once it was in full spate, found many of its main bearers among those who had little connection with the older tradition of alienation. The durability and toughness of the non-Marxist tradition of alienation which came back into a strength fuller than ever after a period of attrition that had lasted for more than a quarter of a century, was striking.[13]

Bohemianism has often been associated with the revolutionaries' antagonism to the existing political and social orders. The new alienation has broadened this relationship. The aesthetic side is far more prominent than in past movements of political alienation. The greater prominence of the aesthetic element has greatly extended and modified the social sources of affiliation to the movement of alienation. Jazz commentators, mod journalists, television comedians, packagers of fun goods, specialists in pornography, cartoonists, interior decorators, "young people" in publishing, advertising executives — all responsive to the fluctuations in style — are new recruits to alienation. To these are joined the "new class" of college and university teachers, clergymen, Negro or Black intellectuals, liberated women, and the university and college students — the very vanguard of the whole movement.

The clergy in the United States, leaving out the self-designated preachers in store-front churches and those who bash the Bible and froth at the mouth in berating the Devil, form an important component in the present-day disorder of the intellectuals. With the aid of Deweyan naturalism, "demythologization," and existentialism, having disposed of their deity or at least placed him in a weak position, Protestant clergymen in the United States have been suffering from the intellectual equivalent of technological unemployment. Superior in attitude toward their benighted flocks, displaced by atheism and psychiatry from the cure of souls, they were for a long time at loose ends. The tradition of "social Christianity" did not arouse their enthusiasm. With the Negro civil rights movement, however, they found something to do; with the war in Vietnam they found much else to do. Reinforced by restless Roman Catholic priests from whom the hand of authority had been lifted and by a rabbinate of doubting piety — all

---

[13] It is true that Marxism has had a small revival, but that has come in a roundabout way rather than through the direct filiation of tradition. It is in part a consequence of revival to halflife of the Communist Party, which has made the writings of Marx and Engel available through its publishing house and partly as a result of the diversity and intellectual randomness of the younger left. It is also a product of the elevation to fame of Professor Marcuse, whose sexual doctrines seem more attractive than his Marxism.

fearful of not being in tune with the times — the clergy has reentered the public life of the intellectual classes.

Negro intellectuals for the first time in American history have gained the attention of the white intellectuals. In the past, worthy Negro intellectuals knocked in vain at the doors of American intellectual life, but outside socialist and communist circles, few attended to them. Then in a short time a handful of Negro intellectuals — a few with some genuine talent, most with little talent and the beneficiaries of a forced levy — appeared on the scene. Their passionate abuse of American society could not have come at a luckier time — without the audience of white intellectuals they could not have been so encouraged.

Finally, the students in higher educational institutions should be mentioned. In an age that praises youthfulness with fewer qualifications than devout Marxists used to praise the working classes, university and college students got whatever benefits there were in being both youthful and intellectual. The hostility against authority — characteristic of adolescence, and in America adolescence is prolonged — was reinforced by their elders' chorus of denunciation of authority — including their own — and by the supineness of authority, both academic and governmental.

When one looks over the list of the alienated one finds that many share one major characteristic of the amateur politician pointed out by Max Weber; they are "wirtschaftlich abkömmlich." [14] Many are not employed at all, or employed irregularly. They have no fixed working hours in general; they come and go as they please. They are more prosperous than the lawyers without briefs and physicians without patients whom Marx saw as the supporters of his rivals. They have much leisure and much flexibility in their work schedules, where they work at all. From all this comes some of their sense of affinity with the *lumpenproletariat*. It also renders them easily available for their characteristic political technique, the demonstration and the mass meeting. The consequence of all this is a spiral of mutually reinforcing animosity against their own society, combining withdrawal and aggressiveness.

The period of incorporation and affirmation generated two convictions among the intellectuals who participated in it. The first — bred by experience and propaganda — was that intellectuals were indispensable to America's functioning. The second, based on this, was that intellectuals were in a crucial position because in various ways the authorities of society were dependent on them. From having felt unwanted and unused, intellectuals moved to the opposite extreme

14 Max Weber, *Politik als Beruf*, 2nd ed. (Munich and Leipzig: Duncker and Humblot, 1926), p. 16.

of a conviction of indispensability. The conviction of indispensability
has been fully compatible with hostility toward those who seem to
deny the rights that come with indispensability. A belief in the power
to command by demonstrative demand has arisen.

PERMEATION OF THE ALIENATED OUTLOOK

The movement from a sense of nullity in making decisions to a sense
of weightiness has not been undone by the movement from denial to
affirmation and back to denial. For one thing, a great many intellectuals have not made the return journey to denial; many have remained
in the positions of authority in decision-making at or connected with
the institutional centers of American society. Economists and scientific
advisors are firmly entrenched and cannot be done away with. They
are, however, simply continuations of positions and outlooks consolidated during the years between 1933 and 1965.

The persistence of the civil attitudes is also evident in its deforma-
tion. The passionate deniers think that they should be part of the
existing central institutional system, which is unique in the history of
the critique of authority. Furthermore the expectations of the deniers
are rendered plausible because they have in fact benefitted by some
partial success in establishing their own view of the matter at the
center where the authority is exercised.[15]

An "intellectualization" of public life has taken place in the United
States. Some values of the alienated intellectuals have become established in the circles of authority. The centuries-long process of the
"civilization" of authority, which entailed authority's becoming modest
in its self-legitimization, restrained in its public declaration of its
claims, responsive in its sensibility to the demands of those it ruled,
has now gone a step further. Elites now quail before the charges of
"elitism." Maintaining law and order and enforcing law, which political and administrative elites have always in the past taken as their
first charge, and which are indeed inseparable from maintaining society and protecting its members, have become matters about which
those who rule are shamefaced. Preventing riots or their restraint, suppression, and dispersal when they do occur, have become thought of
as inadmissible — although in practice they remain drastic and sometimes harsh. Judges and publicists acknowledge a right of violent
demonstration as part of freedom of expression and as a legitimate
procedure when constitutionally provided procedures are unsatisfac-
tory or not immediately effective. In principle and to a great extent,
in fact, the legitimacy of dissent, derived from the freedom of expres-

15 I cite at random the recent opinion of Judge Wyzanski on conscientious objection and the numerous pronouncements of Mr. Justice W. O. Douglas.

sion, is granted even where it involves coercive action and the disruption of institutions.

Penetration of the alienated intellectuals' outlook occurs in a two-fold process. The first, the recruitment of intellectuals with alienated outlooks, is part of the general process of the increased recruitment of intellectuals into intellectual-executive roles. Because the alienated antiauthority outlook is so widespread among the younger generation of intellectuals and those in humanistic and social sciences from where the recruits were drawn, it is only to be expected that in the mass communications, the universities, and in government, too, despite persistent "security clearance" practice, the new recruits bear with them some influence of the alienated outlook. Through their influence as speechwriters and as "idea men," as research workers and as staff members of special investigative commissions, authority has come often to speak — if not equally often to act — in accordance with the voice of the alienated intellectual.

There has also been a penetration into the outlook of incumbents of traditional authoritative roles who themselves are not intellectuals or who, even if intellectuals, have up until recently espoused outlooks conventional to those in authority, the crucial element of which is the belief in the legitimacy of their own authority. For one thing, since the 1950's the sociological sciences have come to dominate this idiom of discourse on public events, not only the terminology but the conceptions of causation and motivation as well as the implicit political outlook of workers in these fields. In addition, intellectuals in the United States have become demonstrators — not by rational argument — but by standing in public places, by covering themselves in buttons and badges, by signing petitions and public declarations. They have come to fill the air and the press. Politicians have been in some measure responsive to this clamor. They have been increasingly deferential to intellectuals ever since the end of the war and the atomic scientists' movement. It was noticeable ever since World War Two in the deference accorded scientists when they testified before congressional committees; the McCarthy procedures were rearguard actions in this respect. The politicians' fear of being out of step with the view they think to be prevalent gives resonance to the demands of the alienated intellectuals.

Because the alienated intellectuals, like ideologists and radicals everywhere, cannot be completely alienated, their claims take the form of the intensification and underscoring of certain elements already present in the central value system of American society. The values of substantive equality are intensified at the expense of the value of an equivalence between reward and exertion. The value of majority rule has long been transformed by a clamorous insistence into the supremacy of uncriticizably virtuous "people," which means, in the vocabulary of those who clamor, numerous Negroes, Puerto Ricans, discontented females, and rebellious university students. The value of individuality has been intensified into the value of the immediate gratification of spontaneous impulse.

Because of this affinity between the central value system and the ideologically exacerbated interpretation of certain elements of this system, the political and publicistic elites who are not often very subtle and who are sometimes easily disoriented, regard these claims as plausible and consistent with what they believed before.

There is more to it than this. Many politicians — omitting the cavemen — feel inferior to intellectuals. They might behave rudely towards them as President Johnson often did, but the same President Johnson after his retirement said that he had not felt qualified to lead the country effectively because he had not gone to one of the major universities. He implied that because of this he could not command the respect of those who had done so.

The mass communications show a similar success for their intellectuals. Although alienated radicals in all countries in the twentieth century have criticized the conduct of the communications media — whether privately or governmentally owned — where they have had the freedom to express their views, the situation today is much different from what it was before World War Two. Although there is still much criticism of the privately owned press in the United States, alienated intellectuals are still strongly represented within the institutions of the press. It is similar in television. The professional tradition of muckraking, the tradition of reportorial vigor, the tradition of sensationalism, and the maxim that "good news is no news" all mean that disorder, failure, and catastrophe are given the greatest prominence. Sympathy with disorder, out of sympathy with its perpetrators and the cause which it purportedly serves, cause the disorder to be much attended to in the mass media.

In book publishing, which is centered mainly in New York, practically all publishers and editors and other intellectuals who are members of the industry are permeated by the alienated outlook, either from conviction or from the desire to be stylish or because of the belief that the spirit of the age requires it. The far-reaching relaxation of censorship and the inclusion of sexual polymorphousness and publicity as part of the culture of the new strata of the alienated intellectuals, as well as some of their older outriders and followers, give the intellectuals in the publishing industry a commercial interest as well as a cultural one in being "with it." Many are reluctant to publish any book that criticizes the alienated view of American society, again out of conviction or from fear of being out of fashion.[16]

The universities, as has been indicated, have become the scene and seedbed of the intellectual life in the United States. Not only do they carry on the traditional functions of the universities of training for the learned, practical-intellectual professions and conducting pure research, but they have accepted the burdens of applied research for government, training for numerous not-so-learned occupations, performed numerous tasks that governments should properly have performed themselves, and provided the support for little magazines and for other activities that in the past were in the bohemian sphere. All these miscellaneous actions, encouraged and applauded on the outside, led to and fed on a form of *Grössenwahn* among university authorities. All this expansion should, one might have thought, been the work of strong characters. Nothing could have been more erroneous. Many of the great university and college administrators who presided over the vast expansion of universities in the indiscriminate service of American society have turned out to be characterless weathervanes facing whichever way the wind blew.

The release of animosity against authority, beginning with the murder of John F. Kennedy, first manifested itself on a trivial issue at the University of California in Berkeley. The University of California after its recovery from the ravages of the loyalty oath controversy had been one of the major pillars of the new structure of co-operation of authority and the intellectuals. Its administrators and teachers were full of pride, justified pride, over their accomplishments. Yet, with the first onslaught, it fell into disorder. The teachers fell out with each other, the presidents and deans were thrown into confusion. The "rightfulness" of the students' cause called forth much support, and those who denied it could not bring the university back to where it was. Similar events occurred with increasing frequency over the ensuing half decade. Finally, even Harvard, which had rebuffed McCarthy, fell before its students. It was only to be expected that the universities which had helped to generate so much of the new culture should be so riddled by it. Presidents, deans, professors, from conviction or cowardice, fell for obviously nonsensical arguments. No authorities under attack had ever gone so far in flattering and beslavering their insatiable antagonists and attempting to placate them.

---

[16] Professor Mathew Hodgart's Swiftian parable of the events at Cornell University in 1969 was refused by thirteen American publishers before it was finally accepted. The book had already been accepted for publication in Great Britain.

ANTIPOLITICAL ACTIVISM

American intellectuals, even more than most intellectuals in most other countries, have inherited an antipolitical tradition. What they have received from their intellectual forebears and what they themselves teach and believe outside scientific research fosters an antipolitical, anticivil outlook. The very favorable structural circumstances of three decades — indulgence by the center, occupational opportunities at the center, and centrality in the world — had put this tradition into the margins of the mind. The first and the third of these circumstances were modified by the deterioration of President Johnson's demeanor in consequence of the resultlessness of the Vietnam war. The tradition reasserted itself when the major politician of the country was rude in tone and ineffective in action. But whereas the older tradition was one of antipolitical withdrawal, the new disposition, although remaining antipolitical, has been far more active. One variant of it resembled, after the outburst of civil political energy on behalf of Robert Kennedy and then Eugene McCarthy, the new politics of the intellectuals under Franklin Roosevelt. The politics of the intellectuals under the New Deal were not electoral or party politics but rather political activity carried on in advisory and counselling capacities under the auspices of a powerful political personage. Some political activists among intellectuals do not now seek electoral office any more now than they did then. They seek programs and grants paid for by the public treasury to work against the government.

Another variant of the new antipolitical politics is part of an older tradition: demonstration. The technique of demonstration was not an intellectual's device until the intellectuals and the communists came together under the auspices of Willi Münzenberg. Demonstrations have now been given up by the working classes because they have trade unions to represent their interests; demonstrations have become once more part of the technique of those who regard themselves as outside the central institutional system in which interests are represented and compromised.

The activist element is at its most extreme in violent, disruptive demonstrations, where the aim is to prevent an institution, usually a defenseless one like a university or a church, from functioning normally. Although there is much talk of power in intellectual circles, the new politics of the intellectuals do not seem to aim to accede to positions of authority either in the existing system or in a new, revolutionarily established system. Hating it and denying its legitimacy as they do, they still seem to acquiesce to its factuality. They seem to count on its continued existence and they anticipate its responsiveness to abusive influence, rather than to influence within consensus. In that sense, the new revolutionary intellectuals — there are some exceptions of course — seem themselves to be the victims of the tentacular powers of the center.

CONFLICT CONTAINMENT
IN PRESENT-DAY SOCIETY

Can a modern society maintain a stable and orderly structure when the political elites and those other sectors of the elite who share power with them have lost their self-confidence and are dominated by a clamorous hostility against that society and those who rule it? An elite that wavers and abdicates the responsibility which is inherent in the roles it fills becomes uncertain of its entitlement to legitimacy. If it cannot claim legitimacy for the actions it undertakes, its actions will be ineffective. Ineffectiveness on the part of an elite breeds disrespect and the refusal of legitimacy. No society, least of all one as complicated as present-day American society, which is so difficult to govern under the best of circumstances, can survive in its ongoing form nor can it develop peacefully from that form if its central institutional system has lost its legitimacy. American society is a noisy and violent society, even in good times. In bad times like the present, it strains the capacities of even the best government.

The containment of conflict in a culture so consecrated to gratifying demands has always been difficult. The institutionalization of class conflict — a by no means perfect institutionalization — was a great accomplishment of the Roosevelt and subsequent administrations. Its continuation depends on the continued legitimacy of authority in government, business enterprises, and trade unions. The evaporation of legitimacy renders the continued institutionalization more problematic than it has been for about a third of a century. Inflation and the demonstration-effect of the successful pursuit of expanded demands place the machinery of collaboration of classes under a heavy burden. The sight of successfully affronted authority is a great stimulant to antinomian impulses.

The ineptitude of governmental institutions in the face of ethnic conflicts — an ineptitude arising from serious disagreements within the government on the merits of the claims and how to treat them, diminished self-confidence in dealing with violence, and particularly violence by some thousands of university students and by a section of the Negro population, whose legitimate moral claims have been usurped and exaggerated by a small, violently inclined group — has further eroded legitimacy.

The inconclusiveness of the Vietnam war has damaged the legitimacy of the federal government more than any other factor. The Russian Czarist government, incompetent and ineffective even in a time of peace, was shaken by revolution (in 1905) only after military defeat at the hands of the Japanese. It was finally overthrown following its disasters on the battlefield in the first two and a half years of World War One.

The Habsburg monarchy was a ramshackle political system but it decomposed only after defeat in World War One. The Hohenzollern regime in Germany was among the most stable in the world until its defeat by the Allies in World War One. The German revolutionaries were feeble indeed — witness the weakness of their creation, the Weimar Republic — but the *ancien régime* had lost its legitimacy. Similarly, the legitimacy of the National Socialist regime that had been so firm in 1943 began to falter when the German allies suffered their first great reverses at Stalingrad and in North Africa.

In short, governments that lose wars are governments that have undertaken to do more than they can. A war is an undertaking that involves national identity, and as such it touches on the deepest roots of the acknowledgement of legitimacy. The loss of a war endangers the real and the symbolic existences of the entire national community and it thereby weakens the readiness to acknowledge the right to rule of those who have taken to themselves the care of the name and safety of that national community.

The American government has not lost the war. It has, however, not won it, and that is almost as bad in some respects because it drags on and on and brings with it an inflation that injures most classes of the population, above all those who are otherwise the most faithful devotees of the legitimacy of government. It also exacerbates class conflict through the continuous demand for higher wages, resulting in strikes and service disruption. All that in turn weakens the legitimacy of government, by further revealing and emphasizing its ineffectiveness.

In this situation of weakened legitimacy, the alienation of the now-pervasive intellectual classes is of consequence. Had intellectuals continued to be as marginal as they were forty years ago both in their functional roles and in their symbolic prominence and appreciation, their alienation would not concern any one but themselves and students of their attitudes. As it is, however, the question merits further scrutiny.

First, the alienation in question here is not universal among intellectuals. Large sections of the intellectual classes do not share in it. Those in the practical-intellectual professions are less alienated than those in the primarily intellectual professions. Those in the scientific and technological professions are less alienated than those in the social science, literary, and humanistic professions. Even in the latter professions, among the social scientists, for example, the economists and the political scientists are less alienated than the sociologists and anthropologists; in the humanistic subjects those concerned with English and American literary studies are most alienated. Certain Negro intellectuals are among the most vociferous, but there are many who do not receive publicity and who are less alienated, although no less critical of the traditional treatment and position of the Negro in American society. The younger generations, especially students in higher educational institutions, are more alienated than the older generations.

The volume of echo that white intellectuals give to the most radical Negroes is likely to diminish, partly because those who do the echoing are creatures of fashion and do not sustain any fashion for long. If this occurs, the more radical Negro intellectuals will have less resonance and their pressure on the more moderate ones will decrease. They will shrink into conspiratorial circles and will be subject not to the laws of movement of intellectual opinion but to those of the security services. These developments depend in part on the capacity of the political and administrative elites to regain control of their nerves and to discriminate between destructive actions and reasonable demands for improvement. It depends on the avoidance of exciting rhetoric. It depends most of all on the restoration of effectiveness and on the image of effectiveness by the government. It depends above all on bringing the Vietnam war to an end, and managing this without generating in sectors of the political elite and in the society at large a "stab-in-the-back" legend.

The intellectuals, sensitive as they are to power, would respond by a renewal of their sense of affinity, as they did under Franklin Roosevelt, even though there is a strong prejudice against any Republican administration. In addition, it should be pointed out that at present, in the ranks of the alienated intellectuals, the most alienated are primarily concentrated in the functionally most marginal roles. Economists and engineers are more important to society than students and teachers and research workers in sociology and English and American literature. Their danger to social stability arises more from their role in the mass communications than from any "direct action" they can take from the inside as a member of executive roles or from the outside as demonstrators and bomb-throwers. Nonetheless, in the present period when intellectuals possess so much prestige and many politicians are inclined to listen to them so deferentially, the most vociferous and most demonstrative, especially in the Negro-white collaboration, are capable of making demands and accusations that rattle the established political and administrative elite; and cause them either to lose self-confidence or to react in an extremely aggressive and repressive manner. Either response threatens to weaken the legitimacy of the established elite among those intellectuals who are inclined to give it the benefit of the doubt; it neutralizes them, weakens their civility, or makes them more sympathetic with the more extremely alienated.

Yet, the fact remains that the American economy — despite the burden of inflation — continues to operate with a most extraordinary effectiveness. The business elite, despite concessions here and there to the mounting lunacy, is more archaic in sentiment and ethos. The leaders of the trade unions continue with an unruffled "business as usual" demeanor. It comes down therefore to whether the political elites in the federal government and in the big cities can reequilibrate themselves, regain their equanimity, reassert themselves by placing confidence in those sections of the population that support them and show initiative in bringing about some noticeable improvement, and in so doing, resume a steady course.

It is a far from easy task. It is encumbered on one side by an alliance with politicians of an irreconcilable outlook, particularly regarding ethnic questions; it is encumbered on the other by many within its own ranks who have been overrun by extremely alienated intellectuals who claim to speak on behalf of "people." What is called for is the reestablishment of a sovereignty deriving ultimately and through representative institutions from "the people" and the reduction of the direct ascendancy of "people," i.e., the "plebiscitary" democracy of a small minority.

The transformation of American society in which authoritative roles came to be linked more intimately with intellectual roles had two major consequences: it brought about the partial suspension of the hostility of the intellectual elites towards the nonintellectual or authority-exercising elites, i.e., toward the executive elites in the broadest sense. It also brought about the incorporation of the intellectuals into a closer and more collaborative relationship with the executive elites. In the course of this intellectuals came in various ways to have great influence on American culture and social structure.

The incorporation of the intellectuals into the center and institutional system is now integral to the structure of American society. The penumbral traditions of the intellectuals have however retained their vitality despite their several decades of submergence, and in the recent troubles of the political, administrative, and military elites, the tradition of alienation has been reactivated. This time, however, as a result of the structural incorporation of the intellectuals into the center of American society, their cultural influence has been great. As a result, the legitimacy of the executive elites — a cultural phenomenon — has been impaired and the effectiveness of these elites has been further damaged with a resultant further deterioration of their legitimacy.

The stability of American society has thus come to depend upon a sector of the society that lives in a tradition of alienation, part of which, in its extreme form, is historically contingent and part of which is almost self-generating in the primary culture of the intellectual role. At the same time, it should be observed that the primary culture of the intellectuals is increasingly generated in academic institutions where there is a delicately poised and not always equally stable balance between, on one hand, a discipline that acknowledges at least the authority of its own traditions and of the institutions which sustain them, and, on the other, a more antinomian and expressive culture. This antinomian culture has a long and deep tradition that developed before it came within academic confines. The stability of the larger society depends, therefore, on maintaining, within the culture and the institutional system of the intellectuals, the predominance of that element which accepts an objective discipline and the integration of academic institutions into the central institutional system of American society.

Proposing a thoroughgoing functional definition of ideology as an inherent constituent of all social systems, Professor Barber indicates the tendencies to variability and evolutionary change in ideological systems themselves in (1) differentiation from other subsystems, (2) generalization or degree of abstraction, (3) systematization, and (4) comprehensiveness. He points also to the variability and change in the role of the ideologist, primarily in its differentiation from other social roles. Finally, Professor Barber examines the role of ideology in the general processes of stability and change in social systems, concluding that ideology may contribute to either one and may be taken as an independent or dependent variable in explaining any process of stability or change. Professor Barber illustrates his theoretical analysis with empirical materials from historical studies and from contemporary public opinion surveys.

Bernard Barber

FUNCTION, VARIABILITY, AND CHANGE IN IDEOLOGICAL SYSTEMS

Although the phenomenon to which it refers is as old and continuing as human social systems, the concept of ideology (and indeed the word itself) is a modern one. Born of the French Revolution and of Napoleon's conflict with his critics, the concept has become pandemic in the language of modern social and political discussion. Everyone, it would sometimes seem, in some terminology or other now talks about ideology: the man in the street, the sociologist and political scientist, the philosopher, and, of course, the ideologist.[1] In all this discussion, there is, inevitably, a modicum of agreement on a defi-

[1] The terminological variants for ideology include such terms as fables, doctrines, lore, myth, beliefs, dreams, mystiques, rhetoric, and so forth. For example, Richard Hofstadter, in *The Age of Reform* (New York: Knopf, 1955), chap. 1, "The Agrarian Myth and Commercial Realities," gives an excellent discussion of an important American ideology.

244

nition of ideology, but the degree of agreement is far less than enough to make the term an easy and accepted entry in the lexicon of social-scientific discourse.[2] Our first task in this essay, therefore (an essay which, because of its brevity, must be viewed also as a prospect for a larger work), must be to establish a definition of ideology that helps us to understand its stable and its changing forms and functions in social systems. With such a definition, we can achieve a better scientific analysis of such other problems as: the variable relations between ideology and other essential functional components of social systems; the variability in the structure of ideological systems themselves; the variability in the role of the ideologist, that is, in the task of making and disseminating ideologies; and, finally, the variable effects of ideology, as against the other essential functional components of social systems, in causing or obstructing change in such systems.[3]

TOWARD A FUNCTIONAL RATHER THAN SUBSTANTIVE DEFINITION OF IDEOLOGY

One persistent and nearly universal difficulty in establishing a social-scientific definition and understanding of ideology has been the

[2] This point is made in many quarters. See, for example, the Introduction by David E. Apter in *Ideology and Discontent*, ed. David E. Apter (New York: The Free Press, 1964), esp. p. 15. See also George Lichtheim, "The Concept of Ideology," *History and Theory*, vol. 4 (1965), p. 164, where he says, in a learned article discussing Destutt de Tracy, Condillac, Helvetius, Hegel, Kant, Feuerbach, Marx, Comte, Durkheim, Weber, Nietzsche, Schopenhauer, Mannheim, and Lukacs, all important contributors to the discussion of ideology: "Few concepts play a larger part in present-day discussions of historical and political topics than does that of ideology, and yet it is not always clear what meaning is applied to the term by those who employ it."

[3] The two largest influences on the analysis of ideology developed here, though they will be among the first to point out differences between us, are Talcott Parsons, *The Social System* (New York: The Free Press, 1951), chap. 8, "Belief Systems and the Social System: The Problem of the Role of Ideas"; and Clifford Geertz, "Ideology as a Cultural System," in *Ideology and Discontent*, ed. David E. Apter. See also Francis X. Sutton, Seymour E. Harris, Carl Kaysen, and James Tobin, *The American Business Creed* (Cambridge: Harvard University Press, 1956). See further the two articles on ideology in the *International Encyclopedia of the Social Sciences* (New York: Macmillan and Free Press, 1968), one by Edward Shils and the other by Harry M. Johnson. None of these analyses rids itself entirely of a substantive definition of ideology, though Geertz goes farthest in this direction. On substantive and functional definitions of ideology, see the next section of this essay. Finally, for a very useful historical account of the concept of ideology, see Norman Birnbaum, *The Sociological Study of Ideology, 1940–1960: A Trend Report and Bibliography*, prepared for the International Sociological Association, with the support of UNESCO (Oxford: Blackwell, 1962).

practice of defining ideology in substantive terms rather than in uncompromisingly functional terms. In this practice, ideology has been defined by the substantive character of the content of ideological statements: whether these statements are, in substance, scientifically true or false or mixed; whether they are logically consistent or inconsistent; whether they are systematically interrelated or not; whether they are "one-sided" and "distorted" or "total" and "comprehensive"; whether they are concrete and sloganistic or highly abstract and sophisticatedly intellectual. Our position is that all these substantive differences may be important for some purposes, some of which we will take up later, but they are not important for indicating the *differentia specifica* of ideology.

The *essential defining characteristic* of ideology, for social-scientific purposes, is its functional role in social systems, its role of justifying or criticizing the value and norm preferences that have to be expressed at nearly every point in the action occurring in social systems. If a statement has this function in social systems — whether its substantive content is scientific or not or partly so, whether it is inconsistent or not, whether it is systematic or not, and whether it is "distorted" or not — then it is to be scientifically described as an ideology under this definition. To be sure, because those expressing or creating ideologies are often strongly committed to justifying or criticizing some value or norm preference, the ideologies they use and develop are often a jumble from any substantive scientific or logical point of view. Ideologies concretely are made up of a mixture of scientifically valid, scientifically indeterminate, and scientifically invalid statements and of a mixture of logically consistent and logically inconsistent statements. Although there are intellectual and social pressures against such jumbles, there are also strong pressures for using and creating them from the forces of the ideological function itself.

However, statements of quite different substance, the one more scientific, the other much less so, may have the identical ideological function in a specified context in a social system, namely, the justifying or criticizing of a value or norm preference in that context. For example, a more scientific statement and a much less scientific one about the genetic characteristics of Negroes compared to whites will both have an ideological function if they are presented to justify or criticize some choice that a body politic as a whole or one of its legislative agencies is seeking to make either about the value of equality in general (for all human beings) or about the norm of equality for whites and Negroes in schools, or work, or public facilities. In another social context, that of the forum of scientific discussion, where there is no reference to a value or norm preference for social policy, these two statements will be described in terms of their relative scientific validity, their relative consistency, their relative degree of systematization, and other substantively scientific and logical characteristics. These scientific and logical characteristics may have some effects on a statement that can be described as ideological because it can be shown to have justifying or criticizing functions in a value preference context. But, by themselves, they are not essential characteristics of an ideology.

Because the essential function of ideologies is to justify or criticize one value or norm preference possibility as against some other possibility, we will find that concrete ideologies contain a mixture of positive and negative implications and explicit statements. Statements by implication only will prevail where an ideology is well established and where there are no felt challenges to it. In new or not well-institutionalized ideologies, both the positive and the negative statements in the mixture will be more explicit. Whether implicit or explicit, the mixture of positive and negative statements is required by the function of an ideology. Where one value or norm preference is being justified, its opposites or alternatives have to be criticized to strengthen the positive justification. Thus, in an ideology justifying the value of equality, not only will some statements show the advantages of this value, but also some statements will detail the social disadvantages of the value and practice of inequality. And where a prevailing value or norm preference is being criticized, an admixture of positive statements will justify some alternative preference and thereby strengthen the criticism. Thus, Marxism does not merely criticize the inequality of Capitalism ("the capitalist" vs. "the proletariat") and its lack of freedom ("the wage slave") but it describes and praises its own creation of a breed of "new men," who will be both completely equal and completely free.[4] A dramatic statement of the positive-negative polarity of Marxism and Capitalism, a statement for which a counterpart on the other side could easily be found, is Lenin's statement:

> the only choice is: either the bourgeois or the socialist ideology. There is no middle ideology, and, moreover, in a society torn by class antagonisms there can never be a non-class or above-class ideology. Hence to belittle the socialist ideology *in any way, to turn away from it in the slightest degree,* means to strengthen the bourgeois ideology.[5]

[4] For the Soviet version of the symbol and ideology of the "new man," see Raymond A. Bauer, *The New Man in Soviet Psychology* (Cambridge: Harvard University Press, 1952).

[5] V. I. Lenin, "What Is to Be Done," *Selected Works,* vol. 1, part 1 (Moscow: Foreign Language Publishing House, 1950), p. 242. Emphasis in original. Cited in Daniel Bell, "Marxism-Leninism: a Doctrine on the Defensive — The 'End of

Lewis Coser has coined the generic term "salvation abroad" to describe the ideological situation in which intellectuals criticize their own society or historical period by praising some other society or historical period. The two examples he treats intensively are "the admiration for Russia and China among a wide group of French intellectuals of the Enlightenment and the Russophilia of English and American intellectuals during the 1930's." [6] Of course, in the opposite phenomenon of "hell abroad," ideologists praise the values of their own time or place by criticizing those of another time or place. American Russophobia during the Cold War period was an example of the "hell abroad" ideological pattern.

Whence the essential function of ideology and hence of ideologies themselves? The functional origin of ideology, it would seem, lies in the basic fact that human social action and human social systems are systems of possible choice between valued alternatives. Compared to the action of other animal species, with at least a very large relative degree of difference, human action endlessly involves choice points. These choice points occur at innumerable phases of action in all types of social system, large or small, societal or dyadic, comprehensive in scope and functions or more limited therein. Choice is ubiquitous and continuing in social system process, and so also are the values and norms that express the patterned principles of these choices. It follows that ideology, defined as the statements that have the function of justifying or criticizing the value and norm choices that have been made, is ubiquitous and continuing in human social systems. In a more scientific discourse about ideology, if we cannot purge the present term of its connotations of "good" and "bad," we might adopt a term like "value-preference-justifications (criticisms)," which is intended to emphasize the functional character of ideological statements and to play down the moralizing about them by different parties as "good" or "bad." Ideology, or value-preference-justifications, will come to be a more valuable term in the social-scientific lexicon when it is accepted that we are dealing with an essential and general function of social systems and not with something that is, in principle, "good" or "bad."

In this sense, then, that the essential characteristics of human social systems require it, ideology is a stable and persistent element in all such systems. In this sense, it is obvious, there could be no "end of

---

Ideology' in the Soviet Union?" in *The Appeals and Paradoxes of Contemporary Marxism*, ed. M. N. Drachkovitch (New York: Frederick Praeger, 1966).

[6] Lewis A. Coser, *Men of Ideas: A Sociologist's View* (New York: The Free Press, 1965), pp. 143 ff.

ideology," a possibility that has been widely but not too fruitfully debated in recent years.[7] All that the assertion of an "end of ideology" could have meant was the provincial claim that some particular ideology (in this debate, chiefly Marxist socialism) was no longer accepted at all, or at least not with a former intensity of conviction, by some particular group. In the essential and general sociological sense, there can be no "end of ideology." Some of those who have substantive definitions of ideology do not, of course, share this conclusion. Especially those with a rationalistic, positivistic view of ideology, those who have defined ideology as bad science, eventually to be completely replaced by good science, might still see an eventual "end of ideology."[8] But, with a functional rather than a substantive definition, this view falls to the ground.

How do we scientifically establish the ideological function of a given statement, whatever its substance? Anyone who insists on a functional definition of ideology must ask himself this question. It is certainly a question which anti-functionalists will ask. Here, as elsewhere in functional analysis, how we establish or measure functionality is not an easy question to answer. That does not mean that it is not the scientific question to ask. Answers to the most important scientific questions are often not easy to answer. In such a situation we do not shift to other, less important questions. We strive to give the best answers we presently can and, further, we strive to improve our answers. We may even accept it as a scientific challenge that the effort to make such improvement will help us in the general social-scientific task of working out better indicators of the existence of functionality in various social contexts.

In ideology, of course, the justificatory or critical function of certain statements is often easy to establish. This is the case in situations where statements are explicitly and self-consciously offered as value or norm justifications and where there is consensus among all the participants, *pro* and *con* a given value or norm, and among objective scientific observers as well that the particular statements do clearly have an ideological function. There are many such situations in

[7] See Daniel Bell, *The End of Ideology* (New York: The Free Press, 1960); and Bell, in Drachkovitch, *The Appeals and Paradoxes of Contemporary Marxism*, where he has qualified somewhat his original statements on the end of ideology in response to various critics.

[8] For a theoretical critique of such rationalistic positivism, see Talcott Parsons, *The Structure of Social Action* (New York: McGraw-Hill, 1937). For more substantive critiques of particular positivistic views, see Vilfredo Pareto, *The Mind and Society*, 4 vols. (New York: Harcourt, Brace, 1935); and the views of L. J. Henderson in *L. J. Henderson on the Social System*, ed. Bernard Barber (Chicago: University of Chicago Press, 1970).

social systems, though because of the bad meaning in which the term "ideology" itself is usually taken, those who make functionally ideological statements are more willing to admit to the justificatory function than they are to describe themselves with this invidious term. Their "opponents," of course, are all too quick to use the term, hoping thereby to score a point in behalf of their value or norm preference.[9] As Clifford Geertz has nicely put it, "It is one of the minor ironies of modern intellectual history that the term 'ideology' has itself become thoroughly ideologized." [10]

But in some social contexts, it is not so easy to see the ideological function of statements. For example, wherever the relationship between means and end, between preference on the one hand and goal or policy or norm on the other, is not terribly clear, as it often is in social systems because of inadequate knowledge or because of the complexity of the system, then it may not be so easy to establish whether a statement is trying to describe such a situation in a relatively objective and orderly way or whether it is expressing a value preference. Much of the content of our daily conversation and of the mass media is of this character. It is also hard to establish functionality in those situations where the intentions of those making certain statements are not clearly expressed. Where intentions are obscure, it is necessary to clarify them before an ideological function can be imputed to those who make statements. We should note, of course, that functions do not have to be intended; they may be unintended as well. Thus, a scientist-teacher making a certain statement about the genetic equality of whites and Negroes, intending no reference to value or policy choices, may find that at least some of his students "hear" the statement as having a certain value or policy preference. A statement that for him has only scientific functions in that context may for some of his students have an ideological function because they are taking it in a different social system context. Much confusion and acrimony may arise in situations of this kind where there are

[9] Russians seem to be an exception in this respect. Because Marxism defines ideology as a general social-political phenomenon, determined in all societies by the structure of class relationships, the Russians gladly accept their own views and those of other societies as ideologies. Of course, they think of their own Marxist-Leninist ideologies as true and good, the ideologies of others as false and bad. For an illuminating discussion of this point, and a comparison with the negative American view of ideology, see Sbigniew Brzezinski and Samuel P. Huntington, *Political Power: USA/USSR* (New York, Viking, 1965, pp. 17–19).

[10] Geertz, "Ideology as a Cultural System," p. 47. Geertz goes on, pp. 49–50, to criticize the negative and implicitly or explicitly invidious definitions of ideology in the work of Werner Stark, Edward Shils, and Talcott Parsons, three modern sociological theorists of ideology.

different intended and unintended functions for the several participants in a social system. The social scientist must be aware of these
different possible functions and describe the situation accordingly.

There are various patterned sources, then, of difficulty in establishing ideological functions for some statements made in social interaction. But there are also patterned sources of relative ease in the same
task, and the difficulties can, both in principle and often in fact, be
dealt with. When social science accepts the definition of ideology as a
persistent and functional component of all social systems, and when
it then improves its methodology for describing and analyzing ideology, we shall have made significant progress in our understanding of
social systems in general.

THE EVOLUTIONARY VARIABILITY
OF IDEOLOGICAL SYSTEMS

Although ideology is analytically a persistent functional component of
all social systems, the relationships that its concrete expressions have
with the concrete forms of other types of idea-systems, is not unchanging. In social systems where there is a relative lack of differentiation
and specialization of the several functional components one from
another, the concrete forms of such various types of idea-systems as
science, ideology, philosophy, religion, and art are very much inter-
woven with one another. Thus, in primitive societies, even in our
primitive contemporaries, or in a society as undifferentiated as
Homeric Greece (witness *The Iliad* and *The Odyssey*), the "myths"
that are told by storytellers around the hearths and campfires and in
the public places are a mixture of what the sociological analyst can
see to be a relatively undifferentiated amalgam of poetry, history, science, cosmology, philosophy, religion, and ideology.

Only very gradually in the history of human social systems, as differentiation and specialization have evolved in one or more of these
idea-systems and in the various social-structural components of social
systems as well, have all these several types of idea-system even
partially become concretely differentiated out from one another. In
the history of science, for example, we see that in the analytic sense
science is a component of all social systems but that physical science
did not emerge as a highly differentiated type of idea-system until the
seventeenth century. Biological science, similarly, emerged only in the
nineteenth century, and social science in the twentieth.[11] In this same
evolutionary perspective, we may think of ideology as emerging in
highly differentiated form only in the beginning of the nineteenth

[11] See Bernard Barber, *Science and the Social Order* (New York: The Free
Press, 1952), esp. chaps. 2, 11.

century. This differentiation has proceeded rapidly during the last one hundred and fifty years, though it is far from being a completed process in any social system and is especially retarded in those systems where general differentiation and specialization have developed more slowly.

We can now understand a little more precisely what is meant when intellectuals sometimes refer to the modern era as "an age of ideology." It may or may not be the case that there is more ideology in the analytical sense than there was in earlier, traditional, less differentiated societies. Probably there is, though any measurement would be very difficult. Probably there is because a more differentiated society produces more choice points for which there have to be more values and norms and more ideologies. But certainly there is "more ideology" today in the sense that whatever there is of it is more highly differentiated out from science and religion, more visible as a differentiated system, and more explicitly the focus of development and controversy.

We should stress that the degree of concrete differentiation of one idea-system from another is a relative and varying matter even in modern social systems. Physical science is today relatively more differentiated out from religion than is social science, though the continuing conflict between religion and science in the seventeenth, eighteenth, nineteenth, and even early twentieth centuries indicates the difficulty, slowness, and variability with which this differentiation was achieved.[12] We shall have to expect that the differentiation of ideology from science, religion, and the other idea-systems will be similarly relative and varying. And probably we shall have to expect, because of the inevitable interaction of these different functional components in changing social systems, that differentiation will never be an absolute matter but only one of a little more and a little more as social science creates a better understanding of social systems and as the conditions in social systems make it possible for differentiation to occur.

VARIABILITY AND CHANGE IN THE STRUCTURE OF IDEOLOGICAL SYSTEMS

The structure of ideological systems varies not only in the relative degree of differentiation from other types of idea-systems, but along other dimensions as well. Like scientific or religious idea-systems, ideological systems may vary in the degree of their *abstractness* (or generalization, as it is sometimes called), their *systematization,* and

---

[12] For a brilliant account of the hard, slow process of differentiating natural science out from ideology and religion, see C. C. Gillispie, *The Edge of Objectivity* (Princeton: Princeton University Press, 1960).

their *comprehensiveness*. The criterion of abstractness is cognizant that ideological systems may range from the very concrete, for example, the justification of the equality norm in a particular dyadic social system, that of Mr. and Mrs. Smith or that of two friends, Jack and Joe, to the highly abstract and general, for example, the justification of the value of equality for *all* participants in *all* social systems in *any* time and in *any* place and of *any* size.

The systematization criterion refers to the extent to which the parts of a concrete ideology are consistently and explicitly interrelated with one another. An inconsistent or unsystematic ideology may not only have statements that are logically inconsistent with one another but, more important, sociologically inconsistent. Thus, an ideology that justifies equality for all is inconsistent if it then justifies inequality for some particular social category or group, such as a particular skin-color category or ethnic group or age bracket. In fact, concrete ideologies do vary considerably along this dimension. Some are a jumble of ill-related and inconsistent elements; others are the result of careful efforts to be explicit and consistent in the values and norms being justified or criticized.[13]

Finally, the criterion of comprehensiveness refers to the fact that concrete ideologies vary in the extent to which they concern themselves with the several subsystems of values and norms or "choice-points" of a given social system. In American society, for example, a thoroughly comprehensive ideology would concern itself with all aspects of "the American system." A less comprehensive one would be concerned only with husband-wife norms, or with the norms of family relations more generally, or with stratification or authority values in American society.[14] Again, in the world of concrete ideologies, we find this type of variation in degree of comprehensiveness.

In the modern world, especially in those social systems that are more differentiated and specialized in their component subsystems, we find that there are ideologies of all kinds when we order them along these three dimensions. A great many are concrete, unsystematic, and highly limited in scope. Some are abstract, systematic, but still highly limited in scope. And a few are highly abstract, systematic, and comprehensive. What is new, probably, in the modern

[13] For an account of the subtly but importantly greater systematization of social and political ideologies in Russia as compared with the United States, see Brzezinski and Huntington, *Political Power,* pp. 19 ff.

[14] For an abstract and systematic, though brief, discussion limiting itself to the authority and stratification values and ideologies in American society, see S. M. Lipset, "Revolution and Counter-Revolution — The United States and Canada," in *The Revolutionary Theme in Contemporary America,* ed. Thomas R. Ford (Lexington: University of Kentucky Press, 1965).

world, as compared with less differentiated societies, is that the tendency in making ideologies is to greater abstractness, systematization, and comprehensiveness. If nothing else would, the greater abstractness, systematization, and comprehensiveness of both natural and social science push ideology in this direction. The makers of ideology, although they do not always use what is available to them in science for their own purposes, can turn the more abstract, systematic, and comprehensive statements of science to their own functional ends.

But more than instrumental borrowing would seem to be involved. The values of generality, systematization, and comprehensiveness pervade all intellectual life in modern social systems. At least to intellectuals, if not to the man in the street, an ideology is better if it is more rather than less abstract, systematic, and comprehensive.[15] Perhaps this is another part of what people who describe modern times as "the age of ideology" have in mind, that never before has the tendency been so strong toward developing ideologies as highly abstract, systematic, and comprehensive justificatory statements for value preferences. Ideologies of this type are certainly more visible and may seem to be much more powerful. Highly abstract, systematic, and comprehensive ideologies such as Marxism or those for Capitalism (both idea-systems viewed here only in their function as ideologies and not also as scientific statements, which they may in part also be) are peculiar to the modern world. Such ideologies are what people have in mind when they speak of "the age of ideology." To many people, such ideologies seem to be entirely different and without any functional similarity to the highly concrete folk tales in which Homer poetically developed the intermixed ideologies, religion, and cosmology of ancient Greece.

One sociological consequence of developing more abstract, systematic, and comprehensive ideologies is that in a social system different ideological forms may now co-exist for the same values or norms. That is, even in a situation of value consensus, there may be "high-

[15] It should be remembered that "professional" ideologists are often writing as much for one another, those who agree with them and those who don't, as for those who are not ideologists at all and who are only one part of their intended audience. On the need to see professional ideologists as a group, interacting with one another both face-to-face and through print, see the classic work, Florian Znaniecki, *The Social Role of the Man of Knowledge* (New York: Columbia University Press, 1940). For an excellent use of some of these ideas of Znaniecki's, very well illustrated with historical and contemporary materials, see Lewis Coser, *Men of Ideas.*

brow," "middle-brow," and "low-brow" versions of the supporting ideologies.[16] A "high-brow" ideology for "the American system," for example, may take the form of an abstract, systematic, and comprehensive discussion that requires a whole book for its expression. A "low-brow" version may express itself in a set of concrete slogans, epithets, and cliché phrases.[17] Insofar as the different forms help to maintain a value consensus, the existence of these different forms is functional. But insofar as the different forms themselves stir mutual fear, hostility, and contempt in those who start from a value consensus, the consequence may be a dysfunctional weakening of the value consensus or an obscuring of what is held in common by the different forms in which it finds expression. An important task, then, in societies where ideologies are structured in various forms along the dimensions of abstractness, systematization, and comprehensiveness is to translate and interpret the various forms one into another for the benefit of those who might lose sight of actual value consensus because of more visible differences of form. "Middle-brow" newspapers, news magazines, television and radio programs, and other forms of public communication probably play a large role in this task of interpretation and translation between "high-brows" and "low-brows," though they do not always find it easy to deal either between these two categories or indeed with either one on their own behalf in an entirely satisfactory way. There are strains in communication between each possible pair of these three categories. Value and ideological consensus is somewhat weakened by the different forms of expression and communication in the three categories.

VARIABILITY AND CHANGE
IN THE ROLE OF THE IDEOLOGIST

All participation in all social systems involves the endless expressing and creating of ideologies. Human interaction systems are a continuing process of making commitments to value and norm preferences

[16] Note the significance of such similar terms as "high culture" and "mass culture," used much by high-brow intellectuals when declaring their ideologies about the superiority of the one to the other. See Winston White, *Beyond Conformity* (New York: The Free Press, 1961).

[17] For quantitative data on this hierarchical structuring of American ideologies, using public opinion survey results, see Angus Campbell et al., *The American Voter* (New York: Wiley, 1964), chaps. 9–10. See also Philip E. Converse, "The Nature of Belief Systems in Mass Publics," in David E. Apter, ed., *Ideology and Discontent.*

and, almost as frequently as making these commitments, of justifying them. More often than not, probably, the participants in social systems take their ideologies for granted. *Ego* and his *alters* share a value consensus, they have learned the appropriate ideologies very well, and there is no self- or other-challenge to the established ideologies. Sometimes, however, there is value dissensus or there is a new interaction situation that requires innovation with regard to values and ideologies. Only in such situations do the participants in social systems become more self-conscious of their ideological activities. The proportion of such self-conscious expressing and creating of ideologies is probably greater in the differentiated and changeful social systems of the modern world than in the less differentiated and changeful systems of earlier times.

The socialization systems of a society or of one of its subgroups are usually fairly effective for teaching its members the established ideologies.[18] The families, the childhood and other peer groups, the storytellers and poets, the general schools, special ideological schools, and, in modern society, the mass and specialized communications media, all socialize people well in the general and specialized ideologies that are taken for granted in the relevant social systems.[19] A large part of human "learning" may be learning rational knowledge of

[18] This is not meant to imply that socialization produces only consensus. On the contrary, the social scientist must always look for value and ideological dissensus in any social system. The amount of consensus and dissensus is always an empirical problem. For an analysis of the types of consensus and dissensus and for the ways in which public opinion survey techniques and data can be used to give empirical accounts of such consensus and dissensus, see V. O. Key, Jr., *Public Opinion and American Democracy* (New York: Knopf, 1961), esp. chs. 2, 3. For another use of public opinion data for these purposes, see Gabriel A. Almond, *The American People and Foreign Policy* (New York: Harcourt, Brace, 1950), chaps. 8–9. For an analysis in non-quantitative terms of a particular case of American ideological dissensus, see Overton Hume Taylor, "The 'Free Enterprise' Ideology and American Ideals and Institutions," *Daedalus*, vol. 92 (1963), pp. 415–432.

[19] On the socializing effects of the family and other agencies for political ideologies, see Herbert H. Hyman, *Political Socialization* (New York: The Free Press, 1959). On the socializing functions of schools, see Key, *Public Opinion*, chap. 13, "The Educational System"; and Herbert Passin, *Society and Education in Japan* (New York: Bureau of Publications, Teachers College, Columbia University, and East Asian Institute, Columbia University, 1965), chap. 7, "Education and Ideology." Passin's account has general relevance for modernizing countries. For the effects of the mass media in instilling ideologies, see Key, *Public Opinion*, chap. 14. For the influence of the "high-brow" media of Victorian England, see Coser, *Men of Ideas*, chap. 7, British Nineteenth-Century Reviews. Finally, for the socializing functions of an American "rightist" ideological school, see Raymond E. Wolfinger et al., "America's Radical Right: Politics and Ideology," *Ideology and Discontent*, ed. David E. Apter, esp. p. 263.

the empirical worlds — physical, biological, and social. But a large part is also learning the ideologies without which the individual participants and the social systems cannot function.

In this sense, then, that human beings in social systems always have been, still are, and always will be the part-time declarers and inventors of ideologies, they are all ideologists. They all play this role in some measure, as they play many other roles on a part-time basis, roles such as child or student or religious participant. But the role of ideologist may take other forms in the division of labor in a society or smaller social system than this part-time, undifferentiated, unspecialized form. The role of ideologist, occupied by some minority of the members, may become a relatively full-time, clearly differentiated, highly specialized role, requiring a definite kind of training and promising certain definite kinds of careers. In short, it may become what we call an occupational role.

Yet if one looks in the standard lists of occupational titles that are compiled by modern societies to help them with their necessary social and economic bookkeeping, one will not find the title *ideologist* as one will find other "modern" roles like business manager, nuclear scientist, or dental technician. This is because of the widespread invidiousness of the terms *ideology* and *ideologist*. If one adopts the substantive definition of ideology as error or distortion by the standards of science, instead of the functional definition in which substance is irrelevant for essential understanding, and if one always thinks of ideology as an erroneous doctrine that one's opponent is offering, never as a description of one's own doctrine, then the terms *ideology* and *ideologist* are bound to be invidious. Instead, where in fact the role of ideologist is being carried on as an occupational role, the occupant of the role is called by a whole range of euphemistic, evasive, or wastebasket titles. Ideologists are government spokesmen, journalists, editorial writers, critics, columnists, public relations officials, intellectuals, social philosophers, staff aides, or speechwriters, not plain and simple ideologists, as they very well may be.[20] To get some sense of the relative size of this occupational group, we may note that there were in 1969 some 6,700 members of the Public Relations Society of America. This compares with some 11 or 12,000 members of the American Sociological Association, another fairly new occupational group. Of course, not all members of the Public Relations

[20] On the ideological functions of various types of intellectuals in labor unions, see Harold L. Wilensky, *Intellectuals in Labor Unions* (New York: The Free Press, 1956), esp. pp. 12, 33, 80, 85, 88, and 102. On art critics as ideologists, see Harrison C. and Cynthia A. White, *Canvases and Careers: Institutional Change in the French Painting World* (New York: Wiley, 1965), p. 119.

Society are ideologists, any more than all members of the American Sociological Association are sociologists, but both figures indicate roughly that a considerable new occupational group is performing its function for a whole variety of modern groups and societies.[21]

IDEOLOGICAL SYSTEMS AND SOCIAL CHANGE

The problem of ideological systems and social change has two important parts that have to be considered separately as well as being related to one another. The first part is the problem of change within ideological systems themselves. Although always in interaction with the other subsystems of a social system, it seems useful for better understanding, as we have seen, to construe ideological systems as having certain structural and processual characteristics of their own and therefore as having a certain margin of functional autonomy from their environment of other social subsystems. That is, because the structure of ideological systems may vary along the dimensions of abstractness, systematization, and comprehensiveness, it seems useful to construe the processes that make up this structure as being dynamic and as having tendencies toward increase in the amount of these three dimensions. Such tendencies are the internal source of changes in the structure of ideological systems. Put more concretely, ideologists, whether less or more specialized in their role, will tend to try to make their ideologies more effective by making them more abstract, systematic, and comprehensive. As the role of ideologist becomes more specialized, this tendency becomes stronger. These internal changes in ideological systems will, of course, given the interaction of ideologies and other social subsystems, have consequences for these other subsystems, which may result in change for them too, though their own margin of functional autonomy may forestall such change in many cases.

This matter of the interaction of ideological and other subsystems in a larger social system raises directly the second important part of the problem of ideological systems and social change. That part has to do with the much-debated question of the relative role of the ideological system as against other subsystems, such as the polity or the economy, in causing social change in a more comprehensive system of which they are the subsystems. In at least one version of Marxism, for example, and also in various non-Marxist "materialist"

[21] Given their greater acceptance of a "scientific" usage for the term ideology, one would expect the Russians to be easier with the use of terms like "ideologue" to refer to members of the Communist Party and the Government structure. For evidence that this seems to be the case, see Brzezinski and Huntington, *Political Power*, pp. 40–41.

theories about stability and change in social systems, the ideological system is never the original source or cause of social change; it is always the dependent, never the independent variable in processes of change; it is always epiphenomenal in social systems.

This view of ideology as always the dependent variable in processes of social change is erroneous. In systems of whatever degree of comprehensiveness, ranging from the low extreme of a specialized dyad to the high extreme of a self-sufficient society, ideological systems may be either independent or dependent variables. They may be independent when their own internal processes of change have changeful consequences for other subsystems and for the system as a whole. Thus, if an ideologist develops a more abstract and more comprehensive justification for the value of equality, this development may cause changes in specific equality norms in many areas of the system where these norms were not formulated previously, or nor formulated with such effectiveness. This seems to be what is happening in the world today. As ideologists for equality generalize their doctrines and make them more comprehensive, the specific norms of equality with regard to ethnic groups, economic groups, age groups, sex groups, and ability groups are changing and causing direct and indirect changes in all these areas and others as well. And ideologies may also be the independent source of social change even when they themselves have not changed but because various ideologists and ideological groups actively propagate the ideologies that already exist. When existing ideologies are brought into direct and active confrontation with existing social structures that in some way deviate or fall short of the values and norms justified in the ideology, those social structures may change because they are now being directly and actively questioned in a way that is new.

As sometime independent, sometime dependent variables in the processes of social change, ideologies do not only work toward fostering social change. They forestall, obstruct, or resist social change as well as cause it. In most concrete ideologies, for example, as we have seen, there is some mixture of positive and negative elements. That is, in a concrete ideology for equality, there will be arguments against inequality, either in general or in some specific form. Or, vice versa, ideologies for inequality, such as prevailed in pre-modern times, argued against equality and thereby helped to obstruct changes in that direction.[22]

In sum, ideologies may have either independent or dependent func-

[22] On various "social class" and equality ideologies in European society from medieval times to the present, see Bernard Barber, *Social Stratification: A Comparative Analysis of Structure and Process* (New York: Harcourt, Brace, 1957), pp. 197–208.

tions in processes of social change; they may either foster or obstruct social change. Some brief examples will illustrate a little further the nature of the interaction between ideological and other subsystems in a larger social system. We may note, first and somewhat ironically, that despite the claim of at least one version that ideologies are always a dependent variable in social systems, Marxism seems to be one of the best cases for demonstrating the independent role of ideologies in social change. As ideology, as an active critic of established "capitalist" values and norms, and as the active propagator of "socialist" values and norms, Marxism may have caused more social change than any other force in the modern world. In both industrial and would-be industrial societies, its consequences have been very great. Only nationalist ideology, which is also a powerful and independent type of ideological system in the modern world and which the universalist values expressed in Marxism have consistently neglected or underrated, might be said to have had an influence on modern social change of the same magnitude as Marxism.[23] It can be argued that Marxist and nationalist ideologies together have caused as much social change as changes arising in the economy or polity.

At a lesser degree of comprehensiveness in social systems, in the structure of family systems, we can again see the independent influence of ideology on social change, in this case the worldwide change toward the greater prevalence of the conjugal family. The influence of an ideological system has been well stated by W. J. Goode in a book that provides a great deal of evidence both for the change and for the influence of the ideology:

> One important source of change is the *ideology* of "economic progress" and technological development, as well as the ideology [*sic*] of the conjugal family, and spokesmen for both appear in non-Western countries before any great changes are observable either in industrial or family areas of life.
>
> Elders may deplore both ideologies, but both appeal to the intellectuals, often trained in Western schools, and to the young, to women, and generally, to the disadvantaged. The ideology of the conjugal family is a radical one, destructive of the older traditions in almost every society. It grows from a set of more general radical principles which also arouse these groups *politically* in perhaps every underdeveloped country. Its appeal is almost as universal as that of "re-

---

[23] Nationalist ideologies play a very large part in modernizing countries that were formerly colonial dependencies. All the top officials of the new nation, and especially the head of state, may play a very large role as ideologists in this situation. For a case of this kind, see Herbert Feith, "Indonesia's political symbols and their wielders," *World Politics*, vol. 16 (1963), pp. 79–97.

distribution of the land." It asserts the equality of individuals as against class, caste, or sex barriers.

The ideology of the conjugal family proclaims the right of the individual to choose his or her own spouse, place to live, and even which kin obligations to accept, as against the acceptance of others' decisions. It asserts the worth of the *individual* as against the inherited elements of wealth or ethnic group. The *individual* is to be evaluated, not his lineage. A strong theme of "democracy" runs through this ideology. It encourages love, which in every major civilization has been given a prominent place in fantasy, poetry, art, and legend, as a wonderful, perhaps even exalted, experience, even when its reality was guarded against. Finally, it asserts that if one's family life is unpleasant, one has the right to change it.[24]

The opposite case, where ideology was developed after social and economic interests had determined action, has been well described by the sociologist-historian, Charles Tilly, in his account of the sources of rebellion in 1793 against the French revolutionary government by groups in the Vendée, in the west of France:

> In the case at hand, it seems that the beliefs about the virtues of the old regime and the intentions of the rebellion which have so often been retroactively imputed to the rebels *actually emerged from the stress of battle*, that once defined they did influence the movement, that they were *later elaborated* by elite apologists of the old regime and powerfully *affected the region's political life in the nineteenth century*. It does not seem that one can explain the counter-revolution by alleging the personal attachment of the peasants to Throne and Altar.[25]

Thus, it was not a pre-established ideology about "Throne and Altar," as Tilly calls these two ideological foci, but subsequent events and the social and economic interests on both sides creating them that caused both the opposition to the revolution and its ideology and support for the ideology justifying Throne and Altar.

A generic situation in which ideologies may play a large role in social change occurs where what we may call "utopian" ideologies

---

[24] William J. Goode, *World Revolution and Family Patterns* (New York: The Free Press, 1963), p. 19. See also p. 369. For a case study of "an ideology that failed," or at least that had only a limited effect on social structure and behavior, see Bernard Barber, "Is American Business Becoming Professionalized? Analysis of a Social Ideology," in *Sociological Theory, Values, and Sociocultural Change: Essays in Honor of Pitirim A. Sorokin*, ed. Edward A. Tiryakian (New York: The Free Press, 1963) and also (New York: Harper Torchbooks, 1967).

[25] Charles Tilly, "The Analysis of a Counter-Revolution," *History and Theory*, vol. 3 (1963), p. 57. Emphasis inserted. See also Tilly, *The Vendée* (Cambridge: Harvard University Press, 1964).

exist.[26] "Utopian" ideologies justify or criticize an imagined social system in which new values or norms prevail in a way that *seems* to current common sense knowledge or social science knowledge to be impossible. (It is important to emphasize *seems* because what may look impossible at one state of knowledge or condition of the social system may be seen as possible later.) The Platonic ideology criticizing the conjugal family as a bastion of social equality and recommending a familyless society, is an example of a utopian ideology. George Orwell's picture of life in *1984* may be another one. Favoring the values of individualism and freedom, Orwell has overdrawn the present possibilities for an un-free, authoritarian, and conformist society, though recent history has shown us that actuality may go a considerable way in the direction that Orwell exaggerated. In both these cases of utopian ideology, the Platonic and the Orwellian, and in many others as well, even when the conditions imagined in the "good" or "bad" utopia are not realizable in fact, the ideology may still have considerable effects for social change short of full realization of the utopia itself. Utopian ideologies are exceptionally dramatic and often powerful systems of ideas that at least tell us the social directions our values and norms do or do not prefer. The Platonic ideology for a familyless society may not bring about the abolition of the conjugal family, but it may aid in changes that considerably reduce the inegalitarian effects of the family, changes such as making property inheritance or access to education more nearly equal. Especially in the Christian and generally Western value tradition, with its future-oriented and perfectionist characteristics, utopian ideologies have been powerful and independent engines for social change.

In conclusion, it is our conviction that the concept and analysis of ideology do not have to be left to the ideologists. The concept and analysis of the functions and forms of ideology in social systems belong to social scientists.

[26] It should be carefully noted that the following definition of "utopian" ideology is different from that given by Karl Mannheim in *Ideology and Utopia*, trans. Edward Shils and Louis Wirth (New York: Harcourt, Brace, 1936), esp. at p. 36.

SOCIAL STRUCTURE, CULTURE, AND PERSONALITY

Technically trained and knowledgeable in both sociology and psychology, Professor Inkeles is an example of what every "social psychologist" should be, a scholar who can treat the relations among the social structural, cultural, and personality systems with an adequate grasp on each and all of them. In this essay, his purpose is to make a programmatic statement about such relations in order to guide future research and theory. Professor Inkeles begins with an account and critique of three important analyses of the role of personality in historical and social change: Erikson and his theory of "identity crises"; McClelland and his theory of "need achievement"; and Inkeles' own cross-cultural work in six countries showing that modernizing social structural and cultural systems causes adult individual personality systems to shift in their needs, dispositions, attitudes, values, and actual behavior toward the "modern" types. Professor Inkeles concludes with thirteen propositions that are at once an outline of and a program for further research on the complex ways in which processes of stability and change in personal and sociocultural systems are related.

Alex Inkeles

CONTINUITY AND CHANGE IN THE INTERACTION OF THE PERSONAL AND THE SOCIOCULTURAL SYSTEMS

To speak of a personal and a sociocultural system is already to assume more than some are willing to grant. Let us begin, therefore, by acknowledging that both concepts are higher level abstractions, or better syntheses, based on the observation of more disparate, concrete, and molecular units of human behavior. The common material of the social sciences is the sum of all the human acts of some delimited population, whether these acts are directly observed or are

265

found embedded in some physical object — as in a house, a plowed field, a law, or a book. Social scientists have found it convenient and appropriate to classify these acts in groups or sets, to attribute the sets to particular referents, to assign names to these sets of acts, and to attribute to them certain systematic properties. Those acts for which the referent is a particular individual are taken collectively to make up the *personal system*. Those which are shared by a relatively enduring group of individuals are considered to make up the *social* or *cultural system*. In this paper, however, I will gloss over what to some social scientists are very vital distinctions, and refer to the sociocultural system as a single entity.

Whether a particular behavior should be assigned to one or another of these systems is often ambiguous, and there is a necessary degree of arbitrariness in the final decision. The law is clearly shared by a population without being in any important sense a property of any person. A man's dreams on the other hand are very distinctly his own.

Even if all other men dream, and even if the content of a man's dream is not unique, his dream is not shared behavior. It does not require an interaction of persons. But if a man tips his hat to a lady as a sign of polite recognition the action is not uniquely his. It has meaning mainly as *inter*-action with the lady, and its content is almost entirely determined by a shared set of social rules governing the situation. Such an individual act is therefore part of the shared system of action of a delimited population. It is part of the social system. Yet it also is an attribute of the person. It establishes the man's "politeness" and his conformity to social rules. Moreover, the act may be carried out in distinctive ways, typical of the personal style of this individual. It is, therefore, also relevant to the personal system. Joint relevance to both the personal and the sociocultural system is a quality manifested by most acts, which enormously complicates any analysis of the interrelations of personality and social structure.

Further difficulties inhere in the concept of system. The term *system* is applied where two conditions can be satisfied. First, a set of behaviors must manifest a consistent pattern or structure such that some more regularly "go with" others. Second, this pattern or structure cannot be ephemeral, but rather should be relatively stable and enduring. How much consistency is required to establish a pattern and how much persistence through time to qualify it as stable is not well agreed upon among social scientists. Yet the concept of system is essential for all personal and sociocultural analysis.

Neither the personal nor the sociocultural system is undifferentiated. One way of describing the differentiation of the sociocultural system is relatively conventional and concrete. We recognize certain standard major institutions and institutional complexes, each generally organized around some central social function — such as the production and distribution of goods and services, or the socialization and training of the young. This analysis identifies the familiar categories of institution cited in all standard sociological texts: the political system, the religious system, and so on. These major systems are themselves congeries of component institutions — the family, the firm, the court, the school. More analytically, each institution may, in turn, be conceived as a complex network of statuses and their associated roles, these last being generally considered the basic conceptual building blocks of institutional analysis.

This more conventional and quite serviceable basis for differentiating the components of the sociocultural system must compete with several others. Most prominent is the functional approach, which centers attention on a series of functions that must be performed if social life is to be maintained through time. Examples would be socialization, control of deviance, provision of essential goods and services, defense against external force, and the like. These functions lead one back to the conventionally defined institutions, but may also aid us to see how far certain problems cut across these institutions. The problem of authority, for example, may be the central issue in political institutions, but it must be faced, as well, in the family, in productive organizations, in agencies of socialization. We are especially in debt to modern anthropology for increasing our sensitivity to the way in which particular cultures reveal a decided pattern in treating such issues as authority, a pattern evident as the issue is approached across a series of different institutions.

By contrast, there is little agreement as to the best strategy for dealing with the differentiation of the personal system. Indeed, numerous approaches and conceptions, most very incomplete and pursued without reference to competing and overlapping conceptions, make personality psychology a veritable Tower of Babel. A substantial source of additional difficulty comes from confusing with the personal system itself certain *processes* out of which the personality merely develops — such as operant conditioning or biosocial maturation. Within this anarchic intellectual domain, however, an outsider not caught up in a fixed commitment to any approach can discern the broad outlines of analytic themes that occur with great regularity in many major schools of personality psychology.

For example, needs or dispositions, such as the need for power, affection, affiliation, and autonomy, emerge as a component of most conceptions of personality. Styles of personal functioning including the cognitive, conative, and affective modes are also generally recognized as critical elements of the personal system. Furthermore, some core or center, some organizational principle or cybernetic system of control, is acknowledged as important in most psychological theories, as the wide use of such concepts as "self," "ego," and "identity" indicates. Finally, the theoretical importance of assessing the interrelation of parts of the personal system and the quality of overall functioning, expressed in concepts such as integration, effectiveness, adjustment and mental health is widely recognized.

Now, how do these two systems interact to ensure continuity or to generate change in one or the other? A logically complete model requires that we consider the case in which neither changes, the case in which either one changes but not the other, and the case in which both change. Any paradigm for analysis will obviously be greatly complicated by the degree to which we take into account levels and subsystems. Changes may occur in the system as a whole, in some major subsystem, or in some single component. In the sociocultural system, for example, the family may change, but not the legal system. In the personal system, personal values may be transformed, but not the level of anxiety. As one elaborates the permutations and combinations, the potentially enormous complexity of the problem becomes apparent. A thorough treatment could be encompassed only within the confines of a very large book. I have sufficient space here for only the sketchiest treatment of highly selected materials, which can serve only to illustrate some dimensions of the problem and some paths we might follow in search of more satisfying answers to difficult questions.

My plan is to describe three substantial efforts to study the role of personality in the process of major sociocultural change. All three are concerned with the emergence in society of that set of institutional arrangements we identify with the "modern" world. Each study, however, is different. It focuses on a distinctive aspect of the modernization process, concerns itself with different elements of the sociocultural and personal system, and represents a different mode of scientific work.

ERIKSON ON RELIGIOUS CHANGE
AND IDENTITY CRISES

The questions that laymen pose about a problem are seldom those that interest, or at least that are dealt with, by the scientist approaching the same problem. This is certainly true in studying personality and social structure. Take, for example, the question: What is the role of the individual in bringing about social change? The issue seems to be vital to almost everyone except the man who attempts a scientific study of the interaction of personality and social structure. Not, I trust, because the social scientists are obtuse, insensitive, or stupid, but rather because the problem simply does not lend itself to science. The question of the role of the individual in history addresses itself to unique, or almost unique, events. Social science is capable mainly of explanation in probabilistic terms. There are simply not enough events, certainly not enough for which we have any substantial body of data, to formulate a generally valid proposition on the role of the individual in making history.

Yet the question is too important to people for them to be put off so easily, and some social scientists have been courageous and responsible enough to attempt an answer within the limits of the very modest supply of facts at our disposal. In the most recent era Erik Erikson has been most assiduous and most successful in explicating the role played by the personality of outstanding individuals in the historical process.

Erikson's key concept is "identity," by which he means, very broadly, a person's sense of himself and his capacity to perform in fulfilling expectations that he and others set on himself. Late adolescence is a critical period in the life cycle, for at this stage an individual's identity is more or less permanently defined. If young people entering this stage of the life-cycle are unable to accept the meaningfulness of the identity offered by their society and time, they may suffer some form of identity crisis. Such crises will affect not merely the occasional individual, but may be experienced by most or all in a particular generation in a given society.

Resolving such crises may occur through the development of a new identity forged and exemplified by the life and teaching of an exceptional person who has experienced the same basic crisis, but whose uniquely creative resolution of it points the way to a new historical identity. Thus, Erikson holds that Luther "bridged a political and psychological vacuum which history had created in a significant portion of Western Christendom." [1] Luther, Erikson continues, helped resolve the crisis that was brought on by the end of the era of absolute faith, as Freud later played a critical role in resolving the crisis brought on by the end of the era of absolute reason.[2]

The analysis of Luther's historic role is an extension of the mode of analysis Erikson had applied earlier to Hitler's role in German history. Before Hitler, the German experience reflected a conflict between orientation to the "narrow" and the "broad," between an identity based either on extreme provincialism or on extreme cosmopolitanism. This persistent conflict was enormously exaggerated by the depressed

[1] Erik Erikson, *Young Man Luther* (New York: Norton, 1958), p. 15.
[2] Ibid., p. 252.

condition of the German economy and society in the wake of the First World War. Under these conditions, the people "began to listen to Hitler's imagery, which for the first time in Reichs-German history, gave political expression to the spirit of the German adolescent." [3]

Erikson thus offers a psychological explanation of historical change. His mode of analysis is distinctively his own, but it bears important resemblance to that undertaken by Erich Fromm, and shares certain features with what may be termed the *psychoanalytic school of modern history*.[4] The general model that guides this sort of analysis is the following: Some massive processes of social change either start or evolve into more or less spontaneous, or at least uncontrolled, forces operating much as do physical events in nature. Such processes include epidemics or disease like the plague; protracted and devastating wars, like the Thirty Years War; and the opening of new trade routes, as with the Orient or the New World. Such events profoundly disrupt well-established patterns of social relationship, lead to a questioning of authority, and an erosion of traditional belief. Personal qualities previously highly valued no longer find a respected and productive outlet in social action. Individuals become frustrated, depressed, angry, disoriented. It is no longer possible to raise young people in the conviction that the standards they are being taught are valid, or in the hope that they will find satisfying ways of using the skills one teaches and of achieving the goals one sets for them. A crisis of meaning afflicts the culture, and is jointly manifested in a crisis of identity in the individual.

A new basis of identity is required to meet the challenge of the new historical situation — an identity that emphasizes at least some new values, one that permits the individual to take a new stand with regard to his past and to orient toward a meaningful future. The necessary resolution of the tension felt by most people in such crises cannot be attained on a purely individual basis. This follows, in part, from the fact that the effective integration of the person requires that his values and beliefs be shared with significant others, a sharing which confers validity on the values held by the individual. The unsuitability of purely individual resolutions of the crisis also follows from the fact that the distress people are experiencing comes in part from their sense that anomie prevails, from their feeling of aloneness, and from the recognition that everyone is adopting his own idiosyncratic resolution of a commonly experienced crisis of identity.

In this situation a critical hero may emerge, an individual *typical* in

---

[3] Erik Erikson, *Childhood and Society* (New York: Norton, 1950), p. 309.
[4] Erich Fromm, *Escape from Freedom* (New York: Rinehart, 1941).

experiencing precisely the common crisis of his time, but *atypical* in developing an unusual personal resolution that can then serve as a model for others. This new identity, disseminated, diffused, widely adopted, eventually institutionalized, becomes the stable core around which individual personality is organized anew. Because this new personality mode is presumably more in harmony with the forms of social organization emerging in the new historical era, individuals become more effective, action is more productive of the ends desired by individuals, meaning is restored to life, personal integrity is reestablished. The crisis of identity is temporarily resolved as individual and community have moved to some new stage of integration between the personal and the sociocultural system.

This analysis faces several critical observations. First, and most notable, the theory offers no explanation for the set of major social forces that initially precipitate the crisis of identity. The nature of the massive social change occurring prior to the appearance of the hero who generates the new group identity is simply taken as given. If personality study is to make a substantial difference in our understanding of social change, we cannot readily settle for a theory that says nothing about what causes the main social changes to which individuals are presumably responding.

Second, we are given no guidance for understanding *differential* responsiveness to the newly offered identity. In some communities the new identity is adopted, but in others, not. Within the same community, some individuals develop the new identity, others do not. Are psychic or social structural factors to explain these differences? If psychic factors play a role, what are the properties of those who do not seem to need a new identity? What are the consequences of not adopting the new identity? For those who do not adopt the new identity, does the crisis remain permanent, or are there other resolutions, including other new identities? What difference does it make to the process of social change that the new identity is of one sort rather than another — say, that offered by Calvin rather than by Luther? And what is the fate of those communities and individuals that do not discover or enjoy a hero in history and are therefore not offered a new identity?

MC CLELLAND ON NEED ACHIEVEMENT
AND ECONOMIC DEVELOPMENT

David McClelland's analysis of the psychological origins of entrepreneurial behavior meets at least one objection we raised concerning Erikson's treatment of Lutheranism and Hitler's Germany. Erikson's analysis deals mainly with individual adjustment to social changes already far advanced. McClelland purports to explain what produces the very engine of social change itself.[5]

The basic social fact with which McClelland begins is the differential economic development of nations. He holds that these differences result from differences in the frequency with which national populations produce individuals with a high "need for achievement," who, in turn, are more likely to undertake the entrepreneurial behavior that leads to economic development. The need for achievement is defined as a basic psychological disposition that is laid down in childhood. McClelland and his co-workers have developed an elaborate theory to define the family constellation assumed to be productive of the need for achievement. History does not, unfortunately, provide source materials appropriate for directly testing the occurrence of these conditions in earlier times. McClelland therefore falls back on other indicators designed to test the prevalence and intensity of the need for achievement. Guided by the principles of "projective" psychological testing, he has sought to measure need achievement by such indirect indicators as the decoration of pottery in ancient Greece and the occurrence of achievement "imagery" in the textbooks used by children in the more recent past.

McClelland has found that there are indeed substantial correlations between his measures of achievement imagery and the level of economic activity in different times and places. Particularly interesting is his finding that children's textbooks show a marked frequency of achievement imagery some twenty years before periods of heightened economic activity in their countries. He has interpreted these facts as fairly conclusive evidence that the pupils' greater need for achievement produced heightened economic activity once these young people entered the managerial and entrepreneurial positions they assumed as adults.

In McClelland's model, therefore, psychological propensities are no longer merely the *response* to social change, as in Erikson, but have become the prime *cause*. A stronger need for achievement in individuals becomes a social imperative. Those possessed of it are seen as more or less driven to undertake entrepreneurial activity, and that activity in turn is assumed to lead to economic development and all the social transformations ordinarily attendant on that process.

Again, it is inevitable that so sweeping a theory should invite much critical challenge. Some challenges apply specifically to the details of McClelland's research design, his techniques, and his conclusions, but others may be raised at the more general level of the model for re-

---

[5] The main theory and supporting evidence are set out in David C. McClelland, *The Achieving Society* (Princeton, N.J.: Van Nostrand, 1961).

lating personality and social structure that McClelland's work represents.

Most critical is the question: How far is the more frequent achievement imagery found in certain times and places a reflection of changed social conditions rather than a cause of them? After all, the children do not themselves write their textbooks. It is therefore logical to assume that certain social changes that had already occurred must have stimulated adults to produce textbooks with more achievement imagery. In that case achievement imagery becomes more the product than the cause of social change. And we are left wondering why men with a propensity to heightened achievement imagery were writing textbooks instead of organizing businesses.

We must also seriously question the link between the imagery found in the textbooks and inculcating the need for achievement in the schoolchildren. The need for achievement is supposed to be a quite basic psychological disposition, a deep-seated and relatively enduring attribute of the personality. Our experience both in life and in research indicates that such traits are not easily inculcated when absent, nor changed when once established. It seems to require prolonged exposure to influence of a very particular kind under very special conditions to affect substantially an individual's standing on a psychological measure of this type. This point is rather dramatically underlined by the difficulties McClelland and his associates have encountered in seeking to discover the specific child-rearing environments and techniques that produce high need achievement in contemporary individuals.

This raises a third challenge, for we must be aware that McClelland, perhaps of necessity, does not establish that such heightened economic activity as might have occurred in various countries was in fact produced by individuals who had been outstanding for the strength of their need for achievement when they were schoolchildren. In his analysis we have only two statistical series that are demonstrated to be correlated — one measuring the amount of achievement imagery in primary school textbooks, the other describing national levels of economic activity as reflected in per capita consumption of electricity. For the periods earlier than the 1950's no individuals were studied. Therefore, no evidence is presented to establish that the graduates of schools using textbooks rich in achievement imagery were, as individuals, strong in their need for achievement. Neither is it demonstrated that the increased economic development noted in certain countries in fact resulted from the activity of specific individuals with higher need for achievement.

Of course, Dr. McClelland was doing historical analysis and so we can hardly expect him to have administered psychological tests to individuals who lived in the past. Nevertheless, our doubts on these points are legitimate and persist. Moreover, studies for the contemporary period in situations roughly comparable to those McClelland examined historically do not yield very convincing evidence for the assumptions he makes about earlier times. There is no persuasive evidence that in contemporary schools the amount of achievement imagery in the textbooks would be a good predictor of the strength of need for achievement in the school's pupils. The evidence that outstanding entrepreneurs are high on need achievement is weak. Such reports as we have showing executives to be higher in achievement imagery are, furthermore, subject to the challenge that the imagery follows from the activity and not the activity from the personal disposition. The critical evidence — that individuals who, when young, showed more need achievement actually *later* more often became entrepreneurs — is totally lacking.

The last reservation we may enter about McClelland's analysis concerns his failure to specify the social conditions under which high need for achievement might or might not result in entrepreneurial behavior, and equally important, in entrepreneurship that was effective in bringing about significant economic change on a society-wide basis. There seems every reason to believe that a need for achievement could find expression in numerous fields of endeavor outside the economic. Unless the need for achievement as measured by McClelland has been mislabeled, and is really the need for economic entrepreneurship, we need an explanation as to why those with this need should be going into economic life rather than into politics, art, or science.

Even if men high in need achievement are attracted to economic entrepreneurship, their effectiveness can hardly rest on their psychological properties alone. Entrepreneurs must work with resources of capital, material, and manpower; they are dependent on markets, and can be effective only if significant economic opportunity is inherent in a given historical situation. We must, therefore, question how far a supply of men high in need achievement is a "sufficient" condition for economic development. Economists incline to give much weight to the importance of opportunity factors in eliciting entrepreneurial behavior, and to view economic development as permitting the use of various substitutes for the usual entrepreneurial role and for other "inputs" as well. We are led to wonder, therefore, how far need achievement is even a necessary condition for economic activity.[6]

[6] See Alexander Gershenkron, *Continuity in History and Other Essays* (Cambridge: Harvard University Press, 1968); Gustav Papanek, *Pakistan's Development: Social Goals and Private Incentives* (Cambridge: Harvard University Press, 1967).

McClelland's study is bold, imaginative, inventive, altogether a signal contribution to the investigation of a classic question in the study of social change that has been the subject of continuous interest and debate ever since Weber opened up the issue in *The Protestant Ethic and the Rise of Capitalism*. As we have seen, it is nevertheless subject to serious challenges, some of which might indeed be considered fatal to the integrity of McClelland's historical analysis. But my purpose in introducing these reservations is not to evaluate the adequacy of this particular research, which in any event deserves and requires more extended discussion. My purpose is rather to highlight some difficulties, ambiguities, perplexities, and frustrations that will beset any effort to use the psychological properties of a small set of individuals to explain a major process of social change such as a marked rise in the level of a nation's economic activity represents.

INDUSTRIALIZATION AND MODERNIZATION OF THE INDIVIDUAL

Both Erikson and McClelland attempt to explain historically important social changes by reference to prior change in the individual psyche. This is inherently a very problematic scientific exercise. Transcendentally important social changes are few. Insofar as we seek to develop a generalizing social science, we need large numbers of cases on which to base our necessarily probabilistic statements. Such social changes as the rise of Lutheranism or burgeoning economic development are inordinately complex phenomena, the limits of which cannot easily be set and the measurement of which tends to be elusive. These phenomena are produced not by a single cause, but by multiple social and personal factors interacting in complex ways. Finally, the fact that these events are located in the past means that critical elements of the relevant evidence will usually be totally inaccessible or extremely difficult to obtain. We are on firmer ground, therefore, when we shift our attention to more contemporary issues and concern ourselves with the impact of social change on the individual.

To illustrate work in this mode, my own research on the impact of industrialization on the modernization of the individual may serve.[7]

[7] The theory guiding the entire research endeavor is set out in compressed form in Alex Inkeles, "The Modernization of Man," in *Modernization*, ed. M. Weiner (New York: Basic Books, 1966). A major product of our empirical analysis will be found in David H. Smith and Alex Inkeles, "The OM Scale: A Comparative Socio-Psychological Measure of Individual Modernity," *Sociometry*, vol. 29, no. 4 (December 1966). A concise summary of our preliminary findings appears in A. Inkeles, "Making Men Modern: On the Causes and Consequences of Individual Modernization in Six Developing Countries," *American Journal of Sociology*, vol. 75, no. 2 (September 1969).

This research seeks to establish how far and in what ways individuals undergo significant psychic change as a result of their contact with those modern institutions presumed to have the ability to influence personality. These include the school, the factory, the city, and the media of mass communication. As potential sources of influence on the personal system these institutions are, in our research, put in competition with other aspects of the sociocultural system, such as religion, ethnic membership, village residence, and employment in agriculture or traditional crafts.

The independent variables in our research are, therefore, certain basic elements of social structure, specifically certain institutions that are a central part of the continuum defining "modern" and "traditional" social systems. The dependent variable is an attribute of the person, a complex or syndrome of qualities that are also conceived as defining a continuum from the relatively more "modern" to more "traditional" personality. This personality syndrome includes *dispositions*, such as a sense of personal efficacy and openness to new experience; *values*, such as favoring planning or believing in fixed time schedules; *cognitive properties*, such as showing an interest in the news and acquiring knowledge of public figures; *conative patterns*, such as steady striving for economic success; and *affective qualities*, such as optimism and trust. Note that all these aspects of the personal system — dispositions, values, cognitive properties, conative patterns, and affective tendencies — are specified as important by our general model of the personal system.[8]

The theory guiding our research specifies that the greater the individual's exposure to the presumably modernizing institutions, the further should be his movement along the psychological dimensions of individual modernization. We challenge the view that childhood experience is the more or less exclusive determinant of adult qualities, and assert that substantial change in the core components of the personality can be effected in adulthood if appropriate conditions exist or resocialization occurs. Furthermore, our theory affirms the capacity of modernizing institutions to effect their changes in the same general direction in all countries, despite the countervailing influence of distinctive traditional sociocultural value systems.

To test the theory we have drawn highly purposive samples from six countries diverse in culture and level of economic development. These samples permit a multiple test of our hypotheses. We may, thereby, avoid being misled by statistical artifacts, and can hope to

---

[8] This model of the personal system is set out and explained in Alex Inkeles, "Social Structure and the Socialization of Competence," *Harvard Educational Review*, vol. 36, no. 3 (1966), pp. 265–283.

establish the true generality of our conclusions. We have further assured the basis for cross-national generalization by keeping the structure of our six samples strictly comparable in the different countries. In each country the subgroups included: cultivators still living in their native villages, migrants just leaving the village, workers with varying degrees of experience in industry, and urban nonindustrials pursuing traditional crafts and services in an urban setting. Separate measures permit us to assess the educational level of individuals, and the extent of their exposure to industrial work, urban living, and the media of mass communication.

Preliminary study of our materials yields a fairly definite picture that, although necessarily tentative at this juncture, seems unlikely to be sharply contradicted on any major point by later and more definitive analysis. The evidence is unmistakable in all six countries that exposure to institutions generally considered part of the modern complex leads to changes in individuals, shifting their needs, dispositions, attitudes, values, and behavior toward what we have defined as more "modern."

Of the modernizing experiences, education is by far the single most powerful. It generally yields an increase of up to three points per year on the overall scale of individual modernization, a scale with a range between 0 and 100. Nevertheless, late socialization variables also prove to be independently powerful influences. For example, each year that a man spends in a factory yields him a gain of 1½ to 2 points on the individual modernity scale. Extensive exposure to the mass media produces equal or more powerful effects. Because industrial work and intensive contact with the mass media come only after the presumably formative early years, these extensive changes give powerful support to the argument that quite basic personality change can occur in adult life. These results also make it clear that the changes in individuals are not random, but rather are systematically related to certain variable features of the social structure.

The differentiation within both our independent and dependent variables permits us to locate subvariables that are often presumed to lead to individual modernization but do not, and to identify personality elements that have been assumed to change upon contact with the modern world but do not. We find, for example, that exposure to urban living, in itself, does not significantly produce individual modernization, despite a widespread assumption to the contrary. On the dependent variable side, neither the vigor with which an individual holds to his kinship obligations, nor the inclination to practice his religion, declines markedly with increasing contact with modernizing institutions.

Although the mode of analysis we have adopted in our research on modernization escapes some difficulties that beset Erikson and McClelland, it too must face some serious critical challenges. As was true for Erikson, our research strategy does not offer an explanation of any prime cause of institutional change; that is, it does not explain why education, mass media, or factory work become more widely diffused in one nation and not in another. In our design, differences between nations in their degree of institutional modernization are taken as "given." The research deals with the consequences for the individual of exposure to such institutions as have already been introduced into developing countries. Indeed, our research design does not even require that there have been changes in the frequency with which the modernizing institutions are found in different countries. It deals only with the consequences of increased contact, by individuals, with these institutions. We do not account for variations in social structure. Indeed, the sort of evidence we have limited ourselves to cannot be used to prove that the increased modernization of individuals has any necessary consequence for structural change. We *assume* that societies that have more modern individuals, or a larger proportion of the population scoring *high* on modernity, will experience accelerated structural change toward increased modernity. But the evidence, at least in the form I have collected it, cannot, for the moment, be effectively brought to bear on that issue. So we know that modern institutions change men, and do so in ways we can predict and measure. But our research cannot yet explain why and how the institutions themselves change, or at least get introduced, into different countries at different rates.

SOME TENTATIVE PROPOSITIONS

The three modes in personality study as it relates to social change that we have examined far from exhaust the roster of either approaches or problems. They are enough, however, to make us aware of the inordinate complexity of the task and the inadequacy of the currently available theory and method to cope with so challenging a problem. Our experience is sufficient, however, to indicate the broad outlines of a theory, or at least a system of propositions, which can do some justice to a substantial part of the variance we have observed.

1. Every social system depends for sustained existence on the presence in its status incumbents of certain psychic characteristics. Most essential among these is the general readiness to conform to a set of social norms. Because all social systems have certain requirements that are extremely general, it follows that in certain respects the psy-

chic structure of all populations must share some psychological properties in common. These constitute the common psychic core of social man.

2. Each major type of sociocultural system will encourage and sustain psychic dispositions that, in some respects, define a distinctive personality profile for the populations of this type of system. These personality types will, therefore, be variants of, or extensions of, the common psychic core of social man. The features of personality having this "system-typed" character will be those more required by or adaptive to, the main features of ecology and economy common to a given type of sociocultural system. Other features of personality in these populations, will however, be relatively free to vary.

For example, societies that depend heavily on hunting large animals in open country will be highly likely to encourage in men physical aggressiveness, individual autonomy, and independence from authority, whereas societies engaging in densely settled agriculture are more likely to inculcate non-assertiveness, dependence, and submission to authority. But there is no particularly compelling reason why the cognitive style should be simple or complex in either system, or why there should be an insistence on or a disparaging of status striving in either system. Given the nature of the ecology and economy, the former qualities are largely predetermined, the latter type relatively free to vary.

2a. It follows from proposition 2 that shifts in the broad features of a sociocultural system must be accompanied by comparable shifts in modal personality patterns in the relevant populations. System malfunctioning will otherwise result, as well as personal strain. Personal strain will *in any event* affect some portion of the population living in a rapidly changing sociocultural system. This strain will have a systematic character that can be specified.

3. Within all populations there will be some systematic diversification of personality types, as a minimum, along sex lines.

3a. The degree of diversification of personality modes, and probably the complexity of individual personality structure, will increase as sociocultural systems increase in internal differentiation, role specialization, and institutional complexity.

4. Changes in sociocultural systems, or of the demands made on them by external forces, are likely to be more frequent, more rapid, and more extensive than shifts in modal personality pattern.

4a. It follows from proposition 4 that pressure for changes in modal personality to meet changed role demands will be more common than demands for the invention of new status-role combinations intended to provide a field of operation for now-variant (as against modal) personality types. Nevertheless, pressure for changes in sociocultural arrangements designed to accommodate existing personality needs will be endemic in all non-static societies. When such pressure takes the form of preserving or reviving statuses being otherwise extinguished, we define it as "conservative"; when the pressure is for elaborating markedly new status-role combinations we define it as "reformist" or "radical."

5. The successful adaptation of a sociocultural system to changed conditions, whether these are externally or internally generated, will depend in substantial degree on the psychic properties of the population.

5a. The more the modal personality of any population is characterized by cognitive complexity, conative flexibility, diverse needs, and affective neutrality, the greater its prospects for successful adjustment to new sociocultural conditions of whatever variety.

5b. The greater the diversity of modal types in the population prior to major changes in social conditions, the greater the probability that some incumbents can be found to fill effectively all important new status-role demands.

5c. Whatever the statistical availability of personality types especially suited to meet new status-role demands, a system's ability to master change will depend on structural features of the system that permit it to identify and to move, or at least not to impede the movement of, appropriate personality types into new statuses.

5d. The long-term mutual adaptation of personality and social system presumes one of two conditions: either relevant long-range planning, so that the socialization of the young today will produce people comfortable with the role demands of tomorrow; or effective and extensive adult socialization to inculcate new personality modes in the short term. The first method seems inherently very problematic; the second difficult to effect. Rapidly changing sociocultural systems, therefore, even if changing in only an evolutionary and not a revolutionary manner, must expect maladaptation to be endemic.

6. System changes induced by personality factors, although less common than the reverse, will also occur frequently. Such changes may follow on the seizure of power by an individual of distinctive personality or by the rise to power of a distinctive class. In addition, strains endemic to a social system may, without prior system change, foster the emergence on a wide basis of new personality types who, in turn, insist on, or directly make, sociocultural system changes.

These propositions, crude and primitive as they may be, indicate how we could scientifically study the interrelations of the personal and the sociocultural systems. Although this field has often attracted imaginative scholars, it has suffered from scarcity of relevant facts, lack of rigor in theory, weakness in instrumentation, and the absence of a systematic means to focus research on critical issues. To bring to fruition work meeting these criteria, our discipline must either wait for *its* particular "hero in history," or we must change the sociocultural system of social science as we now know it. For the all-illuminating flash of insight that we await from the great man yet to come, we must learn to substitute the less intense but steadier enlightenment we may extract from the collective effort of a scientifically mature discipline.

DEVIANCE AND
SOCIAL PROBLEMS

Long noted for his contributions to the theory of social deviance, a realm of sociological theory now in considerable flux, Professor Cohen modestly offers some new "approaches" in this field. Assuming that deviance systems themselves and the social systems of which they are parts are to be construed as dynamic and related, with both stability and change always problematical, he offers a review and critique of several of the present leading "schools" in deviance theory: opportunity-structure theory, differential association theory, reinforcement learning theory, identity theory, and labeling theory. Finally, he offers an analysis of some of the social system sources of constancy and change in "the domain of deviance."

Albert K. Cohen

STABILITY AND CHANGE
IN DEVIANCE

This paper is a prolegomenon — that is, something less than the promise implied in the title but something more, I hope, than a prolonged clearing of the throat. Rather than a theory of stability and change in deviance, this paper offers a redefinition of the subject matter or domain of deviance theory, and some suggested approaches, consistent with this redefinition, to a general theory of stability and change in deviance.

WHAT IS DEVIANCE?

Traditional theories of deviance have generally proceeded from certain common assumptions: that deviance is rule-breaking; that the rules whose violation constitutes deviance are those embodied in the criminal law or in conventional notions about morality and propriety;

I am grateful to Howard S. Becker for reading the first draft of this paper and for his helpful suggestions.

285

that the central theoretical concern of the sociology of deviance is to explain why people break those rules; and that a secondary and practical concern is to appraise the effectiveness of measures for preventing deviance and restoring offenders to conformity.

The newer trends in deviance theory seem to be converging upon a very different definition of deviance, namely, the acquisition of a disvalued or stigmatized status. Deviants are people to whom pejorative labels, usually connoting some moral defect or corruption of the personality, have been successfully applied. The central concerns of the sociology of deviance are the process of defining people as deviant; what people do to and about people who have been defined as deviant; and the consequences to people of being defined and treated as deviant. In the more extreme variants of what has come to be known as labeling theory, rule-breaking becomes a secondary or even irrelevant consideration and may not enter into the definition of the field at all.

These newer theories have arisen in part because serious deficiencies in the traditional sociology of deviance have been exposed by the proliferation of new moralities, new life-styles, and new conceptions of authority. It is a truism that rules are man-made and variable not only between societies but also within societies and that, therefore, deviance *is* in a sense in the eye of the beholder. Writers of texts on crime and deviance usually take note of these truisms, mutter worriedly about the complications they create, and then proceed to sweep them under the rug. However, when the moral scene becomes so diverse and confused that the sociologist can no longer identify with confidence even the "conventional" moral outlook, when the most authoritative spokesmen for the "establishment" cannot agree and seem to wander about in a daze (consider the performance of the Supreme Court vis-à-vis the definition of obscenity), the growing bulge under the rug becomes embarrassing. It becomes increasingly difficult to justify taking any particular set of rules as the criterion for defining deviance. To abandon the study of rule-breaking altogether and to turn instead to the study of labeling appears to be an easy way out.

However, I do not believe that the solution lies in jettisoning a concern with rules or moving them from the center of the stage. It seems to me that a realistic approach to deviance theory must take as its starting point that people orient themselves to what they do and others do in terms of rules, that is to say, rhetorics and formulae that provide directives for acceptable behavior and logics for evaluating and justifying behavior. People may agree or disagree on the rules. Some rules may represent the position of a majority, some of dissident minorities. Some have the backing of constituted authority; some do not. Some may be recognized as valid but bad rules, i.e., as rules that ought to be changed but, until they are changed in accordance with the procedures that confer validity, as rules that may be legitimately enforced. All these situations are social facts that make a difference to the way interaction runs off, and are therefore grist for the sociology of deviance. Deviance theory is not concerned with isolating violations of some particular set of rules and treating these as *the* "dependent variable." It is concerned, rather, with the ways that rules, however they may differ and clash, influence and constrain the course of interaction. People may not recognize the rules that others apply, but they still take into account that others apply them. The sociologist does not have to decide whether the hippie's rules or his father's rules truly define deviance. What matters to deviance theory is that when these parties interact, each defines the other as deviant and that to both of them these definitions matter. I may be convinced that the rules you go by are silly, stupid, devoid of sense or legitimacy, yet I may observe your rules or conceal my violations in order to avoid being branded and to keep peace with you. Or I may flout your rules and flaunt my concept for them in order to delight in your discomfiture and indignation. Whatever we do, and whichever side we are on, our behavior cannot be fully understood without reference to the rules we respectively go by.

These rules include rules for defining and judging the appropriateness and legitimacy of our own and the other's responses to what we or they perceive as deviant. That is to say, labeling and sanctioning are themselves governed by rules. The person who falsely labels another is himself regarded as a particularly nasty species of deviant. Labels are often resisted and they sometimes come unstuck. Labeling itself is a complex social process in which all sorts of motives and interests participate, but the most constant element is the demand for justification. The justification is not only in terms of meeting the criteria that define the label but also in terms of who may legitimately label or who may legitimately sanction the procedures that must be observed, the sanctions that are appropriate, and so on. Cops and robbers is a game with rules for all the participants, and any of them may become deviants.

The category of deviant action is not limited to rule-breaking that is publicly recognized as such. It includes also "secret deviance," and deviance visible only to small circles of "insiders." (The latter probably accounts for the great bulk of deviance, especially of the deviant actions of agents of control.) The very secrecy of deviance is itself testimony to the influence of rules. Furthermore, if the sociologist ignores the distinction between rule-breaking and being publicly defined as a rule-breaker, the man in the street does not. He takes for granted that his world contains secret deviance — crime and criminals, chicanery and scoundrels not yet discovered. He also takes for granted that some labels that people bear, and that he himself credits, are not deserved. He believes that he is sometimes taken in by frame-ups, mistaken identifications, and miscarriages of justice. He knows that there is only a crude relationship between who breaks rules and who bears the label; this bothers him; and he does something about it. He sets up elaborate machinery for bringing undiscovered deviance to light and for preventing and correcting injustice. Despite this machinery, he still knows that the universe of visible or apparent or seeming deviance — what we shall call "virtual deviance" — is not identical with the universe of "real" deviance — that is, deviance defined according to the rules he himself recognizes.

There will be gray areas in the sociologist's scheme because gray areas are in the minds of his subjects. Most rules have fuzzy edges and "the people" themselves may be uncertain at times whether certain acts fall inside or outside their scope. This too is a social fact that makes a difference. It leads to exploratory behavior and test cases, caution on the part of the timid, and experimentation on the part of the avant garde. It yields a category of actions whose deviant status from the standpoint of the student of deviance must be marked "uncertain," signifying not an imperfection in the sociologist's scheme but the fidelity of that scheme to the facts of everyday life. Gray is sometimes the color of the social reality.

The rule system, then, is a complex, differentiated field, containing different versions of what the rules are, what they ought to be, and what they mean. Some deal with defining deviance, and some with what one does about deviance either prospectively or after the fact. Some versions of the rules retreat in time to small beachheads or to extinction, and others grow from the small voices of dissident minorities to the common sense of the average man. Perhaps it can be seen as a set of transparent overlays, each describing a different version of the rules, the relevant overlays depending upon who are the participants in the interaction in question, either as principals or as interested audiences. The transparency is important for the sociologist's scheme because the overlays are transparent for the participants; each has *some* awareness of the other's rules and takes them into account, if only as obnoxious but stubborn facts that he must contend with.

In summary, we are concerned with how the course of interaction is affected by the fact that people assess their own and others' conduct in terms of rules. Our concerns include honoring rules in both the breach and the observance, both openly and secretly, and by both the guardians of the rules and those subject to their surveillance. They include virtual deviance, the output of the labeling process. And they include, as we shall see, making and changing the rules themselves. Because the rules are whatever rules the participants in the interaction process go by, and these rules may be conflicting or fuzzy, it is no paradox that we may at times be able to state unequivocally that a certain action is both deviant and conforming, or that its deviant status is uncertain, or that (in consequence of retroactive changes in the rules) an act that was not deviant when I did it is now deviant.

THE DOMAIN OF DEVIANCE

We are now ready to map more systematically the domain or subject matter of the sociology of deviance. Instead of thinking of this domain as a particular set of events or "dependent variable," we shall think of it as the relationships among several sets of events that interact so intimately that to study them meaningfully seems impossible except as a system or part of a system.

Deviant Action

The first sector of this domain, *deviant action,* is the behavior of the participants classified in terms of the normative rules that they go by. *It is not a description of how the participants actually perceive and define the behavior.* As the participants themselves are aware, their perceptions and definitions are subject to ignorance, error, deception, and distortion arising from various biases. Behavior in this sector is, therefore, to be distinguished from labeling behavior. It bears the same relationship to the labels actually given it as does a woman's "real" age, according to the rules for defining age actually in use, to the age that others think she is. This sector, then, is a description of behavior in terms of deviant, non-deviant, ambiguous, uncertain, and any other categories generated by applying the rules of the participants. If it is deviant from one perspective, non-deviant from another, then that too is part of the description. To some normative rules — e.g., those defining witchcraft — there may be no empirical referents within this sector, although there may be a great deal of vigorous "enforcement."

Control

Our second sector, "the sector of control," may be viewed in two ways. First, if we think of deviant action as shaped by feedback, as undergoing change or being stabilized in consequence of the responses it calls out in its environment, we can think of the control sector as the other pole of the interaction or feedback process. From this view, control consists of the behavior of participants viewed from its contribution to the prevention, deterrence, punishment, rewarding, or facilitation of deviant action. Control in this sense is not to be defined by its intentions, because the intended effects may bear little relation to actual effects, and may actually be the opposite of those intended.

A second way of viewing the sector of control is by actions conceived and legitimized by the participants as "doing something about" deviance — i.e., as "preventing," "punishing," "rehabilitating," and so forth. All sorts of official agencies have activities that are socially legitimated by such "vocabularies of motives." Many of these activities may have little effect, one way or the other, upon actual deviance rates. In such crimes as witchcraft, they can have no effect at all, although they may generate impressive rates of virtual deviance.

These two ways of conceiving the control sector are not coterminous. Provisionally, however, I prefer not to attempt a more rigorous and unequivocal definition. Control in the one sense is so intimately related to control in the other that it seems better, for the time being, to leave open the question of precise demarcation. For example, how an individual or an agency defines and legitimizes what it does is a major determinant of its effects upon the sector of deviant action. How the actual or potential deviant responds to what others do to him depends on whether they do it in the name of punishment, revenge, even-handed justice, *quid pro quo,* painful duty, rehabilitation, protecting society, or friendly assistance in working out his problems, and on the credibility of those claims. In other words, all participants in the interaction process are subject to labeling, and all — ego, alter, and third parties — respond to the ways in which each is labeled.

Neither way of defining the control sector settles the question of the actual motivation or structural determinants of control activity. For example, organizations may be established to cope with deviance. These organizations, like organizations in general, may develop vested interests in their own perpetuation, and these interests may be threatened by the very success of the organization in the performance of its assigned task. It may then attempt to legitimize its perpetuation by "proactively" seeking deviance to control rather than simply reacting to visible and obnoxious deviance. It may even take a hand in generating new rules to create new forms of deviance to provide itself with a raison d'être.

It is important to note that the distinction between the first two sectors is analytical. What we call control is itself classifiable in terms of deviance and non-deviance. It is as fertile a field for deviance as any other and one of the fondest preoccupations of labeling theory is, in fact, to invite attention to deviance committed in the name of combatting deviance.

The Rhetoric of Deviance

These two sectors interact within a larger field that requires more explicit integration into our conceptual scheme. Whatever people do in these sectors they do in part because they operate under the aegis of a particular culture or cultures, with their language, logics, and rules for thinking and talking about deviance. The relevant parts of these cultures I shall call the "rhetoric of deviance" and the "rhetoric of control," the remaining two sectors of the domain of deviance.

The rhetoric of deviance includes the terminology for labeling deviant acts and actors and the rules defining these terms, including rules governing extenuation, aggravation, priorities when more than one rule is applicable, the social categories, subcollectivities, and activities to which they are relevant, and so forth. There may be relative consensus on some rules, dissensus and conflict on others. Our metaphor of transparent overlays is a way of describing this sector. I use the term *rhetoric* rather than rules to identify this sector because it is more suggestive of the variety of ways in which rules operate in determining behavior. It suggests commands, prescriptions, and exhortations; it suggests standards for choosing among alternatives and for passing judgment; and it also suggests formulae that may be invoked, before or after the act, in conversation with oneself or with others, to justify or condemn a course of action. The ways in which the rhetoric can be used depend partly on its clarity and specificity, partly on skill in manipulating it, and on various other factors as well, such as the interests of the various parties involved. However, it is much more than a language for post facto rationalization. It always constrains, in some measure, the labeling process and to some degree limits the range of acceptable or socially defensible courses of action. The substantive criminal law, together with its canons of interpretation, is the archetype of the rhetoric of deviance, but every interaction setting has, in its way, a *corpus juris* of its own.

The Rhetoric of Control

The rhetoric of control consists of the language and rules we use to describe, explain, and justify what we do about deviance. It specifies a division of labor in deviance control: what agents and agencies, under what circumstances, may, must, or must not do this or that to whom. It assigns responsibility: i.e., it charges some people with spelling out their own instructions, exercising surveillance over their own conduct, and administering discipline to themselves. For people in "less responsible" positions, the respective expectations attach to incumbents of other roles. A similar normative division of labor may obtain among collectivities and organizations, some of them success-fully claiming the right to regulate misconduct within their own bound-aries, others being subject to the jurisdiction of external agencies. Universities, professional groups like physicians and lawyers, trade associations, and police departments provide examples of current in-terest. The rhetoric of control also provides a normative context for labeling; it specifies procedures, of which the law of criminal pro-cedure is a model, for applying the substantive rules and affixing labels in concrete cases. Like the rhetoric of deviance, it may vary subcul-turally and may be disputed. The policeman's discharge of his solemn duty may be seen as the illegitimate exercise of arbitrary power.

The two rhetorics must be distinguished because they may vary independently. New legislation may enlarge the field of deviance by creating new crimes and expanding the definition of others, while judicial interpretation may be narrowing and "shackling" enforcing agents.

Most important for our present purposes is that rhetorics are not simply parameters, varying from system to system, or even from time to time, influencing events in the sectors of deviant action and con-trol. They also respond to events in these sectors. Thus, a response to deviance could be a change in the rules defining the deviance, so that the behavior loses its deviant status and becomes deviance of a lesser (or graver) kind. Or it could be a change in the normative rules regu-lating control — a change in the division of labor, in the definition of "due process," in the kinds of sanctions permitted for the offense in question; this in turn could lead to changes in the actual structure and operation of control agencies and in the sector of deviant action itself. (Of course, changes in the rhetoric of control do not necessarily result in corresponding changes in the actual structure of control. They could, for example, result in "business as usual" in the control sector, with the difference that the control sector itself now becomes the locus of newly legislated deviance.) A still different possibility is that, in the face of efforts at repressing deviance, a process of normative differentiation and polarization accentuates and enlarges conflicts in the rhetorics of deviance and control. (Compare the "politicization" and "radicalization" of students in confrontations with police.)

More generally, each of the four sectors interacts, directly or indi-rectly, with each of the others. Together they constitute four phases of a dynamic interaction process.

Other Considerations

To assert that these four sectors interact is to identify a field of investigation, not to offer a theory. Theory would have to specify through what mechanisms and channels influence flows from one sector to another; where, and in what order, the effects of events in one part of the domain will be felt in other parts of the domain; how the different sectors, sensitive, to be sure, to changes in one another, are articulated with and respond as well to the common environment provided by the larger system from which the domain is an abstraction. We have not talked about how interests, power, communication, status, and solidarity relate to interaction among these sectors. Even in the smallest social systems, different members have different stakes in making rules, breaking rules, finding or preventing rule-breakers, and in what is done to or about them. They receive different information about what is going on. They are differently skilled in the arts of the four sectors. Their power to influence outcomes varies in differences in authority, loyalties they can call upon, command of resources of direct instrumental utility or useful for purposes of exchange, bargaining, or coercion. The certain knowledge that all these are somehow relevant does not lead us directly to manageable and parsimonious ways of specifying their place in deviance theory.

One thing, however, must be stressed at this point: these other variables — power, communication, solidarity, and the rest — are abstractions from the same interaction process from which the sectors are themselves abstracted, and their own values may change in consequence of the events they help to produce. For example, it may be agreed that the boldness with which people venture upon deviance depends, in part, on their power to evade sanctions and to neutralize "constituted authority" by punishing authority in return. But deviant tactics may themselves lead to an enlargement of power and a larger voice in rule-making process, in managing the control structure, or both. Not only, then, are the four sectors of the domain interdependent; care must be exercised in treating *any* variable as "independent" and "determining."

INTERACTION PROCESS AND
DEVIANCE THEORY

Each sector of the domain of deviance has its literature and, to a degree, its distinctive language. If the four sectors do, indeed, constitute a single domain for theoretical purposes, we must seek, so far as possible, a common language that enables us to deal with all four as parties to the same interaction process.

This language must also be appropriate for analyzing stability and change in structures of action. The stability of an action structure is not, like that of a house, an equilibrium of solid masses of some perduring material. Action is fleeting and evanescent: a stable structure of action is one that re-creates, as it expires, the conditions that breathe life back into it. Stability is always problematical and should never cease to astonish. But stability is the product of the same kinds of feedback processes that produce change. The differences in outcome may result from small differences in the impact of action upon its environment or the information fed back from the environment. Therefore, a theory of stability must be a theory of change as well and, if a full-blown theory eludes us, we should at least seek to construct conceptual schemes that deal with stability and change in the same terms.

Such theory or schemes are more than we can offer at this time. However, starting from some better known theories of the genesis of deviance, we can illustrate the direction in which theory must move to meet these requirements. The emphasis in these pages will be primarily on the interaction between deviance and control. My own thinking on how these schemes may be further expanded to comprehend the rhetorics of deviance and control is still rudimentary.

Opportunity Structure Theory

Opportunity structure theory, as developed by Merton and by Cloward and Ohlin,[1] treats deviance as a function of legitimate and illegitimate opportunities for realizing cultural goals. In their formulations of the theory, the opportunity structure is treated as though it were a datum, a given, so far as the theory is concerned. However, this opportunity structure turns out to be, for the most part, one way of describing how human action is patterned or organized in ego's milieu — specifically, from the view of how it tends to facilitate or thwart the realization of ego's ends. We should expect this patterning to respond to ego's actions. That is to say, the environment, coded as opportunity structure, is as much a dependent variable as is ego's own behavior. Furthermore, if ego's behavior is determined by his environment coded as opportunity structure, then the action that constitutes this environment must be determined by its environment coded in the same terms, and that environment is constructed, in part, of ego's behavior. In brief, ego, responding to his opportunity structure, does something. What ego does constitutes, from alter's point of view, an enlargement or constriction of legitimate or illegitimate opportunities for the realization of alter's interests. Alter responds accordingly, and this response, in turn, constitutes an enlargement or constriction of ego's opportunities, to which he, in turn, responds. In brief, the interaction between the sectors of deviant action and control is a dialogue between two opportunity structures; events on both sides are handled in terms of the same conceptual scheme; and this conceptual scheme is

[1] Robert K. Merton, *Social Theory and Social Structure,* rev. ed. (Glencoe, Ill.: The Free Press, 1957), pp. 131–194; Richard A. Cloward and Lloyd E. Ohlin, *Delinquency and Opportunity* (Glencoe, Ill.: The Free Press, 1960).

applicable not only to the analysis of single transactions but to the successive phases of an evolving interaction process. Furthermore, the same events that we call opportunity structure are also classifiable as deviant or nondeviant action or both (depending upon whether ego and alter agree on their rules for defining deviance).

The normative rules are themselves subject to change; perhaps we may think of these too as changes in the opportunity structure. Changes in the rhetoric of deviance transform from legitimate to illegitimate, or vice versa, opportunities open to ego (here the sector of deviant action). Changes in the rhetoric of control effect corresponding transformations in the deviant–non-deviant status of opportunities open to alter (here the sector of control). In other words, changes in the opportunity structure may be situational (changes in the means and conditions of action) or normative (changes in the rhetorics).

Differential Association Theory

Edwin H. Sutherland's version [2] of cultural-transmission theory, his theory of differential association, may also be reconsidered from the perspective of interaction process. According to this theory, deviant behavior (or, in Sutherland's own formulation, crime) is something one learns in a process of association with others. Through their actions and words they communicate definitions favorable or unfavorable to the commission of deviant behavior. Ego's propensity to deviant behavior is a function of the relative priority, intensity, frequency, and duration of exposure to deviant and non-deviant definitions in his environment.

This, too, is a very one-sided view. The definitions that alter presents to ego are aspects of alter's behavior. This behavior, like ego's, is learned and, like ego's, presumably in a process of differential association with the definitions in *his* environment. These definitions include those that ego, through his words and deeds, presents to alter even as he is responding to alter. In short, if ego interacts with alter, then alter interacts with ego, and each is learning from an environment that is, in turn, simultaneously learning from him. Again, as in opportunity structure theory, we are dealing with a continuing interaction process and we view what is happening on both sides of this interaction process in terms of the same conceptual scheme.

Specifically, suppose that alter, by performing or applauding a certain kind of behavior, presents ego with a strongly favorable definition of that behavior. Suppose that ego, shocked and incredulous, responds:

2 Albert Cohen, Alfred Lindesmith, and Karl Schuessler, *The Sutherland Papers* (Bloomington: Indiana University Press, 1956), pp. 5–43.

"How can you do (or say) a thing like that!" But ego and alter are, as we say, positive reference objects for one another. Ego, despite his shock, is at least aware of the possibility of seeing that behavior in a new light, and the strength of his conviction about its impropriety may be a bit shaken. Alter, on the other hand, surprised and a bit discomfited by ego's disapproval, is likely somewhat to temper his advocacy the next time around. There is a likelihood that, as the interaction proceeds, ego and alter will both change and eventually stabilize at a consensual definition at some intermediate point. If, by contrast, they are negative reference objects for one another, there is a likelihood that an initial consensus will be disturbed or disrupted, and they may move in opposite directions and restabilize only when each is satisfied that he is not in the same camp as the other. Suppose a third possibility: that ego and alter are positive reference objects for one another and that they have in common interests whose realization is similarly thwarted by the established rules to which, however, they both subscribe. They will likely engage jointly in a sounding-out and exploratory process leading to qualitatively new, subcultural rhetorics and definitions that were not part of the scene at the beginning of the interaction.

In brief, differential association theory in its original form has to do with changes in ego's attitudes in consequence of exposure to alter's definitions, and is concerned with explaining behavior in the sector of deviant action. When we place this theory within an interaction process framework, we get a new theory broader in scope and suggestive of outcomes that could not have been derived from the original theory. Specifically, we have arrived, by a slightly different route, at a formulation of the theory of the emergence of new cultures that I first presented some years ago in *Delinquent Boys*.[3] In its expanded form, the theory is now relevant to transformations in the normative system itself.

Reinforcement Learning Theory

There have been a few attempts [4] to apply reinforcement learning theory to deviant behavior; these too — despite brave remarks about "feedback" — have suffered from onesidedness. For our purposes, the

[3] Albert K. Cohen, *Delinquent Boys: The Culture of the Gang* (Glencoe, Ill.: The Free Press, 1955).

[4] C. R. Jeffery, "Criminal Behavior and Learning Theory," *Journal of Criminal Law, Criminology, and Police Science*, vol. 56 (September 1965), pp. 294–300; Robert L. Burgess and Ronald L. Akers, "A Differential Association-Reinforcement Theory of Criminal Behavior," *Social Problems*, vol. 2 (Fall 1966), pp. 128–147, reprinted in *Delinquency, Crime, and Social Process*, ed. Donald R. Cressey and David A. Ward (New York: Harper and Row, 1969), pp. 531–556.

technicalities of reinforcement theory are not important. The basic idea is that that behavior, deviant or conforming, tends to be repeated that is most strongly reinforced. Reinforcement — positive and negative — is, for the most part, a way of coding the response that the actor's behavior elicits from the environment. In fact, the environment may be conceptualized as a "reinforcement schedule" or a pattern of "contingencies of reinforcement." In the experimental situation, the reinforcement schedule is usually the way in which the environment has been "instructed" or "programmed" to emit or withhold reinforcement contingent on the subject's behavior. The environment is responsive, then, to the subject's behavior, but in the same sense in which a slot machine is responsive to the customer: it will reward the customer with a Milky Way if he pushes one button, with a Hershey bar if he pushes another button, but the fact that pushing a given button will produce a given candy bar is something that has been determined by the man who set up the machine, not by anything the customer has done. In "real life," however, and in many experimental situations as well, the source of reinforcement is not a machine but people, and — if reinforcement theory is really a general theory of human behavior — what these people do is likewise determined by the reinforcement *they* obtain from *their* environment. In brief, the reinforcement schedule — the responses that the environment will emit if the subject does this or that — is itself reinforced or altered by the subject's responses. We are dealing, in effect, with a dialogue between two (or more) reinforcement schedules, each changing — or "learning" — during the dialogue. A simple example would be the parent or teacher who finds certain techniques of moral instruction ineffective or too slow or too costly, i.e., "unrewarding," with a certain child, and so tries other techniques, i.e., schedules of reinforcement, until, hopefully, she discovers something that "works." As with the other two theories we have considered, we are dealing with an extended interaction process, both sides of which are conceptualized in the same terms. Under what conditions this process will stabilize, in the sense that the reinforcement that each party will elicit from the other will tend to maintain, on both sides, a relatively constant pattern of response, is a technical and complex problem in reinforcement theory that I am not competent to pursue.

Identity Theory

Finally, I should like to deal at somewhat greater length with a case of special interest to me, that of role-self or identity theory.[5] The basic

5 Albert K. Cohen, *Deviance and Control* (Englewood Cliffs, N.J.: Prentice-Hall, 1966), pp. 97–102.

premises of role-self theory are that each actor has a self that is a complex of several identities; that these identities can be thought of as a set of claims he makes about himself; that he chooses his actions in such a way as to express, test, or validate those claims; that deviant behavior is selected when it performs or subserves one of those functions. That is to say, either it directly communicates or symbolizes or fulfills one of those identities, in which case we speak, with Grosser, of *role-expressive* behavior; or it helps to create the conditions that make possible role-expressive behavior, in which case we speak, with Grosser, of *role-supportive* behavior.[6]

Now what ego will do in any particular situation will depend, in the first instance, on which one of his several identities is salient or at risk in that situation — which of those identities is being tested or challenged at the moment. The identity at risk will determine the consequences to ego of this or that mode of role-expressive behavior. That is, behavior that expresses or validates one set of role claims may or may not be relevant in a given situation, depending upon the role that is at risk in that situation. Finally, if the behavior that is expressive of the role at risk is not feasible or possible because the conditions that make it possible — the necessary skills or knowledge or other resources or props — are not available, then behavior *supportive* of that kind of *role-expressive* behavior may be motivated. There is, then, a kind of logical hierarchy among these three elements: the identity at risk determines what is role-expressive; what is role-expressive determines what is role-supportive. However, the directions of influence are not that one-sided. For example, if the actor is particularly well equipped to engage in behavior expressive of a certain role or identity, then he may contrive or arrange to place that particular identity on the line, so to speak. That is, the identity at risk depends in part (although only in part) on the kind of person he presents himself as being, the kinds of claims he makes about himself. And he will tend to make those claims about himself that he feels, at the moment, capable of living up to. On another level, there may be several modes of action that are expressive of a certain role. Each, however, requires certain supporting conditions, and some seem easier to create or acquire than others. In general, it seems likely that he will tend to choose those modes of role-expression whose supportive behavior comes most easily or is the least risky or has the greatest likelihood of success. Because these three elements interact in complete ways and seem to constitute a system, we will call them an *identity field*.

This field is not, however, a closed system. What alter says and does

6 George Grosser, *Juvenile Delinquency and American Sex Roles* (Ph.D. dissertation, Harvard University, 1952).

may enter and possibly change the field at any of the three points. For example, if a colleague — a fellow thief, a fellow soldier, or a fellow policeman — asks me to lie on his behalf, my claims to being a loyal comrade are now at risk. I am not "in general" or "by nature" a perjurer, but I may perjure myself because there is no other way of validating that identity in the circumstances.

The behavior by which one attempts to express or validate the identity at risk also depends upon alter. The main reason is obvious. If you want to tell alter something, whether by word or deed, you must talk his language. If the language changes, or varies from one subculture to another, then the actions that will convey the intended message must vary accordingly. But it is not only a matter of the standardized "dictionary meanings," so to speak, of words and deeds. What people take my words to mean depends partly on the fact that *I* say them, and this fact makes them more credible or less credible or otherwise alters their meaning. How the authorship affects the meaning depends on the beliefs that others have previously built up about me, either through personal interaction or report.

Finally, the conditions that support this or that mode of expressive behavior depend likewise on alter, for it is largely what alter does that determines whether I shall have the opportunity to "learn, practice, and perform" the behavior expressive of the roles I claim.

Pursuing the logic of interaction process, we see also that what alter does and how his actions enter into ego's identity field is to some degree a consequence of ego's own behavior. These consequences may be intended and desired. Ego may, for example, actively encourage alter to assume a role that will, in turn, call upon ego to assume a complementary role. Ego may try to influence the role vocabulary of his environment or the specific meanings that alter will impute to his — ego's — authorship. And he may, of course, seek out and solicit alter's tutelage or assistance for role-supportive behavior.

Finally, to round out the implications of the interaction process approach, everything we have said about ego can likewise be said about alter. Alter, too, has an identity field. What he does also depends on how environmental events impinge upon that identity field. And ego, to whom alter is responding, is part of that environment. We may, then, say that ego and alter are both loci of identity fields; that the sociological investigator may code the actions of each in terms of their consequences within the identity field of the other; and that the course of action may be interpreted as a process of interaction between two identity fields.

In identity theory, the normative rules are the legitimate expectations that attach to the roles out of which the participants construct their identities. So far, our treatment has been concerned with the maneuverings of the participants under those rules. The same concern with identity may be pursued on another level, namely, efforts to shape the rules themselves, by contending for a version of the rules that makes it easier to build a case for the identity one claims. The marijuana smoker's limiting of his smoking to private places and sympathetic audiences in order to avoid arrest and public exposure is in the sector of deviant action. His efforts at the same time to legalize marijuana may represent the pursuit of the same value in the sector of the rhetoric of deviance. (A non-smoker may participate also in this crusade, not to bring his behavior out of the shadow of deviance, but to express and validate his claims to being a "liberal," "tolerant," and "progressive" person.) The policeman, by the same token, may seek to enhance his performance in his role by vigorously hunting down pot-smokers (making use, perhaps, of illegal techniques of law enforcement) and/or by promoting legislation to free him from normative restrictions in his pursuit of "criminals." In other words, the interaction that is generated by the struggle for identity includes what may be variously described as rule-making, as role-bargaining, or as renegotiation, so to speak, of the terms of the social contract (with the possibility that the parties may not arrive at an understanding and may end up farther apart than ever). It is a struggle that ranges across all four sectors of the domain of deviance.

I have suggested in a very schematic way, without going into detail, how each of four theoretical frameworks that have been applied to deviance theory may be combined with the idea of interaction process, and I have hinted at some possible fruits of such an approach. At this point, three lines of endeavor suggest themselves. One is working out the refinements and implications of each scheme. Another is their operationalization, derivation of testable inferences, and their empirical validation. Another is the investigation of the relationships among the four schemes in order to determine (1) the extent to which they may be mutually translatable; (2) what important things that can be stated in terms of one cannot be handled by another; and (3) whether their useful elements can be fused into fewer than four and possibly a single, more powerful theoretical system.

STABILITY AND CHANGE

The preceding section has dealt generally with highly simplified paradigms of interaction process, constructed on the basis of social-psychological approaches to deviance theory, applicable for the most part to local and small-scale phenomena, and focussed primarily on the interaction between the sectors of deviant action and social control. We shift our perspectives now to social system and societal levels and consider strategies for constructing comprehensive theories of stability and change in deviance. One strategy, of course, is to try to develop more systematically the implications of the kinds of theories we have just discussed for theories of a broader scale, but it is time to consider other approaches as well.

First, however, let me state more explicitly what I understand by "stability and change in deviance." Let us think of social interaction generally as having the properties of a game. The study of games includes studying the rules of the game and how the game is played. The rules we are especially interested in is the subset known as "normative rules" or what we have called "rhetorics." These provide standards for evaluating or justifying moves or plays, and include rules for dealing with violations of the rules. The way the game is played includes following the rules and breaking the rules, the ways in which the players describe and label, accurately and otherwise, rule-following and rule-breaking, and what the players do about rule-breaking. A description of the rules and of how the game is played at a given time is a description of the domain of deviance at that time. Over time this description may, in one or another respect, remain constant or change. This constancy and change are what I understand by stability and change in deviance.

The Natural History Approach

The most obvious strategy for approaching the problem of stability and change might be called the natural history approach: to study, without commitment to any grandiose, general theory, a series of behaviors considered, at some point in time, deviant; to trace, over an extended period of time, its history *from the point of view of all four sectors;* to identify periods of relative stability and relative change; to try to formulate a typology of patterns, because these will surely show great variation; to identify circumstances associated with each of these patterns; and, finally, to attempt to formulate more general theories capable of accounting for the variety of patterns. An example — and not very many come to mind — of a beginning of such an approach is Jerome Hall's classic study of embezzlement.[7] Such studies could be done, for example, of marijuana and opiate use, antitrust law violations, political corruption, abortion, homosexuality, bank robbery, and so forth. It is unlikely that we shall develop empirically adequate theories on a high level of abstraction that are not grounded on the findings of this kind of research.

[7] Jerome Hall, *Theft, Law, and Society* (Boston: Little, Brown, 1935).

Equilibrium Theory

A very different approach might take its inspiration and perhaps some of its substance from equilibrium theory in economics.[8] Although I am skeptical of the generality that could be achieved with a theory along these lines, it remains to be seen what somebody with the temperament of, let us say, a Homans, and with his passion for conceptualizing action in terms of costs and income, could accomplish. Opportunity structure theory would be relevant to such an approach, because the concept of opportunity, closely considered, resolves itself very largely into terms of probability and magnitude of payoffs, expenditures of effort and resources, costs of failure, and effectiveness and efficiency associated with various alternative courses of action. Any particular mode of activity in the sector of deviant action could be thought of as entailing an investment; additional investments in any one line of action would entail changing increments of revenues and costs. At some point the costs will outweigh the revenues. The curves describing the dependence of "outputs" on costs or revenues would presumably differ for different kinds of deviance; some would be relatively elastic, some would be relatively inelastic. On the control side, alternatives could be similarly conceptualized in terms of investments in money, manpower, technology, and the like, and returns in terms of reduction of deviant action, increases or decreases in virtual deviance, appreciation from a grateful public, and so on. It would presumably be possible to specify, in terms of operationally defined curves and their points of intersection, conditions of instability and points of equilibrium.

From the view of such a theory, some changes on the level of rules or rhetoric might be treated simply as ways of reducing the costs of control. For example, changes in the rhetoric of deviance might simply abolish whole categories of deviant action, and release resources for coping with other forms of deviance. Changes in the rhetoric of control might legitimize more efficient techniques of control.

This discussion is intended only to convey the flavor of a style of thinking. On its face, its greatest promise is its application to those kinds of deviance that produce illicit goods and services for a market. Its greatest difficulties are likely to be those already familiar to economists: the problems of dealing with "normative constraints" and

---

[8] For suggestive analyses of deviance by economists see Simon Rottenberg, "The Clandestine Distribution of Heroin, Its Discovery and Suppression," *The Journal of Political Economy,* vol. 76 (January–February 1968), pp. 78–90: Thomas C. Schelling, "Economics and Criminal Enterprise," *The Public Interest,* no. 7 (Spring 1967), pp. 61–78.

"institutional elements" as variables — not just parameters — in a theoretical system couched in terms of logical means-end behavior.

A *structural-functional approach.* Structural-functional approaches are concerned with the conditions of viability of social systems. Finding ways of fulfilling these conditions defines a set of "system problems." There are many lists of system problems. Most lists, however, make provision for the following: The members of the system must agree on a system goal — a common conception of what the system is for; they must value this goal sufficiently that they are willing to suppress differences and to sacrifice private interests in order to attain it; the structure of action must include arrangements for producing a sense of progress toward this goal; the system must include arrangements for neutralizing environmental threats and for obtaining from the environment needed inputs; it must include arrangements for keeping alive and renewing common perspectives; and it must include arrangements for coordinating its diverse components and for preserving solidarity and mitigating conflict among its members.

However, the normal functioning of any social system, even when organized by like-minded people to achieve some highly valued common purpose, inevitably generates differences over system goals, the pursuit of individual and subgroup interests at the expense of collectivity interests, deterioration of solidarity, and so on. It is not merely a matter of an inherent and ineradicable reluctance of individuals to discipline themselves in behalf of system interests. It is also in the nature of social systems that solutions to all of the system problems cannot be simultaneously optimized, that concentrated and dedicated effort in one area necessarily aggravates problems in another area. For example, concentration on goal attainment brings out differences in the ability of different members to contribute, which results in stratification, social distance, distrust, and the impairment of solidarity.

However, this process of system self-destruction tends also to be self-limiting and self-correcting. Deterioration of system functioning manifests itself in the psychological fields of its members as anxiety, frustration, disabling uncertainty, a sense of meaninglessness, and anomie. This happens because, to some degree, the integrity and viability of the system as a whole are of great value to the members, and also because the realization of individual interests, careers, and emotional security depend upon the stability, coherence, and predictability of the larger structure of action within which individuals plan and organize their lives. Information, then, about threats to the viability of the larger system registers as problems in individual lives and relationships, and results in concerted shifts of emphasis to those system problems that have been neglected in the effort to solve other system problems — i.e., to activities tending to offset, repair, or compensate for the sources of "strain."

The domain of deviance is one setting in which this process manifests itself and works itself out. For example, during phases of the system process when a concern with goal-attainment is dominant, the rhetoric of deviance will be legitimated in terms of system goals, and will tend to define goodness and badness by the effects of behavior upon attaining these goals. Deviant action, so far as it detracts from the attainment of system goals, will be more difficult to defend to oneself as well as to others, and will tend to decline. The rhetoric of control will tend to legitimize strict enforcement and severe sanctions where such behavior is concerned and to cavil little about other considerations. The control process itself will be vigorously directed against such behavior and will engage the cooperation of the unspecialized citizenry with the more formally constituted and specialized agents of control.

A rather dramatic example of the influence of goal-attainment considerations upon the domain of deviance is provided by the role of students in the Delano Grape Strike or the "Huelga," as the movement came to be called. This movement of Mexican-American farm workers has had a strongly religious, and especially Roman Catholic, flavor. The farm workers subscribed to a conventional morality and condemned drug use, intoxication, and sexual license. The immediate objective of the movement was to secure for the workers a fuller share of the material wealth of American society. The students who enlisted in this movement tended to share a value system and life style that have come to be called "hippie" and that derogated and offended, in many ways, their Mexican-American comrades. If they freely pursued this style of life they would have antagonized the Mexican-Americans and impaired or destroyed their usefulness to the cause. They adapted by modifying or abrogating aspects of their style of life.

> At the beginning of the training period for the volunteers they were told that they must remember the priority set by the movement on personal behavior. It was stressed that they had been enlisted to fight for the rights of the farm workers; this was to be their primary concern for the time that they stayed in the movement. Personal preferences about other issues were to be put aside if they interfered with working for the Huelga.
>
> The Huelga had no strong, institutionalized means with which to punish deviance. Violations of the movement's rules could result in a variety of sanctions but they were all arrived at after individual consideration. The degree of punishment depended upon the status of the individual. This, in turn, was dependent upon the person's use-

fulness to the movement. . . . The most severe sanction was expulsion. This was seldom used since most of the volunteers managed to remain within the norms set for them by the leadership.[9]

On the other hand, when solidarity, the security of social-emotional networks, and mutual acceptance and accessibility are impaired (perhaps in consequence of "overemphasis" on goal-attainment), a concern with repairing damage in this area comes to play a larger role in all four sectors. Rules, or the ways in which they are interpreted, place less emphasis on goal attainment and more emphasis on reducing social distance, a more equal and less invidious distribution of rewards, and the quality of "horizontal" or peer-group relationships. Deviant action and the allocation of control efforts will likewise reflect the changing emphasis.

This exposition has concentrated on the functional problems of goal-attainment and integration. A fuller analysis would recognize that it may be necessary to distinguish between different system goals and different aspects of the integration problem, that other system problems are also operative, and that different sectors of the domain of deviance may be differentially sensitive and responsive to stress in different functional areas.

Having indicated the general logic of a structural-functional approach, I must now emphasize some qualifications and caveats, and incidentally make clear some very serious problems that must be worked out before we can say that we have a full-fledged and plausible theory, even on the level of its logical adequacy and without reference to its empirical validation.

This approach does not equate responsiveness to system problems, even the problem of goal-attainment, with the minimization of deviance. Rules are categorical; conditions vary. It is normal in social systems that solving system problems may require violating rules that do not take into account special circumstances, and the willingness to commit deviant acts may at times measure an individual's devotion to collectivity interests rather than "ego-oriented" concerns.

As we have already suggested, insistence upon acceptance of and adherence to a common normative framework legitimized by some set of "ultimate values" or system goals may destroy solidarity. A phenomenon that has frequently been remarked in the study of the family, the tendency to "normalize" deviance — that is, to assimilate deviance to some non-deviant category or label, to allow for "exceptions," and

[9] For the text on which these remarks on the Huelga are based and from which the quotation is taken I am indebted to Miss Cynthia J. Brandt, "Conformity Within a Deviant Movement," a term paper submitted to me in a course at the University of California, Santa Cruz, fall quarter, 1968.

to suffer some deviance gladly — is a way of avoiding the alienative and disruptive effects on family solidarity of stigmatizing and punishing family members or even of insisting on recognition and respect for a single set of rules. Furthermore, quite apart from effects upon solidarity, the material costs of attempting to compel uniformity of belief or practice may divert resources from more threatening sorts of deviance and other system problems.

System goals are not to be taken in a narrow, instrumental sense alone. A collectivity is itself a kind of social object. People have expectations of it. It has an image or reputation. Its members make claims about it. It has a role, a self, an identity. The presentation and validation of such a role is something in which the members have a stake; indeed, it is a system goal. Like other system goals, it is something on which people may agree or disagree. Like other system goals, it becomes a criterion for legitimating rules and conduct. In fact, the rules themselves, the dedication of the members to those rules, and the government of their conduct by those rules may be important components of that organizational or collectivity identity. This, essentially, is the meaning of Kai Erikson's book on the Massachusetts Bay Colony.[10] One function, at least, of the persecution of heretics and the witchcraft trials was to shore up and reaffirm the collectivity identity, the image of the Colony as a "city built upon a hill," a light to all nations, an exemplar of a stern, demanding, quintessentially Christian morality. The deviance toward which the witchcraft trials were directed was virtual deviance. It was an artifact of the control sector. Participation in the crusade against witchcraft was a way, on the one hand, of restating the meaning of the Massachusetts Bay Colony (or, in Erikson's terminology, of defining and underscoring the "system boundaries"), on the other hand, of communicating and validating one's own claims as an exemplary citizen of the Colony. From this view, events in the domain of deviance are to be understood in role-expressive rather than instrumental terms.

A qualification of more serious theoretical import is that no guaranteed wisdom of the body corporate insures that "corrective feedback" will occur as described in the foregoing sketch of the model: that threats in the area of some system problem will register in the form of strain; that if it does so register, the strain will be correctly interpreted; that if it is correctly interpreted there will be consensus on the kind of action that will move the system back to its former state; or that, even if this stage is reached, the point of no return will

[10] Kai T. Erikson, *Wayward Puritans: A Study in the Sociology of Deviance* (New York: Wiley, 1966).

not have been passed and that equilibrium, if it is ever achieved, will not be around a new state of the system.

In particular, what we have called "strain" will not necessarily be experienced and dealt with similarly in different parts of the system. Different participants will differ in the value they place upon system goals and upon particular conceptions of the system goals, in their investments in the reputation or integrity of subsystems, in their attachment to various parochial solidarities as against more inclusive, system-wide solidarity, and so on. What will be experienced as threat in the psychological worlds of the members themselves, and to what action they will therefore be moved, is certain to vary. These differences in the ways in which information will be received, interpreted, and responded to are themselves to some degree inevitable outcomes of what might initially be concerted and consensual pursuit of common goals. This very pursuit may generate the social differentiation that gives rise, in turn, to these differences in perspective; but the strain arising from these differences in perspective may not be enough to override the differences themselves and be capable of resolution simply by turning back the clock.

Finally, this same social differentiation also gives rise to differences in power. Not only is strain differently experienced; what one can do about it also differs. No "Unseen Hand" providentially guides responses to strain. There are many corporeal hands, some gloved in velvet and some in mail, some strong and some weak, some that can summon the help of other hands and some that must work unaided. Whether strain felt at any particular point in the system will result in action and whether that action will be opposed and how effectively depends upon the distribution of power in the system. Whether, for example, responses to strain will be in the direction of restoring a former state or moving toward a new state of the system will depend not only on the interests of different parties but on their ability to do something about them. Furthermore, the power of different groups is not necessarily currency that can be redeemed indifferently in any sector of the domain of deviance. There are, for example, some groups whose power to influence at least the official rhetorics is large relative to that of other groups, but whose power to influence the agents of control may not be correspondingly large.

It seems certain that the role of power is not something that can be simply grafted on, in the form of qualifying statements, to a straightforward structural-functional formulation. It is something that is so pervasive that it must somehow be woven into the very texture of the theory itself. Consider for example a criminal court. The "system goal" is "justice," and the system operates under procedural rules that are plausibly justified by their contribution to the implementation of this goal. All who participate in this system on a routine and everyday basis — judges, prosecutors, defense counsel, bailiffs, and so forth — publicly acknowledge their commitment to this goal and these rules. Indeed, the credibility of their claims is a major determinant of the validity of their actions in the wider system and of the availability of necessary resources from the court's environment. In a very fundamental sense, then, the operation of the court must be "oriented to" and legitimated in terms of these claims, and these operations must be sensitive and responsive to changes in the system goal and its implementing rhetoric originating outside the court. But this is a very far cry from saying that, in any simple sense, they "reflect" the goal and rhetoric.

On the contrary, it is also possible to think of the court as a structure within which various people develop differentiated interests having to do with their livelihoods, careers, reputations, comfort, and convenience. Each is in a position to "do something" for the others; each is in a position to "make trouble" for the others. Each, in other words, has a certain amount of *power* to enlarge or reduce the "payoffs" of the others' "games." These differentiated interests are not, however, necessarily antagonistic and do not necessarily, or even typically, result in gross conflict and contentiousness; i.e., they are not necessarily "centrifugal forces" tearing the system apart. Typically, on the contrary, they result in tacit but powerful understandings — that is to say, rules — whose aim is to serve the interests of the functionaries of the system and which are at many points in conflict with the goals and rhetoric to which all give public obeisance. (Among the rules, and one in which all have a lively interest, is an expectation that all participants will cooperate in maintaining a public image of decorous conformity to the manifest goals and regulations.) The least powerful of the participants, because he does not participate on a regular and quotidian basis, is the criminal defendant. It has been pointed out in numerous discussions of "plea bargaining" and the role of counsel in criminal cases that meting out justice more often than not runs off in a manner for which the manifest rhetoric provides no model and often in flat contradiction of that rhetoric. It is a process that the courts must be able to *reconstruct* in terms of that rhetoric for external consumption; in that sense, it is *constrained* by the rhetoric but not *determined* by it. And the defendant, whose rights are supposed to be safeguarded by the process, may, in many instances, be fairly described as the victim rather than the beneficiary of the system of criminal justice. Furthermore the criminal court has an impressive ability to improvise small changes enabling it to maintain its structure in the face of changing normative directives from "higher levels" of the system, without fundamental changes in the modus vivendi that the court personnel have worked out.[11]

In more general terms, something of the sort could probably be said not only of the criminal court but of most organizations. In fact, this section could probably be read as an alternative model for accounting for stability or homeostasis. In such a model, the steady state of the system, the values around which the variables of the system oscillate, would be determined by the interests and bargaining power of the members of the system. It would contain elements of cooperation, where those interests are congruent or complementary, and of compromise, accommodation, or exploitation where they are not. Events outside or inside the system that disturb the steady state would be experienced as threats to the interests of at least some of the members and would activate power plays, on the part of those threatened, to neutralize, "correct for," or extrude the disturbing factors. On the other hand, changes in the pattern of interests or the distribution of power or both will set off an adjustment process resulting in a new steady state realistically accommodated to the changes in interests and/or power.

However, I do not believe that such a "power model" can stand on its own feet. I will not dwell on the semantic problems of the concept "power" and the difficulties associated with the notion of quanta of power — "A" has so much power but "B" has twice as much — but will go directly to the matter of stability itself. Even if we recognize, as we must, that official rhetoric and public presentations of the organizational self often mask an unacknowledged but tough and resilient network of power relationships, we must recognize also that the stability of the network is more than a matter of checks, balances, and coalitions of power. The very toughness and resiliency of the network depend also on solving "system problems" not unlike those I mentioned in my sketch of a structural-functional model: problems of legitimization in terms of some criterion transcending the immediate self-interest of individual members, problems of trust and solidarity, problems of transmitting and maintaining common perspectives, problems of exchange with the environment, problems of coordination and conflict-resolution, and so on. In other words, a social system conceived according to a power model itself invites analysis in structural-functional terms. I am not minimizing the role of power. I assume

[11] Abraham S. Blumberg, "The Practice of Law as a Confidence Game: Organizational Cooptation of a Profession," *Law and Society Review*, vol. 1 (June 1967), pp. 15–39.

that it is somehow involved in all human relationships and transactions. It is a question of how a theory of broad and ambitious scope can be modified to take account realistically of the pervasive facts of power.

It has not been my intention to say some kind words about a structural-functional approach and then to negate them with warnings, doubts, and reservations. I grant that the discussion amounts, in effect, to saying that this approach to theory is an extremely promising *starting point*, and that, if and when it can be reworked to take account of all these complications, it will have become a very different theory. But this is not an unkind thing to say of any theoretical perspective in sociology, and certainly not in the sociology of deviance.[12]

[12] I am embarrassed to confess that I did not read Leslie T. Wilkins' *Social Deviance: Social Policy, Action, and Research* (Englewood Cliffs, N.J.: Prentice-Hall, 1965) until after I completed this paper. This is one of the few works that deals in an original and stimulating way with a theory of stability and change on a high level of abstraction. Had I read it sooner, my own treatment of the subject would have been significantly affected.

In this essay on ethnic-group relations, Professor Johnson illustrates how complex are the relations between stability and instability in social systems. Stability at one level or in one part of a system may be contributing to conflict and instability elsewhere; conversely, conflict and instability at some levels or in some parts of the system may be essential for achieving stability in others. Contributing to the analysis of stable and unstable outcomes of ethnic group relations within a society, Professor Johnson offers twenty-one variables that are presumptively important in such relations and shows how they have worked in a wide variety of societies. These variables are often involved in unplanned patterns of change in the relations between ethnic groups. In addition, since such change may be affected by "social movements," Professor Johnson offers a brief sketch of Smelser's theory of social movements and its relevance for ethnic group relations. He concludes with a statement on some directions for future research.

Harry M. Johnson

STABILITY AND CHANGE
IN ETHNIC-GROUP RELATIONS

In the narrowest sense, one ethnic group is distinguished from another by both cultural and biological characteristics. In this essay, however, I shall use the term "ethnic group" in a broad sense to refer to any fairly endogamous social category distinguished from another in lan-

This essay draws upon the theoretical part of a book-in-progress on ethnic-group relations, in which besides elaborating the theory of social change, including its social-psychological aspects, I shall describe four cases systematically with reference to the twenty-one variables briefly discussed in this essay. The four cases are black-white relations in the United States; French-Canadian separatism; anti-Semitism in the Soviet Union and the satellites; and the nationalist movement in India, culminating in independence.

311

guage, religion, or tribal or national origin, or in the statistical distribution of such visible genetically determined physical characteristics as skin color or the epicanthic fold. Of course an endogamous group that has a somewhat distinctive culture has a broad tendency over a long time to develop some degree of physical or "racial" homogeneity as well; but for various reasons there are cases of fairly endogamous groups that either are not racially distinctive or are racially distinctive (in a statistical sense) but have few distinctive cultural characteristics.

Membership in an ethnic group is ascribed by birth into a family that is commonly regarded as belonging to the ethnic group in question. Membership, therefore, is not necessarily voluntary. The typical unit of an ethnic group is a family, and an ethnic group therefore includes both sexes and people of all ages. (In a particular society, however, as opposed to the world as a whole, a given ethnic group may have a markedly high or low sex ratio or a skewed age distribution.) The ethnically categorizing cultural or physical characteristics are socially important, even though not all the individual members may have them.

Ethnic ascription partly derives from and partly leads to the psychological identification of group members with one another. The ethnic identity of a person may be a source of pride to him or may occasion negative or low or ambivalent self-esteem. Whether positive or negative in value, shared ethnic identity is always the basis for a varying amount of social organization (apart from families). Ethnically based organizations may include cultural organizations, churches, recreational clubs, various organized social movements, political parties, mutual-aid associations, and business or professional firms.

It should be obvious that the very existence of an "ethnic group" is a matter of degree. To repeat, the defining characteristics of an "ethnic group" are ascriptive status; cultural or physical ("racial") distinctiveness; mutual identification; the practice and presumption of endogamy; and the tendency to form some collectivities, besides families, by ethnic identification.

Ethnic groups are similar to castes and social classes, which are also to some extent culturally distinctive and endogamous; they may involve considerable in-group identification, and may be the basis for the formation of various collectivities besides families. Not all social classes and castes are technically ethnic groups, however, because the social classes in a society — Sweden, for example — may be largely homogeneous in race, language, religion, and nationality, although there will of course be differences in amount and possibly kind of education, in occupational level, and in general life style. Moreover, as a matter of definition, social classes or castes are distinguished from one another in social prestige; as compared with the society as a whole, the member families of a social class or caste fall within a relatively narrow prestige range. Although different ethnic groups in a society frequently do differ in social prestige, families of an ethnic group in the society may have a fairly wide prestige range in social-class terms. This means that some families belonging to different ethnic groups may share important traits in "style of life" that have significance for class position.

Nevertheless, ethnic groups on the one hand and social classes and castes on the other are indeed similar types of group. In some cases class stratification has largely coincided with ethnic-group stratification. Short of perfect coincidence, there are various possible approximations. Different social classes may not speak different dialects in a technical sense, but there are of course considerable class differences within the same broad speech community. Because of statistical differences in education and life situation, different social classes do not have quite the same religion even when they belong to the same church. Different ethnic groups in the same society rarely if ever have the same degree of prestige; even when members of a given ethnic group are widely dispersed in the class stratification of a society, still the different ethnic groups have different class "profiles" — have a different distribution of their members among the strata of the society.[1] Especially if social classes tend to be rigidly endogamous and if there is little class mobility, they may be ideologically and sociologically even more like ethnic groups. In countries with a hereditary aristocracy, many popular stories express the idea that aristocratic blood makes its possessor naturally refined. The princess could feel one hard pea through several soft mattresses. The innate nobility of the foundling prince will shine through, even though he is brought up by humble peasants in ignorance of his ancestry.

Not only do different ethnic groups in the same society ordinarily have differential prestige, but usually there can be said to be a dominant group to which the other ethnic groups are subordinated to varying degrees and in various ways. An ethnic group subordinated to another is often called a minority, regardless of the relative size of minority and dominant group. The terms "dominant group" and "minority" imply high and low status respectively, and a dominant group may to some extent exploit a minority or discriminate against it. In

[1] This aspect of ethnic-group relations is emphasized in one of the best general treatises: Tamotsu Shibutani and Kian M. Kwan, *Ethnic Stratification* (New York: Macmillan, 1965).

any case, the dominant group has more political power than the minority. Dominant group and minority often have "prejudice" toward each other — negative attitudes associated with somewhat simplified and selective ideas, often called stereotypes.[2] It is theoretically possible, however, for different ethnic groups to coexist and to cooperate to a considerable extent without a great deal of mutual discrimination and prejudice. *Pluralism* is the state of affairs in which tolerance and mutual respect between ethnic groups are institutionalized. In a pluralist society, all ethnic groups are permitted within broad limits to keep their distinctive beliefs and practices and to segregate their social life to some extent, but at the same time to participate in the common life of the society to the extent of their desire and ability. Participation in the common life includes full political and economic rights. Pluralism as an ideal may be approximated to varying degrees. Like all other social values it may be structurally important even though it is not fully realized at levels of social structure below the value level. We shall have more to say about pluralism below.[3]

The theory of ethnic-group relations has little or nothing distinctive because ethnic-group relations are often involved in social differentiation, social stratification, collective behavior, and social change. Perhaps the social and political importance of ethnic-group relations, however, warrants a special treatment in which as many aspects of theory as possible will be brought together and focussed upon them. I shall confine my attention to cases of ethnic-group relations *within* a society, but this limitation is arbitrary; it would be just as possible to treat in social-system terms the relations between Israel and the Arab states, or indeed we could treat the whole world as a social system and consider, for example, the relations between the so-called whites and the so-called colored races. (This does not mean that conflict along these lines is inevitable, as some ideologists think.)

STABLE OUTCOMES
OF ETHNIC-GROUP RELATIONS

It has gradually become clearer, partly as a result of Talcott Parsons' work, that the basic structure of a social system is cultural and normative. The *stability* of a social system is primarily stability of social

---

[2] Stereotypes are not necessarily negative. See Shibutani and Kwan, ibid., pp. 83–107. For a good general article, see John Harding, "Stereotypes," *International Encyclopedia of the Social Sciences* (New York: Macmillan and The Free Press, 1968).

[3] The term "pluralism" is being used here in a special sense. For a quite different definition, see Pierre L. van den Berghe, *Race and Racism* (New York: Wiley, 1967), pp. 34–36.

structure. When social structure is relatively stable, we may safely infer that structure-maintaining processes exist and are working well (but these processes can of course be identified and studied). An important implication of structural stability is that the functional problems of the social system are being fairly well met, in the sense that no dissatisfactions ("strain") are serious enough to threaten dissolution of the system or to cause many participants to press for structural change. This is only another way of saying that the basic integrative and adaptive problems of the system are being met. As Parsons has made clear, however, there can be *dynamic* equilibrium, which in his sense means that the value level of social structure (the most general level) remains stable partly because structural change takes place, often rather extensively, at the three lower levels of structure. Dynamic equilibrium combines stability with flexibility. It is not incompatible with a great deal of social turmoil and violence.

Because two interacting ethnic groups often have different cultures, ethnic-group relations are often unstable: that is, we can often expect that they will involve structural change or social strain that could lead to change. Still, the process of change does eventually result in some outcome that is relatively stable. At the extreme of relative harmony, an outcome stable by definition would be *amalgamation* of the interacting ethnic groups: a state in which any pre-existing ethnic problem has been eliminated by the merging of the groups so that they now form one group biologically, culturally, and socially.[4] In China, a small conquering group has more than once been swallowed up by the much more numerous and culturally superior Chinese. In other cases, where it is largely the minority (in the technical sense) that is changed, amalgamation may involve some forced assimilation and acculturation, but the outcome itself is at an extreme of positive relations. At the opposite extreme is a very different "final solution" — *genocide*, which eliminates the ethnic problem by eliminating one of the ethnic groups. This outcome is perhaps never absolute, however. In the two closest approximations in modern times, the Turkish persecution of the Armenians and the Nazi persecution of the Jews, numerous members of

---

[4] "Acculturation" emphasizes the acquisition of part or all of the culture of another group. "Assimilation" emphasizes some sort of incorporation in a social system. "Inclusion" refers to the process by which a group is assimilated to full status in a pluralist society; see Talcott Parsons, "Full Citizenship for the Negro American?" *Daedalus* (November 1965), reprinted in Parsons, *Sociological Theory and Modern Society* (New York: The Free Press, 1967), pp. 422–465. "Assimilation" is a more general term than "inclusion": for example, a tribe might have been assimilated to the caste system in India, but it was not "included" in the society. In the United States, the term "integration" *can* mean inclusion, but it varies in meaning from full amalgamation to mere desegregation.

the minority did survive.[5] Even as a policy, genocide is perhaps never absolute. At least, where violent persecution has occurred it has been accompanied by expulsion or flight from the territory.

A third relatively stable outcome, neither so harmonious as amalgamation nor so inharmonious as genocide or expulsion, is *separation.* A religious sect that fears contamination of its ideas or values might withdraw from the rest of society as far as possible. A more drastic form of separation would be *secession* or *partition.* A minority secedes if it leaves the society of the dominant group altogether, either to form a new society or to join some other existing society. Partition is the outcome in which the territory of the original society is divided between two ethnic groups (or combinations of ethnic groups). Such a division may come about through agreement or may be forced on one group by the other. Separatism is an ideology favoring some one of these forms of separation.

Two favorable circumstances for the relative stability of separation would be, first, agreement on the solution by minority and dominant group and, second, population exchange leaving each separate territory relatively homogeneous ethnically. Even agreement and population exchange, however, may be accompanied by great violence. When British India was divided between Pakistan and independent India, about 5,000 Hindus, Moslems, and Sikhs were killed and 3,000 were seriously injured in riots in the Punjab. About 10.2 million people moved from one country to the other.[6]

At least two other possible outcomes are also relatively stable, although considerable change from either of them is still possible and likely. These outcomes are *pluralism* and *dynamic equilibrium.* Pluralism (in the sense of the earlier discussion) may well, under circumstances of continued friendly interaction, result in a higher rate of intermarriage, hence a movement toward the more definitive outcome of amalgamation. Another possibility, however, is that the normative order underlying pluralism will break down and a new unstable period of conflict will ensue. In any case, pluralism, as a possibly stable outcome, differs from separation in that it involves more, and more friendly, interaction between the different ethnic groups, made possible by their common possession of values that override cultural differences. In principle, ethnic groups in a pluralist society in no way compose a dominant group and minorities.

Dynamic equilibrium, as we have noted, is by definition stable in

[5] On the Turkish-Armenian case, see Marjorie Housepian, "The Unremembered Genocide" (*Commentary Report,* undated).

[6] Joseph B. Schechtman, *The Refugee in the World: Displacement and Integration* (New York: A. S. Barnes, 1963), p. 108 and context.

one sense and unstable in another. But it might involve a relatively steady movement toward pluralism or amalgamation, or (probably less definitively) toward greater segregation and discrimination. Again, it seems likely that dynamic equilibrium is more stable when minority and dominant group agree on the basic policy or ultimate goal of ethnic-group relations. The most likely goals on which there could be agreement are amalgamation, pluralism, and separation (secession or partition).

All these outcomes are relatively stable in that they involve a reduced integrative problem for the society in ethnic-group relations. One theoretical problem to which we might address ourselves, therefore, is identifying the combinations of factors that are most likely to lead to one or another of the more stable outcomes.[7]

SOME IMPORTANT VARIABLES
IN ETHNIC-GROUP RELATIONS

Important variables in ethnic-group relations are those associated with change toward greater harmony or conflict. They affect the goals of dominant group and minority in their relations with each other and ultimately affect the outcome of social movements in ethnic-group relations. A great deal more research will be necessary before we can say which variables, among those that are presumptively "important," are most important of all, and in which combinations of their values.

General sociological theory, as well as specific research in ethnic relations, suggests at least twenty-one variables that we may presume are important in the indicated sense. These variables may be grouped, very roughly, according to the LIGA scheme made familiar by Parsons. Again following Parsons, we use the scheme twice, once with reference to the general action system and then with reference to the social system. Last are certain variables that are below the action system. It will be seen, however, from the following list, that these distinctions are indeed rough as used here.

Variables Presumptively Important in Ethnic Relations

1. Circumstances in which dominance was established
2. Difference in cultural level between dominant group and minority
3. Ethnic ideology of the dominant group
4. Ethnic ideology of the minority

---

[7] This section is influenced by Louis Wirth, although my emphasis is on outcome while his was on the characteristic goal of the minority. See Louis Wirth, "The Position of Minority Groups," in *The Science of Man in the World Crisis*, ed. Ralph Linton (New York: Columbia University Press, 1945), pp. 347–372.

5. Social value system of the dominant group
6. Social value system of the minority
7. Solidarity of the dominant group
8. Solidarity of the minority
9. Vulnerability of the minority to exploitation
10. Vulnerability of the minority to scapegoating
11. Competition between dominant group and minority
12. Presence of other ethnic groups that dominant group uses against the minority
13. Presence of other ethnic groups that join forces with the minority
14. Presence of external governments friendly to the dominant group
15. Presence of external governments friendly to the minority
16. Effectiveness of international organization in the particular case of ethnic-group relations
17. Physical differences between dominant group and minority
18. Relative size of dominant group and minority
19. Amount of spacial segregation between dominant group and minority
20. Sex ratio in the dominant group
21. Sex ratio in the minority

The *circumstances in which dominance was established* may be regarded in part as a cultural variable, because it is through tradition that they affect enduring attitudes taken by the dominant group toward the minority and, especially, by the minority toward the dominant group.[8] Before discussing briefly the significance of this variable, we might run down the list of its possible values. There seem to be five principal types of situation in which dominance is established:

1. Conquest: An alien group gains dominance over an indigenous population. The alien group may or may not be culturally superior. A great deal of violence may be involved, as in the whites' conquest of the Indians in the New World; or the alien group may gain ascendancy with relatively little violence, as the whites did in Hawaii.
2. Slavery: The minority is brought by force to the territory of the dominant group.
3. Peaceful migration: The minority comes of its free will, with

the consent and possibly at the urging of the dominant group,
and at least temporarily and to some extent accepts an inferior
position.

4. Reversal of relations: After being conquered, the indigenous
   population regains its independence and is in a position to
   dominate or drive out its former conquerors. This situation is
   well illustrated in the successful movement for the independence
   of India from British control and in the rise of modern independent Africa states. A special case of reversal of relations is
   illustrated by the present situation of the East Indians in Burma,
   Kenya, Uganda, and Malaysia, and by that of the Chinese in
   Malaysia and Indonesia. In these cases, the original conquerors,
   the British, brought the Indians or Chinese in as peaceful immigrants to put them to work as laborers or to help in administration over the conquered population, and after the conquered
   population regained its independence it confronted not only
   the ousted conquerors but the middle group of immigrants,
   who had enjoyed some degree of dominance under the protection of the conquerors.

5. Groups brought together by redrawing of boundaries: Notably in
   Africa, the European conquerors brought together in the same
   territory (e.g., Kenya, Nigeria) tribes that had been politically
   independent of one another; then after the new territories regained substantial independence from the Europeans, the tribes
   confronted one another and seldom if ever became harmonious
   and equal partners. Striking cases are the relations between the
   Kikuyu and Luo in Kenya; and between the Yoruba and Hausa,
   on one hand, and the Ibo, on the other, in Nigeria. In these and
   similar cases, both dominant group and minority are indigenous.

In general, a conquered population on its "own" territory is slow
to take over the culture of the conquerors or to accept its subordinate
position gracefully. Although its culture and social system may be
badly disrupted, they do remain as sources of solidarity against the
conquerors. To some extent, preservation of the original culture may
serve as a form of defiance, an expression of resentment. As Lieberson
points out, being "indigenous" is a relative matter. The French in
Canada were alien invaders from the point of view of the Indians,
but to themselves, vis-à-vis the English, the French were an indigenous
group and the English were the alien invaders. The French Canadians
are likely to refer to themselves simply as *les canadiens* and to the
non-French Canadians as *les anglais*. The French were in Algeria so
long that they had come to regard it as home, and they resisted the

Muslim independence movement with the ferocity of men who were defending their homeland against intruders. They were willing to resist an army from France itself. Similarly, the English in South Africa, and even more the Afrikaans-speaking South Africans of Dutch ancestry, regard themselves not as colonists but as native South Africans, as indeed most are. For that reason alone, they are not likely to give up their dominance gracefully.

Slaves are of course likely to be resentful, but as compared with a conquered indigenous population or peaceful immigrants in a subordinate position, they are likely to have little control over their culture and social life. Consequently they are likely to take over the culture of the dominant group. Today the so-called Negroes in the United States are culturally American and scarcely more African in culture than the so-called white population. Even the Greek slaves in Rome were hardly an exception, for if they retained Greek culture and taught it to the Roman masters, this could happen only because the Romans were eager to make some aspects of Greek culture their own: the slaves in effect were conforming to the cultural control of the masters. Whether slaves retain their original culture to some extent, as in Brazil, or lose it almost altogether, as in the United States, the point is that the dominant group is largely in a position to decide.

Peaceful immigrants are likely to adopt the culture of the dominant group for different reasons. They have come voluntarily, presuming the new country to be more advantageous than the old. In many cases, they are free to return if they are disappointed; or, if not free to return, they may be grateful for refuge. It is interesting to compare the French in Canada or Algeria with the French Huguenots in South Africa. The latter, as grateful refugees from persecution, were comparatively quick to accept the culture of the dominant group. Perhaps another reason that peaceful immigrants accept the culture of the dominant group is that they have little objective possibility of imposing their own culture on an unwilling dominant group. A dominant group controls not only the number of immigrants to its territory but also the selection of immigrants by country of origin. When the whites gained ascendancy in Hawaii, they invited in many immigrants for labor, but they took care to take these immigrants from *several* countries (notably Japan, China, and Portugal). E. K. Francis reminds me, however, that some religious sects, especially, have emigrated mainly to *preserve* their cultural differences. He himself has written up the case of the Mennonites for a forthcoming book on minorities. As he shows, however, the Mennonites have had great difficulties resisting cultural change; Mennonite groups have gone first to the

Ukraine, then to Canada or the United States, and then to Paraguay or Mexico (always leaving a segment behind).

The reversal of ethnic-group relations need not be accompanied by gross vengeance for past humiliation and exploitation. Among the possible reasons for the fairly good relations that may ensue between the former colonial power and the newly independent state we might mention the following:

1. The colonial power is not necessarily decisively beaten in violent rebellion, so that it is at the utter mercy of its former subjects; rather, the colonial power just gives up, with opportunity to protect the actual colonists to a considerable extent.

2. Closely connected with this point, the colonial country may well have become sharply divided over colonialism, so that the former subject people owes its independence, in part, to efforts by the old dominant group itself.

3. Closely connected with these two points, the former colonial power, even after it has given up its dominance, may extend considerable economic and military help to the independent state. This policy may spring in part from self-interest, the desire to salvage as much as possible from the wreckage of empire — economic investments, political influence, and cultural prestige. But there is no need to discount altogether a sense of responsibility in the old dominant group, a feeling of duty toward the "backward" that may mask selfish interests to some extent but that also may be to some extent genuine. The colonial power in its role as tutor has been likened to parents who profess to want their children to be independent but who never think the children are ready, till finally the children themselves assert their independence by vigorous rebellion. Taken in one way, this comparison might be offensive to the peoples who were subordinated by Western imperialist powers; but, if properly understood, the comparison need not be offensive at all; for there is no doubt that, as a result of complex factors, the Western powers were in some respects culturally superior to the peoples they came to dominate, yet these peoples as individuals need have no sense of shame whatever. As Max Weber showed, the basic direction of cultural development is largely an unanticipated result of factors that do not depend upon differences in native ability.

4. Another reason that the new dominant group, freshly master again in its own house, may not be very hard on the aliens who intruded, is that the newly independent government may strongly desire to keep the country attractive to individuals from the former colonial

power, technical experts for example, whose help may be needed in meeting the difficult problems of independence. Experts from the former colonial power may be preferable to experts from other "advanced" countries, because the former already know something of the problems at first hand.

5. Closely connected with this felt need is the more general fact that the attitude of the former "minority," even when it was actually oppressed, was seldom simply negative toward the oppressive dominant group. There was of course a good deal of resentment, but there was also recognition of the actual cultural superiority, in some respects, of the dominant group. This recognition was sometimes implicit and repressed, sometimes grudging, and sometimes self-abasing and exaggerated. In any case, some part of the former minority is able to accept the fact that they still have something worthwhile to learn from the masters whom they have just overturned. This recognition is likely to be especially strong among the leaders because they have probably become acculturated beyond the average. The East Indians and Africans who were trained in English universities, for instance, were by that training better qualified to become leaders of revolt.[9]

Tolerance for the formerly dominant group, however, is somewhat brittle, for progressive leaders in the newly independent states are in danger of being caught in what Parsons calls the restorationism-colonialism dilemma.[10] On the one hand, they must counteract the desire of some segments of the traditional upper class to "restore" the social structure that existed before colonialism; this desire is romantic (unrealistic) because it is incompatible with both economic growth and the maintenance of national independence. On the other hand, the progressive leaders must guard against the charge that they are restoring colonialism — a charge to which they are ideologically vulnerable because of their Western education and their desire for economic development. If the restorationism-colonialism dilemma is erroneously accepted as a realistic definition of the situation, it tends to polarize intellectuals between traditional restorationists (reactionaries) and some variety of Marxian radicals. As Parsons points out, the

[9] See, for example, F. X. Sutton, "The Social Basis of New States in Africa," a paper given for a Conference under the auspices of the Committee on Comparative Politics of the Social Science Research Council, Gould House, June 8–12, 1959; also M. N. Srinivas, Caste in Modern India and Other Essays (New York: Asia Publishing House, 1962).

[10] See "Some Reflections on the Institutional Framework of Economic Development," especially pp. 116–126, in Talcott Parsons, Structure and Process in Modern Societies (Glencoe, Ill.: The Free Press, 1960).

false dilemma can be forestalled to some extent; other possibilities exist and are sometimes relatively successful; but the point here is that the type of ideology that comes to predominate can affect the status of individuals and groups from the former imperialist country.

As for the groups of East Indians and Chinese who in various countries had been "imported" by the colonial power, their situation has been less favorable after the conquered indigenous population has regained dominance. Presumably they were resented in the first place because they were aliens brought in without the consent of the indigenous population and given a somewhat favored position in the middle. They were resented also because they considered themselves superior to the indigenous population and remained aloof from it. They prospered in business, partly at the expense of the indigenous population but in any case to a greater extent, partly because they had certain cultural as well as social advantages. Their position of relative, low-level dominance made them highly visible as alien "exploiters," with little solidarity with the original population from which they prospered. When the tables were turned, they were vulnerable as scapegoats, partly because their countries of origin were themselves relatively backward economically and could provide neither a model to be emulated nor help in the task of modernization. It may be that the ambivalent feelings of the indigenous population toward the dominant groups were to some extent directed so that the more positive feelings flowed to the prestigious former colonial power, for the reasons just given, while the more negative feelings were displaced onto the middle groups. In any case, the East Indians in Burma, Malaysia, Kenya, and Uganda have been discriminated against, dispossessed, or driven out to a large extent, and the Chinese in Malaysia and Indonesia have been feared and persecuted by the populations to which they were once superior. After these populations gained independence, it appeared to them that these middle groups, in the new circumstances, were a greater obstacle to their gaining full control of their own countries than the original conquerors were.

This brief discussion demonstrates that the first variable, *circumstances in which dominance was established,* is quite complex; in particular, the cultural aspect, conceived as operating through the crystallization and transmission of early attitudes, is typically mixed with situational and social-structural factors.

The second cultural variable, *difference in cultural level between dominant group and minority,* is obviously important to common sense, but its importance until fairly recently has been obscured by the reluctance of some social scientists, because of popular prejudice and ethnocentrism, to regard any culture as superior to any other. The fairly recent revival, on a new plane, of interest in social (and cultural) evolution has put social science closer to common sense, but of course has also gone well beyond it in making necessary distinctions.[11] In any case, the common popular tendency is to attribute cultural inferiority to a more general inferiority of native capacity, so that, for instance, the backwardness in some respects of African tribal cultures has been erroneously regarded as evidence of Negro innate intellectual inferiority. In other cases, an immigrant minority even from such a culturally advanced society as Italy has been at first regarded as inferior because the immigrants themselves were not well educated. Many such minorities have changed their "image," of course, through acculturation and assimilation. But popular misconceptions about the relation between cultural level and innate capacity are not confined to the dominant group. Culturally backward conquered peoples, and uneducated immigrants stigmatized as inferior, have to contend with their own doubts about their capacities. These doubts frequently appear as self-deprecation, boastfulness, or defensiveness, and they may constitute a culturally and socially determined personality handicap in the effort to gain self-esteem and social acceptance.[12] They may also, however, be a goad to achievement.[13]

The third and fourth variables are *ethnic ideology of the dominant group* and *ethnic ideology of the minority*. An ideology is a more or less coherent set of ideas about the nature of a particular social system or class of systems — its place and effect in a larger social world, its mechanisms of functioning, and the causes of its alleged defects if any. An ideology is thus closely bound up with a value system and a complex of social interests. Ideologies frequently contain a considerable amount of cognitive distortion — selectivity of facts and objec-

---

[11] See Talcott Parsons, "Evolutionary Universals in Society," *American Sociological Review* (June 1964); reprinted in Parsons, *Sociological Theory and Modern Society*, pp. 490–520. See also Parsons, *Societies: Evolutionary and Comparative Perspectives*. Foundations of Modern Sociology Series, Alex Inkeles, general editor (Englewood Cliffs, N.J.: Prentice-Hall, 1966). For an earlier discussion bearing more on cultural systems than on social systems, see Robert K. Merton, "Civilization and Culture," *Sociology and Social Research*, vol. 1 (1936): pp. 894–904.

[12] Thomas F. Pettigrew points out that Americans were once very defensive about their cultural inferiority vis-à-vis Europe; see his *Profile of the Negro American* (Princeton, N.J.: Van Nostrand, 1964), chap. 1.

[13] See Everett E. Hagen, *On the Theory of Social Change* (Homewood, Ill.: Dorsey, 1962). Hagen's theory, of course, suggests only one possible route to economic growth or social or cultural change in general, and probably not the most important route. (In general, Hagen's references to Max Weber are quite superficial.) For the route that Hagen does stress to run to its creative conclusion, moreover, Hagen sometimes allows a very generous amount of time — in one case, several centuries.

tively untenable interpretations.[14] In the frequently tense relations between ethnic groups, ideological distortion is common on both sides. In the United States, perhaps the most common idea used by whites to justify differential treatment of Negroes is that Negroes are biologically inferior in intelligence and, if intermixed freely with whites, would undermine the biological basis of civilization. This gross ideological distortion is rapidly losing currency, but it has of course been very common in the recent past. Another ideological defense of segregation and discrimination has been the idea, allegedly drawn from both the Old and New Testaments, that God created Negroes inferior and meant them to be slaves.[15] In South Africa, it was "obvious" to the Dutch Calvinists that the blacks are inferior, and in the struggle for control of the land they developed the idea, suggested by the Old Testament, that they were God's Chosen People, destined to bear witness and to endure great trials in holding the Promised Land against the surrounding heathens. Thus opposition and trouble were to be expected.[16] The minority also develops ideological distortions. Some (apparently not a great many) Negro leaders in the United States today have (or at least vigorously express) the idea that whites as such are nothing but vicious hypocrites and that

[14] See Talcott Parsons, "An Approach to the Sociology of Knowledge," vol. 4, pp. 25–49 in World Congress of Sociology, Fourth, Milan and Stresa, *Transactions* (Louvain, Belgium: International Sociological Association, 1959); and the two separate articles on ideology by Edward Shils and Harry M. Johnson in the *International Encyclopedia of the Social Sciences*, vol. 7, pp. 66–85.

[15] Slavery in the Bible is of course a complex topic. See the discussion by Jerald C. Brauer, *Protestantism in America: A Narrative History* (Philadelphia: Westminster Press, 1963), chap. 11, especially pp. 172–174. Slavery is certainly contrary to the *spirit* of the basic Christian message as most people have interpreted it. To be sure, Paul did send a runaway slave back to Philemon, the slave's master, with a letter urging Philemon to receive the slave, whom Paul had converted, as a "beloved brother." One is tempted to think that defense of slavery in America in the nineteenth century, by reference to the Bible, was at least selective and at best desperate. As Brauer points out, it is significant that the Northern and Southern churches split when the issue of slavery became hot enough to bring about the Civil War. See also John Hope Franklin, "The Two Worlds of Race: A Historical View," *Daedalus*, vol. 94, no. 4 (Fall 1965), pp. 899–920.

[16] Jan J. Loubser, "Calvinism, Equality, and Inclusion: The Case of Afrikaner Calvinism," a paper presented at the annual meeting of the Society for the Scientific Study of Religion, New York, October 1965. See also Pierre L. van den Berghe, "Apartheid, Fascism and the Golden Age," originally published in 1962; reprinted in *Africa, Social Problems of Change and Conflict*, ed. van den Berghe (San Francisco: Chandler, 1965), pp. 502–513. Van den Berghe makes it clear that within the white Afrikaaner dominant group itself the value system stresses austere Calvinism, individualism, democracy, "pastoral" life (agriculture), and benevolent despotism (vis-à-vis the blacks). But the difficulty of "excluding" the blacks has led to "fascist" features.

they will be moved to redress black grievances only by fear. (This extreme idea, used to advocate or condone violence, is often mixed, however, with other ideas that are inconsistent with it, and one cannot be sure exactly what it means.) In any case, more rational Negro leaders such as Whitney Young, Roy Wilkins, and Bayard Rustin warn that this idea or anything very close to it, as a serious definition of the blacks' situation in the United States, could have tragic consequences for the whole population, white and black alike.[17]

Ideology is largely shaped by other factors, some of which are included among the variables listed previously; but once ideological distortions are clearly crystallized as part of culture they work in ethnic-group relations as causes as well as effects.

The next two variables are the social *value system of the dominant group* and the social *value system of the minority*. Following the usage established by Parsons, "values" are the most general conceptions of ideal or desirable states of a certain class of objects. Thus there are many types of value.[18] Social values (ideal conceptions of a class of social systems) are cultural insofar as they are shared; they are social-structural insofar as participants in the social system are committed to realizing the values — to making the social system conform, or keeping it in conformity with the ideal conception. Realizing the values means attempting to make the lower levels of social structure carry out or fulfill the general ideal conception with increasing specificity, allowing for the increasingly specific and constraining features of the environment of the social system. The levels of *societal* structure below the value level are social institutions (norms governing whole classes of collectivities, relationships, and status-roles), the varying structure of specific collectivities, and the structure of specific (unique) status-roles. Thus the societal value system is at the top of a

---

[17] See, for example, Bayard Rustin, "The Anatomy of Frustration," an address given on May 6, 1968, and printed as a pamphlet by the Anti-Defamation League of B'nai B'rith (315 Lexington Ave., New York, N.Y. 10016). This short speech contains an excellent interpretation of the feelings of Negro Americans today. Another piece by Rustin is also very good and relevant: " 'Black Power' and Coalition Politics," a *Commentary Report*, undated.

[18] See Talcott Parsons and Winston White, "The Link Between Character and Society," in *Culture and Social Character*, ed. Seymour Martin Lipset and Leo Lowenthal (New York: The Free Press, 1961), pp. 89–135; reprinted in Parsons, *Social Structure and Personality* (New York: The Free Press, 1964), chap. 8 (but see especially pp. 193–198); Parsons, "An Approach to Psychological Theory in Terms of the Theory of Action," in *Psychology: A Study of a Science*, ed. Sigmund Koch, vol. 3, pp. 612–711, esp. pp. 659–671; Parsons, "On the Concept of Value Commitments," *Sociological Inquiry*, vol. 38, no. 2 (Spring 1968); and, in the same issue, the article by Rainer Baum on "Value and Democracy in Imperial Germany," pp. 179–195.

hierarchy of control and is the relatively stable aspect of the dynamic equilibrium of the society. Because the basic social institutions governing all subcollectivities in the society must be legitimated by the value system (or else be unstable), obviously the value system of the dominant group affects what rights the minority may have, e.g., the extent to which the minority has the right to a separate cultural and social life, the right to social mobility, the means by which grievances may be legitimately expressed and remedied.

Some of the highest values of American society, such as democracy and equality of opportunity, are so far from being carried out perfectly that some members of some groups, notably Negroes and college students, question whether the United States is seriously committed to these values or whether the commitment is hypocritical. It is necessary to stress, therefore, that values do not work alone to determine action. Neither a straight "idealist" nor a straight "realist" position in theory is realistic. Although Max Weber seems to have established this point once for all, and Parsons has made it a basic part of his theory, not all social scientists yet take it for granted. Among the most important obstacles to the full realization of a societal value system are: (1) lack of complete institutionalization of the value system in the relevant population; (2) "fundamentalism"; (3) vested interests; (4) often deep-rooted ideological distortion; (5) ignorance, on the part of many people, of many of the fillable gaps between values and lower-level social arrangements; (6) ignorance, often even on the part of experts, of what must be done to remove existing gaps; and (7) the fact that there are many social problems and inadequate resources for dealing fully with them all at the same time or solving them all quickly. We will comment briefly on each of these major obstacles to full realization of societal value systems, especially if the latter are very demanding.

1. The dominant value system of a society may not be the only one. Groups in the population may persist in their commitment to some *other values*, other groups may have become alienated, or groups of recent immigrants may not have had time to internalize the dominant value system.

2. Even people who have internalized it may have that kind of rigidity about it that Parsons calls *fundamentalism*, by which he means the tendency to identify societal values with particular social institutions. Fundamentalists react to threats to lower-level patterns as if the highest-level values were being threatened, and fundamentalists may react this way even though the threatened lower-level patterns may actually have become obsolete.

3. Fundamentalists may or may not have *vested interests* in the threatened social arrangements. Vested-interest groups in any case are of course likely to be unenthusiastic about proposals that appear likely to reduce their income, power, prestige, or privilege. Thus, reforms needed to carry out the value system may be successfully resisted. On the other hand, as Parsons has pointed out, vested interests are not necessarily altogether conservative. When pressure for change is obviously great a vested-interest group may initiate some change to forestall more; it may give up something in the hope of not losing everything.[19]

4. Vested interests, of course, are often defended by *ideological distortions*. Ideological distortion, however, may just as well arise from any other limited perspective. People with serious, long-standing grievances, who may also have to devote most of their time to the basic tasks of keeping alive, may become so much obsessed by their own social situation that they have little interest in the varied problems of the whole society; their intense experience of their own plight causes them to ignore many other aspects of social reality or to perceive them in a highly selective way, amounting sometimes to paranoid distortion.

The pressure of vested interests and the prevalence of ideological distortion may lead to a gross perversion of the value system, at least for some time and for some people. The historian Stanley Elkins has argued that the strict Calvinist value system of many Southern whites in the United States came into sharp conflict with their economic interest in maintaining and extending slavery. According to Elkins, the value system, if carried out, would have forced them to abolish slavery; renouncing the wealth that slavery made possible was, however, too difficult to contemplate. In this conflict, the Southern whites developed the ideological distortions we have already mentioned, with the result that the treatment of Negroes was perhaps harsher than it would have been if the value system had been less demanding.[20] The rigid ideological distortions were a kind of tribute

[19] Parsons, "Some Reflections on the Institutional Farmework of Economic Development."

[20] Stanley M. Elkins, *Slavery: A Problem in American Institutional and Intellectual Life* (Chicago: University of Chicago Press, 1959). Gunnar Myrdal, in *An American Dilemma* (New York: Harper, 1944), p. 591, makes a similar point, as we are reminded by Louis Schneider and Arthur J. Brodbeck in "Some Notes on Moral Paradoxes in Race Relations," *Phylon*, Second Quarter (1955), pp. 149–158, an article that goes on to make some other interesting observations. We must not suppose, of course, that social inequality of opportunity, which may come to be regarded as injustice, is more likely to occur when egalitarian ideals are smothered by ideological distortion than it is when inequality is institutionalized. In pre-

to the value system. In time the value system would assert itself in a less perverted form. We should note, however, that even in cases of extreme value perversion the value system may still operate widely and without distortion for other issues and, for many people, even for the very sensitive issue that led to distortion.

The same kind of perversion occurred in South Africa, with even more serious distortion of the basic Calvinist value system. The ideological distortions justifying exploitation and segregation became so rigid that many observers would be inclined to say that white supremacy and racial segregation are among the actual social values of the whites of Dutch ancestry. Jan Loubser has argued, however, that the policies of white supremacy and racial segregation are symptoms of pathology and are perversions of the whites' underlying value system.[21] There are indications that Loubser's interpretation is correct. Along with the racial oppression in South Africa, there has been growing opposition to it on moral grounds, not only from the blacks

---

British India there was little embarrassment about the very great inequality of the caste system; and institutionalized inequality was stable in ancient Greece, the Roman Empire, Confucianist China, and many other societies. On the other hand, inequality that depends upon covering over democratic and egalitarian ideals ideologically, as in the United States and the Republic of South Africa, is always uneasy and unstable. The frustration of the value system is terribly costly. The Civil War in the United States would not have occurred if there had not been strong moral feelings against slavery. On this point, writers such as Arthur Schlesinger, Jr., and the Dutch historian Peter Geyl have quite cogently answered such so-called revisionists as James G. Randall and Avery Craven; see pertinent selections in Edwin C. Rozwenc, ed., *The Causes of the American Civil War, Problems in American Civilization* (Boston: D. C. Heath, 1961). True: the South objected to the tariff policy put into effect by the votes of the more populous industrialized North; and the South had locked itself in by its elaborate ideological defense of slavery, leading in time, in opposition to the North, to the development of Southern nationalism, which was given a certain legitimation by the South's position on the constitutional issue of the sovereignty of the states: but it was on moral grounds (the value system), not economic interest, that the North would not allow the extension of slavery into the new states and territories; and many of the Northern abolitionists took their stand despite their misgivings (not so reproachable then as now) that Negroes might not be biologically qualified for full participation in a civilized democratic society. An institutionalized value system can be hampered and to some extent frustrated, and it can be overturned or drastically modified by revolution; but as long as it *is* the institutionalized value system, it *will* be heard, like Lloyd Garrison protesting against slavery. The value system may be said to have ups and downs. In the 1890's and early 1900's, during a particularly "low" period in the United States, the "Jim Crow" system was established in a complex national episode of scapegoating; see C. Vann Woodward, *The Strange Career of Jim Crow*, rev. ed. (New York: Oxford University Press, 1957).

[21] See also Van den Berghe, "Apartheid, Fascism and the Golden Age."

but from whites. In particular, the South African Council of Churches and the interdenominational Christian Institute of South Africa declared, in September 1968, that the present social order in South Africa is incompatible with Christianity. By July 1969, 132 leading South African citizens had joined in a study project, the purpose of which, in the words of the director, is to answer the question, "Is it possible to create a basic order in South Africa based on integrative thrusts of love and association? . . . how do we suggest realistic ways of bringing about integration in our educational system, our political structures, our economic system?" [22]

5. Ideological distortion is possible, though not inevitable, because many people who are committed to the value system are ignorant of the extent to which existing lower-level social arrangements are incompatible with it. *Ignorance* of the actual plight of Negroes in the United States is still widespread, despite increasing attention to it in the mass media. Herbert J. Gans, among others, has argued, first, that the political institutions of the United States imperfectly carry out the principle of majority rule but, second and more fundamentally, that the principle of majority rule is an imperfect criterion of democracy anyway. He argues that actual social arrangements are such that many numerical and ethnic minorities are in effect largely without political power and are left with no alternative but violence and disruption as a means of expressing their political demands. Many political scientists have pointed out that the modern ideal is not pure democracy but constitutional democracy, which sets certain limits to the possibly tyrannical rule of the majority. Gans is of course correct in emphasizing that democracy is ill served by present social arrangements for financing political campaigns and nominating candidates, by stacking things so that rural votes count more than urban votes, by gerrymandering large cities in such a way as to neutralize the Negro vote, by some of our taxation policies, and by the seniority rule for determining the chairmen of important Congressional committees. He is of course correct also in emphasizing the importance of perceived self-interest in people's voting choices. But I should emphasize more than he does that as long as the great majority erroneously assumes that our political institutions on the whole are acceptably democratic, the majority will inevitably remain imperfectly aware of the legitimate needs of minorities and will not have an adequate chance to see that social values to which this majority are perhaps sincerely committed are far from being carried out as well as they might be. Social injustice is not due only to the fact that selfish people

[22] *The New York Times,* July 27, 1969, p. 101.

have most of the power and can afford to be callously indifferent to the needs of minorities. Social injustice also depends, to some extent, upon the fact that existing social arrangements do not provide adequate means of communication from minorities to the dominant group and thus make it possible for the dominant group to vote and otherwise act on the sincere, complacent, and partly erroneous assumption that they are expressing their values. Some of our economic and political institutions, as Gans makes clear, operate in such a way that the interests of the majority, unknown to them, are ill served. These same institutions, however, also prevent the majority from seeing that their own social *values* are also imperfectly carried out.[23] Our institutions, however, are by no means totally inflexible, and there is reason to assume that the present tide of criticism will eventually bring about change. Once enough people become convinced that social injustice is widespread, and can see a way of rectifying it, they will press for action to do so. Commitment to social values, informed by a more accurate knowledge of the situations, is likely to be far more effective than fear in bringing about social justice for minorities in the United States.

6. Ignorance of gaps between values and lower levels of social structure is an impediment to full realization of the value system. Even if these gaps are perceived, however, another kind of ignorance also keeps our capacity to realize the value system lower than it might be: this is *ignorance of* what *measures* would be most *effective* for solving the social problem. Most people, for example, would take it for granted that Negroes in the United States attend public schools that on the average are inferior to those the whites attend; this belief strongly suggests that improving the quality of schools for Negroes (integrated or not) would be a good policy for preparing Negroes for competition in our complex society. In 1966, however, the Coleman report cast some doubt on this belief that Negro schools are inferior to those attended by whites.[24] The investigation directed by Coleman did show that the average performance of Negroes in public schools is lower than that of whites, but gave little or no support to the view that the quality of the schools themselves explains the difference. More recently a group at the Harvard School of Education has checked out the criticisms that were leveled against the Coleman report; Christopher Jencks, a member of the Harvard group, reports

[23] Herbert J. Gans, "We Won't End the Urban Crisis Until We End 'Majority Rule,'" *The New York Times Magazine,* August 3, 1969, p. 12.

[24] James S. Coleman, *Equality of Educational Opportunity,* Office of Education, United States Department of Health, Education, and Welfare (Washington, D.C.: U.S. Government Printing Office, 1966).

that a more careful sifting of the evidence makes Coleman's conclusions even firmer than before. Jencks says that the difference in average performance between Negroes and whites is not due to differences in textbooks, the training of school teachers, the average size of classes, or other such factors, but seems to be due to factors outside the classroom. He suggests that basic reforms are necessary in the wider society, that these reforms should be such as to make it possible for more Negroes to develop "middle-class" virtues of self-respect and self-discipline, and that these virtues are also probably more important than book learning for employability in most of the jobs in the society.[25] Here we see an example of how "common knowledge" and even expert "knowledge" might be wrong. This does not mean, of course, that the schools could not be improved. It may still be true that the public schools are better adapted to helping middle-class children learn than they are to helping lower-class children. On the other hand, the intensive Coleman report, the Harvard intensive restudy of it, and other evidence such as that set forth in the Moynihan report strongly suggest that the public schools, if they were to be reorganized to meet the needs of the lower class, would certainly have to make up for defects in training outside the school and also for defects in political and economic institutions and in welfare policies that in turn are responsible for defective training in many lower-class homes.[26]

7. The last obstacle to the full realization of the social-value system is the existence of *too many* complex *problems* to solve all at once. This point needs little elaboration. The list of social problems in the United States includes inadequate medical and dental services, inadequate legal services for the poor, long delays in the courts, inadequate prisons, air and water pollution, inadequate consumer protection and protection against crime, inadequate public transportation facilities, inequitable tax burdens, and many more. In addition, neither our value

[25] Christopher Jencks, "A Reappraisal of the Most Controversial Educational Document of Our Time," *The New York Times Magazine,* August 10, 1969, p. 12.

[26] Daniel P. Moynihan, *The Negro Family: The Case for National Action,* Office of Policy Planning and Research, Department of Labor (Washington, D.C.: U.S. Government Printing Office, 1965). Some hypersensitive Negro critics of the Moynihan report objected to it because they thought it blamed the backwardness of Negroes on the Negroes themselves (for their having such a high percentage of broken families). Actually the report was an indirect criticism of *American society* from the perspective of the American value system.

It is possible that "fundamentalism" is the result of vested interests, ideological distortion, and ignorance. To these we might add the resentment of segments of the population who have already lost something through social change and are opposed to further change in the same direction.

system nor pure national interest could allow us to neglect many foreign problems. No call for a reassessment of national priorities, however successful and much needed it might be, could drastically change the fact that we have more problems than we can effectively handle in a short time.

We have been speaking of the dominant societal value system. It is hardly necessary to emphasize that the value system of an ethnic minority also faces all these obstacles to full realization, but on the whole the obstacles will tend to be greater if the value system is different from that of the dominant group.

Given the hierarchy of control in the action system, the social value system strongly affects the personality value system. There is much evidence that the average level of motivation for personal achievement differs from one ethnic group to another.[27] This is important because if the minority lags in achievement motivation, it will have a harder time winning the respect of the dominant group. On the other hand, if the average personality of the minority has a greater stress on achievement than the average personality of the dominant group, the minority will be exposed to resentment and possible defensive discrimination.[28] The classical example, of course, is the Jewish minority in various countries ever since the Dispersion. But there are many other examples. One basic reason for the tribal conflict in Nigeria seems to be that the Ibo (the main tribe in Biafra) are more ambitious and successful, on the whole, than the Yoruba or Hausa. The resentment of these other tribes lead them to persecute the Ibo, whereupon the Ibo respond by their attempt to secede. Ibo individuals have also been very successful in other African countries, such as Ghana and Cameroon.[29]

The next two variables in ethnic-group relations are the *solidarity of the dominant group* and the *solidarity of the minority*. The ability of the minority to improve its position depends to some extent on its solidarity. At the same time, the dominant group can more easily keep the minority in an inferior position if the members of the dominant group agree on this objective. Solidarity of course depends in part on shared values and a shared normative order, but it also depends on interests. The dominant group may be divided by religion or class con-

[27] Some of the relevant studies are summarized in David C. McClelland, *The Achieving Society* (Princeton, N.J.: Van Nostrand, 1961).

[28] See Robert K. Merton, "The Self-Fulfilling Prophecy," *Antioch Review* (Summer 1948); reprinted in Merton, *Social Theory and Social Structure*, enlarged ed. (New York: The Free Press, 1968), pp. 475–490, especially pp. 480–484.

[29] See James S. Coleman, *Nigeria: Background to Nationalism* (Berkeley and Los Angeles: University of California Press, 1960).

flict or different sectional interests. Vis-à-vis a particular minority, the dominant group may be rather heterogeneous even ethnically, as for instance the whites are vis-à-vis the Negroes in the United States. Similarly, the minority may be divided into subgroups, which was true of the Jews in the United States following the immigration from Poland and Russia in the 1890s. For some years these Eastern Jews were to some extent looked down upon by the Jews already here, who were mostly from Germany. The more acculturated German Jews were not perfectly sure that they wanted to be identified with the new-comers. In time, of course, attitudes in such cases are likely to change. In long-term perspective, ethnic groups are gradually being formed and gradually dissolving into others.[30]

Cultural and social differences are relative. Before they came to the United States, Italians were more likely to think of themselves as Milanese or Neapolitans or whatever and not to identify very closely with people from other cities; Northerners tended to look down on the backward South. In the United States, however, these differences lost their importance in comparison with the fact that the dominant group, knowing nothing about the prejudices in Italy, treated all Italians more or less alike. Thus the development of a self-conscious Italian minority in the United States took time. The same thing was true of the Negroes. To most white Americans, Africa was Africa; to the blacks it was, at first, the home of their particular tribe and its neighboring tribes, who might speak different languages and practice different religions. In time, of course, Negroes here forgot about their particular tribes, and all became members of one minority, member-ship in which was ascribed on the general basis of known black-African ancestry.

Probably the most important aspect of the solidarity (or lack of it) of the dominant group is whether it agrees on a policy about the minority. Here the value system and ideology are especially important. Wherever democracy and pluralism are accepted as ideals, a part, at least, of the dominant group will be in favor of better treatment of an oppressed minority. However strong vested interests in oppression may be, this division of the dominant group will tend to encourage the minority to try to win freedom or equality. This *social* encourage-ment will reinforce the cultural influence of the dominant group's value system on the minority. It has often been pointed out that one weakness in the colonialism of some Western European countries was that democratic ideals grew stronger in the very centers of empire; divided the dominant group, at home and in the foreign possessions,

[30] See Shibutani and Kwan, *Ethnic Stratification*, pp. 200–208.

HARRY M. JOHNSON 335

over imperialism; and eventually spread to the "inferior" populations themselves. The same process has been very strong *within* a (relatively) democratic society such as the United States.

The next variable we consider is *vulnerability of the minority to exploitation,* which has to do with all the factors, taken together, that make it objectively profitable (or not) for the dominant group to exploit the minority. One of the most striking illustrations of the variability of these factors is the change that occurred in the attitude toward slavery after the invention of the cotton gin in 1792. The movement for abolishing slavery had been gaining strength, but the cotton gin, combined with certain improvements in the machinery for making cotton cloth, for which there was a good world market, made it profitable to plant cotton in new areas of the South, and the price of slaves shot up. The pressure of greed was perhaps most strikingly shown in the difference in attitudes toward slavery that developed between the religious groups of the South as compared with those of the North. Whereas the Northern churches, in keeping with the sentiment of the world at large, increasingly found slavery repugnant, the Southern churches seized gratefully the idea that God meant Negroes to be slaves; argued that the business of the church is to save individuals, not to reform society; and urged their members to treat in a kindly way the "inferior" slaves in their care.[31] One possible reason that slavery was more easily abolished in Brazil than in the United States was because the sugar industry of Brazil declined in the nineteenth century. It was on the sugar plantations that most of the slaves had been used.

In the United States today, exploiting the Negro or black minority is still common, but today the progress of mechanization and cybernation has gone so far that Negroes are more fearful of unemployment (or effective *exclusion*) than they are of direct exploitation. This is another example of the variability of the minority's vulnerability to exploitation.

The next variable, *vulnerability of the minority to scapegoating,* has been well treated by Parsons himself.[32] Psychologically, the main mechanism involved in scapegoating is displacement, although projection may also be involved. Displacement is primarily a defense mechanism; the subject directs feelings toward an object inappropriate from a purely rational point of view, as if he might have the unconscious purpose of concealing from himself his feelings toward a more

[31] See Brauer, *Protestantism in America.*
[32] Talcott Parsons, "The Sociology of Modern Anti-Semitism," in *Jews in a Gentile World: The Problem of Anti-Semitism,* ed. Jacques Graeber and Steuart H. Britt (New York: Macmillan, 1942), pp. 101–122.

appropriate object; or he recognizes the true object of his feelings but conceals from his conscious mind some reasons for his having those particular feelings, thus displacing them in another sense. In scapegoating, however, although an "inappropriate" object may be chosen, the aspect of psychological defensiveness may be no more important than the "need" for relieving feelings by expressing them. This need for relief seems to have been involved in the scapegoating of Japanese and Japanese Americans on the West Coast, following the Japanese attack on Pearl Harbor. Surely, the white Americans who participated in this persecution of Japanese or who condoned it were well aware that it was not the Japanese in the United States who had attacked Pearl Harbor. Nevertheless, there may have been some displacement, in that some white Americans may have been seizing the opportunity to get rid of people whose economic success they resented. This displacement element, however, could slip in only because of strong (and quite conscious) feelings of anger against the real Japanese attackers and fear of Japanese in general (who, it was felt, might attack again or might betray important information to the enemy). In the background was a weak or lacking sense of identification by many white Americans with the Japanese ethnic group. (This is what Neil Smelser would call "structural conduciveness." [33])

Scapegoating thus requires: (1) strong feelings seeking relief; (2) inability on the part of the scapegoater to recognize the true object of his feelings or to recognize some aspect of the object that in part occasions those feelings; and (3) the availability of another object altogether, or of some pretext for attacking the true object. Behind the inability to recognize the true object may lie sheer ignorance (the actual causes of frustration may be quite complex). Or it may be too dangerous to recognize the true object. Behind the inability to acknowledge the true *aspect* of the object that, at least in part, has occasioned negative feeling, may lie the fact that the subject, underneath, regards his feelings as unworthy of him and recognizes that they are not entirely fair. Thus a pretext must seem to be more acceptable from a moral point of view.

For example, the whites could say the Japanese on the West Coast had to be removed because they were dangerous and disloyal and we were at war with their relatives. (So many white Americans thought, although there was little or no objective basis for fearing the Japanese on the West Coast.) Another background factor permitting the particular object to be chosen as a scapegoat is that the scapegoater

[33] Neil J. Smelser, *Theory of Collective Behavior* (New York: The Free Press, 1963).

can get away with it (he need not greatly fear retaliation). In turn, a specific aspect of this factor is that the scapegoater has little sense of identification with the scapegoat. (In minor cases, however, the scapegoat can "choose" the particular object just because close identification makes the relationship safe.)

Parsons emphasized two related facts: first, the source of frustration and the choice of scapegoat, in collective episodes of scapegoating, involve objective aspects of social structure, however much distortion there may be in the scapegoater's definition of the situation; and, second, that the scapegoat chosen, although the choice is not rationally justified, is symbolically appropriate in that the scapegoat can readily be associated with the actual source of frustration. Thus, according to Parsons, although Jews were definitely not responsible for the failure of non-Jews, Jews *could* readily be associated with success because they had been remarkably successful in a short time and in conspicuous fields. According to this view, modern anti-Semitism was in part due to resentment against *all* successful people, and the Jews were "selected" as a scapegoat because a high proportion of them were among the successful people and because, being an "inferior" ethnic group, they could easily be accused of having used unfair means in reaching their success. Where scapegoating of others is not possible, perhaps because the necessary distortions have been too thoroughly exposed, frustrated people must cope with their negative feelings in other ways. For example, they can turn their aggression against themselves, or they can redefine their life goals or perspectives in such a way that their failure ceases to be so important. Parsons's treatment of anti-Semitism is more complex than we have space to indicate here, but if it be taken as paradigmatic, it needs and deserves much further investigation. There is little doubt that scapegoating is common in ethnic-group relations and that vulnerability of the minority to scapegoating is a complex *variable*.

Competition between dominant group and minority has long been recognized as an important variable. Like vulnerability to scapegoating, it is complex. The *amount* of competition depends on at least the following factors: the kinds and consistency of discrimination practiced by the dominant group against the minority; the extent to which the dominant group may exclude itself from certain activities by branding them as too low; the extent to which cultural differences between dominant group and minority may disqualify one or the other for competition, at least in a relative sense; and the extent to which cultural differences may attract one group to an activity but give the other no interest in it. Competition, moreover, is a very general phenomenon; it may occur, for example, not only for jobs but also for places in school. The *effect* of competition on dominant group hostility toward the minority depends, also, upon the state of the market; if the market for employment is tight, the dominant group may resent competition more, and if the market becomes tight enough, the dominant group may begin to covet jobs hitherto thought too low, or may begin to discriminate more severely.

Competition has a double aspect. On the one hand, following the principle stated by Merton, that an "inferior" minority is expected (in one sense) to have inferior achievement, successful competition by the minority in valued activities tends to arouse resentment and envy in the dominant group; it opens the way for scapegoating. On the other hand, a culturally inferior minority with relatively few achievements to its credit can hardly gain greater prestige and be socially accepted by the dominant group unless the minority members engage in competition with members of the dominant group and unless they sometimes succeed more than the latter. This is especially important in the modern world for occupational achievement. Thus we must distinguish the short-run and the long-run effects of competition.[34] Perhaps a fairly general phenomenon is that the dominant group tends to resist the attempt by a minority to get into a field or a level from which it has hitherto been excluded but that, once access has been gained, competition in that field or at that level comes to be taken more nearly as a matter of course and the minority as a whole tends to acquire, directly or by reflection, whatever advantages may come with successful competition. Among such advantages are increased prestige and improved means for further competition and for further assaults on remaining barriers. As we have noted, however, retrogression also occurs. Competition, then, is a particularly good example of a variable that is not "straight line." [35]

The next two variables may be considered together; they are *presence of other ethnic groups that the dominant group uses against the minority* and *presence of other ethnic groups that join forces with the minority*. As we have noted, the dominant "group," vis-à-vis a particular minority, may actually be composed of several ethnic groups.

[34] Distinguishing short-run and long-run effects was one problem that complicated the heroic attempts by two different researchers to formulate propositions about competition, conflict, and discrimination. Robin M. Williams, Jr., *The Reduction of Intergroup Tensions: A Survey of Research on Problems of Ethnic, Racial, and Religious Group Relations* (New York: Social Science Research Council, 1947); and Hubert M. Blalock, Jr., *Toward a Theory of Minority-Group Relations* (New York: Wiley, 1967).

[35] Blalock, ibid., passim, discusses this problem. On p. 193, Blalock lists the following difficulties in causal models of complex processes: indirect measurement, nonlinearity, nonadditivity, reciprocal causation, and delayed feedback.

In general, if there are three or more ethnic groups in a society they may combine in various ways for political purposes. The dominant group may use the principle "Divide and rule." One minority may wish to dissociate itself from another, or it may join with one or more other minorities to fight for common objectives. What tactics are likely to be used will depend on other variables. For instance, joining with another minority may make sense if the normative order of the society and the spacial distribution of minorities are such as to give them voting strength. The existence of several minorities tends also to provide precedents. What one minority has done, another may come to feel it can do too. By now, the experience of "including" minorities in the United States has created the strong presumption that any minority that has not yet been fully included can be, provided the right kind of effort is made.

Many cases dramatically show the importance of *external governments friendly to the dominant group* and *external governments friendly to the minority*. Both moral and material support may be involved. The Nigerian government received both from England, and Biafra (composed of minorities attempting to make secession stick) received help from France. It is perhaps equally important that most African countries have tended to remain neutral or have even opposed Biafran secession, while perhaps urging the Nigerian government to make some concessions to the Ibo and other minority tribes. (Many other African countries have discontented minorities, and they do not like the possibility that the Ibo secession might be taken as a precedent.) The actions and attitudes of other countries have also contributed on the whole to stabilizing (in a relative sense) the dominance of the whites in South Africa. It has been very controversial that British and American business firms help to strengthen the economy of South Africa, hence presumably to strengthen white rule. These firms have the support of the governments of their countries. At least, although most countries in the United Nations disapprove of the racial policies of the present government of South Africa, there has been no success in sharply reducing foreign investment there. Some people feel, however, that the stronger the South African economy, the more must whites allow blacks to participate in it and benefit from it, even with continued great discrimination. These people feel either that the gradual assimilation of blacks into the economy, together with growing moral sentiment against apartheid, will eventually bring about an important change of government policy in South Africa, or else that the whites in South Africa will probably not change enough, and soon enough, to prevent an eventual violent rebellion, the outcome of which would be better, they feel, the more chance the blacks have had to acquire some Western education and skills. Whatever the merits of this line of thought, religious groups in Western countries are increasingly moving toward the position that any form of support for the present racist government of South Africa is wrong.

The white supremacists of Rhodesia and the Portuguese African territories give support to the white supremacists of South Africa, and vice versa. On the other hand, all these white governments must contend with the fact that all black Africa opposes in principle white supremacy anywhere. This moral and emotional stand of the African countries in which blacks are dominant (and not only numerous) is darkened, however, because these countries have many other problems to contend with and are themselves still economically dependent, to some extent, on South Africa. The present South African government has deliberately sought to neutralize black governments by offering attractive trade agreements.

In Cyprus, both principal ethnic groups, the Greeks and the Turks, are supported by outside governments — in this case, of countries whose populations are involved in the same ethnic conflict but to a lesser extent. That is, Greece has a small Turkish minority, and Turkey has a small Greek minority.

In some cases, the minority would have different aspirations entirely if it had no ethnic brothers in some external country. Just before World War Two, the ethnic Germans in Czechoslovakia and Poland were separatist only because the Nazis in Germany strongly encouraged them. It is hardly necessary, however, for a foreign government to encourage irredentism in a minority group; it is probable that many German-speaking Italians near the border of Austria would be separatist whatever attitude the Austrian government might take.

Closely connected with the actions and attitudes of particular governments about ethnic problems in other countries is the variable *effectiveness of international organization in the particular case of ethnic-group relations.* In general, the United Nations has been able to take a strong moral stand against the oppression of minorities in any country, but in particular cases the effectiveness of the United Nations seems to depend upon whether the great powers have some common interest or different but harmonious interests in cooperating. In South Africa, the great powers (that would have to bear the costs of vigorous intervention in any form) do not agree; hence the United Nations in this case is relatively ineffective. In Cyprus, on the other hand, both the United States and the Soviet Union would like to forestall the danger that world conflict might grow out of the ethnic-group conflict on the island; hence a United Nations peace-keeping military force has intervened and has been able to keep armed conflict at a minimum while negotiations go on. In Nigeria, although the disposition of great-power interests is complex and confused, apparently the Western powers would like to keep the Soviet Union out of the conflict if possible, and the Soviet Union apparently does not mind too much because she favors the stronger ethnic-group coalition backing the central government. Hence the relatively inactive role of the United Nations results from a certain measure of agreement between the Western powers and the Soviet Union. The fact that in some cases the international *organization,* the United Nations, does not intervene very vigorously does not mean that the balance of world *opinion* is unimportant. It would be difficult to measure the "force" of world opinion, but there is no doubt that every government has to take it into account in its actions toward its minorities. Undoubtedly the churches of South Africa are gradually being brought to themselves, restored to their "true" values, partly by the expostulation of *international* religious organizations to which they belong.

Physical differences between dominant group and minority are important for at least three reasons. First, they may help to distinguish the members of one group from those of another. Physical, social, and cultural differences that enable people to identify one another's ethnic group make up what is usually called visibility. Without visibility it would not be possible to have ethnic groups at all.

Second, physical differences eventually come to symbolize inferiority (or superiority). This symbolization in some cases is rather general; one handicap Negroes in the United States or South Africa have to overcome is the tendency to regard black skin color as an indicator of inferior intellectual capacity, therefore of a rather general inferiority. The question is still open, for some people, whether "racial" differences are associated, statistically, with actual differences in capacities; but on a rational basis the question is not open whether any differences there may be would justify differential treatment of ethnic groups. All qualified observers have to agree on the basic fact that in observable intellectual characteristics there is enormous overlapping between "racial" groups whenever social and cultural factors are controlled reasonably well. For the most part, then, physical differences (which are themselves not absolute but statistical differences) have little if any intrinsic importance, and their importance lies in their being the focus of rather tenacious cultural beliefs. Roughly speaking, such traits as skin color sum up, symbolically, the social and cultural experience of two ethnic groups in the history of their interaction with each other. Groups such as the Spanish and Portuguese, who experienced years of interaction with dark-skinned Africans of equal or superior culture and social position, do not to the same extent as Anglo-Saxon groups regard black skin as a mark of innate inferiority. In Brazil, people of Portuguese ancestry are the beneficiaries of this broader history, but at the same time they are also affected by the fact that there were "Negro" slaves in Brazil for over three centuries. To some extent, Brazilians are also affected by the prejudices of the "Anglo-Saxons" from the United States. Still more broadly, the social and cultural superiority of "white" peoples over "colored" peoples in the world as a whole for three or more centuries has subtly affected the attitudes of people everywhere. White people tend to think of themselves as superior to colored people, and colored people tend to be ambivalent toward whites.[36]

The third respect in which visible distinguishing physical traits are important is that they are difficult to change quickly. Some individuals of "inferior" ancestry can "pass" over into the "superior" group, but this depends on their not having the negative stigmata to a great extent. Most individuals cannot change their ethnic-group memberships during their lifetime. Moreover, from the perspective of an individual, the cultural symbolic meaning of ethnic physical traits is slow to change.

Nevertheless, the symbolic meaning does change in time. Taking Negro Americans as an example, we can mention at least five factors that will affect the cultural meaning of Negroid characteristics.

1. More and more Negroes and whites will probably come to understand that the connection between skin color and culture is largely adventitious.

2. The intermarriage rate will probably go up to some extent; a few very prominent cases could have a considerable influence.

3. Successful Negro leadership in the moral crusade to eliminate all injustice from our society would certainly give Negroes a more solid basis for positive ethnic identity and would create a massive historical fact that whites in time could only regard with admiration.[37]

4. The average educational level of Negroes will probably continue to rise, and more and more Negroes will probably have great creative achievements, increasing the prestige of the ethnic group as a whole; in an ethnically conscious society, even humble individuals are able to take pride in identifying with the great achievers of their ethnic group.

5. Black African countries will probably become increasingly important on the world stage.

Of these five factors, which are most important? We can only speculate. Even though people may know in a bookish way that cultural

---

[36] See the Spring 1967 issue of *Daedalus*, "Color and Race."
[37] See Parsons, "Full Citizenship for the Negro American?"

and social attainments are only adventitiously associated with ethnic physical traits, the association seems to have a very strong influence on the symbolic meaning of these physical traits. A reasonably observant person will be struck by the great emphasis given in propaganda to the real or alleged achievements of members of the allegedly inferior ethnic group whose general position it is sought to improve. A belief in the existence of native *capacity* gives pale reassurance, apparently, in comparison with *actual* known achievement. The first is somewhat speculative; the second is hard fact. If this point is sound, then of the five factors mentioned, probably the most important is the cumulation of cultural and social achievement by individual Negroes. Given the particular content of existing stereotypes, *intellectual* achievement is especially important. Occupational achievements in general, however, depend on opportunity. In this perspective, achieving social justice, largely as a result of the efforts of Negroes themselves, is also important. Two things are necessary: the platform of equal opportunity and the take-off of actual achievement.

The *relative size* of dominant group and minority is obviously important, yet difficult to be precise about. A small ethnic group is more likely to be absorbed. A small minority is more likely to make concessions. A large minority is more likely to become free or dominant in the long run. Therefore, a small dominant group is likely to live in some fear, either making concessions or using repressive measures to keep control.

The *amount of spacial segregation* between dominant group and minority is like relative size — important but difficult to be precise about. How large is "large"? How diffuse is "diffuse"? A thinly scattered minority will presumably have more contacts with the dominant group, create less fear, and thus find it harder to prevent acculturation and assimilation. A concentrated minority is perhaps more likely to think of secession than one that is scattered. Concentration near a border is especially favorable to thoughts of secession, and more favorable still is concentration near a border separating the minority from ethnic brothers who are dominant in an adjacent country. This is the situation of the Somali in Ethiopia and Kenya, and they clamor for secession. The fact that the Turks, on the other hand, have enclaves all over Cyprus makes secession and partition more difficult for them than it would be for the French Canadians, who are largely concentrated in the province of Quebec. The Turks in Cyprus, however, show that this variable is not simple; on the one hand, the Turks are too scattered to make partition feasible or easy; on the other, their scattered enclaves are large enough to make it difficult for the Greeks to absorb them. No one variable, "simple" or "complex," operates alone, of course:

the value system and the international situation of the Greeks in Cyprus, for example, make it impossible for them to use utterly ruthless measures, such as the Turks used against the Armenians in 1915–1916.

The *sex ratio* of a fairly large ethnic group is likely to be fairly normal, but the sex ratio of a small ethnic group is often skewed, usually toward having a relatively large number of men. When the Portuguese first came to Brazil, they were almost all men, because the voyage was difficult and the land was little known and dangerous. Portugal at that time was spreading herself rather thin, colonizing not only Brazil but also India and Africa. In Brazil, where the Indian population was very primitive, the Portuguese men were encouraged to marry Negro slave women to create a population loyal to Portugal. Similarly, when the Dutch first went to South Africa, they were mostly men, and many married Hottentot women, thus creating the nucleus of the group now known as the Coloreds. (Later the sex ratio of the Dutch became more normal, and intermarriage was discouraged.) In these cases the low *sex ratio in the dominant group* led to a high rate of intermarriage. If this continues long enough, the dominant group will hardly want to establish a fixed color line between themselves and the minority, because many dominant group members would then find themselves discriminating against their own legitimate children. By contrast with the Portuguese who went to Brazil, the English who came to the country that later became the United States brought their own women with them, intending from the first to settle permanently, or they soon sent to England for women to marry. Thus in the United States a more castelike line could and did develop. Many white men had children by Negro slave women, but these children remained illegitimate.

If it is the minority rather than the dominant group that has a low sex ratio, the outcome as far as intermarriage is concerned is more problematic. The early Chinese immigrants to the United States were almost all men, but the rate of intermarriage was extremely low, because the unacculturated Chinese men had little prestige and low occupations. (The position of the Chinese minority in the United States has greatly improved in recent years.) The Chinese immigrants to Thailand, on the other hand, intermarried with the Thai women to a much greater extent. The Chinese immigrants were mostly men, but the main thing was that Thai women found them in some ways more attractive than Thai men. China had never conquered Thailand; relations between the two countries were usually cordial; and Chinese culture had great prestige throughout the East. The men who emigrated from China to countries in Southeast Asia usually went into business and were more successful, on the average, than the native populations. Even in these favorable circumstances, the usually high rate of intermarriage fluctuated according to numerous other variables, such as the number of unmarried Chinese women who came into Thailand, the number who were not prostitutes, the compatibility of Chinese dialects of the Chinese men and the available Chinese women, the ease or difficulty (depending on political conditions) with which Chinese men in Thailand could send back to China for a wife or go back in person, and still other factors.[38]

ETHNIC-GROUP SOCIAL MOVEMENTS

All "action" in the technical sense is goal-directed consciously or unconsciously; but in treating social change in a society we can distinguish between change that takes place without *social movements* organized to effect it and social change that does involve organized social movements. Social change that need not involve social movements includes, for example, change in the rural-urban balance of the Negro population, change in the rate of Negro literacy, change in the average number of completed years in school, the gradual formation of a new ethnic group, the establishment of a new ethnic newspaper, a change in the per capita number of ethnic journals. The twenty-one variables we discussed briefly in the previous section are involved in much change of this sort. For example, increased vulnerability of a minority to scapegoating might affect the intensity of discrimination against minority publications or the degree of minority support for them. Factors not directly mentioned might affect one or more of the twenty-one variables and thus in turn affect kinds and rates of social change in ethnic-group relations. For example, invention of the cotton gin affected the vulnerability of Negro slaves to exploitation, and this in turn intensified the internal trade in slaves and the importation of Negroes from Africa, and reduced the appeal of the abolitionist movement.

As I remarked close to the beginning, no special theory of ethnic-group relations marks it off sharply from sociological theory in general. For the study of ethnic-group change that does involve organized social movements, we probably could do no better than start with Smelser's *Theory of Collective Behavior*, especially those chapters that deal with norm- and value-oriented movements. Smelser's components of social action are very similar to the four levels of social structure, and like them compose a hierarchy of control and conditioning. Smelser's first component, it will be recalled, is values (L); the second is norms (I); the third, "mobilization of motivation," corresponds to collectivities with more or less specialized goals (G); and the fourth, fa-

[38] G. William Skinner, *Chinese Society in Thailand: An Analytical History* (Ithaca, N.Y.: Cornell University Press, 1957), especially pp. 126–127.

cilities, is a broadened form of status-roles (A), which Parsons regards as adaptive in the sense that role performances or services in roles are the chief means (facilities, in a broad sense) for collective goal-attainment. Smelser's six determinants of collective behavior (including social movements) are all individually familiar under various names; they are structural conduciveness, strain, generalized belief, precipitating factor, mobilization of motivation, and social control. One of Smelser's basic contributions is his clear-cut conception of episodes of collective behavior as *value-added* processes; this conception implies: (1) that the factors that enter collective behavior as determinants may have been *created* in a variety of possible temporal sequences; but (2), that the six determinants, analytically, must be *activated* in the "proper" sequence: structural conduciveness, strain, generalized belief, precipitating factor, mobilization of motivation, and social control; and (3) that an episode of collective behavior of a certain kind becomes more likely as the determinants are "added" one after the other (although two or more may occur concretely together); but (4) that the episode will not occur unless all six are activated in the appropriate order and form.

Smelser distinguishes three broad types of social movement: the norm-oriented movement, the value-oriented movement, and the general social movement. Here we may mention examples without formally defining these three types. The movement to get the Civil Rights Act of 1964 passed was a norm-oriented movement; the Indian independence movement was a value-oriented movement; the labor movement in the United States, or the broad movement for "the advancement of colored people," is a general social movement. Any one of these types may be positive or negative: that is, a positive norm-oriented movement, for example, would seek to change some aspect of social structure at the norm level, whereas a negative norm-oriented movement would seek to prevent this change at the norm level. A positive value-oriented movement may be active or relatively passive. The active type, if successful, would involve changing the whole society at the value level, thus setting in operation a new hierarchy of control that would constantly press for changes at all three lower levels of social structure, to make them consistent with the change that has taken place at the value level. The relatively passive type of value-oriented movement would seek to establish its hierarchy of control securely for only a segment of the population, the participants in the movement and their successors, not for the society as a whole; it would be relatively "passive" in the sense that it would aim for a secure withdrawal from the larger society.

Applying these important distinctions to ethnic-group relations, and bearing in mind the relatively stable outcomes we have already outlined, there can be active social movements for assimilation or amalgamation, pluralism, reversal of dominance, expulsion of a minority, or genocide; and there can be passive movements for separation (withdrawal, secession, or partition).[39] Either the dominant group or the minority may be either for or against assimilation or amalgamation, pluralism, reversal of dominance (e.g., a movement for national independence), or separation. (We have to remember, of course, that many ethnic-group movements may attract and mobilize only some members of dominant group or minority, and that in some movements some dominant group members and some minority members may be on the same side). A movement for expulsion could be favored or opposed by either the dominant group or the minority, provided we regard a minority's possible goal of secession as roughly equivalent to a dominant group's possible goal of expulsion. There may be a dominant-group movement for or against genocide, but presumably a minority can only be against genocide. The case of the Hutu in Rwanda is not an exception, for after the Belgians left the old Ruanda the Hutu were no longer a minority subordinated to the Tutsi; they had become the dominant group.[40]

Readers of Smelser will remember that his six determinants determine the occurrence of episodes of collective behavior; they do not determine whether a social movement, for example, will be successful or not. Smelser does have much to say about the probability of success or failure, but it will also be useful, as always, to keep in mind the treatment of social change in Parsons.[41] With regard to structural

[39] Amalgamation may be a vague policy, as in Brazil, but a more likely goal of a social movement would be assimilation (see Wirth, "The Position of Minority Groups)"; movements toward assimilation would probably have to precede amalgamation as an outcome. Dominance reversal is such an important goal in some nationalist movements and, if achieved, is such an important turning point in ethnic-group relations, that it must be mentioned here even though it starts a new cycle and in that sense is not a stable outcome. Dynamic equilibrium is a relatively stable outcome, but in ethnic social movements it would be represented in movements toward assimilation, pluralism, or separation.

[40] See Elspeth Huxley in *The New York Times Magazine*, May 19, 1963.

[41] Some of Parsons' main contributions to the theory of social change are *The Social System* (Glencoe, Ill.: The Free Press, 1951), chap. 11; "An Outline of the Social System," in *Theories of Society*, vol. 1, ed. Talcott Parsons, Edward Shils, Kaspar D. Naegele, and Jesse R. Pitts (New York: The Free Press, 1961), pp. 30–79; "Some Considerations on the Theory of Social Change," *Rural Sociology*, vol. 26, no. 3 (September 1961); *Societies: Evolutionary and Comparative Perspectives*, Foundations of Modern Sociology Series, ed. Alex Inkeles (Englewood Cliffs, N.J.: Prentice-Hall, Inc., 1966); and "On the Concept of Value Commitments," *Sociological Inquiry*, vol. 38, no. 2 (Spring 1968).

conduciveness, both Parsons and Smelser emphasize the importance of the question whether the first two levels of social structure are fused or differentiated. *Fusion* is conducive to value-oriented movements; *differentiation*, to norm-oriented. Fusion makes the social structure relatively rigid; differentiation, relatively flexible. Both Parsons and Smelser treat social strain as a source of possible structural change, and both emphasize that the hierarchy of control, as it affects social structure, generally tends toward integration but, under some circumstances, can also contribute to social strain. (For example, the strain presently felt by blacks in the United States, with the sympathetic support of many whites, partly derives from the fact that discrimination is incompatible with the value system of the society.) With regard to the determinant "generalized belief," Smelser points out that the ideology of a social movement always involves what he calls "short-circuiting": the goals of the movement, even if attained, will not remove all the felt strain. In many cases, the goals are quite unrealistic. Parsons emphasizes at least five broad interrelated factors that help to determine success or failure.

1. The proposed change must be reasonably definite and capable of finding a place in the total social structure.

2. It is of great importance whether the movement can legitimate the proposed change; this means showing that the proposed change "realizes" the next higher level of social structure better than existing arrangements do.

3. The movement must have adequate means — for example, financial resources and contributions of effort.

4. In particular, the movement must be able to overcome resistance.

5. If the proposed change is to "stick," the eventual balance of rewards and punishments must favor the new structure.

Both Parsons and Smelser also emphasize the importance of resourceful leadership. Some of these factors are obviously important for success (or eventual failure) in the mobilization of motivation, Smelser's fifth determinant. The factors of legitimation and ability to overcome resistance are involved in "social control" in the very broad sense of Smelser's sixth determinant.[42]

[42] Readers of Smelser will remember that the sixth determinant, social control, is a little different from the others in that, although it comes into operation after mobilization of motivation, in the value-added process, it also operates throughout the process. Parsons's concepts of demand and supply, as used in his *Daedalus* article on inclusion of Negro Americans ("Full Citizenship for the Negro American?"), are similar in this respect and are related to Smelser's concepts of mobilization of motivation and social control. "Demand" and "supply" refer to pressures

My brief statements here by no means adequately summarize the theories of Parsons and Smelser that are relevant to analyzing change in ethnic-group relations. It should be obvious, however, that these theories do apply. The basic concepts, perhaps, are social system; hierarchy of control and conditioning; social strain (exogenous and endogenous); and various possible reactions to strain, of which one, pressure for structural change, is always met by resistance. The twenty-one variables briefly treated in an earlier section can easily be fitted into this scheme. As far as the determinants of social movements are concerned, almost all the variables can be related in various ways to structural conduciveness, strain, mobilization of motivation, and social control. Some variables have more direct or obvious relevance to one or two of the six determinants than to the others. For example, the circumstances in which dominance is established and the relative size of dominant group and minority are especially relevant to structural conduciveness and generalized belief.

What is the role of conflict in ethnic-group relations and the place of social-psychological concepts in analysis? "Conflict" has of course been used to refer to a wide range of phenomena, all the way from a difference of opinion about tactics between people committed to the same values and goals, to efforts at mutual destruction between groups whose values are incompatible, who have strong opposing interests and few interests in common, and who cherish various grudges against each other. As we approach the latter extreme, conflict is not functional for a social system; rather, it poses an integrative (functional) problem for the system. In such a case, it is the *resolution* of conflict that may be said to be functional, in that it may bring about a new (and perhaps "higher") integration. But where the resolution of conflict (a process that necessarily *involves* conflict) occurs in social systems, it has required organization, cooperation, solidarity, and the operation of one or more hierarchies of control in the Parsonian sense; the organized forces that succeed in imposing their will have had to be integrated to some extent; and if the outcome is a compromise, the other side has been able to gain concessions because it too was to some extent integrated and cooperative. Conflict of course is involved in virtually all social change, if not all social action. The obstacles to the realization of a value system are at the same time occasions of

---

from both dominant group and minority and to reactions to those pressures, also from both dominant group and minority. It should be pointed out that the demand-supply analysis could also be used in connection with social movements toward goals other than inclusion — in particular, assimilation, separation, or dominance reversal.

conflict. One essential condition of the success or partial success of a social movement is the ability to overcome resistance, which involves conflict.

In ethnic-group relations, which often involve exploitation, discrimination, and resentment, *violence* (which again leads to conflict) may well become an important mode of communication between the minority and the dominant group. Violence by itself is not a very precise mode of communication, however, and it may fail utterly if it is misunderstood. "Understanding," in the full sense that implies empathy if not sympathy, requires both interpretation of the violence to the dominant group and, not necessarily justification of the violence itself, but justification of the minority's sense of grievance. Justification involves reference to both the value system and the objective situation. If the sense of grievance is already known, violence can still serve a function analogous to that of negative situational sanctions in the exercise of "power": as Parsons has pointed out,[43] the negative situational sanctions that stand behind power symbolize, first, the fact that the authority exercising power "means it" when he demands compliance with a binding decision, and second, symbolize, more remotely, the *importance* of compliance to collective goal-attainment. Therefore, a minority (some of its members, of course), after expressing grievances in more pacific ways, may, even in unpremeditated violence, be expressing and actually communicating (to some members of the dominant group, of course) that they "mean it" (they really feel deeply aggrieved), and *demonstrating* that the solidarity embracing dominant group and minority has reached a tenuous condition. When violence is *organized* by a subgroup of the minority, it *is* an exercise of power, and involves, for the subgroup itself, binding (authoritative) decisions and collective striving for goal-attainment, and signals, to the dominant group, minority alienation and interest demands. Violence is never really meaningless, although its meaning may not be clear to everyone; indeed, its meaning may at first not be fully clear to the violent themselves.

This leads us to social psychology. Following Parsons, we may regard psychology as the science having to do with the structure and functioning of personalities as systems. *Social* psychology is concerned with learning and motivational processes and "establishments" (Murray's term) that may be very similar for many personalities as a result

[43] Talcott Parsons, "On the Concept of Political Power," originally published in Proceedings of the American Philosophical Society, VII (June 1963); reprinted in *Sociological Theory and Modern Society* (New York: The Free Press, 1967), pp. 297–354.

of (1) their similar participation and situation in a social system and (2) the laws of personality functioning. Social psychology is also concerned with the personality variables that may lead different people to react differently to similar conditions. *Similar* processes and establishments, abstracted from the concretely unique personalities, may pose problems or facilitate solutions for the social system.

Smelser, in his treatment of collective behavior, largely ignores psychology. This was no doubt a conscious decision and may be justified by the fact that there are different levels of organization in the action system and the social-system level controls the personality level. Thus it is possible to treat the social-system level without explicit attention to the lower level, taking it for granted that psychological processes are going on. Nevertheless, there is no possible objection, of course, to taking the social-psychological level into account explicitly; and there is every reason to expect that doing so will supplement Smelser's analysis rather than supplant it. We have already mentioned scapegoating, which often involves the psychological mechanism of displacement, projection, and rationalization. One or more Freudian mechanisms may well be involved in all six determinants of collective behavior treated by Smelser, as he of course knows perfectly well. The mechanisms of defense have to do with the integration problem of the personality. Recently, social psychologists have extended Freud's work. The theory of cognitive dissonance or more broadly expressed, "balance theory," takes account of the fact (not unknown to Freud, of course) that the pressure of conflict in the personality may lead to "genuine" as well as "spurious" integration or balance — to actual problem-solving as well as to "defenses." This is important in ethnic-group relations in no doubt many ways. For example, to preserve self-esteem, people who are forced to act in a nondiscriminatory way despite their prejudice, may, to be sure, rationalize their compliance, but they may also become sensitive to good arguments for compliance and may actually lose their prejudice to some extent. Another social-psychological concept is *relative deprivation*, which seems to have been given prominence by Samuel Stouffer. As Robert K. Merton has pointed out, relative deprivation depends on one's reference groups, and these in turn depend upon the kind and extent of one's participation in social systems.[44] More generally, the sense of deprivation is relative to one's expectations. More and more acutely, many Negro Americans feel relatively deprived although Negroes on the average

[44] Robert K. Merton and Alice S. Rossi, "Contributions to the Theory of Reference Group Behavior," chap. 10, in Merton, *Social Theory and Social Structure,* enlarged ed. (New York: The Free Press, 1968).

have been doing better than in the past, and their chance of going to college is actually better than that of whites in most of Europe.[45] The whites in Europe, however, are not an important reference group for blacks in the United States, whereas the whites in the United States are; and white Americans are progressing even more rapidly than blacks.[46] Moreover, in various ways black Americans have been led to expect greater and more rapid improvement than has occurred. It is itself an important indicator of social change that has already taken place, however, that blacks in the United States now take whites as a reference group in a way that, only a few years ago, they did not.[47]

SOME DIRECTIONS OF FUTURE RESEARCH

1. It would be awkward to have to continue to treat societal values as unique in each case. Instead, we can expect that more and more sociologists will follow Parsons' lead and deal with values in a systematic comparative way. A great deal of work will be necessary, however, to make the more abstract approach useful for research.[48]

2. Comparative study will become easier when more acceptable indicators and indices are developed for complex variables such as value systems, vulnerability to scapegoating, and the degree of effectiveness of international organization.

3. We need systematic comparison of as many cases of ethnic-group relations as possible. Every case, that is, should be described with reference to the same variables, defined in the same way as far as possible.[49] The "values" of the twenty-one variables described above will not be combined at random. Only comparative study, however,

[45] See the admirably succinct and intelligent appraisal by an English editor, Norman Macrae, "The Neurotic Trillionaire," *The Economist* (London), May 10, 1969; reprinted in part and partly summarized in *Current* (August 1969), pp. 25–32. This article also prescribes a four-point program of urgent action needed now in the struggle for inclusion of Negro Americans.

[46] See *Daedalus* (Fall 1965), especially Rashi Fein, "An Economic and Social Profile of the Negro American," pp. 815–846, and James Tobin, "On Improving the Economic Status of the Negro," pp. 878–898.

[47] After writing this article, I discovered a new essay by Smelser in which he fills to some extent the psychological gap in *Theory of Collective Behavior*. See "Social and Psychological Dimensions of Collective Behavior," chap. 5, in his *Essays in Sociological Explanation* (Englewood Cliffs, N.J.: Prentice-Hall, 1968). In the same book, chap. 8, "Toward a General Theory of Social Change," is also of interest for the treatment of ethnic-group relations.

[48] Rainer Baum used systematic analysis of a sample of novels as a basis for characterizing value systems; see reference in footnote 18. Jan Loubser is working on a questionnaire concerning social values, following Parsons' theory.

[49] An early work that compares cases with respect to the same variables is Charles Wagley and Marvin Harris, *Minorities in the New World: Six Case Studies* (New York: Columbia University Press, 1958).

can reveal how the values actually do combine. One strategy would be to compare many cases with known outcomes (amalgamation, pluralism, separation, reversal of dominance, genocide, expulsion). It could be hypothesized that such and such a syndrome of values of the variables, with such and such variants, would be found for cases that ended, for example, in separation; another syndrome for cases that ended in reversal of dominance. Only by the careful study of cases would it be possible to note the interaction of variables in time. What are the characteristic steps and processes that lead to a particular type of outcome? It might also be found that certain variables are largely dependent upon others, or that variables not included among the twenty-one are more important than some that are.

4. For sociological theory in general, as well as studying ethnic-group relations, it will of course be desirable to consolidate the different approaches now used. In particular, the various approaches stemming from Mead, Cooley, and Simmel, all loosely called *symbolic interactionism*, should be compared systematically with the structural-functional-processual theory of the action system (a theory that actually is also "symbolic interactionist"). Such a project would be especially valuable because very few sociologists appear to be, at present, intimately familiar with both "symbolic interactionism" and the structural-functional theory developed in the work of Talcott Parsons.

NATIONALISM AND
NATIONAL SOCIETIES

The analysis of revolutions has been a classic part of the study of social change. In this essay, pointing out that from 1945 to 1968 some sixty-six countries successfully revolted from colonial rule, Professor Geertz asks what kinds of social change resulted from these revolutions and what problems of social change remain. He examines the role of nationalism both in the making of these revolutions and in the conditions for stability and change in the newly independent countries. He shows how these new nation-states are now confronted by the choice between two ways of defining their national identities, what he calls "essentialism" and "epochalism." Finally, Professor Geertz concentrates on analyzing another general question: what is the role of ideology in the historical processes of stability and change in social systems?

Clifford Geertz

AFTER THE REVOLUTION: THE FATE OF NATIONALISM IN THE NEW STATES

Between 1945 and 1968 sixty-six "countries" — the actualities demand the quotation marks — attained political independence from colonial rule. Unless one counts the American engagement in Vietnam, an ambiguous case, the last great struggle for national liberation was that which triumphed in Algeria in the summer of 1962. Though a few other collisions are apparently still to come — in the Portuguese territories of Africa, for example — the great revolution against Western governance of Third World peoples is essentially over. Politically, morally, and sociologically, the results are mixed. But from the Congo to Guyana the wards of imperialism are, formally anyway, free.[1]

[1] The term "new states," indeterminate to begin with, becomes even more so as time passes and the states age. Though my main referent is the countries that have gained independence since World War Two, I do not hesitate, where it suits

Considering all that independence seemed to promise — popular rule, rapid economic growth, social equality, cultural regeneration, national greatness and, above all, an end to the ascendancy of the West — it is not surprising that its actual advent has been anticlimactic. It is not that nothing has happened, that a new era has not been entered. Rather, that era having been entered, it is necessary now to live in it rather than merely imagine it, and that is inevitably a deflating experience.

The signs of this darkened mood are everywhere: in nostalgia for the emphatic personalities and well-made dramas of the revolutionary struggle; in disenchantment with party politics, parliamentarianism, bureaucracy, and the new class of soldiers, clerks, and local powers; in uncertainty of direction, ideological weariness, and the steady spread of random violence; and, not the least, in a dawning realization that things are more complicated than they look, that social, economic, and political problems, once thought to be mere reflexes of colonial rule, to disappear when it disappeared, have less superficial roots. Philosophically, the lines between realism and cynicism, between prudence and apathy, and between maturity and despair may be very broad; but sociologically, they are always very narrow. And in most of the new states right now they have thinned almost to the vanishing point.

Behind the mood, which is of course not unmixed, lie the realities of post-colonial social life. The sacred leaders of the national struggle are either gone (Gandhi, Nehru, Sukarno, Nkrumah, Muhammed V, U Nu, Jinnah, Ben Bella, Keita, Azikiwe, Bandaranaike), replaced by less confident heirs or less theatrical generals, or have been diminished to mere heads of state (Kenyatta, Nyerere, Bourguiba, Abderrahman, Sekou Touré, even lately Nasser and Castro). The near-millennial hopes of political deliverance once invested in a handful of extraordinary men are not only now diffused among a larger number of distinctly less extraordinary ones but are themselves attenuated. The enormous concentration of social energies that charismatic leadership can, whatever its other defects, clearly accomplish, dissolves when such leadership disappears. The passing of the generation of prophet-liberators in the last decade has been nearly as momentous, if not quite as dramatic, an event in the history of the new states as was their appearance in the thirties, forties, and fifties. Here and there, new ones will doubtless from time to time emerge, and some may make a considerable impact upon the world. But, unless a wave of Communist uprisings, of which

---

my purposes and seems realistic, to extend the term to cover states like those of the Middle East, whose formal independence came earlier, or even those, like Ethiopia, Iran, or Thailand, which in the strict sense were never colonies at all.

there is now little indication, sweeps through the Third World throwing up a cloud of Che Guevaras, there will not soon again be such a galaxy of successful revolutionary heroes as there were in the Olympian days of the Bandung Conference. Most new states are in for a period of commonplace rulers.

In addition to the reduction in the grandeur of leadership, there has been a solidification of the white collar patriciate — what American sociologists like to call "the new middle class" and the French, less euphemistic, call *la classe dirigeante* — which surrounds and in many places engulfs that leadership. Just as colonial rule tended almost everywhere to transform those who happened to be socially ascendant (and submissive to its demands) at the time of its advent into a privileged corps of officials and overseers, so independence tended almost everywhere to create a similar, though larger, corps out of those who happened to be ascendant (and responsive to its spirit) at its advent. In some cases, the class continuity between the new elite and the old is great, in some less great; determining its composition has been the major internal political struggle of the revolutionary and immediate post-revolutionary periods. But accommodative, parvenu, or something in between, it is now rather definitely in place, and the avenues of mobility that for a moment seemed so wide open seem now, to most people, distinctly less so. As political leadership has slipped back toward the "normal," or anyway appearing such, so too has the stratification system.

So too, indeed, has society as a whole. The consciousness of massive, univocal, irresistible movement, the stirring to action of an entire people, that the attack upon colonialism almost everywhere induced has not wholly disappeared, but it has powerfully lessened. There is much less talk, both inside the new states and in the scholarly literature concerning them, about "social mobilization" than there was five, not to say ten years ago (and what there is seems increasingly hollow). And this is because there is in fact much less social mobilization. Change continues, and indeed may even be accelerating under a general illusion that nothing much is happening, an illusion in good part generated by the great expectations that accompanied liberation in the first place.[2] But the general forward motion of "the nation as a

2 For an incisive, if anecdotal, discussion of the way in which contemporary social conditions in the Third World hamper the recognition of change on the part of "the natives" and foreign observers alike, see A. Hirschman, "Underdevelopment, Obstacles to the Perception of Change, and Leadership," *Daedalus*, 97:925–937 (1968). For some comments of my own relative to the tendency of Western scholars — and, inferentially, Third World intellectuals — to underestimate the present rate (and to misconceive the direction) of change in the new states, see "Myrdal's Mythology," *Encounter* (June 1969), pp. 26–34.

whole" has been replaced by a complex, uneven, and many-directioned movement by its various parts, which conduces to a sense less of progress than of agitated stagnation.

Yet, despite the sense of diluted leadership, renascent privilege, and arrested movement, the force of the great political emotion upon which the independence movement was everywhere built remains but slightly dimmed. Nationalism — amorphous, uncertainly focused, half-articulated, but for all that highly inflammable — is still the major collective passion in most new states, and in some it is virtually the only one. That, like the Trojan War, the world revolution may not take place as scheduled, that poverty, inequality, exploitation, superstition, and great power politics are going to be around for a while, is an idea, however galling, that most people at least can somehow contrive to live with. But, once aroused, the desire to become a people rather than a population, a recognized and respected somebody in the world who counts and is attended to, is, short of its satisfaction, apparently unappeasable. At least it has nowhere yet been appeased.

Actually, the novelties of the post-revolutionary period have, in many ways, exacerbated it. The realization that the power imbalance between the new states and the West has not only not been corrected by the destruction of colonialism, but has in some respects increased, while at the same time the buffer colonial rule provided against the direct impact of that imbalance has been removed, leaving fledgling states to fend for themselves against stronger, more practiced, established states, renders nationalist sensitivity to "outside interference" just that much more intense and that much more general. In the same way, emerging into the world as an independent state has led to a similar sensitivization to the acts and intentions of neighboring states — most of them likewise just emerged — that was not present when such states were not free agents but, as oneself, "belonged" to a distant power. And internally, removing European rule has liberated the nationalisms within nationalisms that virtually all the new states contain and produced as provincialism or separatism, a direct and in some cases — Nigeria, India, Malaysia, Indonesia, Pakistan — immediate threat to the new-wrought national identity in whose name the revolution was made.

The effects of this persistent nationalistic sentiment amid national disappointment have been naturally varied: a withdrawal into don't-touch-me isolationism, as in Burma; a surge of neotraditionalism, as in Algeria; a turn toward regional imperialism, as in pre-coup Indonesia; an obsession with a neighboring enemy, as in Pakistan; a collapse into ethnic civil war, as in Nigeria; or, in the majority of the cases where the conflict is for the moment less severe, an underdeveloped version of muddling through, which contains a little of all these plus a certain amount of whistling in the dark. The post-revolutionary period was envisioned to be one of organizing rapid, large-scale, broadly coordinated social, economic, and political advance. But it has turned out to be rather more a continuation, under changed, and in some ways even less propitious circumstances, of the main theme of the revolutionary and immediate pre-revolutionary periods: the definition, creation, and solidification of a viable collective identity.

In this process, the formal liberation from colonial rule turns out not to have been the climax but a stage; a critical and necessary stage, but a stage nonetheless, and quite possibly far from the most consequential one. As in medicine the severity of surface symptoms and the severity of underlying pathology are not always in close correlation, so in sociology the drama of public events and the magnitude of structural change are not always in precise accord. Some of the greatest revolutions occur in the dark.

FOUR PHASES OF NATIONALISM

The tendency for the velocities of outward change and inward transformation to be out of phase with one another is clearly enough demonstrated in the general history of decolonization.

If, keeping all the limitations of periodization in mind, one divides that history into four major phases — that in which the nationalist movements formed and crystallized; that in which they triumphed; that in which they organized themselves into states; and that (the present one) in which, organized into states, they find themselves obliged to define and stabilize their relationships both to other states and to the irregular societies out of which they arose — this incongruence comes plainly into view. The most obvious changes, those which caught and held the attention of the entire world, occurred in the second and third of these phases. But the bulk of the more far-reaching changes, those altering the general shape and direction of social evolution, occurred or are occurring in the less spectacular first and fourth.

The first, formative stage of nationalism consisted essentially of confronting the dense assemblage of cultural, racial, local, and linguistic categories of self-identification and social loyalty that centuries of uninstructed history had produced with a simple, abstract, deliberately constructed, and almost painfully self-conscious concept of political ethnicity — a proper "nationality" in the modern manner. The granular images into which individuals' views of who they are and who they aren't, are so intensely bound in traditional society, were challenged by the more general, vaguer, but no less charged conceptions of collective identity, based on a diffuse sense of common destiny, that tend to characterise industrialized states. The men who raised this challenge, the nationalist intellectuals, were thus launching a revolution as much cultural, even epistemological, as it was political. They were attempting to transform the symbolic framework through which people experienced social reality, and thus, to the extent that life is what we make of it all, that reality itself.

That this effort to revise the frames of self-perception was an uphill battle, that in most places it was hardly more than just begun, and that in all it remained confused and incomplete goes without saying — or would, had not the contrary so often been asserted. Indeed, the very success of the independence movements in rousing the enthusiasm of the masses and directing it against foreign domination tended to obscure the frailty and narrowness of the cultural foundations upon which those movements rested, because it led to the notion that anticolonialism and collective redefinition are the same thing. But for all the intimacy (and complexity) of their interconnections, they are not. Most Tamils, Karens, Brahmins, Malays, Sikhs, Ibos, Muslims, Chinese, Nilotes, Bengalis, or Ashantis found it a good deal easier to grasp the idea that they were not Englishmen than that they were Indians, Burmese, Malayans, Ghanaians, Pakistanis, Nigerians, or Sudanese.

As the mass attack (more massive, and more violent, in some places than others) upon colonialism developed, it seemed to create, in and of itself, the basis of a new national identity that independence would merely ratify. The popular rallying behind a common, extremely specific political aim — an occurrence that surprised the nationalists nearly as much as it did the colonialists — was taken for a sign of a deeper solidarity, which produced by it would yet outlive it. Nationalism came to mean, purely and simply, the desire — and the demand — for freedom. Transforming a people's view of themselves, their society, and their culture — the sort of thing that absorbed Gandhi, Jinnah, Fanon, Sukarno, Senghor, and indeed all the bitter theorists of national awakening — was identified, to a large extent by some of these same men, with the access of such peoples to self-government. "Seek ye first the political kingdom" — the nationalists would make the state, and the state would make the nation.

The task of making the state turned out to be exacting enough to permit this illusion, indeed the whole moral atmosphere of the revolution, to be sustained for some time beyond the transfer of sovereignty. The degree to which this proved possible, necessary, or even advisable, varied widely from Indonesia or Ghana at one extreme to Malaysia or Tunisia at the other. But, with few exceptions (as I write, the main ones are Nigeria and Vietnam), by now all the new states have organized governments that maintain general dominion within their borders, and well or badly, function. And as government shakes down into some reasonably recognizable institutional form — party oligarchy, presidential autocracy, military dictatorship, reconditioned monarchism, or, very partially in the best of cases, representative democracy — it becomes less and less easy to avoid confronting the fact that to make Italy is not to make Italians. Once the political revolution is accomplished, and a state, if hardly consolidated, is at least established, the question: Who are we, who have done all this? reemerges from the easy populism of the last years of decolonization and the first of independence.

Now that there is a local state rather than a mere dream of one the task of nationalist ideologizing radically changes. It no longer consists in stimulating popular alienation from a foreign dominated political order, nor with orchestrating a mass celebration of that order's demise. It consists in defining, or trying to define, a collective subject to whom the actions of the state can be internally connected, in creating, or trying to create, an experienciable "we" from whose will the activities of government seem spontaneously to flow. And as such, it tends to revolve around the question of the content, relative weight, and proper relationship of two rather towering abstractions: "The Indigenous Way of Life" and "The Spirit of the Age."

To stress the first of these is to look to local mores, established institutions, and the unities of common experience — to "tradition," "culture," "national character," or even "race" — for the roots of a new identity. To stress the second is to look to the general outlines of the history of our time, and in particular to what one takes to be the overall direction and significance of that history. There is no new state in which both these themes (which, merely to have names for them, I shall call "essentialism" and "epochalism") are not present; few in which they are not thoroughly entangled with one another; and only a small, incompletely decolonized minority in which the tension between them is not invading every aspect of national life from language choice to foreign policy.

Language choice is, in fact a good, even a paradigmatic, example. I cannot think of a new state in which this question has not in some form or other risen to the level of national policy.[3] The intensity of the disturbance it has thereby generated, as well as the effectiveness with which it has been handled, varies quite widely; but for all the diversity of its expressions, the "language issue" turns precisely on the essentialism-epochalism dilemma.

[3] For a general review, see J. A. Fishman et al., eds., *Language Problems of Developing Nations* (New York: Wiley, 1968).

For any speaker of it, a given language is at once either more or less his own or more or less someone else's, and either more or less cosmopolitan or more or less parochial — a borrowing or a heritage; a passport or a citadel. The question of whether, when, and for what purposes to use it is thus also the question of how far a people should form itself by the bent of its genius and how far by the demands of its times.

The tendency to approach the "language issue" from the linguistic standpoint, homemade or scientific, has somewhat obscured this fact. Most discussion, inside the new states and out, concerning the "suitability" of a given language for national use has suffered from the notion that this suitability turns on the inherent nature of the language — on the adequacy of its grammatical, lexical, or "cultural" resources to the expression of complex philosophical, scientific, political, or moral ideas. But what it really turns on is the relative importance of being able to give one's thoughts, however crude or subtle, the kind of force that speaking one's mother tongue permits as against being able to participate in movements of thought to which only "foreign," or in some cases "literary," languages can give access.

It doesn't matter therefore whether, in concrete form, the problem is the status of classical as against colloquial Arabic in Middle Eastern countries; the place of an "elite" Western language amid a collection of "tribal" languages in sub-Saharan Africa; the complex stratification of local, regional, national, and international languages in India or the Philippines; or the replacement of a European language of limited world significance by others of greater significance in Indonesia. The underlying issue is the same. It is not whether this or that language is "developed" or "capable of development"; it is whether this or that language is psychologically immediate and whether it is an avenue to the wider community of modern culture.

It is not because Swahili lacks a stable syntax or Arabic cannot build combining forms — dubious propositions in any case [4] — that language problems are so prominent in the Third World; it is because, for the overwhelming majority of speakers of the overwhelming majority of languages in the new states, the two sides of this double question tend to work out inversely. What, from the ordinary speaker's view, is the

[4] For the first (not accepted, but attacked), see L. Harries, "Swahili in Modern East Africa," in Fishman et al., *Language Problems*, p. 426. For the second (accepted during an incisive discussion along the general lines here being developed), see C. Gallagher, "North African Problems and Prospects: Language and Identity," in *Language Problems*, p. 140. My point, of course, is not that technical linguistic matters have no relevance to language problems in the new states, but merely that the roots of those problems are much deeper and that expanding lexicons, standardizing usages, improving writing systems, and rationalizing instruction, though valuable in themselves, do not touch the central difficulty.

natural vehicle of thought and feeling (and particularly in cases like Arabic, Hindi, Amharic, Khmer, or Javanese — the repository of an advanced religious, literary, and artistic tradition to boot), is, from the view of the main current of twentieth-century civilization, virtually a patois. And what for that current are the established vehicles of its expression, are for that ordinary speaker at best but half-familiar languages of even less familiar peoples.[5]

Formulated this way, the "language problem" is only the "nationality problem" writ small, though in some places the conflicts arising from it are intense enough to make the relationship seem reversed. Generalized, the "who are we" question asks what cultural forms — what systems of meaningful symbols — to employ to give value and significance to the activities of the state, and by extension to the civil life of its citizens. Nationalist ideologies built out of symbolic forms drawn from local traditions — which are, that is, essentialist — tend, like vernaculars, to be psychologically immediate but socially isolating; built out of forms implicated in the general movement of contemporary history — that is, epochalist — they tend, like lingua francas, to be socially deprovincializing but psychologically forced.

However, rarely is such an ideology anywhere purely essentialist or purely epochalist. All are mixed and one can speak at best only of a bias in one direction or another, and often not even of that. Nehru's image of "India" was doubtless heavily epochalist, Gandhi's doubtless heavily essentialist; but because the first was the disciple of the second and the second the patron of the first (and neither managed to convince all Indians that he was not, in the one case, a brown Englishman, or, in the other, a medieval reactionary) demonstrates that the relation between these two routes to self-discovery is a subtle and even paradoxical one. Indeed, the more ideologized new states — Indonesia, Ghana, Algeria, Egypt, Ceylon, and the like — have tended to be both intensely epochalist and intensely essentialist at the same time, whereas countries more purely essentialist like Somalia or Cambodia, or epochalist like Tunisia or the Philippines, have been rather the exceptions.

The tension between these two impulses — to move with the tide of

[5] The main exception so far as the Third World generally is concerned is Latin America, but there — proving the rule — language issues are very much less prominent than in the new states proper and tend to reduce to education and minority group problems. (For an example, see D. H. Burns, "Bilingual Education in the Andes of Peru," in *Language Problems*, pp. 403–413.) To what degree the fact that Spanish (or, more, Portuguese) is just enough of a carrier of modern thought to be felt to be an avenue of it and just marginal enough a carrier of it not actually to be a very good one has played a part in the intellectual provincialization of Latin America — so that it has in fact had a language problem without quite realizing it — is an interesting and separate question.

the present and to hold to an inherited course — gives new state nationalism its peculiar air of being at once hell-bent toward modernity
and morally outraged by its manifestations. There is a certain irrationality in this. But it is more than a collective derangement; it is a
social cataclysm in the process of happening.

ESSENTIALISM AND EPOCHALISM

The interplay of essentialism and epochalism is not, therefore, a kind
of cultural dialectic, a logistic of abstract ideas, but a historical
process as concrete as industrialization and as tangible as war. The
issues are being fought out not simply at the doctrine and argument
level — though there is a great deal of both — but much more importantly in the material transformations that the social structures of all
the new states are undergoing. Ideological change is not an independent stream of thought running alongside social process and reflecting
(or determining) it, it is a dimension of that process itself.

The impact within any new state society of the desire for coherence
and continuity on the one hand and for dynamism and contempora-
neity on the other is both extremely uneven and highly nuanced. The
pull of indigenous tradition is felt most heavily by its appointed and
these days rather besieged guardians — monks, mandarins, pandits,
chiefs, ulema, and so on; that of what is usually referred to (not altogether accurately) as "the West," by the urban youth, the troubled
schoolboys of Cairo, Djakarta, or Kinshasa who have surrounded
words like *shabb, pemuda,* and *jeunesse* with an aura of energy, idealism, impatience, and menace. But stretching out between these all-
too-visible extremes is the great bulk of the population, among whom
essentialist and epochalist sentiments are scrambled into a vast confusion of outlooks, which because the current of social change produced it, only the current of social change can sort it out.

As illustrative cases, compressed to the dimensions of historical an-
ecdotes, of the generation of this confusion and of the efforts now
being made to dissolve it, Indonesia and Morocco can serve as well
as any. My reason for choosing them is that they are the cases I
happen to know first hand and, in dealing with the interplay between
institutional change and cultural reconstruction, the degree to which
one can substitute a synoptic vision for an intimate one is limited.
Their experiences are, as all social experiences, unique. But they are
not so different either from one another or from those of new states as
a whole as to be unable to reveal, in their very particularity, some generic outlines of the problems faced by societies struggling to bring
what they like to call their "personality" into a workable alignment
with what they like to call their "destiny."

In Indonesia, the essentialist element is, and long has been, extremely unhomogeneous. To an extent, this is true for virtually all the new states, which tend to be bundles of competing traditions gathered accidentally into concocted political frameworks rather than organically evolving civilizations. But in Indonesia, the outlands at once of India, China, Oceania, Europe, and the Middle East, cultural diversity has been for centuries both especially great and especially complex. The edge of everything classical, it has been itself shamelessly eclectic.

Up until about the third decade of this century, the several ingredient traditions — Indic, Sinitic, Islamic, Christian, Polynesian — were suspended in a kind of half-solution in which contrasting, even opposed styles of life and world outlooks managed to coexist, if not wholly without tension, or even without violence, at least in some sort of usually workable, to-each-his-own sort of arrangement. This *modus vivendi* began to show signs of strain as early as the mid-nineteenth century, but its dissolution got genuinely under way only with the rise, from 1912 on, of nationalism; its collapse, which is still not complete, only in the revolutionary and post-revolutionary periods. For then what had been parallel traditionalisms, encapsulated in localities and classes, became competing definitions of the essence of the New Indonesia. What was once, to employ a term I have used elsewhere, a kind of "cultural balance of power" became an ideological war of a peculiarly implacable sort.

Thus, in apparent paradox (though, in fact, it has been a nearly universal occurrence in the new states) the move toward national unity intensified group tensions within the society by raising settled cultural forms out of their particular contexts, expanding them into general allegiances, and politicizing them. As the nationalist movement developed, it separated into strands. In the Revolution these strands became parties, each promoting a different aspect of the eclectic tradition as the only true basis of Indonesian identity. Marxists looked mainly to the folk melange of peasant life for the essence of the national heritage; the technicians, clerks, and administrators of the *classe dirigeante* to the Indic aestheticism of the Javanese aristocracy; and the more substantial merchants and landholders to Islam. Village populism, cultural elitism, religious puritanism: some differences of ideological opinion can perhaps be adjusted, but not these.

Rather than adjusted they were accentuated as each strand attempted to graft a modernist appeal on to its traditionalist base. For the populist element this was Communism, and the Indonesian Communist party, professing to discern an indigenous radical tradition in the collectivism, social egalitarianism, and anti-clericalism of rural life, became the chief spokesman for both peasant essentialism, especially Javanese peasant essentialism, and for a revolutionary epochalism of the usual "rise of the masses" sort. For the salaried element the modernist appeal was industrial society as found (or imagined) in Europe and the United States, and it proposed a marriage of convenience between oriental spirituality and occidental drive, between "wisdom" and "technique," that would somehow preserve cherished values while transforming the material basis of the society out of which those values had arisen. And for the pious, it was naturally enough religious reform, a celebration of the effort to renovate Islamic civilization in such a way as to regain its lost, rightful leadership of the moral, material, and intellectual progress of mankind. But, in the event, none of these things — Peasant Revolution, The Meeting of East and West, or The Cultural Resurgence of Islam happened. What happened was the mass slaughter of 1965–66 in which somewhere between a quarter and three-quarters of a million people lost their lives. The blood bath in which the Sukarno regime with painful slowness drowned was the result of a vast complex of causes, and it would be absurd to reduce it to an ideological explosion. Yet, whatever the role of economic, political, psychological, or for that matter accidental factors in bringing it on (and, what is even harder to explain, sustaining it), it marked the end of a distinct phase in the progress of Indonesian nationalism. Not only were the slogans of unity ("one people, one language, one nation"; "from many, one"; "collective harmony"; and so on), which had not been easy to credit in the first place, now rendered implausible altogether, but the theory that the native eclecticism of Indonesian culture would yield easily to a generalized modernism clamped on to one or another element of it was definitively disproved. Multiform in the past, it would seem also to have to be multiform in the present.

In Morocco, the main obstacle to defining an integral national self has not been cultural heterogeneity, which in comparative terms has not been so very great, as social particularism, which in comparative terms has been extreme. Traditional Morocco consisted of an enormous, ill-organized field of rapidly forming and rapidly dissolving political constellations on every level from the court to the camp, every basis from the mystical to the occupational, and every scale from the grand to the microscopic. The continuity of the social order lay less in any durability of the arrangements composing it or the groups embodying it, for the sturdiest of them were fugitive, than in the constancy of the processes by which, incessantly reworking those arrangements and redefining those groups, it formed, reformed, and re-reformed itself.

Insofar as this unsettled society had a center it was the Alawite monarchy. But even in the best times the monarchy was hardly more than the largest bear in the garden. Embedded in a patrimonial bureaucracy of the most classic sort, a haphazard assortment of courtiers, chieftains, scribes, and judges, it struggled continuously to bring competing centers of power — of which there were literally hundreds, each resting on slightly different ground than the next — within its control. Although between its founding in the seventeenth century and its submission in 1912 it never altogether failed in this, it also never more than very partially succeeded. Not quite an anarchy and not quite a polity, the Moroccan state had, with its endemic particularism, just enough reality to persist.

Initially the effect of colonial domination, which only formally lasted about forty years, was to eviscerate the monarchy and turn it into a kind of Moorish *tableau vivant;* but intentions are one thing and events are another, and the ultimate result of European rule was to establish the king as the axis of the Moroccan political system rather more emphatically than had originally been the case. Though the earliest movements toward independence were undertaken by an uneasy, and as it turned out unstable, coalition of Western-educated intellectuals and neotraditional Muslim reformers, it was the arrest, exile, and triumphant restoration of Muhammed V in 1953–55 that finally secured the independence movement, and, in securing it, turned the throne into the focus of Morocco's growing but still intermittent sense of nationhood. The country got, revived, ideologized, and better organized, its center back. But, it soon turned out, it also got, similarly improved, its particularism back.

Much post-revolutionary political history has demonstrated this fact: that however transformed, the crucial struggle still consists in an attempt by the king and his staff to sustain the monarchy as a viable institution in a society in which everything from landscape and kinship structure to religion and national character conspires to partition political life into disparate and disconnected exhibitions of parochial power. The first such exhibitions came with a series of so-called tribal uprisings — in part foreign stimulated, in part the result of domestic political maneuvering, in part a return of the culturally repressed — that harried the new state during the first few years of independence. These were eventually put down with a combination of royal force and royal intrigue. But they were merely the first, rather elemental indications of what life was going to be like for a classical monarchy that, returning from the limbo of colonial subservience, had to establish itself as at once the authentic expression of the nation's soul and the appropriate vehicle of its modernization.

As Samuel Huntington has pointed out, the peculiar fate of traditional monarchies almost everywhere in the new states is to have also to be modernizing monarchies, or at least to look like such.[6] A king content merely to reign can remain a political icon, a piece of cultural bric-a-brac. But if he wants also to rule, as Moroccan kings have always very much wanted to do, he must make himself the expression of a powerful force in contemporary social life. For Muhammed V, and, since 1961, his son Hassan II, this force has been the emergence for the first time in the country's history of a Western-educated class large enough to permeate the entire society and discrete enough to represent a distinctive interest. Though their styles have been somewhat different — Hassan is remote where Muhammed was paternal — they have each struggled at once to organize and to place themselves at the head of The New Middle Class, The Intermediate Sectors, *La Classe Dirigeante*, The National Elite, or whatever this forming crowd of officials, officers, managers, educators, technicians, and publicists ought properly to be called.

Suppressing the tribal rebellions was thus less the end of the old order than the end of an ineffective strategy for dominating it. After 1958, the essentials of what has become the palace's established approach to securing a firmer grip on the Moroccan half-polity emerged — the construction of a constitutional monarchy, constitutional enough to attract the support of the educated elite and monarchical enough to maintain the substance of royal power. Desiring the fate of neither the English monarchy nor the Iraqi, Muhammed V, and even more Hassan II, have sought to create an institution which, invoking Islam, Arabism, and three centuries of Alawite rule, could draw its legitimacy from the past and, calling for rationalism, *dirigisme*, and technocracy, its authority from the present.

The stages in the recent history of this effort to turn Morocco, by a kind of political miscegenation, into what can only be called a royalist republic — the separation of the secularist, religious, and traditionalist wings of the nationalist movement and the consequent formation of a multiparty system in 1958–59; the failure of the king's own coalition

[6] Samuel P. Huntington, "The Political Modernization of Traditional Monarchies," *Daedalus*, 1966: 763–768; see also his *Political Order in Changing Societies* (New Haven: Yale University Press, 1968). With Huntington's general analysis, too much influenced, in my opinion, by the analogy of the king vs aristocracy struggle in premodern Europe, I am, however, in some disagreement. For Morocco anyway, the image of a populist monarchy "out of style in middle-class circles," appealing over the heads of "local privilege, corporate autonomy [and] feudal power" to the masses in the interests of progressive reform, seems to me very nearly the reverse of the truth. For more realistic views of post-independence Moroccan politics, see John Waterbury, *The Commander of the Faithful* (London: Weidenfeld and Nicolson, 1970).

party, the Front for the Defense of Constitutional Institutions, to gain a parliamentary majority in the 1963 general elections; the royal suspension, ostensibly temporary, of parliament in 1965; the dime novel murder (in France) of the major opponent of the whole project, Mehdi Ben Barka, in 1968 — need not be traced out here. The point is that the tension between essentialism and epochalism is as observable in the vicissitudes of the post-revolutionary Moroccan political system as in those of the Indonesian; and if it has not as yet attained so flamboyant a denouement, and one may hope never will, it has been moving in the same direction of increasing unmanageability as the relationship between what Edward Shils has called the "will to be modern" and what Mazzini called the "need to exist and have a name" grows steadily more involved.[7] And though the form it takes and the speed at which it moves naturally vary, the same process is occurring in, if perhaps not all, at least the overwhelming majority of the new states as, the revolution accomplished, the point of it is sought.

CONCEPTS OF CULTURE

Until Talcott Parsons, carrying forward Weber's double rejection (and double acceptance) of German idealism and Marxist materialism, provided a viable alternative, the dominant concept of culture in American social science identified culture with learned behavior. This concept can hardly be called "wrong" — isolated concepts are neither "wrong" nor "right" — and for many, rather routine purposes it was, and remains serviceable. But it is now clear to virtually everyone whose interests extend any distance beyond the descriptive that it is very difficult to generate analyses of much theoretical power from such a diffuse, empiricist notion. The day when social phenomena were explained by redescribing them as culture patterns and noting that such patterns are handed down from generation to generation is very nearly past. And Parsons, insisting in his grave and toneless voice, that to interpret the way a group of human beings behave as an expression of their culture while defining their culture as the sum of the ways in which they have learned to behave is not terribly informative, is as responsible for its passing as any single figure in contemporary social science.

[7] Edward Shils, "Political Development in the New States," *Comparative Studies in Society and History*, vol. 2 (1960), pp. 265–292; 379–411. For a general discussion of these somewhat clashing ambitions in connection with religious, ethnic, linguistic, racial, cultural diversity in the new states, see my, "The Integrative Revolution: Primordial Sentiments and Civil Politics in the New States," in *Old Societies and New States*, ed. Clifford Geertz (New York: The Free Press, 1963), pp. 105–157.

In place of this near-idea, Parsons, following not only Weber but a line of thought stretching back at least to Vico, has elaborated a concept of culture as a system of symbols by which man confers significance upon his own experience. Symbol systems, man-created, shared, conventional, ordered, and indeed learned, provide human beings with a meaningful framework for orienting themselves to one another, to the world around them, and to themselves. At once a product and a determinant of social interaction, they are to the process of social life as a computer's program is to its operations, the genic helix to the development of the organism, the blueprint to the construction of the bridge, the score to the performance of the symphony, or, to choose a humbler analogy, the recipe to the baking of the cake — so the symbol system is the information source that, to some measurable extent, gives shape, direction, particularity, and point to an ongoing flow of activity.

Yet these analogies, which suggest a pre-existing template stamping form onto a process external to it, pass rather facilely over what has emerged as the central theoretical problem for this more sophisticated approach: namely, how to conceptualize the dialectic between the crystallization of such directive "patterns of meaning" and the concrete course of social life.

There is a sense in which a computer's program is an outcome of prior developments in the technology of computing, a particular helix of phylogenetic history, a blueprint of earlier experiments in bridge building, a score of the evolution of musical performance, and a recipe of a long series of successful and unsuccessful cakes. But the simple fact that the information elements in these cases are materially separable from the processual — one can, in principle anyhow, write out the program, isolate the helix, draw the blueprint, publish the score, note down the recipe — makes them less useful as models for the interaction of cultural patterns and social processes where, a few more intellectualized realms like music and cake-baking in part aside, the very question at issue is precisely how such a separation is, even in thought, actually to be effected. The workability of the Parsonian concept of culture rests almost entirely on the degree to which such a model can be constructed — on the degree to which the relationship between the development of symbol systems and the dynamics of social process can be circumstantially exposed, thereby rendering the depiction of technologies, rituals, myths, and kinship terminologies as man-made information sources for the directive ordering of human conduct more than a metaphor.

This problem has haunted Parsons' writings on culture from the earliest days when he regarded it as a set of Whiteheadian "external objects" psychologically incorporated into personalities and thus, by

extension, institutionalized in social systems, to the most recent where
he sees it more in the control mechanism terms of cybernetics. But nowhere has it come home more to roost than in discussing ideology; for,
of all the realms of culture, ideology is the one in which the relationship between symbolic structures and collective behavior is at once
the most conspicuous and the least clear.

For Parsons, an ideology is but a special sort of symbol system:

> a system of beliefs held in common by members of a collectivity . . .
> which is oriented to the evaluative integration of the collectivity, by
> *interpretation of the empirical nature of the collectivity* and *of the
> situation in which it is placed,* the processes by which it developed
> to its given state, the goals to which its members are collectively ori-
> ented, and their relation to the future course of events.[8]

Yet, left at that, this formulation fuses together modes of self-inter-
pretation that do not entirely go together, and, glossing over the moral
tension inherent in ideological activity, obscures the interior sources
of its enormous sociological dynamism. In particular, the two clauses
I have underscored, the "interpretation of the empirical nature of the
collectivity," and "[the interpretation] of the situation in which [that
collectivity] is placed," are not, as I hope I have by now demonstrated,
as coordinate as practical enterprises in social self-definition as the
mere "and" conjoining them might suggest. So far as new state nationalism is concerned, they are in fact very deeply, in some places irrec-
oncilably, at odds. To deduce what the nation is from a conception of
the world-historical situation in which it is thought to be enclosed —
"epochalism" — produces one sort of moral-political universe; to di-
agnose the situation with which the nation is faced from a prior
conception of what it is intrinsically — "essentialism" — produces quite
another; but to combine the two (the most common approach), produces a confused assortment of mixed cases. For this reason, among
others, nationalism is not a mere by-product but the very stuff of social
change in so many new states; not its reflection, its cause, its expression, or its engine, but the thing itself.

To see one's country as the product of "the processes by which it
developed to its given state," or, alternatively, to see it as the ground
of "the future course of events" is, in short, to see it rather differently.
But, more than that, it is to look in rather different places to see it:
to parents, to traditional authority figures, to custom and legend; or,
to secular intellectuals, to the oncoming generation, to "current events,"
and the mass media. Fundamentally, the tension between essentialist

---

[8] Talcott Parsons, *The Social System* (Glencoe, Ill., The Free Press, 1951), p.
349. Italics added.

and epochalist strains in new state nationalism is not a tension between intellectual passions but between social institutions charged with discordant cultural meanings. An increase in newspaper circulation, an upsurge of religious activity, a decline in family cohesion, an expansion of universities, a reassertion of hereditary privilege, a proliferation of folklore societies are — like their contraries — themselves elements in the process by which the character and content of that nationalism as an "information source" for collective behavior are determined. The organized "systems of belief" propagated by professional ideologists represent attempts to raise aspects of this process to the level of conscious thought and so deliberately control it. But, no more than consciousness exhausts mentality does nationalist ideology exhaust nationalism.

What it does, selectively and incompletely, is articulate it. The images, metaphors, and rhetorical turns from which nationalist ideologies are built are essentially devices, cultural devices designed to render one or another aspect of the broad process of collective self-redefinition explicit, to cast essentialist pride or epochalist hope into specific symbolic forms, where more than dimly felt, they can be described, developed, celebrated, and used. To formulate an ideological doctrine is to make (or try to make; there are more failures than successes) what was a generalized mood into a practical force.[9]

The scuffle of political sects in Indonesia and the shifting foundations of monarchy in Morocco, the first so far an apparent failure, the second so far an ambiguous success, represent such attempts to draw the intangibilities of conceptual change into articulate cultural forms. They represent also, of course, and even more immediately a struggle for power, place, privilege, wealth, fame, and all the other so-called "real" rewards of life. Indeed, it is because they also represent this that their ability to focus and transform men's view of who they are and how they should act is so great.

The "patterns of meaning" by which social change is formed grow from the processes of that change itself and, crystallized into proper ideologies or embedded in popular attitudes, serve in turn, to some inevitably limited degree, to guide it. The progress from cultural diversity to ideological combat to mass violence in Indonesia, or the attempt to dominate a field of social particularisms by fusing the

---

[9] I have commented in more but still insufficient detail on the role of symbolic formulation in ideological activity in "Ideology as a Cultural System," in *Ideology and Discontent,* ed. David Apter (New York: The Free Press, 1964), pp. 47–76. See also in this regard almost any of the works of Kenneth Burke, but especially *The Philosophy of Literary Form* (Baton Rouge: Louisiana State University Press, 1941).

values of a republic with the facts of an autocracy in Morocco are without doubt the hardest of hard political, economic, and stratificatory realities; real blood has flowed, real dungeons have been built — and, to be fair, real pain relieved. But they are also without doubt the record of those would-be countries' efforts to breathe intelligibility into an idea of "nationhood," in terms of which these realities, and worse to come, can be confronted, shaped, and understood.

And this is true for the new states generally. As the heroic excitements of the political revolution against colonial domination recede into an inspirational past to be replaced by the shabbier, but no less convulsive movements of the dispiriting present, the secular analogues of Weber's famous "problems of meaning" grow more and more desperate. It is not only in religion, that things are not "merely there and happen," but "have a 'meaning' and are there because of this meaning," but in politics as well, and in new state politics in particular. The questions "what is it all for?" "what's the use?" and "why go on?" arise in the context of mass poverty, official corruption, or tribal violence as much as in those of wasting illness, defeated hope, or premature death. They get no better answers, but insofar as they get any at all it is from images of a heritage worth preserving or a promise worth pursuing, and though these need not necessarily be nationalist images almost all of them — Marxist ones included — are.[10]

Rather like religion, nationalism has a bad name in the modern world, and, rather like religion, it more or less deserves it. Between them (and sometimes in combination) religious bigotry and nationalist hatred have probably brought more havoc upon humanity than any two forces in history, and doubtless will bring a great deal more. Yet also rather like religion, nationalism has been a driving force in some of the most creative changes in history, and doubtless will be so again in many yet to come. It would seem, then, well to spend less time decrying it — which is a little like cursing the winds — and more in trying to figure out why it takes the forms it does and how it might be prevented from tearing apart even as it creates the societies in which it arises, and beyond that the whole fabric of modern civilization. For in the new states the age of ideology is not only not over, but, as the

[10] The question of the relationship between Marxism and nationalism is a vexed one which it would take another essay even to outline. Suffice it here to say that, as far as the new states are concerned, Marxist movements, Communist or non-Communist, have almost everywhere been heavily nationalistic in both aim and idiom, and there is very little sign that they are becoming any less so. Actually, the same point could be made about religio-political movements — Muslim, Buddhist, Hindu, or whatever; they too tend to be as localized in fact as they are placeless in principle.

inchoate changes of self-conception wrought by the dramatic events of the past forty years emerge into the public light of explicit doctrine, only just beginning. In preparing ourselves to understand and deal with it, or perhaps only to survive it, the Parsonian theory of culture, suitably emended, is one of our most powerful intellectual tools.

In this essay, Professor Bellah asks how we shall explain the apparent paradox that contemporary Japanese society is made up of some elements that have been stable since the seventh century and of others which are not only the products of recent massive social changes but which seem to be functionally inconsistent with the former. Professor Bellah believes that the continuity in the Japanese social system appears mainly in values and the structure of group life, that the change is mainly in cultural content and in large-scale institutional and organizational forms. According to his analysis, the change is not only consistent with the continuity but has been stimulated by it. Moreover, the processes of social change have been different in Japan and in the modern West. The "particularistic groupism" of the former and the "universalistic activism" of the latter have led to partly similar contemporary outcomes but by different paths, resulting in somewhat different potentialities for future change. This analysis reminds us again that the processes of social change in societal systems are not single or simple.

Robert N. Bellah

CONTINUITY AND CHANGE IN JAPANESE SOCIETY

How does it happen that the nation with the highest average economic growth rate for the last hundred years is also the only complex society with a Bronze Age monarchy, where the emperor until recently was believed to be the lineal descendant of the Sun Goddess and himself in some sense divine? [1] How does it happen that in the nation with

[1] This article has been influenced by two recent books: *Japanese Society* by Ishida Takeshi of Tokyo University which will soon be published by Random House, and *Tate Shakai no Ningen Kankei* (Human Relationships in a Vertical

the third highest gross national product the most important modern novel, Tanizaki Junichiro's *The Makioka Sisters*,[2] resembles the great eleventh-century novel of Murasaki Shikibu, *The Tale of Genji*,[3] not only in its sensitivity to nature and human feeling, but also in the structure of personal relations and the anxiety about gossip and criticism? How does it happen that in spite of the industrial revolution, life in the agricultural villages is so much like that of the late prehistoric period some fifteen centuries ago? [4] These questions are meant to suggest only a few dimensions along which the great continuities of Japanese life can be measured, even when one must also note the drastic series of structural changes that characterize Japanese history. The paradox of continuity and change in Japan stretches to the limits any functional theory of society and any theory of change in terms of structural differentiation. If societies are functioning systems how can the same structural features accommodate such major organizational and cultural changes? If structural differentiation accounts for the changes what explains the immunity of so many important features of Japanese society from this process?

Talcott Parsons has developed with considerable subtlety a conception of Western social development that involves long-term continuity at the level of value orientations combined with great structural change.[5] This example may not be entirely relevant because the element of universalism, so important in allowing this process to occur in the West, is singularly weak in Japan, and besides the continuities are by no means limited to the highest level of value orientations. Nevertheless it may be useful to try to unravel this apparent enigma by considering the Japanese value system where indeed continuity has been most impressive.

Society), Kōdansha Gendai Shinsho, 1967, by Nakane Chie, also of Tokyo University. Professor Nakane's book has been published in translation by the University of California Press under the title *Japanese Society*. Among many other books which might be mentioned one perhaps stands out: Maruyamo Masao's *Nihon no Shisō* (Japanese Thought), Iwanami Shinsho, 1961. The title essay was published originally in 1957.

[2] Translated by Edward G. Seidensticker (New York: Alfred A. Knopf, 1957).

[3] Translated by Arthur Waley (New York: Modern Library, 1960).

[4] See Richard K. Beardsley, "Japan Before History," *Far Eastern Quarterly*, vol. 19 (1955).

[5] See Talcott Parsons, "Christianity and Modern Industrial Society" in *Sociological Theory, Values and Sociocultural Change*, ed. Edward A. Tiryakian (New York: The Free Press, 1963); "Christianity," in *International Encyclopedia of the Social Sciences* (New York: Macmillan, 1968); and *Societies: Evolutionary and Comparative Perspectives* (Englewood Cliffs, N.J.: Prentice-Hall, 1966).

THE JAPANESE VALUE SYSTEM

In *Tokugawa Religion*[6] I characterized the values of the Tokugawa Period in terms of the pattern-variables of particularism and performance, a combination that according to action theory can be seen as "political." Although at that time I believed this pattern was considerably older than the Tokugawa Period (1600–1868), more recently Randall Huntsberry has shown convincingly that at least from the formation of the Japanese state in the seventh century "political" values of particularism and performance were central, though he points out certain variants and alternatives that were also influential.[7] Ezra Vogel has found the same pattern virtually unchanged in the post-war new middle class.[8] Thus, this pattern seems to be almost continuously dominant from the beginning of historic times to the present.

Rather than repeat the technicalities of the description of Japanese values in *Tokugawa Religion* I would like to cite a later somewhat more discursive statement:

1. Value is realized in groups which are thought of as natural entities. The community (*Gemeinschaft, kyōdōtai*) is the locus of value.

2. These groups are thought to be integrated with the structure of reality and thus are endowed with a sacred quality.

3. There is a divine-human continuity in which the symbolic heads of groups have an especially important place, being especially endowed with a sacred quality. One of their functions is to relate the group to the divine ancestors and protective deities. This pattern applies at many levels: e.g. family (and its ancestor worship), village (and the local deity, *ujigami*), and ultimately the whole country at whose head is the emperor (and above him the imperial ancestors).

4. Individuals exist because of a continuous flow of blessings from spirits and ancestors through the symbolic heads of groups. The individual is obligated to work in order to repay in small measure the blessings he has received and to sacrifice himself for the group if necessary.

5. Science, ethics, philosophy, virtually all aspects of culture are valuable only insofar as they contribute to the realization of value in the group, not as ends in themselves. Ethics consist mainly in acting as one should in one's group — there is no universal ethic.

[6] Robert N. Bellah, *Tokugawa Religion* (Glencoe, Ill.: The Free Press, 1957), chaps. 1 and 2.

[7] Randall Huntsberry, "Religion and Value-Formation in Japan" (Ph.D. dissertation in Comparative Religion, Harvard University, 1968).

[8] Ezra Vogel, *Japan's New Middle Class* (Los Angeles: University of California Press, 1963). The analysis of Nakane Chie (see footnote 1) also confirms the continuation of the earlier pattern into the contemporary period.

6. In spite of how completely the individual is merged in group life there is one place where he can be relatively independent: the realm of personal expressiveness including art, mysticism, recreation, skill. But this sphere does not legitimize failure to fulfill group expectations. It actually helps reconcile the individual to group demands.[9]

Despite the importance of this pattern certain elements within the Japanese tradition do not entirely fit. Especially significant are the universalistic and individualistic components of what I have called the "tradition of submerged transcendence." [10]

JAPANESE GROUPS AND
NATIONAL INTEGRATION

The earliest Japanese groups of which we have knowledge, the warrior bands who carried out the conquests establishing the primacy of the Yamato Court in central Japan, illustrate the value pattern described previously. Society was divided into tightly knit local groups known as *uji* and *be* whose members were united by strongly particularistic ties. There was a kinship group at the core but non-kinsmen were included as well.[11] Heroic action was defined by selfless devotion to the defense or aggrandizement of one's group. The Japanese state as we see it crystallizing in the early historical records, the *Kojiki* and the *Nihon Shoki*, capitalized on these values by concentrating loyalty on the Yamato ruling family and regulating the status of other groups by service they rendered to the Yamato court.[12] Part of the formative structure of the new Japanese state was partly provided by a system of court ranks and bureaucratic offices of Chinese inspiration. This was superimposed on the *uji* system, which continued to provide the real vitality in Japanese social organization. Even though the behavior of particular groups toward the imperial family did not always meet the ideal standards of the mythographers, the inner coherence of groups and the integration of the national polity tended to be mutually reinforcing. As John Hall has written, "In its most generalized form, perhaps, the sense of group served to heighten the Japanese consciousness of the political community as a whole, reinforcing that particular pattern of unity around the imperial family which the Japanese have labeled 'the polity' (*kokutai*)." [13] On the other hand, with the con-

---

[9] Robert N. Bellah, "Values and Social Change in Modern Japan," *Asian Cultural Studies*, Tokyo, vol. 3 (1962), pp. 32–33.

[10] Ibid., pp. 34–39.

[11] On early Japanese social and political organization see the extremely helpful book by John Whitney Hall, *Government and Local Power in Japan, 500 to 1700* (Princeton: Princeton University Press, 1966).

[12] On this point see Huntsberry, "Religion and Value-Formation in Japan."

[13] Hall, *Government and Local Power in Japan*, p. 12.

tinuity of the imperial family it has been possible to form and reform
other groups beneath it. The later rise of the feudal lords and their
groups of warriors (*bushi*) completely destroyed the old *uji-be* system.
But the feudal groups had the same basic value pattern as the earlier
groups, namely, one that stressed particularism and performance —
group loyalty and selfless service to its ends. Hall explains how the circulation of elite groups could combine with strong national continuity:

> Historically the imperial family was once a party to the violent
> struggle for power in Japan. But once the initial hegemony was estab-
> lished, and although the imperial family gradually lost real military and
> political power, its symbolic position as mediator between the mem-
> bers of the oligarchy and as the prime source of legitimacy remained of
> such importance that the emperor could never be assailed. . . . Five
> times powerful military families arose to political hegemony in Japan.
> . . . Yet in each instance these families achieved their victory as the
> result of a military conquest which carried through from within the
> oligarchic structure rather than attacking it from without. . . . Even
> during the age of great feudal wars no group was able to obtain a base
> of power outside the polity from which it might have attacked and
> destroyed the system of legitimacy over which the emperor presided.
> In the fifteenth and sixteenth centuries the emperor was reduced to a
> condition of near oblivion and outright economic distress, yet the idea
> of the national hierarchy remained. As new military leaders fought to
> the top they looked to the emperor for tokens of legitimacy and to the
> system of court ranks over which he presided for a means of ritualiz-
> ing the pyramid of power. It is no accident that Japan entered the
> modern era following a political coup d'etat carried out in the name of
> the emperor.[14]

One important difference between the *bushi* groups and the earlier
uji and *be* is that the element of kinship was of less importance in
their organization. The family line of the feudal lord was focal, but
the followers were united to the lord through loyalty rather than kinship. It was possible to organize new feudal alliances and extend their
power rather more easily than in the earlier system. From about the
tenth century on, the feudal organization penetrated even the remotest
parts of Japan and provided the basic social organization for many
centuries.

In the Tokugawa Period the group structure characteristic of the
bushi permeated wider sections of the population and notably influenced both the townsmen and the peasants. The same type of tie that
linked feudal lord and *samurai* also came to characterize the relation
of merchant and clerk. In many parts of Japan the village consisted

[14] Ibid., p. 13.

of one or more *dōzoku,* a hierarchically organized group of families not necessarily linked by kinship. Thus the pervasive influence of tightly organized hierarchical groups extended throughout the population.

The Meiji Restoration of 1868 completely abandoned the feudal system and introduced modern economic and political organization. But within the pores, so to speak, of government ministries and industrial firms Japanese group life continued to thrive. Tightly organized all-embracing groups demanded the complete loyalty and devoted service of their members. As in the past such groups formed and reformed, justifying their existence by the larger polity. The power struggles between elite groups went on largely within the framework of the imperial system, though in recent decades, especially with the American occupation, political elements entirely outside the traditional *kokutai* finally began to enter the scene. But even such groups as the Zengakuren factions who are currently battling for control of the university campuses exhibit much the same group structure which has been so typical in Japan, though their ideology questions every accepted tenet of Japanese society. Tightly cohesive and all consuming in their demands, they receive intense loyalty and devoted service from their members.

We now can summarize some implications of the Japanese group life pattern for the problem of continuity and change. The basic loyalty in Japan is to the group rather than to a status or an abstract ideal or a notion of self-fulfillment. This means that many particular status systems such as the *uji-be* system of ancient Japan or the feudal class system of Tokugawa times could be abandoned without changing the basic value pattern. Indeed particular groups themselves were not considered eternal. As total as any group's demands might be, the group itself was justified by its performance and might be displaced by other groups if it did not succeed. Further, groups were not closed or isolated. They were linked in vertical chains of loyalty that ultimately brought them all within the structure of the national polity. This meant that when there was strong direction from the top, Japanese groups could be mobilized for vigorous new lines of action. Nonetheless it is hard to see in this structure, either in its value or its organizational components, any powerful internal drive toward innovation and differentiation. Indeed the universalism and individualism that are usually associated with strong rationalizing tendencies were severely limited by this pattern. If we look at the periods of most rapid and radical change in Japan, the seventh and eighth centuries and the nineteenth and twentieth, we see that they are associated with the wholesale importation of a more rationalized foreign culture. This phenomenon requires further inquiry.

JAPANESE CULTURE AND FOREIGN CULTURE

No complex society has maintained a stronger sense of what is native and what is foreign than Japanese society. This consciousness did not begin in modern times but goes back to the centuries immediately after the large-scale importation of Chinese culture. It seems likely that if a statistical comparison were made Japan would be found to have "borrowed" no more than other countries have, and possibly Japan would be well below the average on a "borrowing index." The concern with this issue is in the meaning of native and foreign culture, not in the amount of borrowing. The heart of specifically Japanese culture is the value system and group structure described previously. The native religion, Shinto, can be seen as the religious dimension of every Japanese group, but especially of the nation itself with its divinely descended emperor. Part of the problem in defining Shinto, or indeed of defining purely Japanese culture, is that it seems to be contentless. This "contentlessness" led Nishida Kitarō to define Japanese culture as a "formless form" (katachi ga nai katachi)[15] and Maruyamo Masao to call Japanese tradition an "empty bag," or an "unstructured tradition."[16] Japanese culture as the "container" is less easy to define than the heterogeneous "contents" of largely foreign origin, but it is the container that tenaciously persists while ever-new contents are received and often later abandoned. This pattern has led Maruyamo to say that there is no history of Japanese thought as such but only a history of the reception of various foreign systems.[17] These systems have existed for a while, usually in isolation from each other, and then have either died out or continued as the property of small and specialized groups. The same arguments can to some extent be extended to institutions as well.

The first great period of receiving foreign culture was in the seventh and subsequent centuries when Chinese thought and institutions were consciously and deliberately imported on a massive scale. It was

[15] In "Nihon Bunka no Tokushitsu" (The Characteristics of Japanese Culture), Miki Kiyoshi Zenshū, vol. 17, Iwanami (1968), p. 476. This article is actually an interview with Miki Kiyoshi and was published in Miki's collected works rather than of Nishida. Its omission from the collected works of Nishida may be because its editors felt the words were not necessarily Nishida's or it may be that the nationalist sentiment in this interview, stronger than in most of Nishida's writings, was offensive to the editors.

[16] Maruyamo Masao, Nihon no Shisō, pp. 11 ff.

[17] Ibid., pp. 2 ff.

perhaps the most systematic effort in world history before modern times of a less developed society to learn from a more developed one. A written language, a classic literature, a complex religion, a political theory, a legal system, an elaborate bureaucracy, a system of coinage, forms of land tenure, and much else were imported wholesale. Some of these cultural importations became so indigenized that they merely gave conscious expression to the native tradition. This is obviously the case where abbreviated forms of certain Chinese characters were used to write the Japanese syllabary (*kana*), but it was also true in the realm of thought where Confucianism supplied the rationale for the close personal bonds of kinship and loyalty which were already central in Japanese social organization. Other elements borrowed from China added a new dimension to the generalization of social communication and social control, as in the bureaucracy and the legal system. Even where the Chinese patterns were eroded by Japanese particularism a residue remained that left Japan permanently different from and more differentiated than Japanese society in late prehistoric times.

Much the same argument can be made for the massive reception of Western culture in the last hundred years. Political, legal, economic, and educational systems have been imported, largely replacing previous institutions in these areas. New philosophical, religious, and artistic movements have entered the country and have competed with earlier systems of thought. All these new importations have been indigenized to some extent but all bear the clear marks of their foreign origin. As a result of conscious systematic importation and adaptation Japan has been transformed from a poor agricultural society to a powerful industrial one. Once again importing foreign culture has gone hand in hand with a rapid advance in structural differentiation. It should be noted that this second transformation, like the first, was carried through under the aegis of the emperor system by groups organized in typically Japanese ways.

The lack of individualism and universalism in the Japanese pattern and the subsequent weakness of the drive toward rationalization would seem to be made up for by the ease with which it has been possible to import and adapt more rationalized forms from other cultures. Because the indigenous pattern, being relatively "formless," is not committed to any dogmatic set of beliefs or institutions but only to a pattern of group life, it does not place any barriers to importing foreign culture, as Islamic or Confucian orthodoxies did. The native Japanese pattern was simple and flexible, sufficiently generalized to sustain new and complex features and not so specialized as to limit new developments.

Of course, Japan's geographical position helped to make this mode of adjustment possible. Japan was just far enough from the continental mainland to make conquest extremely difficult, as the Mongols learned to their cost. On the other hand Japan was close enough so that she was within easy reach of the latest cultural advances in China and, indirectly, India as well. This continuous borrowing (the seventh and nineteenth centuries are only the most dramatic instances) kept Japan from ever getting too far behind the more "advanced" societies so that she was not in great danger of being overwhelmed by sheer technological superiority.

Japan's pattern of particularistic groupism not only allowed the relatively smooth acceptance of more rationalized thought and institutions, but it also provided the motivation for it. The constant effort to improve the position of one's own group relative to others within the society was generalized to a competitiveness between Japan and other societies. The necessity for Japan's equality with or superiority to other nations is not a product of modern nationalism. Concerns of this sort lie deep in Japanese history. They are related to the national integration under the emperor mentioned previously and helped provide in Japan an apparently easy fit with the model of the Western nation-state, though in fact the basic structure was quite different. In particular it should be noted that rationalization and rational forms are in the traditional Japanese view merely means to nonrational ends given by the immutable structure of Japanese group life.

Another dimension in understanding the paradox of continuity and change in Japan should now be evident. The continuity is mainly in the realm of values and the structure of group life. The change is mainly in cultural content and large-scale institutional and organizational forms. The relatively isolated, insular Japanese position accounts for some continuities, particularly in material culture, but the nature of Japanese society accounts for many more. On the other hand the rapid change and increase in structural differentiation result from importing and adapting more complex patterns developed abroad.

FUNCTIONS AND DYSFUNCTIONS
IN THE JAPANESE PATTERN

Many positively functional features of the Japanese pattern have already been mentioned — its flexibility, openness to adaptive improvements, and at least incipient national integration. The tight discipline of the groups over the individual allowed a ready mobilization of effort when required, though it caused strains for personality that require a later section for their consideration. Two features which have had severe dysfunctional consequences and which seem to be inherent in the Japanese pattern are *factionalism* and *xenophobia*.

The essence of the tightly organized Japanese groups is that they are linked primarily through vertical loyalty ties.[18] Between groups of the same order that are not linked together by a relatively close superordinate power there is apt to be competition verging on open conflict. This feature of Japanese society has its positive side because the competition and conflict of various groups have contributed to the dynamism of Japanese society and the circulation of Japanese elites. But, especially when the higher levels of integration are weak, the resulting factionalism can have severe consequences. Civil disturbances caused by the rivalry of the most prominent *uji* and *be* were common in the ancient period. Conflict between feudal lords kept the whole country in endemic warfare from about the tenth to the sixteenth centuries. Even when such group conflicts did not result in actual violence, as they tended not to do in the Tokugawa Period and in modern times, they have produced many situations of insubordination and lack of responsible control. The great feudal domains of Satsuma and Choshu actually endangered the national safety by attacking foreign warships against the orders of the Tokugawa regime toward the end of its rule. In the period from the 1931 Manchurian incident through World War Two numerous examples of factional strife and insubordination could be cited, actions that rendered leadership ineffective so that the nation first drifted into a war that nobody planned and then fought it less effectively than was possible.

Xenophobia too seems to be an inherent feature of the Japanese group. Students of Japanese village life have noted that even neighboring villages may view each other with grave suspicion. The tight group structure makes a sharp distinction between "us" (*uchi no mono*, literally "inside persons") and "them" (*yosomono*, outsiders).[19] The feeling is so strong that the outsider is sometimes considered less than human. When generalized to the national level this tendency can result in extreme xenophobia. Two periods of xenophobia had severely pathological consequences for Japanese society: the closing of the country (*sakoku*) near the beginning of the Tokugawa Period and the period of ultranationalism in the 1930's and early 40's. We have noted the usual openness of Japanese society to foreign culture and have linked this to the strong competitiveness associated with the performance values in the Japanese pattern. Foreign culture is endlessly assimilable as long as it does not affect the Japanese pattern itself — as long as it is only "contents" and not disruptive to the container. But when the foreign threat seems to endanger the fundamental pattern

[18] Nakane Chie, *Tate Shakai no Ningen Kankei,* especially chaps. 3 and 4.
[19] Ibid., pp. 49 ff.

itself the reaction can be extreme — in early Tokugawa times almost total withdrawal after a period of vigorous intercourse with and borrowing from the West, and in the 1930's and early 40's external aggression, again after a period, the so-called "Taisho Democracy," of exceptional openness. These extreme reactions were not mainly triggered by foreign aggression, though both periods were dangerous for Japan. Other periods of foreign danger have had the opposite effect. Rather what seems decisive is the fear that significant groups within the country have been converted to ways of thinking incompatible with the traditional structure of Japanese society. Thus both periods of xenophobia were marked by vigorous persecutions. The persecution — including the large-scale execution — of Christians in early Tokugawa Japan was among the greatest religious persecutions in world history. The ban on Christians continued throughout the Tokugawa Period and even the first Christian converts at the end of the Tokugawa Period still had to face the irrational hostility that Christianity aroused. In the later period, severe persecution of liberals and Marxists followed. In both cases a renunciation of the alien commitment and a return to purely Japanese group life were primarily demanded. Only if the victim refused to recant was he executed or imprisoned. In both cases the persecuted groups were felt to have had loyalties that transcended and were incompatible with the Japanese *kokutai*.

These xenophobic periods were dysfunctional or pathological not merely because of persecution, unpleasant though that is. In both cases communication with the outside world broke down, leading to serious miscalculations that endangered the whole society. At the beginning of the Tokugawa Period, Japan was a military match for any European power and the strongest nation in East Asia, having overwhelmed Korea and undermined the Ming regime in China. At the end of it Japan was so weak, comparatively speaking, that she could have been successfully invaded by any determined second-rate power in Europe. The complete isolation from the development of Western scientific and democratic thought from the beginning of the seventeenth to the middle of the nineteenth centuries probably had even more severe consequences. The disastrous consequences of Japan's military adventures in the 1930's and 40's hardly need mention.

In less powerful doses Japan's xenophobia has undoubtedly been functional in promoting national pride and a vigorous effort to maintain national independence and autonomy. But Japan has also suffered from an opposite malady — extreme xenophilia. On occasion at least some Japanese, overwhelmed by a sense of Japan's backwardness, have seemed willing to jettison the entire national heritage. There were those, for example, in the early Meiji Period who wanted the nation to abandon the Japanese language and learn English instead or to abandon Buddhism in favor of Christianity. More common has been a gnawing doubt and self-derogation about Japanese culture. On the whole a moderate amount of self-doubt and a willingness to learn from others have been greatly beneficial to Japan's cultural advancement.

To point out certain dysfunctions in the Japanese pattern is certainly not to derogate it. Every society has severely dysfunctional elements as Americans at the present moment know very well. Over the long haul the Japanese pattern has produced a dynamic, flexible, and effective society. This does not mean that it has not, as have all such patterns, exacted its price.

PERSONALITY IN PREMODERN JAPAN

Japanese groups place very great demands on the personality of the individual. They also provide very great rewards. Considering the infrastructure of Japanese groups is necessary to obtain further insights about stability and change in Japanese society.

We have spoken of the hierarchical nature of Japanese groups. Concretely this means that a primary group is composed of a leader and his followers, often conceptualized as a pseudo-kinship relation as when the leader is referred to as a parent-person (*oyakata*) and the followers as children-persons (*kokata*). It is worth pointing out that the leader in this terminology is called "parent" rather than "father" (in ancient Japanese "*oya*" probably meant "mother" first and "parent" only as a derived meaning, but this is forgotten today) and his functions are diffuse, having to do with the general welfare of his followers. A high degree of dependency on the mother is generated by Japanese socialization patterns and this dependency is later partially transferred to the leader who must "care for" his followers and not merely direct them in specific tasks. Secondary groups in Japan are composed by linking together vertical chains of loyalty. A national political leader today, or a feudal lord of old, has his direct followers who in turn have their followers down to the lowest level primary groups. Although great initiative and dynamic activity of a very "masculine" sort are necessary to put together large groups organized in this way, and such a leader may develop a great following because of his ability to come through for his followers or to coerce them into obedience, such masculine dynamic leaders are not greatly loved. The leadership that excites the strongest emotion and the greatest devotion is more passive and even feminine. Symbolically this more emotionally positive leadership focusses on the mother at the family level and the emperor at the national level. Both stand for nurturance and benevolence rather than domination and control. Those who dominate and direct gain their legitimacy as defenders or protectors of the more feminine leader type. Even when the hierarchical dimension is not strong, as in some traditional groups and perhaps increasingly today, the group itself is felt as nurturant, accepting, and in a sense feminine.[20]

All this means for individual personality that high levels of performance are demanded by and supported by nurturant, accepting groups and leaders. Instead of being crushed by despotic patriarchal authority the individual is encouraged to work hard to gain maternal favor. He is manipulated more by rewards than by threats and punishments. Although completely dependent on the group and its leader he is nonetheless not crushed by external authority but may exhibit remarkable initiative and creativity. This pattern helps to explain how the strong Japanese emphasis on the group nonetheless goes along with rapid adaptiveness and flexibility.[21]

Despite the great rewards, the rigors of group life are considerable. Social obligations may directly contravene personal feelings and needs, and there was no justification in pre-modern times for any outcome but personal submission to the group. The conflict between love based on personal feeling and marriage based on the convenience of the family line epitomized this kind of conflict and the only possible outcome other than submission to the social demands was love suicide. But the group could be frustrating not only because it frustrated personal feelings but also because it aroused but did not fulfill the need for perfect fusion, loss of personal identity in the group. When human relations prove frustrating, Japanese for many centuries have thought of merging with nature as a solution to personal problems.[22] The benevolent all-encompassing beauty of nature in which one can completely submerge one's own identity has been a symbol of personal fulfillment. Much in the Japanese aesthetic tradition has concentrated on this kind of expression. But even the aesthetic appreciation of

[20] I have in an unpublished paper referred to the Japanese emperor as a "mother-figure." On the whole question of the feminine dimension of Japanese culture see Huntsberry, "Religion and Value-Formation in Japan," and Matsumoto Shigeru, *Motoori Norinaga* (Cambridge: Harvard University Press, 1970).

[21] On the relation between family structure and achievement in Japan see Kamishima Jirō, *Kindai Nihon no Seishin Kōzō (The Spiritual Structure of Modern Japan)*, Iwanami (1961), part 3; and George De Vos, "The Relation of Guilt Toward Parents to Achievement and Arranged Marriage Among the Japanese," *Psychiatry*, vol. 23, no. 3 (1960).

[22] Ienaga Saburō, *Nihon Shisō-shi ni okeru Shūkyōteki Shizenkan no Tenkai (The Development of the Religious View of Nature in the History of Japanese Thought)*, Sōgensha (1944).

nature has not always been satisfactory and the Japanese have many times been led to a religious quest for enlightenment to overcome the last remnants of the troublesome individual self.

In our discussion of Japanese values we have already seen that aesthetic and religious pursuits did not undermine the commitment to the group but actually reinforced it by providing a means for handling unbearable tensions that the group itself could not absorb. But this is not quite the whole story; the social structure of aesthetic and religious life in Japan should be further considered.

It would certainly be a mistake to give the impression that the aesthetic sphere was one of purely personal expression divorced from a social context. Poetry, the most ubiquitous Japanese literary expression, was a form of social communication. This is clearly true in the Heian Period when love affairs were carried on through indispensable poetic exchanges, but even in modern times when, as Tanizaki shows in the relation between Sachiko and her husband in *The Makioka Sisters,* poetry continues to play a role. Indeed the brevity and allusiveness of Japanese art forms are in part explained by the fact that they are not meant to be taken as isolated objects set apart for solitary contemplation but are part of an ongoing stream of interaction and take their meaning only from that context. A simple ink painting hung in the appropriate spot in a Japanese room says something about the season, the character of its owner, and the nature of the occasion. It will frequently be replaced by other pictures for other contexts, unlike a Western painting that exists as an independent element in a room. Thus, no "frame" separates the Japanese work of art from its surroundings. In poetic diaries, a peculiarly Japanese art form, prose and poetry are intricately related and flow out of each other.[23] In a Japanese room the painting is complemented by the flower arrangement, the bamboo and wood of the interior architecture, and the view of the garden. The boundary between art and life is blurred and ideally life itself is turned into art so that everything, from the clothes one wears to the way one enters a room, has a kind of formal perfection and expressive subtlety. Then group life and artistic expression have no break and each intimately reflects the other.

Except that perfection of artistic form always carries a certain autonomy. The more completely the individual was committed to artistic expression the more he tended to withdraw from the normal group obligations of Japanese life. In the Heian Period the greatest writers

[23] See the introduction to Earl Miner, *Japanese Poetic Diaries* (Los Angeles: University of California Press, 1969). Miner's suggestive treatment of poetic diaries has quite general implications for the place of the aesthetic in Japanese life.

tended to be widowed or semi-retired gentlewomen of the lower nobility. In the Middle Ages the greatest painters and poets were Buddhist monks. The great seventeenth-century *haiku* poet Bashō ran away from his feudal post and spent much of his life in wandering and semiseclusion. Even in the modern period one can think of Tanizaki Junichirō writing *The Makioka Sisters* during World War Two, utterly unaffected by the current nationalist propaganda, or Nagai Kafū writing his petulant and utterly apolitical diary entries in the same years.[24] The pervasive Japanese groupism is the organizing principle of the artistic world as well — schools of painting, flower arranging, tea ceremony, as well as such professions as acting, dancing and music tend to be organized along kinship or pseudo-kinship lines. Even in the modern period the Japanese art world has divided into the usual collection of warring cliques. Yet the greatest artists and the most innovating ones have seldom been produced by the conventional schools. They have usually been those who, like Bashō, broke loose from some earlier life course to devote themselves to a new and autonomous expression.

Although artistic expression was integrated with the ongoing pattern of everyday life perhaps more completely than in any other advanced society, it often took the form of a covert protest against that life. The poetic tradition is full of disillusionment with human society and often reflects the turn to nature or religion as a consolation. Both the drama and the novel have frequently focussed on the conflict between social obligation and human feeling. This is not to say that social protest or social analysis has an artistic tradition. The social problem drama or novel has received only uncertain experimentation in the modern period and did not exist at all traditionally. Japanese art forms generally concentrate on feelings more than ideas, but feelings may rebel against a social order even when no set of ideas supports them. This is exactly what happens in the longer literary forms where such situations become most explicit. The unhappy protagonists have no hope of openly challenging their sad fate and go to their death amid the tears of the audience. But even a seventeen syllable poem or a flower arrangement may be an expression of and an emotional protest against personal unhappiness.

No culture has more richly cultivated the life of feeling and its aesthetic expression, and only here Japanese culture transcends its particularism and speaks to the universal human spirit. In poetry and painting, novels and plays, as well as in house architecture, garden

---

[24] See Edward Seidensticker, *Kafū the Scribbler* (Stanford: Stanford University Press, 1965), chap. 8.

design, and flower arrangement, Japanese culture breaks through the limitations of its social organization and has exercised far-reaching influences on other cultures.

Religion is the one other sphere where Japan has been able to transcend its cultural particularism and for much the same reason. For many centuries the religious life was a refuge, often the only refuge, from the unbearable pressures of group life. It was always possible for even the most distinguished person to shave his head and enter a monastery when faced with an irresolvable dilemma or when overcome with unbearable remorse. The upper classes were more apt to follow the meditation practices of Zen Buddhism, perhaps in some exquisite mountain temple where each change of season brought new beauties of nature. The masses were more apt to cast themselves on the mercy of Amida, the Boddhisattva who vowed never to enter nirvana till all sentient beings are saved. Japanese religion like Japanese art is aesthetic and emotional rather than intellectual, but it too provides an oasis of personal autonomy and of access to universal values in a desert of particularism.

I have called that aspect of the Japanese artistic and religious tradition that stands in tension with the existing social reality the "tradition of submerged transcendence." It is transcendent because it breaks through the strictures of the given social order but submerged because it lacks the ability to call forth any alternative. It is expressive of dissatisfaction without providing the basis for constructing anything new. The continuity of this tradition from Murasaki Shikibu to Tanizaki Junichirō or from Shōtoku Taishi to Suzuki Daisetsu itself indicates the basic continuity of the Japanese group structure to which it is so closely and so ambiguously related.

THE RELATION BETWEEN TRADITION AND MODERNIZATION IN JAPAN

The relation between tradition and modernization in Japan is peculiarly complex. I would argue, though this is not the place to marshall the evidence, that no inherent trend toward modernization existed in any of the current usages of that term in Tokugawa Japan. Social change in the Tokugawa Period can best be understood as the working out of the pattern possibilities of the Japanese culture of approximately 1600 through two hundred and fifty subsequent years of peaceful isolation. I see no fundamental challenge to the basic pattern of Japanese culture nor any inherent drive toward a radically different society. On the other hand much dynamism of Japan's modernization can be attributed to the traditional culture and society *once it had sustained the material and psychological shock of the Western impact.*

This means that potentialities that did not in the Tokugawa Period drive toward modernization could be mobilized in its support once new necessities and new models entered the picture. This limits the usefulness of Japan as an "example" for other modernizing nations with quite different traditional cultures.

Let us review quickly the elements that made the transition from feudalism to nation-state (the chief unit and vehicle of modernization in the West),[25] an at least superficially easy one for Japan. Japan already had a semicentralized government in the Tokugawa Shogunate. It also had an ancient tradition of national political unity as well as a tradition of reshuffling actual power under the unchanging legitimacy of the emperor. A political elite had a strong Confucian ethic of governmental responsibility and considerable experience of government at the local and provincial level. This elite (the *bushi* class) had already become a salaried bureaucracy and thus was disembedded from the involvements in local landholding that limited the effectiveness of its Chinese counterpart. No significant regional, linguistic, religious, or cultural divisions stood in the way of national integration and national geographical boundaries were of the most unambiguous sort. The general populace was schooled in the discipline of tightly organized groups, competitive but open to direction, and quickly responsive to strong leadership. There was no significant tradition of organized opposition to political authority. Except for an occasional peasant revolt, usually brought on by extreme famine conditions and utterly lacking in political program or organization, there was no form of alienation from authority other than purely private withdrawal and escape.

By and large the early Meiji state was built on these elements. It can be said to resemble the Western European nation-state only superficially for these reasons: There was no way of changing the top effective leadership (under the emperor) except through the open violent clash of political power groups. The choice of national goals depended entirely on the intelligence of the top leadership — there were few regular channels of representation, interest aggregation, or even consultation. Only the *bushi* class was conscious and responsible at the national political level, and members of that class could enter the government only with personal connections, often involving coming from the same feudal domain, with the top leadership. Communication flowed easily from the top down but with difficulty the other way. There was no ideal of the political participation of a nation of citi-

25 S. N. Eisenstadt in a talk at the Institute of International Studies, University of California, Berkeley, in July 1969 emphasized the dominance of the nation-state model in most existing conceptions of modernization and the many ways in which non-Western polities differ from that model.

zens, but rather the political role of the general population was limited to that of self-sacrificing subject. The whole modern Japanese political history is the history of attempts to open up this structure (which as described would apply only to early Meiji Japan) to new groups and new modes of political communication and participation and of opposition to such attempts. The major problem in any substantial alteration of this structure was that this structure itself was the very basis of Japan's rapidly growing national strength. Thus measures to strengthen the traditional pattern often went hand in hand with efforts to increase participation and develop the mechanisms of democratic government. *Both* these tendencies were seen as aiding modernization at least insofar as that is measured in wealth and power. Thus strengthening tradition in Japan was a component of modernization rather than necessarily in opposition to it.

Strengthening the traditional components of Japanese society took place at two primary points — the *kokutai* or national polity, and the primary group, whether in family, village, or factory. Through the mass media and compulsory education the *kokutai* ideology of the family state [26] was widely inculcated. It stressed the obedient subject and very secondarily the participant citizen. Through the civil code and governmental sponsorship of various associations, such as youth groups and veterans groups, the state attempted to reinforce the tight hierarchical nature of Japanese primary group relations. Also from the second decade of Meiji the government attempted strictly to repress any ideology or group that seemed openly to challenge the *kokutai*. But at the very same time important steps were made in the direction of representative government. A constitution was granted to the people by the emperor in 1890 that opened the way to legislative participation in government and eventually (1919) to a party cabinet. Although effective participation was only opened to a relatively small group, the trend was for gradually increasing inclusion. But at virtually every step strengthening the traditional structure went in hand with growing participation, as when in 1925 universal suffrage was passed at the same time as a Peace Preservation Law that outdid all previous Japanese legislation in limiting free speech and repressing allegedly subversive groups.

During the 1930's and early 40's the balance was tipped toward the "traditional," though it should be remembered that this was a period of continued economic development and growing egalitarianization of Japanese life. Since 1945 the balance has shifted toward representative government and popular participation, though the cohesive pri-

[26] See Ishida Takeshi, *Meiji Seiji Shisō-shi Kenkyū* (*Studies in the History of Meiji Political Thought*), Miraisha (1954), part 1.

mary group is far from dead and even a shadowy form of *kokutai* lingers on. The most interesting questions about Japan's modern century are: How far has the traditional *kokutai* and primary group really been undermined? How far have genuinely alternative modes of organization been established? And how have the traditional forms survived in modern guise? If we could answer these questions we would begin to know whether the centuries-old Japanese pattern with its balanced stability and change is still viable or whether it may be shifting in a radically different direction. The evidence is certainly insufficient but some speculations may perhaps be allowed.

CULTURAL RESOURCES FOR VARIANT PATTERNS

We have already commented at length on one aspect of Japanese tradition, the "tradition of submerged transcendence," which is deeply ingrained at the very heart of Japanese culture and personality, especially in the aesthetic and religious spheres, but which has only an ambiguous relation to the central value system focussing on the predominance of the group. On one hand, these aesthetic and religious activities have provided a safety valve for the dominant system, in that alienative motivation has been drained off without threat to the social order. On the other hand the deep-going universalism and individualism of the tradition of submerged transcendence cannot help but implicitly call into question the dominant pattern. There has been, however, no political means whereby this subversive potentiality could be realized. The religious-aesthetic tradition has been not only apolitical but almost amoral. This does not mean that resources from this tradition cannot be utilized to construct an alternative system of social values, but it does mean that most work in such an enterprise is still to be done.

Another element in Japanese tradition, however, was strongly political and ethical in orientation but was not entirely at peace with the dominant pattern. Confucianism also contains an element of "submerged transcendence," even though it existed in some tension with the religio-aesthetic components of the tradition for which earlier in this paper I have reserved that term. Much in the Confucian tradition does reinforce and rationalize the dominant pattern. Confucian ethics stresses particularistic obligations to parents, teachers, and rulers. It has been used to justify existing social orders in all East Asian societies. But at the same time in its notion of Heaven (*Ten*) and of the Way (*Dō*), Confucianism contains universalistic overtones that have clear political and moral implications. Moreover in the Confucian tradition, the conception is that the man of moral virtue, whatever his worldly position, may act to embody the transcendent moral order no matter what existing authorities may say. This freedom of moral action was very closely hedged and denied altogether by the most establishment-oriented Confucians, but it was not entirely lacking in China or Japan. It combined with a Confucian pragmatism enjoining retainers to act in the "best interest of" their superiors even when the superiors didn't know it, to provide an intellectual and moral justification for many great innovators at the end of the Tokugawa Period who had to engage in dangerous missions often expressly forbidden by parents and feudal lords.

Confucianism provided much of the scaffolding for the modern ideology of the *kokutai* or emperor system. It is also true that explicit reference to Confucianism in modern Japan has been almost exclusively the property of the right-wing. Confucianism almost nowhere in East Asia has been able to disentangle itself from its involvement with the old regime. But we must also point out the many ways in which Confucianism supplied a bridge to Western universalistic ideologies like Christianity, liberalism, and even socialism. It is well known that the Puritanical Yankee missionaries made such an impression on many young samurai in the late nineteenth century because they seemed the very embodiment of Confucian self-mastery and ethical idealism. Most early liberal and socialist thinkers had started as rather idealistic Confucians. Even as late as World War One, Yoshino Saku-zō's term *minpon-shūgi* (literally "people-as-the-basis-ism" but more loosely "democracy"), has a distinctly Confucian ring.

Nor, indeed, was Confucian universalism entirely confined to ideology. It was to some degree embodied in institutions, particularly in the educational and bureaucratic institutions of Tokugawa Japan. And of course the universalism embodied in those and other institutions of modern Japan has to some extent this same Confucian lineage. Both here and in the ethical idealism that has such a long history in Japan our figure, "container and contents," cannot be taken too literally. The particularistic "container" has been permanently bent by the centuries-old "content" of Confucian universalism. Nevertheless, for reasons already stated, Confucianism lacked either the dynamism or a sufficiently clear alternative model to challenge fundamentally the basic pattern of Japanese values. Those fundamental challenges that have arisen in modern times may draw from Confucian universalism or from the religio-aesthetic tradition of submerged transcendence, but they have always also involved some significant influence from the newly available Western culture.

Maruyamo has made the case for the largely instrumental use to which borrowings from Western culture have been put [27] — means at the service of group goals but without value in themselves — but he is quite aware that that is not the whole story. At least some components of Western culture standing in tension with Japanese group values have evoked profound commitment, including Christianity, Liberalism, German Idealism, and Marxism. To give a complete account of these four tendencies would be to write much of the intellectual history of modern Japan. Here we can consider only a few ways that they combined with or challenged the Japanese tradition.

German Idealism more closely resembles the Japanese tradition of submerged transcendence than any other of these four tendencies. It is no accident, therefore that Nishida Kitarō, Japan's most influential modern philosopher, combined an attachment to Zen Buddhism and the "Oriental" philosophy of absolute negativity with an interest in German Idealism. The particular synthesis that Nishida developed has been called the "orthodoxy of emperor system thought," but this seems gratuitous. It is true that Nishida never developed a social or political ethic and never openly criticized the status quo. In this apolitical stance he resembled much of the German philosophy that had influenced him. Yet his espousal of a Kantian personalism clearly extended the implications of the Japanese religio-aesthetic tradition in an ethical direction and was an important first step toward an altered conception of society even if it never went any further. These implications remained implicit and some of Nishida's disciples wrote the most intellectually respectable apologetics for the Japanese war policy. But it would be as absurd to blame Hitler on Kant as to blame Tōjō on Nishida. Nishida Kitarō and other ethical personalists who flourished in the 1920's remain an important resource for building an ethic both genuinely Japanese and genuinely universalistic.

Christianity has had a perennial appeal in modern Japan. Christianity made more explicit the transcendental implications of Confucianism and demanded an ultimate loyalty to Christ rather than the emperor or the state.[28] Christianity also contained certain resemblances to the Pure Land tradition of Buddhism, as Uchimura Kanzō recognized when he said that he worshipped Christ not as Wesley and Moody did but as Hōnen and Shinran worshipped Amida. Christianity, at least in the American Protestant strand that had the most influence, carried a much more explicit social ethical concern than did German

---

[27] Maruyamo, *Nihon no Shisō*, Introduction.

[28] See Takeda Kiyoko, *Ningenkan no Sokoku (Conflicting Views of Man)*, (Kōbundō), 1959, for the similarities and differences between Japanese traditional thought and Christianity as they appeared in the Meiji Period.

Idealism. Japanese Christians have been involved in every reform movement for the last century and were especially in the vanguard in the Meiji Period. Modern Japan has produced at least one authentically new Christian movement — the so-called Non-church Christianity of Uchimura Kanzō. Especially interesting about this movement is that although starting as a protest against the dominance of the missionary church even as a model for Japanese Christianity, it has developed a deep-going criticism of Japanese group structures as well.[29] Paradoxically, organized on a teacher-disciple basis, it yet demands of its followers that they worship Christ directly without mediation through the teacher. One leading Non-church teacher, a former president of Tokyo University, dissolves his Bible class every year so that the students will not form too strong and permanent a relation to him. Though small, the Non-church movement has had influence out of all proportion to its numbers, like the Quakers in America.

Liberalism, a somewhat vaguer tendency than the other three, has been of pervasive influence in modern Japan. It has produced such important government leaders as Shidehara Kijūrō and such influential social thinkers as Kawai Eijirō. Although the Marxist critics accuse the liberals of not being "thorough" in their criticism of the emperor system, undeniably most liberals were committed to universal ethical values that transcended the Japanese nation. They tried to interpret the Meiji Constitution in a liberal direction and to reduce the emperor's role to that of a conventional constitutional monarch. They contributed much to the genuine successes of pre-war Japanese democracy. They were unable to halt the drift to Fascism, a tendency that many courageously fought, less because of defects in their ideology than because of the structural weakness of their political position and their lack of allies in defending parliamentary democracy.

Marxism has been a very powerful movement in modern Japan. Since World War One, it has been the largest movement whose value position stands outside the traditional *kokutai*. Marxism is based on a theoretical understanding of reality in general and history in particular that grants no special position to the Japanese people and its emperor. It has also represented to many Japanese a struggle for social justice often at great personal sacrifice to those involved, which has deep ethical meaning. Marxism is explicitly anti-individualistic, but at least in pre-war times considerable individualism was necessary to persevere in the Marxist movement. The Japanese have not been entirely satisfied with the objectivist and cognitive stance of orthodox

[29] Carlo Caldarola is making an extremely interesting study of the contemporary Non-church Christians in a doctoral dissertation in sociology at the University of California now in progress.

Marxism, and the somewhat heterodox Marxist Miki Kiyoshi even before the war discussed *"shutaisei"* or "subjectivity" in social life and political action.[30] Since the war this element has come to be more and more emphasized so that Marxism too has contributed to a kind of ethical personalism.[31] Present-day student groups are very much concerned with this issue. Just as Christianity has been far more influential than the Christian Church so the Marxist influence in Japan has been far wider than the Communist or Socialist Parties.

All these tendencies were well established in pre-war Japan and all helped to give some grounding to "Democracy," the officially proclaimed new value system after the war. The minor success in institutionalizing liberal democratic values had been made by the 1920's was partial and almost completely swept away during the period of ultranationalism. Nonetheless, the new institutional order, which was derived largely from American liberalism and established by command of the occupation authorities, had some real grounding in previous Japanese experience. No direct challenge to the traditional *kokutai* from within has ever succeeded. The post-war institutional system did not result from the maturation of an alternative value pattern that finally gained the social support to institutionalize itself, but was imposed from without — and that imposition by no means destroyed the *kokutai* or the traditional Japanese group structure. Both were too amorphous and too pervasive to be annihilated by a mere change in official ideology or even by changes in the legal order. The confession documents written by Japanese Marxists and liberals in the 1930's when they renounced their former errors show that they do not by and large expand on the superiority of a native Japanese *ideology*. They tend to renounce ideology altogether and signal their intent to return to the primordial loyalties of family and nation.[32] They ceased being Marxists not to become some other kind of "-ist," but to be once again simply Japanese. Because the traditional Japanese pattern has never rested primarily on explicit verbal formulation (has never had, for example, a formal creed), it cannot be considered abandoned when

---

[30] Miki expounded his views in a number of books the most comprehensive and influential of which was *Kōsōryoku no Ronri* (*The Logic of the Power of the Imagination*), vol. 8 of *Miki Kiyoshi Zenshū* (*Collected Works*), Iwanami (1967). This work was first published serially from 1937 to 1943. Miki died in prison in 1945 but has enjoyed a great post-war vogue.

[31] A convenient summary of some of these issues in post-war thought can be found in Matsumoto Sannosuke's Introduction to the August 1966 (vol. 4, no. 2) issue of the *Journal of Social and Political Ideas in Japan*, pp. 2–19.

[32] Patricia Golden Steinhoff has treated these documents extensively in a 1969 doctoral dissertation on *tenkō* (recantation) submitted for a degree in sociology at Harvard University.

new verbal formulations are adopted. Only changes in ways of thinking and feeling and in patterning interpersonal relations can tell us that the traditional pattern is changing. Here the evidence remains ambiguous.

VALUE CHANGE IN POSTWAR JAPAN

So far we have been discussing cultural resources for constructing a new value system. Now we must consider how structural changes and historical experiences affected value change in postwar Japan.

Defeat in the Pacific war and foreign occupation were unprecedented experiences for the Japanese people. Not in historic times had the Japanese islands been successfully invaded. Never before had Japanese society been at the mercy of a foreign power. The entire modern fabric of ideology known as emperor-system thought collapsed before these eventualities, and the personal charisma of the emperor was dealt a severe blow. The explicit ideology of the pre-1945 period is most unlikely ever to be successfully revived again, though nostalgic echoes of it have been heard increasingly in recent years. But the basic value system in Japan, including the *kokutai* broadly understood, has never depended primarily on explicit formulation and, as we have seen, is able to survive ideological collapse.

Perhaps the profoundest change in postwar Japan has been the shifting balance between public and private values, which has had wide repercussions. When the terrible sacrifices that the state had exacted from the people, especially in the closing phases of the war, proved to be utterly without meaning or effect a terrible revulsion set in.[33] Whereas before the war any pursuit of purely private happiness was considered almost criminal, postwar society has been heavily oriented to a family-centered consumer hedonism. A good job, a pleasant home (with television, refrigerator, automobile, etc.), and a happy marriage have become the great desiderata. This exaltation of private ends has been criticized as selfish and materialistic not only by the old right but by the new left. Yet unlike private values in earlier times the new emphasis on the private sphere is not apologetic, does not defend itself as a mere complement to public values, and is much more closely integrated into the main centers of social life. Even the sense of Japan as a nation, which continues very strong, has been affected by the new values. Japan's economic productivity is proudly compared to other nations, not its military might nor its imperial rule. The events that concentrate and symbolize national

[33] See Oda Makoto, "The Meaning of 'Meaningless Death,'" *Journal of Social and Political Ideas in Japan*, vol. 4, no. 2 (1966), pp. 75–85. This is a translation of an article which appeared in *Tenbō* (January 1965).

identity are things like the 1966 Olympics or Expo '70. The competitive element is strong in these occasions but they symbolize consummatory gratification more than political domination. This shift from sacrifice for public ends to private gratification has been clearest in the relation between state and people, but it has influenced group life at every level. One way to say this is that the vertical dimension of Japanese group life has been weakening. The ubiquitous "boss" in Japanese society has not disappeared, but it has become necessary for him to moderate the nature and extent of his demands.

To some extent this tendency has gone hand in hand with the institutionalization of a democratic political order and an egalitarian legal system. In recent years attempts to strengthen the arbitrary powers of the state have been consistently resisted as possible infringements on the growing sphere of private interest. But the shift toward the importance of the private sphere is not to be interpreted as identical with an institutionalized individualism. Consciousness of individual rights remains relatively low. In many ways the individual is as dependent on the group as ever but group power is exerted through conformist pressure from peers more than through hierarchical authority.[34] In many spheres vertical controls remain strong but are exerted in a more subtle and roundabout way than would formerly have been the case. In other words, the typical structure of Japanese life is by no means broken. Nor is it quite right to say that the national collectivity has been smashed and Japanese society has been split into its constituent groups, for national consciousness remains strong and a powerful bureaucracy continues to provide direction over a surprisingly wide range of activities.

Many aspects of structural change in modern Japan seem to favor individualism and universalism, the perennial solvents of Japanese group particularism. Universalistic criteria have long been fundamental in the vast educational system as well as in much of the legal and governmental system. Though pockets of particularism held out in the economy even there universalistic criteria are becoming ever more decisive. All these changes are bound to have a long-run influence on values. And yet exposure to urban life, modern industry, and advanced education does not in itself create universalistic and individualistic values. "Mass society" theorists have shown how these advanced conditions can lead to the creation of pseudo-Gemeinschaft and "other-direction." In Japan where Gemeinschaft, pseudo-Gemein-

---

[34] On this point see Yoshiharu Scott Matsumoto, "Contemporary Japan: The Individual and the Group," *Transactions of the American Philosophical Society,* New Series, vol. 50, part 1 (1960); and Ishida Takeshi, *Gendai Soshiki-ron, (Contemporary Organization Theory),* Iwawami (1961).

schaft, and other-direction have always been strong, much in modern society strengthens rather than undermines them. Thus, structural conditions alone do not seem to be determinative. They reinforce traditional patterns as well as providing some support for alternatives. The future of the Japanese value system will be determined by the creative action of the Japanese people and will not simply be dictated by existing economic and social structures, important though they may be.

As part of the shift from public to private dominance has come the increasing unwillingness to put up with the traditional split in consciousness between personal desire and social duty. The issue of subjectivity (*shutaisei*) referred to here has been raised by those who insist on integrating personal impulse and public action. Many educated Japanese have come to rebel against living in a society where social obligations act like steel cables pulling and controlling one's acts regardless of what one's own feelings are. One element in the student revolts is an almost apocalyptic desire to determine the social conditions under which one will live, rather than docilely accept a fixed and pre-existing network. The most constructive expression of this new impulse is the growth of genuine voluntary associations in post-war Japan. Much so-called "voluntary association" has been in fact government-inspired and government-dominated. Long before the war various government ministries cultivated special interest groups that they then patronized and subsidized. This pattern is still very much alive. Veterans groups, farmers groups, even religious groups tend to gravitate to the appropriate ministry and obediently accept direction. Yet more and more in recent years genuinely autonomous groups have emerged to give a social expression to the private sphere and to nurture a genuine individualism.[35] But for many who have little hope of reconciling personal desire and group obligation Japanese society continues to provide a range of the most exquisite aesthetic and sensual diversions, sufficient perhaps in themselves to explain why Japan has never had a social revolution.

Some Japanese intellectuals have recently realized that abstract ideologies, particularly of Western origin, can have little hope of transforming Japanese life unless they are deeply indigenized so that they affect the feelings and unconscious thoughts of the masses.[36] However true this may be, indigenization has almost always meant in Japanese history the loss of universalism and the submergence of transcendence. From Buddhism to Christianity, from Confucianism

[35] See Ishida Takeshi, *Japanese Society*, ch. 9.
[36] See Matsumoto Sannosuke, "Introduction." Takeuchi Yoshimi has been especially influential in applying this lesson of the Chinese revolution to Japan.

to Marxism, the more the foreign ideology has penetrated Japanese group structure the more it has come to serve the interests of Japanese particularism. This situation has made the "synthesis of East and West" illusory in modern Japan, for the synthesis has almost always involved the loss of vitality of the more universalistic partner. And, this situation has tended to divide Japanese intellectuals between Japanese purists and thorough Westernizers. Although some at least partially successful syntheses have been achieved — for example in the work of such philosophers as Nishida Kitarō and Miki Kiyoshi, of such novelists as Soseki, Akutagawa and Tanizaki, of such a religious leader as Uchimura — the very limitations in these syntheses as well as their rarity leads one to be cautious about the future. Japan continues to be Asian but not Asian, Western but not Western, and in the very paradoxicality of its situation, acutely self-conscious.

At the moment what must be said about Japanese values is that there is a variety of competing possibilities. Socially effective particularistic values continue to contradict proclaimed universalistic ones. A society that talks a great deal about individualism continues to be dominated by groupism. The present ambiguities can continue partly because of delicate balances in political forces both within and outside the country. But history is unlikely to allow such tightrope-walking forever. Political or economic crises could force decisions that would propel the society in a more decisive direction. Several possibilities suggest themselves.

One possibility that seems partially to be realizing itself is the classic Japanese response to periods of weakening central control, namely the emergence of several strong competing power centers. This situation in the past has led to open power struggles in the country. At the moment only the radical student groups seem bent on an all-out challenge to governmental authority. It does not seem likely that this tendency will spread to broader segments of the population, but the possibility exists. A tightly structured and totalistic group like Sōka Gakkai, for example, is a potential base for an independent power-play. Another possibility is that the conservative government party, which is far from weak, may exert a more overt effect on ideology by resurrecting some old slogans and jettisoning some of the democratic rhetoric, which could be done without resorting to the extremism of the ultranationalist period. Still another possibility is that a coalition of reformist forces spearheaded by the newer voluntary associations and the more democratic elements in the Diet might succeed in seriously weakening the hold of particularistic and especially hierarchical groupism through both formal political changes and informal behavioral changes.

It is possible, then, that certain deep patterns of Japanese social life, which have existed since the formation of the Japanese state, may be breaking up and quite different patterns may be emerging. But the enormous tenacity and adaptability of the Japanese pattern indicate that any such conclusion is quite premature. In any case the conflict is not between "tradition" and "modernity," for the traditional pattern has been highly favorable for many kinds of modernization. Rather the question is What kind of modernity? Only the Japanese people themselves can answer that question.

METHODOLOGY

The development of sociology since World War II has been marked by great advances not only in theory but also in the logic and methodology of empirical research. Unfortunately, these two advances have not often enough been brought together for their mutual advantage. Theory has used research too seldom, and research has tended not to study the dynamic character of social systems. Too much emphasis in empirical research, especially in the use of that great invention, the cross-section survey, has been placed on the study of individuals rather than social systems, and on single-time points in these systems rather than on their continuing process.

In this essay, Professors Riley and Nelson demonstrate in detail and very successfully the large present possibilities and future potentialities for bringing closer together the theory of dynamic social systems and empirical research on those systems. They show the advantages and limitations of many empirical research logics and techniques for studying both stability and change in social systems.

Matilda White Riley and Edward E. Nelson

RESEARCH ON STABILITY AND CHANGE IN SOCIAL SYSTEMS

Despite the early preoccupation of sociologists with research on social stability and change, much of today's research is *neither* dynamic *nor* oriented to social systems. In exactly these aspects, the history of sociological research since World War Two is in itself a notable instance of the impact of social change. For one unanticipated conse-

This chapter was written in association with Marilyn Johnson, Beth Hess, and Bernice Starr; with advice and assistance from Anne Foner, Patricia Mysak, and Mildred G. Aurelius. The following persons have been kind enough to read and make helpful comments on earlier versions of the manuscript: Albert D. Biderman, Donald T. Campbell, Otis Dudley Duncan, Irving L. Horowitz, Everett C. Hughes, Phillip S. Hughes, John Knodel, Wilbert E. Moore, and John W. Riley, Jr.

quence of the general scientific and technological advance has been the spawning of research procedures, notably the cross-section survey, which, though rigorous, are all too often incongruent with the sociologist's fundamental notions about the dynamic character of society.

The emergent strain between theory and narrow empiricism in sociology, and the consequent danger of misleading interpretation of data, is apparent when contemporary "scientific" methods are subjected to critical comparison with earlier "softer" procedures for studying social dynamics. For example, contrast the cross-section survey with participant observation. How do the two methods differ in scientific rigor? How compatible is each with sociological theories about the group, about the individuals who interact within the group, or about the dynamic processes that can result in social stability or social change?

The relative precision of the cross-section survey is evidenced in such refinements as population sampling or attitude measurement. But the typical survey or poll can be open to the charge of theoretical incongruence when used by sociologists. Relying as it does on questioning for obtaining data, the survey focuses most naturally on the individual rather than on the group or on the individual's role in the group. Moreover, by emphasizing a single time period, the results of countless surveys have tended to hold our view of society suspended at a given moment, giving the illusion of a static structure that may be quite at variance with both theory and reality.

By contrast, participant observation makes little claim to precision. It is typically restricted to a single case of a group or small-scale society. Frankly unsystematic, it substitutes intuitive description for the scientific exactitude of measurement and statistical analysis. Yet the method can be highly appropriate for the sociologist's theories. Not only does it focus directly on the group, rather than on the individual. It also treats the group *as* undergoing process and change and *as* consisting of interacting persons and subgroups who contribute to these processes.

In respect to rigor, then, it is small wonder that modern sociologists are loath to rely heavily upon participant observation or upon many other soft or undeveloped procedures characterizing earlier sociological research,[1] but choose instead to utilize the more sophisticated techniques of the cross-section survey. In respect to theoretical congruence, however, it is difficult for the sociologist to translate back

---

[1] The contemporary effort to establish sociology as a science may in itself create a reluctance to utilize the intuition or the hunches that are an essential ingredient in the discovery process, as suggested by Melville Dalton, "Preconceptions and Methods in Men Who Manage," in *Sociologists at Work*, ed. Phillip E. Hammond (New York: Basic Books, 1964), pp. 50–95.

into the antecedent processes the particular configurations viewed in cross section at a single time. And it is difficult for him to apply the refinements that have been developed for individual analysis without either reifying the group or else reducing the group to a mere "contextual" aspect of the individual.

What would a future sociologist of knowledge find if he were to investigate the sociological research of the mid-twentieth century? What evidence might he uncover of a willingness to forego theoretical congruence for technical rigor? — to place the empirical emphasis on the static rather than the dynamic? — on the individual rather than on the group? He would certainly find traces of a spate of textbooks, often addressed specifically to sociologists, that begin and end with survey research.[2] He might well happen upon remarks that the survey is accepted as "a fundamental instrument of sociological research," [3] or that, following World War Two, survey analysis "became the language of empirical social research." [4] He might encounter an analysis of articles published in two leading sociological journals in 1965–66, in contrast to articles published twenty-five years earlier,[5] in which the evidence seems clear: contemporary research is both overwhelmingly quantitative and overwhelmingly synchronic. Further, the majority of the recent reports, based on large samples, derive their data from questioning and thus center most directly on the individual rather than on the group or society. And, according to this analysis, all these emphases are more pronounced now than in the early 1940's.

Armed with such evidences, the future sociologist of knowledge may well conclude that, in these decades, empiricists and theorists talk past one another. Indeed, he may infer that technology has sometimes led us to test hypotheses that are not central to our thinking, or to misinterpret certain data because they were obtained by inappropriate procedures.[6]

---

[2] Such books range from Herbert Hyman's *Survey Design and Analysis* (Glencoe, Ill.: The Free Press, 1955), written by a social psychologist for marketing and opinion research as well as for social research, to treatments by such sociologists as Bernard S. Phillips, *Social Research: Strategy and Tactics* (New York: Macmillan, 1966); Charles Y. Glock, "Survey Design and Analysis in Sociology," in *Survey Research in the Social Sciences* (New York: Russell Sage Foundation, 1967), pp. 1–62; or Morris Rosenberg, *The Logic of Survey Analysis* (New York: Basic Books, 1968).

[3] Rosenberg, ibid., p. xi.

[4] Foreword by Paul F. Lazarsfeld to Rosenberg, ibid., p. vii.

[5] Julia S. Brown and Brian C. Gilmartin, "Sociology Today: Lacunae, Emphases, and Surfeits," *The American Sociologist*, vol. 4 (1969), pp. 283–291.

[6] The criticism has often been made of course, as by Herbert Blumer, "Public Opinion and Public Opinion Polling," in *Public Opinion and Propaganda*, Daniel Katz et al. ed. (New York: Dryden Press, 1954), pp. 70–84; and Raymond Boudon, "Secondary Analysis and Survey Research: An Essay in the Sociology of the Social

To forestall any such regrettable verdict on the twentieth century, contemporary sociology faces a severe challenge: How can those methods for studying social dynamics which are theoretically relevant become imbued with the technical sophistication of the less relevant methods? How can the more primitive research designs early employed by sociologists be so modified as to retain their conceptual strengths while ameliorating their empirical weaknesses? In short, how can we at once achieve rigor and relevance?

Types of Research Methods

As a necessary beginning in meeting this challenge, we will examine in this essay the theoretical relevance of particular designs for research on stability and change in social systems. Whereas a wide array of research methods, of varying empirical precision, will ultimately be required for any full understanding of social dynamics, we shall select as illustration a few strands from the sociological literature of the past century. In regard to technical refinement, we shall merely suggest, through occasional reference and example, the vast potential that is currently emerging both in sociology and in several related fields.[7]

Thus we shall think of research methods in terms of their congruence with a theory that focuses *both* on dynamics *and* on groups or societies treated as social systems. For this purpose, we can roughly categorize all empirical methods (see Figure 1) on two dimensions: use of time and treatment of the group. In respect to time, one empirical approach corresponds to our conceptual model: it is diachronic, so that the research observations directly reflect the time sequence. The contrasting research approach is, instead, synchronic or cross sectional (restricted to a single point of time, or designed without reference to time).[8] Similarly, in respect to the group as the research case to which the data refer, the group can be treated empirically as a system with clearly identified parts (subgroups or individuals in roles), or the group

---

Sciences," *Social Science Information,* vol. 8 (1969), pp. 7–32. Our effort is to deal constructively with such criticisms.

[7] Unfortunately, there are many evidences of disciplinary provincialism, such as the sharp decline over the past twenty-five years in the citations by sociologists of journals in the fields of psychology, and the consistently small number of citations in anthropology. Brown and Gilmartin, "Sociology Today," pp. 286–287.

[8] The terms "diachronic" and "synchronic" have been adapted from the field of linguistics (cf. Joseph H. Greenberg, "Saussure, Ferdinand de," in *International Encyclopedia of the Social Sciences,* ed. David L. Sills (New York: Macmillan and The Free Press, 1968), vol. 14, pp. 19–21) to refer to the empirical use of time in research, in contrast to the conceptual definition of social systems as "dynamic" rather than "static."

FIGURE 1
Scheme for Classifying Empirical Approaches
to Stability and Change in Social Systems

Treatment of the group

Use of time	As an entity	As a system with identified parts
As a single point (synchronic)	(a) Synchronic group designs	(c) Synchronic system designs
As a sequence (diachronic)	(b) Diachronic group designs	(d) Diachronic system designs

can, instead, be treated as an entity, without emphasis upon its internal structure.

Figure 1 shows the four broad types into which research designs are classified by these two cross-cutting dimensions. Each cell represents an ideal type that comprises diverse designs. Any design has its own special limitations: it selects for attention only certain aspects of the conceptual model at hand (just as in some respects it sacrifices scientific rigor). In general, those approaches occupying cell *d,* the diachronic system designs, clearly constitute the optimum type because they are congruent with the conceptual model on both dimensions. However, these methods are not always feasible, or they may suffer from shortcomings that can be offset by other methods. Thus each of the other three cells contains compromise approaches that afford certain advantages for particular objectives, as our discussion will suggest. At the same time, we shall emphasize the implications of incongruence between theory and method, especially the dangers of interpretative fallacies resulting from how each of these three types falls short of the optimum approach.

We will examine these four ideal types in the two major sections of this essay. In the first section, the use of time in research designs, we use as examples mainly studies that are based on the group or society as an entity rather than as a complex system. In the second, we will examine — both for synchronic and diachronic designs — empirical methods of treating the group as a system of interdependent parts. In the concluding section we will allude to the potential of existing methods and data for the rapid future enhancement of research on social stability and change.

USE OF TIME IN RESEARCH

On the time dimension in Figure 1, research procedures are needed to test sociological theories of the group or the society conceived as essentially dynamic, not static. As Barber has said, "there is nothing static" in the concept of social system or social structure, "except in the sense that all process is assumed to have an analyzable structure at any moment in a time series." [9]

To be sure, theories requiring empirical test differ widely in defining and specifying the dynamic character of the group. For example, Parsons observes two types of processes, those that maintain the stability of the system, and those that change it.[10] Smelser identifies two dimensions on which theories may differ: short-term versus long-term processes, and disintegrative versus reconstructive processes.[11] Other theories distinguish explicitly between processes that are endogenous to the particular social system being examined, and exogenous processes or interchanges across the system boundaries.[12] Yet whatever sociological theory is under immediate research scrutiny, the underlying conceptual model is dynamic.

How, then, can this essentially dynamic model be examined by empirical procedures that sometimes do, but often do not, build the passage of time into the research design? We shall consider this question first by scrutinizing the simpler research approaches that treat the group or society as an entity (with little attempt to identify the parts or members within each group), contrasting synchronic group designs with diachronic group designs — cells *a* and *b* in Figure 1 — for research on social change.

[9] Bernard Barber, "Structural-Functional Analysis: Some Problems and Misunderstandings," *American Sociological Review*, vol. 21 (1956), pp. 129–135.

[10] Talcott Parsons, *Societies: Evolutionary and Comparative Perspectives* (Englewood Cliffs, N.J.: Prentice-Hall, 1966), pp. 20–21.

[11] Neil J. Smelser, *Essays in Sociological Explanation* (Englewood Cliffs, N.J.: Prentice-Hall, 1968), pp. 195 ff. As might be expected, Smelser finds few theories of social decline in contrast to the vast literature stressing such constructive changes as economic development or the rise of civilizations. See Robert A. Nisbet, *Social Change and History* (New York: Oxford University Press, 1969) for an analysis of "the metaphor of growth" as applied to society, including an attack on the "neo-evolutionists" from Durkheim to Parsons and Smelser.

[12] See, for example, Talcott Parsons and Edward A. Shils, "Value, Motives, and Systems of Action," in *Toward a General Theory of Action*, ed. Talcott Parsons and Edward A. Shils (Cambridge: Harvard University Press, 1951), pp. 230–233; and Parsons, "An Outline of the Social System" in *Theories of Society*, ed. Talcott Parsons et al. (New York: The Free Press, 1961), pp. 71–72.

Escape from the Static Bias

The synchronic group study slices through the social process at a given point in time. The data range from complete censuses to sample surveys; from reports of interviewers or observers to tribal artifacts or historical documents. Not all synchronic studies are strictly cross-sectional; many comparative analyses, such as those based on ethnographic reports, simply disregard the diverse times to which the data refer.[13]

The results of synchronic analysis typically consist of static correlations or associations among properties of groups [14] such as: industrialization may be correlated with urbanization in a sample of countries; [15] literacy rates for Census areas of the United States may be negatively related to the proportions of Negroes in the area; [16] large firms may be more likely than small firms to hire older workers.[17] Does the static character of such correlations thereby restrict the researcher to static interpretations that have little relevance for his dynamic model? Not entirely. Because the synchronic approach has many advantages, methodologists have clung to it although struggling prodigiously to escape the cross-section straitjacket. They have invented some ingenious devices that can often tease out of the static correlations clues to suggest the underlying dynamic processes.

It will aid our assessment of these devices to distinguish among three elements of research on dynamic processes: (1) the association among variables, (2) the time sequence of these variables, and (3) the linkages (or "causal" mechanisms) producing the association. Of these

[13] As in any typology, the decision to classify a given design as synchronic, rather than diachronic, is arbitrary.

[14] In contrast to these simple illustrations are many more sophisticated examples, such as the factor analyses used to map major dimensions of variation among cities or regions. See, e.g., Carl-Gunnar Janson, "Some Problems of Ecological Factor Analysis," in *Quantitative Ecological Analysis in the Social Sciences*, ed. Mattei Dogan and Stein Rokkan (Cambridge: The MIT Press, 1969), pp. 301–341.

[15] Kingsley Davis and Hilda Hertz Golden, "Urbanization and the Development of Pre-Industrial Areas," *Economic Development and Cultural Change*, vol. 3 (1954), pp. 6–24.

[16] W. S. Robinson, "Ecological Correlations and Behavior of Individuals," *American Sociological Review*, vol. 15 (1950), p. 352. Of course, Robinson cites this material to illustrate his "ecological fallacy." We want to emphasize, however, that such data are entirely appropriate for an analysis based on groups. See, e.g., Erik Allardt, "Aggregate Analysis: The Problem of its Informative Value," in *Quantitative Ecological Analysis in the Social Sciences*, ed. Mattei Dogan and Stein Rokkan (Cambridge: The MIT Press, 1969), pp. 41–51.

[17] W. Willard Wirtz, *The Older American Worker: Age Discrimination in Employment, II*, Report of the Secretary of Labor (Washington, D.C.: U.S. Government Printing Office, 1965), p. 5.

three, the associations among variables (element 1) are *empirical* regularities found in the data. By contrast, the connecting linkages (element 3) are not examined empirically, but rest upon *interpretation* in terms of sociological theory or knowledge. Moreover, the time sequence (element 2), which can be established empirically through diachronic studies, is also left to interpretation in the synchronic designs.

The peculiar difficulties of synchronic studies seem to inhere, then, in the dual burden of interpreting both the time order of variables and their causal linkages. Many devices that attempt to handle such difficulties direct special attention to elements 1 and 3. Some empirical procedures can, for example, add to the initial evidence about the association among variables (element 1), thereby suggesting certain causal explanations (element 3) as more likely than others. Other interpretative procedures add to the plausibility of the results by using logical or mathematical models to predict the shape of the data if the researcher's assumptions about causal processes are true. All such procedures appear, however, to require a theory (whether based on a priori assumption or on outside information) that states the time order of the particular variables under analysis. Thus, at best, synchronic designs seem most suitable for exploring and suggesting dynamic processes.

Addition of variables. One approach to the dynamic interpretation of synchronic findings examines the synchronic interrelationships among several, rather than just two, variables. Its aim is to uncover all possible empirical relationships among the explanatory variables by controlling potentially confounding factors; at the same time, it postulates (but does not test) a time sequence of the variables.[18] This approach was early formulated by Durkheim for the more complex analysis of social systems — cell *c* in Figure 1. In the forms widely utilized by survey researchers for study of individuals,[19] this approach seems applicable to certain group analyses as well.

[18] Compare Samuel A. Stouffer, "Some Observations on Study Design," in *Social Research to Test Ideas*, Samuel A. Stouffer (New York: The Free Press, 1962), p. 294.

[19] See Matilda White Riley, *Sociological Research*, 2 vols. (New York: Harcourt, Brace & World, 1963), vol. 1, pp. 408–421 for examples; and vol. 2, pp. 143–146, for the logic of the procedure. Empirical operations range from cross tabulation and subgroup comparison to rapidly developing computer procedures for multiple regression and multiple discriminant analysis, and for detecting interaction effects. See Hanan C. Selvin, "Survey Analysis: Methods of Survey Analysis," *International Encyclopedia of the Social Sciences*, ed. David L. Sills (New York: Macmillan and The Free Press, 1968), vol. 15, pp. 414–417; and James N. Morgan, "Survey Analysis: Applications in Economics," in ibid., pp. 432–433.

For many years, survey analysis of multiple variables has been greatly influenced by Lazarsfeld's typology of the "elaborations" occurring when an initial relationship between two variables, X and Y, is examined separately for the subgroups of people classified on a third variable, T.[20] His typology derives from two dichotomous dimensions. The first, which deals with actual empirical outcomes, focuses on whether, under the varying conditions of T, the original XY relationship varies sharply or whether it disappears (our element 1). The second dimension, which is purely conceptual and cannot be tested directly by the data, deals with the crucial factor of time (our element 2). This dimension states alternative assumptions about the position of variable T in the time order, as either antecedent to X or intervening between X and Y. (In the scheme it is also assumed that X precedes Y, and that T does not follow Y.) Thus, by isolating some possibilities on these two dimensions, Lazarsfeld directs attention to a simplified set of possible "modes of explanation" of the connecting mechanisms (our element 3).

An example is Murdock's finding, from ethnographic reports on some two hundred societies, that political integration transcending the community is more likely to occur in societies in which people are settled in villages than in societies composed of migratory tribal bands.[21] Although Murdock does not attempt statistical analysis of a third variable he does speculate further about facilitating political organization by personal relationships beyond the community (through local exogamy, safe conduct, or market peace). Imagine, however, that he had introduced facilitation of personal relationships as a third variable, T, in order to elaborate the original relationship between village settlement, X, and political unification, Y. And imagine that, of the many possible empirical outcomes, he had found that, with T controlled, the original XY relationship disappeared.

How might such a configuration of the data aid the student of social change? The synchronic findings permit interpretation — notice carefully! — only to the extent that a priori reasoning or outside information can support definite assumptions as to the time order of variables. Following Lazarsfeld's scheme, it must be assumed that settlement in villages (X) is antecedent to political unification (Y), and that T either precedes X or intervenes in time between X and Y. Then it is this assumption about the timing of T that governs the explanation attributed to the disappearance of the XY relationship once T is introduced. If T is believed to intervene, then T is said to suggest the

20 See Paul F. Lazarsfeld, "Survey Analysis: The Analysis of Attribute Data," in ibid., pp. 419–428, for a revision of many of his earlier discussions; for the use of time, see especially pp. 425–426.

21 George P. Murdock, *Social Structure* (New York: Macmillan, 1949), p. 85.

nature of the causal linkages. However, if T is believed to precede X (as well as Y), then the apparent XY relationship is to be explained away as "spurious" — much like Yule's often-cited "nonsense correlation" between high birth rates and the presence of storks. Thus the utility of Lazarsfeld's scheme for interpretation of dynamic processes is contingent upon outside information about the time order of the variables.

Intercorrelation of variables. Another means of bringing synchronic data to bear on social dynamics compares the relative magnitudes of the correlations between pairs of items in order to suggest the ordering of these items over time.

Driver and Massey,[22] in a synchronic study of two hundred and eighty North American Indian tribes, used this procedure in an attempt to predict the empirical outcome on the basis of their conceptual model. Concerned with the relative merits of evolutionary rather than diffusionist theories of culture, these authors examined the intercorrelations among several culture traits (such as division of labor, postnuptial residence, land tenure, and descent). In an ingenious approach to this hoary problem they postulated that, if the traits succeed one another in a particular causal sequence (so that $W \rightarrow X \rightarrow Y \rightarrow Z$), then as a result of time lag those traits closer together in time should be more highly correlated than those widely removed. And indeed their results proved consistent with the hypothesized sequence.

However, a re-analysis of this study conducted by Blalock [23] stresses the need for caution in such interpretations. Blalock's reassessment applies a more general mathematical solution to the problem of drawing causal inferences from the intercorrelation of a set of variables, which Simon, drawing upon the econometric literature, had published in 1954.[24] Blalock shows not only that an alternative theory fits the data even better than the original theory, but also — of even greater importance for dynamic research — that "we need not assume that

[22] H. E. Driver and W. C. Massey, "Comparative Studies of North American Indians," in *Transactions of the American Philosophical Society* (Philadelphia: The American Philosophical Society, 1957), n.s., vol. 47, pt. 2, pp. 427–434.

[23] Hubert M. Blalock, Jr., "Correlational Analysis and Causal Inferences," *American Anthropologist*, vol. 62 (1960), pp. 624–631. Blalock's solution depends on the assumption that certain causal relationships do not hold and that all "additional uncontrolled variables . . . have an essentially random effect" on the variables under consideration (p. 625). See also Blalock, *Causal Inferences in Nonexperimental Research* (Chapel Hill: University of North Carolina Press, 1964), for a more extensive treatment of causal inferences in nonexperimental research.

[24] Herbert A. Simon, "Spurious Correlation: A Causal Interpretation," *Journal of the American Statistical Association*, vol. 49 (1954), pp. 467–479.

the pattern among correlations is primarily due to a time lag factor." Just as with Lazarsfeld's method, the more general Simon method [25] rests upon a whole set of assumptions not themselves tested in the analysis. Thus, each of these models requires some external knowledge of time sequences if it is to serve its highly useful function in selecting among available causal models or in suggesting new ones.

Use of Guttman scales. The Guttman scale, one mathematical model that can be tested for consistency with the data, has been employed by several sociologists for interpreting synchronic group findings. As an example, Freeman and Winch,[26] using ethnographic reports on some fifty societies, found that six items postulated to reflect a single dimension of societal complexity did appear consistent with the scalogram model, with the less frequent traits appearing only in those societies where the more frequent traits were also observed. Thus, a formal legal system was found only if a money economy was also present; or written language, the least frequent item, was found only in societies where all five other traits occurred.

Guttman's scalogram pattern, because of its cumulative or transitive character, often seems useful for uncovering situations where traits have developed over time, particularly in exploring unilinear theories of evolution. In addition, several elaborations or variations of the model [27] have been developed that may accommodate the more complex evolutionary theories currently in vogue (to allow for wide variations within a particular evolutionary stage, for bypassing particular

[25] The methods of interpretation opened up by applying path analysis, as developed in genetics, also require assumptions as to ordering of the variables, as noted by Otis Dudley Duncan, "Path Analysis: Sociological Examples," *The American Journal of Sociology,* vol. 72 (1966), p. 7.

[26] Linton C. Freeman and Robert F. Winch, "Societal Complexity: An Empirical Test of a Typology of Societies," *The American Journal of Sociology,* vol. 62 (1957), pp. 461–466. Among others who lay even greater stress on a sequential interpretation are Robert L. Carneiro, "Scale Analysis as an Instrument for the Study of Cultural Evolution," *Southwestern Journal of Anthropology,* vol. 18 (1962), pp. 149–169; Richard D. Schwartz and James C. Miller, "Legal Evolution and Social Complexity," *American Journal of Sociology,* vol. 70 (1964), pp. 159–169; and the analysis of Parsons' "evolutionary universals" undertaken by Gary L. Buck and Alvin L. Jacobson, "Social Evolution and Structural-Functional Analysis: An Empirical Test," *American Sociological Review,* vol. 33 (1968), pp. 343–355.

[27] See, for example, Guttman's image analysis or Stouffer's H-technique, published in Matilda White Riley, John W. Riley, Jr., and Jackson Toby, *Sociological Studies in Scale Analysis* (New Brunswick, N.J.: Rutgers University Press, 1954), pp. 372–389 and 410–415; or the scale proposed by Robert K. Leik and Marilyn Matthews, "A Scale for Developmental Processes," *American Sociological Review,* vol. 33 (1968), pp. 62–75, for acquiring and dropping traits in an ordered sequence.

stages or traits, or for dropping earlier traits after acquiring later ones).

However, although the finding of a scalogram pattern can suggest a time ordering of the items or can indicate that particular cumulative sequences are unlikely, it is in no sense to be taken as clear proof of a diachronic ordering. Imagine, for example, that only three types of societies are found: those having both a legal system and a money economy; those having a money economy only; and those with neither. That is, a legal system is found only where a money economy also exists. Such a patterning of traits is consistent with the idea of social complexity as unidimensional; it means that societies can be arranged along a continuum (as from rural to urban, or from *Gemein-schaft* to *Gesellschaft*). However, no explanation of this unidimensional patterning is given in the data. The pattern *may* reflect a particular sequence in the development of societies, so that those societies with both traits have previously experienced the two earlier stages now represented by the other two types. Alternatively, the pattern may reflect a process of diffusion, in which the simultaneous adoption of both traits has occurred in some societies through the assimilation of the culture pattern of another society.

The Guttman scale, then, does not escape the limitation of synchronic data: time sequences are not empirically established, but are open to interpretation. Because the occurrence of a scale pattern can arise in various ways, it does not in itself demonstrate time order.

Problems of interpretation. In sum, such devices for comparing different groups at a single time period seem poorly adapted for research on societal stability and change. Two stubborn problems beset the dynamic interpretation of the synchronic data. First, the static findings cannot in themselves establish the time sequence. Second, there is all too often, as Stouffer [28] has put it, "a wide-open gate through which other uncontrolled variables can march"; hence the causal linkages are open to some doubt.

In some situations, nevertheless, the synchronic design is the most practical, perhaps even the only, approach to certain aspects of social dynamics.[29] But it is a second-best approach. To be sure, it can be highly suggestive of dynamic theories. It can tell the researcher whether or not he has identified some pieces that may be linked in the

[28] Stouffer, *Social Research to Test Ideas*, p. 294.

[29] See, for example, Goode's discussion of the revival of the comparative method, which had earlier fallen into disrepute. William J. Goode, "The Theory and Measurement of Family Change," in *Indicators of Social Change*, ed. Eleanor Bernert Sheldon and Wilbert E. Moore (New York: Russell Sage Foundation, 1968), pp. 303–304.

process under scrutiny. But it excludes the master variable, time, which is essential for arranging such pieces in their proper sequence.

Because of such restrictions, synchronic designs, if overinterpreted, can lead to mistaken conclusions. Many examples of *cross-section fallacies* are widely familiar. For example, Kuznets [30] has shown that an attempt to derive dynamic processes directly from "Engel's law" could lead to an erroneous result. This famous nineteenth-century generalization that Engel derived from the LePlay studies [31] states the synchronic principle for households within a society that: the larger the household budget, the smaller the share of the total budget that will be spent on such "necessities" as food, and the larger the share that will be spent for such items as clothing or recreation. Over time, however, quite to the surprise of the economists, budgetary patterns have not conformed to this "law." Rather, as Kuznets has demonstrated for the United States between the 1920's and the 1950's, despite a marked rise in consumer expenditures per capita, the share spent for food has remained constant instead of declining; similarly, the share spent for clothing has declined instead of increasing. Clearly, other factors (such as changes in technology or in conditions of life) are at work *over* time in addition to the consumer preferences revealed by budget studies at a given time. Thus, to predict or to interpret the antecedent sequences entirely by the synchronic Engel curve would be fallacious.[32] In this instance, as in many others, we cannot assume a social analogue of the principle that ontogeny repeats phylogeny.

Diachronic Group Designs

In contrast to the synchronic study, which consistently gives the illusion of flatness, the diachronic study reflects the patterning of stability and change over time. Cross-section findings, as we have seen, reveal empirical regularities only in the association among variables, leaving to interpretation the questions of time order and causal linkages. Diachronic studies, on the other hand, move the time dimension from the realm of speculation and into the realm of fact. The data themselves can show the succession of variables. Furthermore, one diachronic design, the experiment, can directly test questions of causal

[30] Simon S. Kuznets, "Income Distribution and Changes in Consumption," in *The Changing American Population,* ed. Hoke S. Simpson (New York: Institute of Life Insurance, 1962), pp. 50–53.

[31] For subsequent use of this law in economics, see H. S. Houthakker, "Engel, Ernst," in *International Encyclopedia of the Social Sciences,* vol. 5, p. 63.

[32] For other types of cross-section fallacies, such as the "life course fallacy" and the "generational fallacy," see Matilda White Riley, Marilyn E. Johnson, and Anne Foner, *A Sociology of Age Stratification,* vol. 3 of *Aging and Society* (New York: Russell Sage Foundation, 1971), chap. 2.

linkages. Patently, then, the over-time approach is the natural way to study over-time interactions and changes. It reduces the necessity for relying on interpretative procedures.

This special advantage of diachronic studies applied to groups — cell *b* in Figure 1 — can be illustrated by an analysis in which Davis and Golden [33] plot the growth of urbanization for each of a sample of countries over the past century and a half. Merely by looking at their charts, one can see how, as the authors claim, the rapid urbanization experienced in recent times in pre-industrial areas tends to parallel that experienced at earlier periods in the now industrialized nations. Here it is no longer necessary to speculate, as one must from synchronic comparisons of industrial with non-industrial societies, about what history might show. The historical record itself demonstrates the similar patterns of change for the several societies, and the temporal lag of some countries behind others in entering upon this process.

Because of obvious difficulties in studying dynamic processes in their entirety, simplifications of a full diachronic design have been devised, all of which utilize data that are ordered in time though they organize or analyze these data in differing ways. One approach focuses directly on *processes*, describing particular short-term or long-term trends, or measuring the association or concurrence among trends. Another design focuses on *structural sequences*, subjecting the variables to synchronic analysis at each of two or more separate time periods, and comparing cross-section views to see what changes may have occurred. Thus, if the former approach starts with diachronic description or correlation, the latter starts with a series of synchronic descriptions or correlations.

For example,[34] a processual analysis might show how the changes in the homicide rate are positively correlated with trends in the prosperity of a country, tending to parallel the rise and fall in the business cycle; whereas the changes in the suicide rate are negatively correlated with trends in prosperity. In a structural sequence, by contrast, two cross-section studies, the first conducted in a period of depression and the second in a period of prosperity, might examine the synchronic relationship of socioeconomic status to suicide and homicide respectively, to ask: Is it the high status segment that is disposed toward self-destruction during economic depression (at time 1)? — the low status segment that is disposed toward killing during

[33] Davis and Golden, "Urbanization and the Development of Pre-Industrial Areas," pp. 6-24.

[34] With apologies to Andrew F. Henry and James F. Short, Jr., *Suicide and Homicide* (Glencoe, Ill.: The Free Press, 1954).

prosperity (at time 2)? Such structural sequences, when they (like panel studies) study the *same* cross-section sample repeatedly,[35] are forms of social system analysis that will be discussed later in relation to cell *d* in Figure 1.

Both processual analyses and structural sequences are congruent with the sociological view of the system as dynamic. Moreover, they form natural counterparts to theoretical analysis. Some theorists (such as Simmel) begin their analysis with social processes, like conflict or adjustment. Other theorists (such as Parsons) begin with structure as the practical starting point. But both are entering, through different doors, into the same continuing dynamic of social interaction.[36] As Parsons and Shils [37] put it, "organization" and "dynamic process" are "the two aspects of the same phenomenon."

Processual analysis. Sociology affords many classic examples of trend analysis. The studies vary in such respects as the time intervals between observations, the total length of time covered, the number of properties examined, or the number or groups included in the sample.[38] Thus, for instance, Durkheim [39] examines trends in suicide rates for different countries, utilizing published statistics. Or Bales observes interaction as it progresses through phases in a small-group session,[40] developing a procedure that Strodtbeck [41] carries out of the laboratory into the Navaho reservation and the Mormon village. Particularly noteworthy as an illustration of research on values and meanings — so crucial a factor in social change — is Sorokin's *Social and Cultural Dynamics.*[42] Sorokin, who treats the whole system of

[35] Structural sequences can also be based on *different* cross-section samples.

[36] Compare Barber, "Structural-Functional Analysis: Some Problems and Misunderstandings," pp. 133–134.

[37] Parsons and Shils, "Values, Motives and Systems of Action," p. 233.

[38] The conceptual models used in the research typically include many interrelated processes. For example, Parsons, noting that any processual outcome results from the operation of plural factors that are mutually interdependent, describes earlier single-factor theories as belonging to the "kindergarten stage" of the development of social science. Parsons, *Societies: Evolutionary and Comparative Perspectives,* p. 113.

[39] Emile Durkheim, *Suicide,* trans. John A. Spaulding and George Simpson (Glencoe, Ill.: The Free Press, 1951).

[40] Robert F. Bales, "Some Uniformities of Behavior in Small Social Systems," in *Readings in Social Psychology,* rev. ed., ed. Guy E. Swanson, Theodore M. Newcomb, and Eugene L. Hartley (New York: Rinehart and Winston, 1952), pp. 146–159.

[41] Fred L. Strodtbeck, "Husband-Wife Interaction over Revealed Differences," *American Sociological Review,* vol. 16 (1951), pp. 468–473.

[42] Pitirim A. Sorokin, *Social and Cultural Dynamics* (New York: American Book Company, 1937).

Western Europe as his research case, deals with numerous aspects of social and cultural change (art, science, law, wars and revolutions, economic conditions, and so on) over a period of some 2,500 years. His data range from many thousands of works of art to all the historical figures mentioned in the *Encyclopaedia Britannica*.

Among the pioneering trend analyses, Ogburn and Thomas' *Social Aspects of the Business Cycle*[43] opened up a broad area of social research to subsequent technical refinement. In this early study the researchers aimed to discover how, over a fifty-year period in the United States, the fluctuations in economic prosperity are associated with the fluctuations in such social phenomena as marriage rates, divorce rates, or — following Durkheim's treatment of anomic suicide[44] — suicide rates.[45] Borrowing from methods developed by economists for quantitative description of the business cycle, Ogburn and Thomas construct curves that disentangle long-term trends from short-term oscillations around these trends. This procedure enables the researchers to control (or hold constant) the secular trend, in order to measure the relationship between annual fluctuations in business conditions and in each social phenomenon in turn. For example, the coefficient of correlation between marriage-rate fluctuations and the business cycle turns out to be +0.66, indicating a general tendency for the marriage rate to increase in prosperity and diminish in depression. Thus these researchers contend with two central methodological problems: first, the systematic description of a single trend, by separating long-term movements from oscillatory changes of shorter duration; and second, the systematic analysis of concurrence among trends.

Such early examples suggest the potential of time-series analysis[46] for permitting dynamic generalizations about groups.

The problem of confounding factors. If diachronic designs can clearly uncover sequential changes, does it follow that they also indi-

---

[43] William F. Ogburn and Dorothy S. Thomas, "The Influence of the Business Cycle on Certain Social Conditions," in *Social Aspects of the Business Cycle*, Dorothy S. Thomas (New York: Knopf, 1927), pp. 53–74.

[44] Durkheim, *Suicide*, p. 241.

[45] Compare the refinements of such subsequent analyses as Henry and Short, *Suicide and Homicide*.

[46] The methods of time-series analysis available to sociologists today, which are applicable particularly to studies of a single group, include a wide range of statistical techniques as well as probabilistic (or stochastic) models developed since the 1930's for estimating the underlying processes. See, for example, Wayne H. Holtzman, "Statistical Models for the Study of Change in the Single Case," in *Problems in Measuring Change*, ed. Chester W. Harris (Madison: The University of Wisconsin Press, 1967), pp. 199–211; Gerhard Tintner, "Times Series: General," in *International Encyclopedia of the Social Sciences*, vol. 16, pp. 47–57; and Herman Wold, "Time Series: Cycles," in *International Encyclopedia of the Social Sciences*, vol. 16, pp. 70–79.

cate the underlying mechanisms and the causal connections? Does a correlation between the business cycle and fluctuations in the birth rate, for example, mean that changes in the birth rate are due to the business cycle? Obviously not. The bugaboo of potentially confounding factors [47] still lurks in the wings, to be dispelled only to the extent that features of the experimental design can be approximated.

One useful substitute for experimental control of selected extraneous factors is *standardization* in trend analyses. For example, if demographers want to describe a single trend, as in the proportions of the population who are married, they may want to control the age distribution, because age affects the marriage rate and the proportion of persons of marriageable age is also changing. The objective, then, is to examine changes in marriage when changes in age are held constant. To effect such control, the age composition of a "standard population" (which is fixed) is substituted for the actual age composition (which is changing); and the marriage rates are recomputed to show what they *would have been* if the actual population had the same age composition as the standard.[48] Standardization can be used, of course, to control several extraneous factors in order to facilitate analysis of the relationships between trends.

Various *quasi-experimental* designs can also aid the effort to grapple with confounding factors. Campbell,[49] who provides a superb assessment of such designs, isolates two or three that can be regarded as usable for "moving from description of change to inferring causes of change." In the "interrupted time-series design," periodic measurements are made on some group and an experimental change is introduced into this time series of measurements; the findings, if they show discontinuities in this series, can suggest that the experimental change had some effect on the time series. A second design, which adds the improvement of a "control group" that is not subjected to the experimental change, is often useful in eliminating rival hypotheses. This improved design, though still inferior to the classical model in its

---

[47] Ogburn and Thomas point to the marriage rate, for example, as a potentially confounding factor in this instance.

[48] Cf. Amos H. Hawley, "Population Composition," in *The Study of Population,* ed. Philip M. Hauser and Otis Dudley Duncan (Chicago: University of Chicago Press, 1959), p. 376; Donald J. Bogue, *Principles of Demography* (New York: Wiley, 1969), pp. 121–123.

[49] Donald T. Campbell, "From Description to Experimentation: Interpreting Trends as Quasi-Experiments," in *Problems in Measuring Change,* ed. Chester W. Harris (Madison: The University of Wisconsin Press, 1963), pp. 212–242; see especially pp. 220–221 and 232–234. Campbell also commends (pp. 235–242) the "cross-lagged panel correlation," although the difficulties of this design have been spelled out by Otis Dudley Duncan, "Some Linear Models for Two-Wave, Two-Variable Panel Analysis," *Psychological Bulletin,* vol. 72 (1969), pp. 177–182.

failure to use random procedures, can be important where manipulating a sociological variable is restricted to only a single group or society.

As sociologists accumulate sequential information from trend studies, and as they accumulate causal hypotheses from the effort to interpret descriptive results in terms of theory, they will undoubtedly make wider and more imaginative use of *experimental designs* in the classical tradition of Fisher.[50] The experiment, as the optimal design for interpreting change in causal terms, requires not only (1) systematic manipulation of the experimental variable, but also (2) randomization in the assignment of the experimental factor (or treatment). Randomization is crucial because the researcher can never be sure that he has recognized and held constant *all* the extraneous factors that may be associated with the dependent variable, Y, or with the XY relationship.[51]

Numerous practical or ethical difficulties in meeting these two criteria have impeded any widespread use of experiments in studying social change, especially because hypotheses referring to the group must be tested on experimental and control samples comprised not of individuals, but of groups. Thus the sociologist must seek out experimental variables that are feasible to manipulate, such as mass communication to Boy Scout Troops, distributing contraceptive devices to villages, or administering health treatments to municipal districts. He must search for situations where it is possible to assign the experimental factor to certain groups, while withholding it from others, on the seemingly arbitrary random basis — as in introducing new products to markets, the racial integration of military units, or the variation of curricula or pedagogy in schools. Such illustrations suggest that a considerable potential for experimentation is available to the sociologist who is imaginative in finding ways to adapt various experimental and quasi-experimental designs to research on social systems. For, if diachronic studies (conducted at two or more time periods) are essential for establishing temporal sequences in the data, experimentation can add greatly to a fuller understanding of the mechanisms governing these sequences.

[50] R. A. Fisher, *The Design of Experiments* (Edinburgh: Oliver and Boyd, 1937), especially pp. 20–24. For a simple statement of experimental design as used in sociology, see Riley, *Sociological Research,* vol. 1, pp. 570–642. See also Donald T. Campbell, "Reforms as Experiments," *American Psychologist,* vol. 24 (1969), pp. 409–429, for the use of experimentation in programs of social reform.

[51] The "magic of randomization," as Campbell puts it, "renders implausible innumerable rival explanations of the observed change by cutting the lawful relationships which in the natural setting would determine which person gets which treatment," in "From Description to Experimentation," p. 213.

USE OF THE GROUP IN RESEARCH

Having considered the various ways in which research designs deal with the dimension of time, and the degree to which these are congruent with sociological theories of society, let us now turn to the other major dimension: treatment of the group as the research case (see Figure 1 above). The dynamism that underlies social processes is not unrelated to the sociological view of societies as systems of interrelated parts composed, at the simplest level, of individuals in roles vis-à-vis other group members.

So far we have confined discussion to studies where the group can properly be treated as a simple entity, with properties referring to the group as a whole. Often, however, sociological theories emphasize a more complex notion of the group as a system. Within this system the lower level parts — the individuals in varied roles, the differentiated sub-groups, the several strata — fit together to form the more inclusive, higher level society. It is the interaction of these parts with one another and with the environment that results in social stability or social change. Thus the concept of a single-level group may be sufficient for *describing* many social processes; but for *explaining* the operation of such processes — a task that requires identifying the mechanisms connecting key processual elements and tracing the responses to environmental pressures for change — one cannot leave out the interrelationships of the people who do the thinking, feeling, and acting within the group.

It may seem obvious that the actors must be incorporated into the social system, conceptually as well as empirically, if the ideas generated by any sociological theory are to permit empirical test. Yet, continual protestations over many years attest to the difficulties of implementing this principle. Thus in 1922 Weber contends that statistical uniformities "constitute 'sociological generalization' only when they can be regarded as manifestations of the understandable subjective meaning of a course of action." [52] Parsons and Shils [53] caution in 1951 against thinking that "the analysis of the processes of [social] maintenance or change can proceed at any stage without referring to components and mechanisms of personalities." Inkeles [54] calls in 1959 for a "psycho-sociology" that would explain the functioning and

[52] Max Weber, *The Theory of Social and Economic Organization,* trans. A. M. Henderson and Talcott Parsons (Glencoe, Ill.: The Free Press, 1957), p. 100.

[53] Parsons and Shils, "Values, Motives and Systems of Action," p. 224.

[54] Alex Inkeles, "Personality and Social Structure," in *Sociology Today,* ed. Robert K. Merton, Leonard Broom, and Leonard S. Cottrell, Jr. (New York: Basic Books, 1959), pp. 249–276.

change of social systems in terms not only of properties of the social system but also of the modal personalities of the participants. And ten years later Smelser [55] deplores the bifurcation between psychological and sociological approaches, quoting (from his own earlier work) an instructive description of an interactive model

> whereby various social-structural factors are seen as impinging on the psyche, which processes these factors, gives them new meaning, and modifies them. The social factors, thus redefined, excite new psychological tendencies, which in turn further condition the social factors.

The conceptual confusion over system levels and their interrelatedness presents problems to the researcher who attempts to treat the group empirically as a multilevel system with identifiable parts. Another difficulty arises because each level has its characteristic properties for which empirical indicants must be found. At a lower level, data are required that reflect the properties of individual role players: their characteristics, motivations, and orientations as persons. At higher levels, data are required to index properties of subgroups or of total societies, such as integration or division of labor. Even more challenging are the methods of cross-level analysis that must be devised to relate these diverse properties, while avoiding both the Scylla of reifying the group and the Charybdis of reducing the group to a contextual characteristic of the individual. For individuals, subgroups, strata, and society are all interdependent with one another in the same system, as each one changes or remains stable over time.

How, then, can the sociologist translate into research operations the conceptual model of a social system? How can he explore the cross-level interdependencies among system processes? A few selected designs will be mentioned in this section of our essay that can only hint at the emerging potential for a theoretically congruent approach. In each instance, the design will be expected to satisfy a special *criterion of congruence:* It must maintain a focus on the group as the inclusive system; but it must, at the same time, identify the parts of the system as they relate to each other and to the whole.

Synchronic System Designs

Some possibilities, as well as problems, of research approaches to social systems can be seen in synchronic studies that are conducted at a single point in time — cell *c* in Figure 1.

[55] Neil J. Smelser, "Some Personal Thoughts on the Pursuit of Sociological Problems," *Sociological Inquiry,* vol. 39 (1969), p. 165.

A cogent example is the study by Inkeles [56] of the effect of modernization on the individual in six developing countries that differ widely in the level of development. Inkeles, by using selected samples of young men in each country, can show that those men exposed to modernizing influences (such as education or factory experience) are more "modern" in their attitudes and values than are men with little or no such exposure. Most important for social (in contrast to individual) change, this finding tends to obtain *within* each country, regardless of the degree of modernization.[57] Thus it is not alone the macrostructural forces reflected in the development of the country, but also the new microstructures (schools, factories, mass media) that men have devised inside each country, that, as Inkeles suggests,[58] "may in turn shape the men who live within the new social order."

Individual as participant in change. The method of obtaining this profound insight into social change is doubly instructive. First, it illustrates an important device for studying change through the eyes of group members who are themselves participants in the process. This device is especially useful when the research focuses on a group at a moment of immediate crisis or of fundamental transformation.[59] Thus Thomas and Znaniecki [60] analyze the letters of Polish peasants to assess the impact on the immigrant family of societal changes at the end of the nineteenth century. Or Cantril [61] examines public opinion polls that reflect responses to the vicissitudes of World War Two by different types of individuals in various countries.

Structural analysis. Inkeles not only utilizes for a whole set of

[56] Alex Inkeles, "Making Men Modern: On the Causes and Consequences of Individual Change in Six Developing Countries," *American Journal of Sociology,* vol. 75 (1969), pp. 208–225.

[57] Although no measure of the modernization of the country is reported in this article, such a measure could be developed from available statistics on per capita energy consumption, for example, or on proportion of the labor force in agriculture.

[58] Inkeles, "Making Men Modern," pp. 224–225. As in all synchronic studies, these data alone cannot demonstrate temporal sequence or causality. Indeed, Max Weber might have argued that a change in attitudes and values precedes the psychological readiness to accept modernizing influences. See *The Protestant Ethic and The Spirit of Capitalism,* trans. Talcott Parsons (New York: Scribner's, 1952), pp. 35–39.

[59] Such strategic timing of the research is, of course, generally useful for studies of social stability and change, whether the research case is the social system, the group, or the individual. See, for example, Bernard Barber, *Social Stratification* (New York: Harcourt, Brace, and World, 1957), pp. 488 ff.

[60] William I. Thomas and Florian Znaniecki, *The Polish Peasant in Europe and America* (Chicago: University of Chicago Press, 1918), vol. 1.

[61] Hadley Cantril, *Public Opinion, 1935–1946* (Princeton, N.J.: Princeton University Press, 1951).

groups this familiar device of observing change through the eyes of participants. He also improves upon this technique by *identifying* within each group those members who are participating directly in the change, and then comparing these participants with the nonparticipants. This improved strategy directs attention to the mechanisms of change. It begins to specify some connecting processes between modernizing the country and modernizing the individual.

This strategy can be reformulated as an instance of the design developed by Riley and her associates and called structural analysis.[62] In its synchronic version, a structural analysis focuses on the group, but (in contrast to the single-level group analysis) makes reference to the differentiated roles that interrelate to form the group's internal structure — thereby meeting the criterion of congruence with a social system model. The data for a structural analysis (illustrated here for the two levels of group and individual) can be diagrammed schematically as in Figure 2, which utilizes concepts from the Inkeles study. The (fictitious) data are first arranged as follows to refer to the appropriate levels of the social system:

1. The countries (large squares in Figure 2) are arrayed by degree of modernization (a group property, Xg).

2. Each country is subdivided into segments [63] by exposure to modernizing influences (a segmental property, Xs, in the sense that each group segment is composed of individuals who are similar in this respect).

3. The proportion of individuals who are modern (Y) [64] is obtained for each segment separately — as indicated by the circles in Figure 2.

These data are then used to carry out the two different aspects of structural analysis: within-group analysis, for exploring relationships between Xs and Y when Xg is controlled; and segmental comparison,

[62] For a more complete treatment of structural analysis as a modification of a full social system analysis, and the related fallacies, see Matilda White Riley, *Sociological Research*, vol. 1, pp. 700–738; Riley, "Sources and Types of Sociological Data," in *Handbook of Modern Sociology*, ed. Robert E. L. Faris (Chicago: Rand McNally, 1964), pp. 1014–1022; Allardt, "Aggregate Analysis: The Problem of Its Informative Value," pp. 41–51. Notice that Peter Blau, in "Structural Effect," *American Sociological Review*, vol. 25 (1960), pp. 178–193, uses the term "structural effects," in quite a different sense in relation to contextual, rather than structural, analysis.

[63] Note that this step, which constitutes a *segmentation* of each case (the group), is not to be confused with the stratification of an aggregate of cases as widely used in survey analysis. Cf. Lazarsfeld, "Survey Analysis: The Analysis of Attribute Data," pp. 425–428.

[64] Depending on the interpretation, Y refers either to the individual or (as a rate) to the segment composed of similar individuals.

FIGURE 2

Schematic Illustration of Fictitious Data[a]

for a Structural Analysis (of selected countries)

Degree of modernization of the country (Xg)

Most modernized country								Least modernized country	

	E	NE		E	NE			E	NE
M	90	(60)	M	85	(55)		M	30	(15)
NM	10	40	NM	15	45	· · · ·	NM	70	85
	100	100		100	100			100	100

Classifications within each country:

E = exposed to modernizing influences; NE = not exposed;
M = modern men; NM = not modern men.

[a] Adapted from Inkeles, 1969.

for exploring relationships between Xg and Y when Xs is controlled.[65]

Within-group analysis is accomplished by comparing the two circled figures for each group separately. If the exposed segment (the shaded circle in Figure 2) invariably contains a higher proportion of modern men than the unexposed segment, this finding provides consistent support for the hypothesis that modernizing institutions are connected with individual modernization — regardless of the cultural and economic level of the country. Alternatively, if this pattern obtains in some countries but not in others, such a result could lead the researcher to seek additional variables that might explain such differential success of modernizing institutions in the two types of countries. This important feature of within-group analysis is illustrated by the Inkeles finding that one country, Israel, differs from the others: only here are the new workers "as well informed as the experienced." [66] As a possible explanation, Inkeles mentions the potential for rapid diffusion of information in Israel; it is easy to imagine an extensive analysis of many countries where (as in Figure 2) the capacity for rapid infor-

[65] See Riley, *Sociological Research*, vol. 2, pp. 145–146.
[66] Inkeles, "Making Men Modern," p. 214n.

mation diffusion might be introduced as an explanatory group-level variable.

It is noteworthy that such within-group analysis is precisely the method invented by Durkheim for examining suicide rates by religious segments "in the heart of a single society." [67] Durkheim found much the same patterns in all the groups. But here again, had he found some countries in which the Protestant rates were *not* higher than the Catholic rates, the within-group analysis would have enabled him to look for additional factors that might explain the difference.

The second aspect of structural analysis, *segmental comparison,* can be illustrated for the Inkeles study by rearranging the same ficti- tious data so as to compare similar segments across the several coun- tries.[68] Comparison of unexposed segments (the unshaded circles in Figure 2), for example, can show whether or not the proportions of modern individuals rise concomitantly with the degree of moderniza- tion of the country — even when all individuals are alike in having less exposure to modernizing institutions than other members of their societies.

These two forms of structural analysis combined may yield various possible outcomes that help the researcher to disentangle the joint effects of two independent variables that refer, on the one hand, to the group, and, on the other hand, to the component individuals — or, more properly, to similar individuals as they form segments of the group.

Reification or reductionism.[69]   Inappropriate treatment of the group in a research design can often cause inadequate or erroneous interpre- tation, just as inappropriate use of time can sometimes suggest er- roneous inferences about temporal sequence. Two rather common fallacies are reification of the group and contextual reductionism. Reifi- cation is defined here as an inappropriate use of a group analysis that treats the group as a single-level entity even though the conceptual model refers to the internal arrangement of parts within a system. Thus reification is failure to meet the special criterion of congruence with the social system model. And "contextual reductionism" is a term we have devised for an inappropriate use of individual analysis, which treats group properties as mere background characteristics of the indi- vidual even though the conceptual model refers to the group. Both

[67] Durkheim, *Suicide,* pp. 152–154, especially Table 18.

[68] A personal communication from Inkeles indicates that this step is not yet possible with the present measures, which are not constructed to be comparable across countries, but were dichotomized at the median for each country separately.

[69] We refer to these more generally elsewhere as "sociologistic" and "atomistic" fallacies respectively. For a fuller discussion, see Riley, *Sociological Research,* vol. 1, unit 12; Riley, "Sources and Types of Sociological Data," pp. 1014–1022.

these fallacies can be illustrated as failures to utilize a structural analysis in situations where this design seems congruent with the theory that the researcher wants to test.

The nature of *reification* [70] is suggested by the data in Figure 2, if one imagines that the researcher, though theoretically interested in the societal *processes* whereby men become modern, had examined the relationship between just two variables: the degree of modernization of the country (Xg); and the overall proportion of men in each country who are modern (a collective property of the group, Yg, obtained from the marginals in Figure 2). This procedure, by reverting to the single-level group analysis, entirely omits the segmental factor, exposure to modernizing influences. By failing to identify *which* individuals in the group are subjected to the new educational or occupational influences, the group analysis does not translate into operations the researcher's theoretical concern with such intrasocietal influences. Hence it obscures entirely those intervening mechanisms that turn out to be crucial in the Inkeles study. [71]

Contextual reductionism occurs when the researcher states theories about the group but mistakenly organizes his group information around the individual as the research case. [72] For example, a contextual analysis that would be appropriate for the study, not of groups, but of individuals [73] could be performed from the data in Figure 2. One would first classify all individuals as inhabitants of either modernized or underdeveloped countries, and then examine separately for each class of individuals the relationship between exposure to modernizing institutions and becoming a modern man. By this procedure, modernization of the country, which was used in the structural analysis as an overall characteristic of the group, is now attributed to the individual as a "contextual characteristic"; individuals from many similar groups are

[70] See also the Second Section of this paper.

[71] Reification can consist also of arbitrarily attributing to the group as a whole a process in which only *segments* of the group are actually participating or being affected. Thus in any situation where a structural analysis would have shown that the group factor Xg is no longer related to the dependent variable once the segmental factor is controlled, use of the simplified group analysis might nevertheless suggest an interpretation in terms of the extraneous group factor.

[72] The researcher's use of either the group, the group segment, or the individual as the research case is ordinarily apparent from his operation, because he must make an explicit decision as to *what* units he is sampling, tabulating, using as the base for his percentages, and the like.

[73] See Blau, "Structural Effect," pp. 178–193; James A. Davis, Joe L. Spaeth, and Carolyn Huson, "Analyzing Effects of Group Composition," *American Sociological Review,* vol. 26 (1961), pp. 215–225; and David L. Sills, "Three 'Climate of Opinion' Studies," *Public Opinion Quarterly,* vol. 25 (1961), pp. 571–573.

aggregated; and the focus of analysis shifts from group to individual.

What are the pitfalls in using such a contextual analysis to examine theories about social systems rather than about individuals? There are at least two sources of possible error or misinterpretation. First, the contextual analysis cannot reveal the differing group patterns observable from the full array of distinct groups (as in the structural analysis in Figure 2). It cannot show differences among countries in the success of their modernizing institutions, for example, nor relate differences in success to the degree of modernization of the country as a whole. Hence, contextual analysis cannot lead the researcher directly to group-level interpretations, or to the search for additional variables that might explain differences among groups. Second, a contextual analysis can sometimes yield empirical results quite different from the results of a structural analysis of the same data. Even when a structural analysis would show a particular pattern for the majority of groups, the existence of a few atypical groups — if sufficiently large — could produce in the aggregated contextual analysis exactly the reverse of this particular pattern.[74] Here the contextual analyst, if he were to interpret such findings as referring to groups, would be entirely wrong.

Contextual reductionism comes most naturally to the researcher accustomed to survey analysis, who often clings to the familiar strategies for studying individuals even when he turns his attention to *groups* as composed of individuals. Thus, when he should collect his information on individuals to measure the group properties in which he is interested, he may inadvertently use group information to measure contextual properties of individuals aggregated from many different groups. In one example, the theory refers to small study groups, postulating a relationship between their role structure and their ability to survive.[75] In another example, the theory refers to local unions, postulating a relationship between the size of a local and its tendency to vote against the incumbent candidate as president of the international organization.[76] Ideally, for each of these theories a congruent design would use the study groups or the union locals as the research case, treating the drop-out rate or the direction of the majority vote as group-level characteristics. Only such a design could show, for example, whether certain study groups survive despite the failure to meet functional requirements of the system; or whether certain locals vote in contrary fashion to others of their size. Only such a design could indicate how

[74] See Riley, *Sociological Research*, vol. 1, pp. 720–723.

[75] James A. Davis, *Great Books and Small Groups* (Glencoe, Ill.: The Free Press, 1961), pp. 575–583.

[76] Seymour Martin Lipset, Martin Trow, and James Coleman, *Union Democracy* (Garden City, N.Y.: Doubleday-Anchor, 1962), pp. 410–422.

many of the groups fit the researcher's conceptual model, or could facilitate an examination of those groups that deviate from this model. Actually, however, in both instances, the analysis is not based on groups at all, but on individuals aggregated from various groups. Both analyses are directed to answering questions, not about social systems, but about the *individual's* staying power as a study group member [77] or about the *individual's* voting behavior.[78] In neither study, then, is the research design congruent with the theory. The sociologist, although aiming to study the group, erroneously chose the individual as his research case.

Thus, if reification fails to maintain the identity of the component individuals, contextual reductionism fails to maintain the identity of the groups. Either fallacy can bring the research findings into question, or can force the interpretation into theoretically untenable positions.

Diachronic System Designs

Studies conducted over time — cell d in Figure 1 — encounter many of the same problems as synchronic approaches in treating groups as systems. Yet sociologists have succeeded in various ways in tracing the dynamic processes of differentiated parts of a system, as these parts interact with one another and with the environment to produce stability and change. Thus Sorokin accounts for the long-term societal trend in prosperity by plotting the component trends for each of the main classes in the society (the clergy, the nobility, and so on). [79] Or Coleman, Katz, and Menzel account for short-term trends in the diffusion of a new drug through a medical community by measuring the "simultaneity" of adoption among sociometric pairs of doctors.[80] We shall first discuss examples that relate closely to the structural analysis we have been considering, and then turn to more extensive designs that either reach back into the past or that comprise entire societies.

[77] For a discussion of this example, see Riley, *Sociological Research*, vol. 1, pp. 718–724.

[78] Lipset, Trow, and Coleman, *Union Democracy*. Despite the group-level statement of findings (pp. 421–422), Table 38 is based, as the note on p. 423 states, not on the local as the research case to which the theory refers, but on individuals aggregated from all the locals of a given size. Note also that, despite the opportunity for diachronic analysis, the data are treated synchronically — another instance, perhaps, of the entrenchment of cross-section survey methods.

[79] Sorokin, *Social and Cultural Dynamics*, vol. 3, pp. 230–236. See also Matilda White Riley and Mary E. Moore, "Sorokin's Use of Sociological Measurement," in *Pitirim A. Sorokin in Review*, ed. Philip J. Allen (Durham, N.C.: Duke University Press, 1963), p. 218.

[80] James S. Coleman, Elihu Katz, and Herbert Menzel, "The Diffusion of an Innovation Among Physicians," *Sociometry*, vol. 20 (1957), pp. 253–269.

Structural sequences. A diachronic strategy similar to synchronic structural analysis illustrates certain principles of studying change in social systems. By comparing two or more cross-section views of the same sample of groups, the structural sequence design not only shows group-level changes; it also relates these changes to shifts in the internal structure of each group. Thus the design meets the criterion of conceptual congruence by identifying the parts of each group in terms of the properties under study, and by tracing the changes in these parts from one period to the next.

The building block in such analysis of structural sequences is the powerful *panel* design [81] developed by Lazarsfeld and his collaborators for studying individuals. Panel analysis is a widely used and highly refined [82] extension of survey analysis that examines the same sample of individuals at two or more time periods to see which ones have changed and in what direction (that is, the "turnover" of individuals can be analyzed). Not only can the researcher observe in the data the frequencies with which certain patterns of change occur, but he can also, with the aid of a mathematical model,[83] make predictions based on the specific rules assumed to govern such individual change.

This panel design is well adapted for diachronic analysis of *single* social systems.[84] By changing the research case from the individual to the group, and selecting a sample of individuals from the group, the full power of the design can be adapted to the study of internal shifts within the social structure.

[81] See, for example, Bernard Levenson, "Panel Studies," in *International Encyclopedia of the Social Sciences*, vol. 11, pp. 371–379.

[82] For example, in a panel analysis where two variables are used at both time periods, Lazarsfeld suggests a method for assessing the relative "strength" of one variable on the other; see Paul F. Lazarsfeld and Robert K. Merton, "Friendship as Social Process: A Substantive and Methodological Analysis," in *Freedom and Control in Modern Society*, ed. Morroe Berger, Theodore Abel, and Charles H. Page (New York: Van Nostrand, 1954), pp. 45–46.

[83] For applications to panel analysis of stochastic models, which define the transition probabilities of moving from one to another set of specified states, see T. W. Anderson, "Probability Models for Analyzing Time Changes in Attitudes," in *Mathematical Thinking in the Social Sciences*, ed. Paul F. Lazarsfeld (Glencoe, Ill.: The Free Press, 1954); Leo A. Goodman, "Statistical Methods for Analyzing Process of Change," *American Journal of Sociology*, vol. 68 (1962), pp. 57–87; or the more recent work by James S. Coleman. For example, Coleman's "The Mathematical Study of Change," in *Methodology in Social Research*, ed. Hubert M. Blalock, Jr., and Ann B. Blalock (New York: McGraw-Hill, 1968), pp. 428–478, describes models for different configurations of change, using such dimensions as continuous versus discrete time, and continuous variables versus attribute data.

[84] Even for study of a single group, like most designs, the panel has limitations. Using a *fixed* sample of individuals, though reflective of individual shifts *within* the group, may not reflect the relevant group-level changes where there is movement of individuals in or out of the population.

TABLE 1
Number of Individuals in Each of Two Communities
Voting Republican (R) or Democrat (D)

	Community M				Community N		
	Time 1				Time 1		
Time 2	D	R	Total	Time 2	D	R	Total
D	300	300	600	D	500	100	600
R	200	200	400	R	0	400	400
Total	500	500		Total	500	500	

Thus in a simplified example, two communities as in Table 1 show identical group-level changes in voting behavior between Time 1 and Time 2 (a net increase of one hundred Democrats); but the separate panel analysis of each community distinguishes two clearly different internal patterns of individual shifting. In Community N, all individuals either remain the same or switch to a Democratic position. But in Community M, there is considerable internal realignment, although the large number switching from Republican to Democrat is nearly counterbalanced by sizeable shifts in the opposite direction. These differences in individual-level patterns signal very different processes of change for the two communities.

The extension of this two-group example to a sample of groups, which might take a form parallel to Figure 2, suggests various analytic possibilities. Thus additional group-level factors (such as degree of industrialization or rate of social mobility) might be introduced to explain differences among communities in their patterns of internal party shifting. Or the panel data on individuals can be used for within-group analysis, while segmental comparisons can be made across groups, to answer such specific questions about the disposition to change parties as: Within communities, is either the initially Republican or the initially Democratic segment any more likely to change? When communities are compared, and party alignment is controlled, is there an association between degree of industrialization and disposition to change? Or a full social system analysis might be developed for examining the interrelationships among group-level and individual-level changes.[85]

Reification again. The dangers of either reification or reductionism,

[85] A design for such a social system analysis has been worked out for very small (two-person) groups in Riley, *Sociological Research*, vol. 1, pp. 728–732. See also the scheme for panel analysis of marital dyads developed by Levenson, "Panel Studies," p. 377. In practice, however, such designs have rarely been utilized.

TABLE 2

Number of Communities Which Were Predominantly
Democratic (D+) or not Democratic (D-)

Time 2	Time 1		
	D+	D-	Total
D+	45	20	65
D-	5	30	35
Total	50	50	100

however, are the same in the diachronic as in the synchronic analyses previously discussed. Table 2 continues the voting example to highlight the dangers of superimposing upon groups the conventional procedures for panel analysis of individuals, while ignoring entirely the potential relevance of system levels within each group. In Table 2, each of a sample of communities, as in Table 1, has been classified as predominantly Democratic or not (by the proportion of its inhabitants who voted the Democratic ticket). For group analysis — cell b in Figure 1 — this procedure can be highly fruitful. Table 2 shows (in the marginals) the even division of communities at Time 1 and the net shift toward a preponderance of predominantly Democratic communities by Time 2. In addition, it shows (in the cells) the pattern of this group shifting. However, Table 2 uses only the group-level information from the marginals of Table 1.[86] It thus conceals entirely the information on internal shifts within each community, as originally shown in the cells of Table 1. Yet these internal shifts may be crucial for understanding changes in the communities as systems. For example, Communities M and N, which were shown in Table 1 to have very different internal change processes, would be classified in the same cell in Table 2. Needless to say, the sociologist whose model specifies such intracommunity role processes would have difficulty in making correct interpretations from Table 2, in which the roles played by individuals are obscured.

Although this example is entirely fictitious, such dangers of dubious analysis or misleading interpretation may be quite real. Despite explicit warnings over a decade ago against applying the scheme for individual panel analysis directly to social system models,[87] experts on

[86] This marginal information is characteristic of the material used for many trend analyses based on groups, as discussed in the first section of this paper.

[87] Matilda White Riley and Mary E. Moore, "Analysis of Two-Person Groups: Some Notes on Lazarsfeld's Formalization," paper delivered at the annual meetings of the American Sociological Association; Riley, *Sociological Research*, vol. 1, pp. 728–729, and vol. 2, pp. 134–137.

panel analysis today still claim — entirely disregarding the internal shifts often involved in system change — that "the determinants of organizational change could be analyzed by the same methods that are used in analyzing panels of individuals." [88] Once again the refinements developed for research on individuals require careful scrutiny and many modifications if their benefits are to be transmitted to sociological research on social systems.

Historical analysis. In addition to structural sequences, which focus on changes in the state of contemporary structures, groups can be analyzed as dynamic systems even in the preindustrial past.

As one example, Smelser [89] demonstrates the feasibility of historical social system analysis for testing a conceptual model of the increasing *structural differentiation* that results from rapid social change. He applies this model (which might also be tested in a whole range of situations) to changes in the working class family that occurred in Great Britain during the Industrial Revolution, examining the process by which economic aspects became differentiated from the other facets of family life. In line with his model, but contrary to accepted belief, he shows how the initial crises of urbanization and industrialization wrought little change in the traditional relationships within the working class family. He explains this unexpected finding by the fact that, despite the long hours of work and the exploitation of child labor in the early decades of the Revolution, the whole family could continue to work together as a unit either in the factory or in the domestic putting-out system. It was not until economic and legal developments threatened to split parents from their children, so that the two could no longer work side by side, that the furious strikes and protests began that were prologue to the ultimate separation of home and factory.

The elements in Smelser's analysis are noteworthy. He seeks out data (on factory legislation, union regulations, economic organization, agitation to limit hours, and so on) that enable him to trace the interdependent changes in two distinct parts of the society: the industrial sector and the families of workers employed in industry. Meeting our criterion of congruence with a social system model, he maintains the identity of each of these parts throughout the historical account. He is not content, for example, to plot the trends in labor disturbances for the whole society; he must, rather, distinguish between those workers who were caught up in the factory and those who remained in domestic industry, showing how disturbances arose as the family relation-

[88] Allen H. Barton, "Organizations: Methods of Research," in *International Encyclopedia of the Social Sciences*, vol. 11, pp. 341.
[89] Smelser, *Essays in Sociological Explanation*, pp. 76–91.

ships of each were threatened in different ways at different stages of the development of industry.[90]

A potentially fruitful approach to historical research on social systems is the analysis by demographers and sociologists of *family histories,* either reconstituted by the social scientist from parish records of births, marriages, and deaths, or taken directly from genealogical studies. In several European countries,[91] for example, longitudinal records of the families in entire villages have been reconstructed as far back as the seventeenth or even the sixteenth centuries. These records can supply information, as in an analysis by Knodel,[92] on changes in age at marriage, frequency of remarriage, bridal pregnancy, illegitimacy, family size, birth intervals, or infant mortality. Where the records include occupation, this information can be used to study intergenerational mobility and changing occupational structure of the community.[93] Moreover, the family data can be coupled with reports of historical events in the society, such as wars or famines. Of special relevance for studying social systems, the genealogical data are "nominative," referring to each family member by name and tracing the linkages within the kinship networks. Thus the approach avoids the restrictions of census data or vital statistics in their usual aggregative form, and gives fresh impetus to research that, as Revelle [94] puts it, allows "longitudinal studies of the ties between successive generations . . . to take the place of cross-sectional studies."

Cohort analysis. At the level of the large-scale modern society, cohort analysis holds great promise by tracing a succession of cohorts over their life course.[95] When a cohort is defined as the aggregate of indi-

[90] A similar systemic focus is maintained in a study of several revolutions by James C. Davies, "Toward a Theory of Revolution," *American Sociological Review,* vol. 27 (1962), pp. 5–19. Davies arranges his data to refer specifically to those segments within the society whose rising expectations may be frustrated or to those segments who may act as initiators of the disturbance.

[91] E. A. Wrigley, "Morality in Pre-Industrial England: The Example of Colyton, Devon, Over Three Centuries," *Daedalus* (Spring 1968), pp. 547–548; Goode, "The Theory and Measurement of Family Change," p. 331.

[92] John Knodel, "Two and a Half Centuries of Demographic History in a Bavarian Village," *Population Studies,* vol. 24 (1970), pp. 353–376.

[93] For example, a study by Heinz Wülker, *Bevölkerungsbiologie Niedersächsischer Dörfer* (Leipzig: Hirzel, 1940), traces the occupational history of the sons of farmers (and the social class of their wives) as they migrate to the city.

[94] Roger Revelle, "Introduction to the Issue 'Historical Population Studies,'" *Daedalus* (Spring 1968), p. 361.

[95] For an extended treatment, see Riley, Johnson, and Foner, *A Sociology of Age Stratification,* vol. 3 of *Aging and Society,* especially chaps. 2 and 8. See also, for example, Norman B. Ryder, "Cohort Analysis," in *International Encyclopedia of the Social Sciences,* vol. 2, pp. 546–550; Mervyn Susser, "Aging and the Field

FIGURE 3

Process of Cohort Formation and Aging
Showing Selected Cohorts over Time

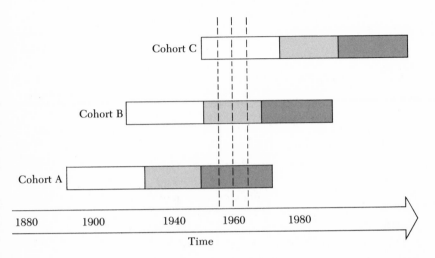

Stages in life course

| Early years | Middle years | Later years |

viduals within a society who were born at the same time and who age together,[96] then the changing society can be viewed as comprising the overall succession of cohorts.

Figure 3 represents schematically the life spans of three selected cohorts, for which particular processes might be described and compared in any given analysis. Three features of the method can be visualized. First, it can trace the life-course patterns of individuals *within* each cohort, as they undergo the processes of aging within the system.

---

of Public Health," in Matilda White Riley, John W. Riley, Jr., and Marilyn E. Johnson, eds., *Aging and Society*, vol. 2, *Aging and the Professions* (New York: Russell Sage Foundation, 1969), pp. 137–146.

[96] Not only total societies, but any social system that persists through the continual replenishment of personnel, can be effectively analyzed as a succession of cohorts. Thus the cohort can be defined as an aggregate of individuals who share, not a common date of birth, but a common date of entry into the particular system (such as a college class, or persons admitted to a mental hospital in a given year); and the notion of "aging" can refer to duration of exposure to the system.

TABLE 3

Characteristics of Successive Cohorts: Fictitious figures show
proportions of persons in each stratum having a given characteristic
(age in parentheses)

Date of birth	Period of observation					
	1900	1920	1940	1960	1980	2000
1940				(20) 50	(40) 50	(60) 50
1920			(20) 40	(40) 40	(60) 40	
1900		(20) 30	(40) 30	(60) 30		
1880	(20) 20	(40) 20	(60) 20			

Second, it can compare the differences *among* cohorts in these life-course patterns. Because each cohort lives at a unique period of history, the progress of individuals over their lifetime varies for different cohorts of individuals, as they encounter the particular role sequences and the particular environmental events and conditions of the differing era in which they live. And third, the method can show how the consecutive cohorts, each one lagging behind its predecessor in the process of aging, all *fit together* to form the changing structure of the society.

These three features can be illustrated from Table 3 which, corresponding in form to Figure 3, presents fictitious data for a cohort analysis. *First,* the patterns (of income, for example, or of life satisfaction) that are associated with movement through the life course are observed in Table 3 by reading across each row.[97] In these fictitious data, there are no changes across the rows. *Second,* by comparing several rows, one can also observe the similarities and differences in the ways the various cohorts think or behave over their respective lifetimes. (Because each cohort starts at a different date, differences among rows are observed by reading along the diagonals from lower to upper right, to compare cohorts when they are at similar ages.) The data for particular cohorts can differ from one another in a great variety of ways: in the shape of their life-course patterns, for example, or in the rates at which they change with aging. In this simplified example, the age patterns for the several cohorts have clearly apparent differences and similarities (in respect to the proportion with a given amount of education, for example). They *differ* in general level: at the starting age (which happens to be 20), each more recent cohort is increasingly likely to have the characteristic in question. But beyond the starting age, the life-course patterns of all cohorts are *alike* in their stability. *Third,* the composite of cohorts at any given period of time

[97] These are net figures for each cohort, not tracing the shifts made by particular individuals unless each cohort is subjected to a special panel analysis.

forms the cross-section data within each column: [98] thus the differences among age segments at each period (in labor force participation, for example, or in political attitudes) can be observed by reading down each column, and structural change can be examined by comparing the columns age-for-age for the several time periods.[99]

In practice, a number of studies have demonstrated that cohort analysis can yield distinctive results that specify the involvement of actors in the dynamics of social systems. In one such study, Taeuber,[100] by using lifetime residence histories to reconstruct the migration patterns of successive cohorts, succeeds in determining whether individuals as they age have followed the societal trend of population away from the farm and toward the city. This analysis discovers that the cohorts of people now old have, indeed, tended to follow the overall pattern; whereas recent cohorts are more likely to move *away* from larger cities to suburbs.[101]

Quite clearly, then, this approach meets the criterion of relevance for a social system design: it identifies the cohorts [102] as parts of the society and follows them through the analysis. Each cohort constitutes a segment of the population that links the microlevel processes affecting individual members to the macrolevel processes affecting the society. Beyond this, the peculiar virtue of cohort analysis for research on social dynamics is its translation into operations of the crucial differences between societal timing and individual (or cohort) timing. The

[98] These columns have been staggered to facilitate the cohort analysis. Notice also the truncated form of the data (complete only for 1940 and 1960 in this example), which illustrates a characteristic difficulty of the method.

[99] This third feature of cohort analysis — the examination of age-specific social-structural change — is significant because it is analogous to many changes in the state of the system that interest the student of social process. Such examination (frequently called "period analysis" or "current analysis" to distinguish it from the tracing of particular cohorts) is reminiscent, for example, of the structural sequence designs (discussed in the second section of this paper), insofar as these designs focus on processes that are related to aging or to duration of membership within the system. But the cohort analysis (as in Table 3) surpasses the usual analysis of social-structural changes in its capacity to tie these changes directly to the underlying life-course processes.

[100] Karl E. Taeuber, "Cohort Population Redistribution and the Urban Hierarchy," *Milbank Memorial Fund Quarterly*, vol. 43 (1965), pp. 450–462.

[101] In another study, John Crittenden, by using samples of successive cohorts and controlling the impact of societal shifts in political response to particular elections, is able to demonstrate the individual's increasing identification with the Republican party as he ages. Crittenden, "Aging and Party Affiliation," *Public Opinion Quarterly*, vol. 26 (1962), pp. 648–657.

[102] The cohort can also be subdivided by sex, socioeconomic origins, or other factors that influence the way it ages or its relationship to other cohorts. In this fashion, cohort membership is added to the set of potentially explanatory segmental variables.

society as a system — with its culture and its structure of roles and collectivities — moves through historical time along its own path of stability and change.[103] For example, it may move through a sequence of states from 1955 to 1960 to 1965 (as suggested by the vertical lines in Figure 3). Meanwhile, the successive cohorts follow their special rhythm of aging over the life course from birth to death. Cohort analysis views these cohorts, not in the cross-section sequences that refer to the society, but along the paths of their respective lives and the respective portions of history in which their lives are inscribed. It enables the researcher to deal diachronically both with the overall system and with the constituent members.

Thus cohort analysis can add to understanding of the subtle interplay between societal stability and change and the progress of individuals through successive roles over their life course. For, as Ryder [104] points out, the sequence of cohorts is a major channel for transforming society. Not only do successive cohorts differ in their impact on society because of their size, composition, early socialization, and the singular period of history to which each is exposed; but in addition, intrinsic strains for both individual and society result from the difference between societal timing and individual timing. The society, itself undergoing process and change, must continually allocate and socialize new cohorts of individuals, just as aging individuals must continually adjust to societal demands to learn new roles and to relinquish old ones. Application and extension of cohort analysis may increase our capability for examining such strains, the equilibrating mechanisms, and the potentially innovative consequences.[105]

OUTLOOK FOR THE FUTURE

To the extent that sociologists are concerned with social systems, then, and with social dynamics leading either to stability or to change, great advances will be required in the type of diachronic system approach suggested in cell *d* in Figure 1. The examples reviewed in the second

[103] For a theoretical synthesis of the phasing of social change see Smelser, *Essays in Sociological Explanation*, pp. 260–280.

[104] Norman B. Ryder, "The Cohort as a Concept in the Study of Social Change," *American Sociological Review*, vol. 30 (1965), pp. 843–861.

[105] Compare the view of society as a tension-management system outlined by Wilbert E. Moore, *Social Change* (Englewood Cliffs, N.J.: Prentice-Hall, 1963), pp. 10–11. See also Robert K. Merton's analysis of the pressure toward change engendered by an excess of dysfunctional over functional consequences in *Social Theory and Social Structure*, rev. ed. (Glencoe, Ill.: The Free Press, 1957), pp. 40–41; and the discussion by Harry C. Bredemeier and Richard M. Stephenson of the special adaptive-integrative problems posed by the differing levels of the social system, in *The Analysis of Social Systems* (New York: Holt, Rinehart and Winston, 1962), pp. 51–58.

section on using the group in research indicate how designs of this type can approximate the required optimum of congruence with both the dynamic and the systemic aspects of the sociologist's conceptual model. Yet, although these examples demonstrate the feasibility and high potential of a diachronic system approach, each is limited in certain respects. Some work with only a single group, without confronting the difficulties of analyzing an entire sample of groups. Others are restricted to the present era or to a confined area (such as a community or a formal organization). Only the rare study deals with total societies, or reaches back into the prestatistical or the preliterate past. If the important strategies incipient in these studies are to become highly developed and to attain the requisite precision, greater heed must be paid to refining certain little-used methods of gathering new data, to formulating a methodology for use of existing data, and to bringing research more closely into line with theory.

Collecting New Data

Two highly useful methods that are little exploited for studying social systems are direct observation of interaction and questioning of individuals as members of groups. Despite the obvious theoretical congruence of the method of *observation*, few contemporary sociologists rely upon it.[106] Yet observation (structured or unstructured, with or without the participation of the researcher) can often deal successfully with the whole system in the round and with its dynamic processes, revealing action patterns and role structure changes that the actors themselves do not fully comprehend. Various clues to technical improvement and wider application of this method can be found, for example, in numerous insightful studies by participant observers,[107] in the interaction process analysis introduced by Bales,[108] or in the several "unobtrusive" procedures examined by Webb and his associates.[109]

Another sociologically relevant approach uses *questioning* for the study, not of individuals per se, but of the several individuals whose

106 Brown and Gilmartin, "Sociology Today: Lacunae, Emphases, and Surfeits," pp. 283–291.

107 For example, William Foote Whyte, *Street Corner Society*, 2nd ed. (Chicago: University of Chicago Press, 1955); A. W. Gouldner, *Patterns of Industrial Bureaucracy* (Glencoe, Ill.: The Free Press, 1954), and *Wildcat Strike* (Yellow Springs, Ohio: Antioch Press, 1954); Howard S. Becker et al., *Boys in White: Student Culture in Medical School* (Chicago: University of Chicago Press, 1961); Herbert J. Gans, *The Levittowners* (New York: Pantheon, 1967); Erving Goffman, *Asylums: Essays on the Social Situation of Mental Patients and Other Inmates* (Garden City, N.Y.: Doubleday-Anchor, 1961).

108 Bales, "Some Uniformities of Behavior in Small Social Systems."

109 Eugene J. Webb et al., *Unobtrusive Measures: Nonreactive Research in the Social Sciences* (Chicago: Rand McNally, 1966), chaps. 5 and 6.

roles fit together to form a social system. Questioning, which may include recollections or may be repeated over time, provides a complement to observation in understanding social process and change. It has the peculiar merit of reflecting directly the orientations and feelings of the actors about the group, for example, about their own roles in it, or about the interaction as they themselves observe it. When skillfully used as a sociological tool, questioning frequently reveals dormant aspects of the system and changing orientation patterns, which are not displayed as the observer watches and which may even be concealed from the other group members. Because questioning typically starts with the individual, however, inferences about social systems depend upon finding means of fitting together data about individuals into *collective data* — a challenging problem that has already been partially met in several social system designs discussed in the last section. Thus an avenue for studying the latent structure of orientations consists, first, of questioning many (or all) the group members individually, and, second, of combining these individual points of view (using a matrix, for example, a map, or a scheme for structural analysis) to refer to the larger system.[110]

Toward a Methodology of Secondary Analysis

No researcher can personally observe social change for a period longer than his own lifetime. And respondents to questioning can recollect only the recent past (Sorokin,[111] for example, was able to gather new data from a sample of families that covered the occupational changes over a span of four generations). If inquiry into social change is to transcend the capabilities of the investigator who goes into the field himself to observe interaction directly or question individuals at first hand, it must exploit the untapped resources of relevant data that already exist in one form or another.[112] And it must perfect new methods of secondary analysis for utilizing such data.

---

[110] For a discussion of this method, see Riley, *Sociological Research*, vol. 1, especially units 4 and 12. See also the research methods developed for analyzing formal organizations, as in the collection by James G. March, ed., *Handbook of Organizations* (Chicago: Rand McNally, 1965); or as summarized by Barton, in "Organizations: Methods of Research," pp. 334–343.

[111] Pitirim A. Sorokin, *Social and Cultural Mobility* (New York: The Free Press, 1959), pp. 419–424. Compare Riley and Moore, "Sorokin's Use of Sociological Measurement," p. 219.

[112] See the case for using available data set forth by John W. Riley, Jr., "Reflections on Data Sources in Opinion Research," *Public Opinion Quarterly*, vol. 26 (1962), pp. 313–322. See also Matilda White Riley, *Sociological Research*, vol. 1, unit 5. However, only a minority of current papers appear to utilize secondary sources — see Brown and Gilmartin, "Sociology Today: Lacunae, Emphases, and Surfeits," pp. 283–291.

The *diversity* of material that can be used for diachronic studies of social systems seems limited only by the ingenuity of the investigator. The sociological researcher can start with data (like family case records, tribal artifacts, or mass media communications) that were not originally produced for research purposes; or he can use for his own objectives research data initially compiled by another researcher (like ethnographic reports or interviews conducted by an outside polling agency). He can also choose between verbal and nonverbal data. Thus, on the one hand, Thomas and Znaniecki [113] use letters and diaries in their study of changes encountered by Polish peasants; Merton [114] analyzes the minutes of the Royal Society to link socioeconomic factors with scientific development in seventeenth-century England; or Erikson [115] utilizes court records of the Massachusetts Bay Colony, along with diverse historical documents, to investigate the association between societal change and the amount and type of socially recognized deviance. On the other hand, Barber [116] uses style and quality of clothing and other things people do or possess as symbolic indicators of social class position in several historical settings; and Webb and associates develop, among other novel "unobtrusive measures," an entire catalogue of nonverbal indicants.[117] Moreover, available data may be found at any of the several stages of research processing: from raw data, to partially processed data already coded and punched, to published statistics not yet fully analyzed or interpreted, to the findings from completed studies which may be reanalyzed or reinterpreted.[118]

[113] Thomas and Znaniecki, *The Polish Peasant in Europe and America.*

[114] Merton, *Social Theory and Social Structure*, pp. 607–627. Compare also Lawrence Stone's use of archives to reconstruct the British aristocracy in *The Crisis of the Aristocracy: 1558–1641* (Oxford: Clarendon Press, 1965); or Sir Francis Galton's use of archives to determine the eminence of persons defined as "geniuses" and the eminence of their relatives, in *Hereditary Genius* (New York: Appleton, 1870), cited by Webb et al., in *Unobtrusive Measures: Nonreactive Research in the Social Sciences*, p. 60.

[115] Kai T. Erikson, *Wayward Puritans: A Study in the Sociology of Deviance* (New York: Wiley, 1966).

[116] Barber, *Social Stratification*, pp. 146–151.

[117] Webb et al., *Unobtrusive Measures: Nonreactive Research in the Social Sciences*, especially chap. 2.

[118] As aids to such analysis, see: the series of *Studies in Comparative International Development*, edited by Irving Louis Horowitz (Beverly Hills: Sage Publications, 1965–); also the bibliography of survey research devoted to social change in various countries, compiled by Frederick W. Frey, *Survey Research on Comparative Social Change: A Bibliography* (Cambridge: The MIT Press, 1969). Examples of systematic reanalysis and reinterpretation are Bernard Berelson and Gary A. Steiner, *Human Behavior* (New York: Harcourt, Brace and World, 1964); Matilda White Riley, Anne Foner, and associates, *Aging and Society*, vol. 1, *An Inventory of Research Findings* (New York: Russell Sage Foundation, 1968).

Particularly valuable for diachronic analysis are the *accumulating stores* of data that have been continually produced in a consistent form over a period of time. Many international, national, and local agencies have long maintained records of vital statistics, labor force participation, voting behavior, and the like. Often these data are comparable for several societies, or for several subsections (such as small territorial units) within a society, permitting analysis based on samples of groups rather than on just a single group. In recent decades, too, cross-section surveys and opinion polls have often been repeated, using standard concepts and measurements, at successive time periods or in several countries. Plans for developing "social indicators," [119] to parallel the widely accepted economic indicators, involve amassing data on societal trends (reconstructed for the past and projected for the future) in education, the family, religion, welfare, and other sectors of social life.[120] Because the expanding volume of data raises problems of accessibility to scholars, data archives [121] have been established in many locations here and abroad that contain machine-readable information on various topics. These materials have been collected from their original sources, processed for general usability, documented, and prepared for distribution to users.[122]

Widespread exploitation of available materials by sociologists undertaking trend analyses, cohort analyses, and other types of diachronic studies should generate *new strategies* and new techniques for

[119] See Raymond A. Bauer, ed., *Social Indicators* (Cambridge: The MIT Press, 1966); American Academy of Political and Social Science, *The Annals*, vol. 371 (May 1967) and vol. 373 (September 1967), "Social Goals and Indicators for American Society," 2 vols.; Eleanor Bernert Sheldon and Wilbert E. Moore, eds., *Indicators of Social Change* (New York: Russell Sage Foundation, 1968); Otis Dudley Duncan, *Toward Social Reporting: Next Steps* (New York: Russell Sage Foundation, 1969).

[120] The proposed analysis meets the criteria of the diachronic system approach advocated in this essay, for it aims to trace the changing organization of society to accomplish social functions, and to show how the changing social desiderata and deprivations are redistributed to the different segments of the population.

[121] Compare David Nasatir, "Social Science Data Libraries," *The American Sociologist*, vol. 2 (1967), pp. 207–212.

[122] At this writing, archives are established, for example, at the National Opinion Research Center at the University of Chicago, the Roper Public Opinion Research Center at Williams College, and the Inter-University Consortium for Political Research centered in the University of Michigan's Institute for Social Research. Even the Human Relations Area File — originally established at Yale University to comprise reports, bibliographies, and texts on a large number of societies — now contains machine-readable information. Moreover, the United States Bureau of the Census has made many of its materials available for general use on cards and tapes.

improved understanding of social dynamics. Each type of available data has its peculiar problems, from the lack of comparability in the samples for sequential opinion polls [123] to the invalidities of trends in the crime rate as published by the Federal Bureau of Investigation.[124] And the value of each important new method undoubtedly lies (as Coleman once put it) in the "innovations that have not yet been made." [125]

A crucial asset to the developing strategies for secondary analysis is the *computer*, together with the "intellectual technology" that Bell describes as the accompaniment to the post-industrial society.[126] Computers, already essential for data processing and statistical analysis, can also be programmed to use sociological data and knowledge for *simulation* of social structures and processes. In simulation, as Coleman describes it:

> the program can be conceived of as a set of social and psychological processes, combined to constitute a system. The program acts through time; thus it can represent a sequence of behavior in a system. It consists of a very flexible set of logical as well as mathematical operations, so that processes difficult to put into mathematical form can nevertheless be simulated.[127]

Thus the computer can be used to perform a function related to that of the mathematical model — with the added advantage that many variables may be interrelated over extensive time periods. To utilize this potentially powerful tool, the sociologist must be able to state assumptions (for testing or further exploration) that include precise definitions (to which numerical values may be attached) of the several relevant variables and their interrelationships. Ideally, too, he must have access to empirical data against which he can later compare the output of the machine to see how closely his assumptions fit the real situation. Although there are comparatively few sociological topics on which these requirements for computer simulation can be approximated, the possibilities are illustrated by studies of changing attitudes

[123] Norval D. Glenn and Richard E. Zody, "Cohort Analysis with National Survey Data," *The Gerontologist*, vol. 10, no. 3, Part I (1970), pp. 233–240.

[124] Albert D. Biderman, "Social Indicators and Goals," in *Social Indicators*, ed. Raymond A. Bauer (Cambridge: The MIT Press, 1966), pp. 115–128.

[125] James S. Coleman, *Models of Change and Response Uncertainty* (Englewood Cliffs, N.J.: Prentice-Hall, 1964), p. 1047.

[126] Daniel Bell, "The Measurement of Knowledge and Technology," in *Indicators of Social Change*, ed. Eleanor Bernert Sheldon and Wilbert E. Moore (New York: Russell Sage Foundation, 1968), pp. 157–158.

[127] Coleman, *Models of Change and Response Uncertainty*, p. 1050.

during an election campaign,[128] for example, or of urban dynamics over a 250-year period into the future.[129] This urban project drama- tizes the use of simulation as a kind of "controlled experiment" to trace the consequences of alternative courses of action when various "interventions" (such as additional construction of low-rent housing) are introduced into the system.

In short, the future advance of dynamic research in sociology will require specification of theoretically relevant procedures for utilizing sociological knowledge that already exists. Studies of social change cannot always start from a tabula rasa. And the vast stores of pertinent data and the high-speed potential for manipulating them demand new levels of sophistication and inventiveness.

Convergence between "Theory" and "Methodology"

Finally, the full enhancement of a future methodology of dynamic social research is contingent upon breaking down the artificial barriers between theory and empiricism. Numerous guideposts toward social system designs point in this direction, as we have suggested in this essay. And yet, strong evidences remain of frequent failure to match research to conceptual models of central sociological concern. We have illustrated the kinds of fallacies engendered by such incompati- bilities — when synchronic designs are given inappropriate dynamic interpretations, or when analyses of the group as an entity (or even of the individual) are mistakenly interpreted to refer to the multilevel system.

Perhaps it is no accident that sociology has been for so long caught in the snare typified by the cross-section survey, with its emphasis on the static rather than the dynamic, and on the individual rather than the group. The investigator who — without a strong emphasis on theory — undertakes to study social systems can understandably be seduced by the elegance of survey designs. And indeed, many influential schol- ars have concentrated their primary efforts upon methodology as such, thereby creating an unnatural schism between empirical techniques and sociological theory — a schism that has been widely reinforced in the sociological curriculum. Yet the cleavage must be healed if we are to prevent erroneous interpretation, to minimize the prodigality of research that neither assays the validity of old ideas nor suggests new ones, to forestall untested and untestable theorizing, and to avoid the

[128] W. N. McPhee, *Formal Theories of Mass Behavior* (New York: The Free Press, 1963), chap. 4; James S. Coleman and F. Waldorf, "Study of a Voting System with Computer Techniques" (Baltimore: Johns Hopkins University, 1962, mimeo.).

[129] Jay W. Forrester, *Urban Dynamics* (Cambridge: The MIT Press, 1969).

sterile posturing and political wrangling of those "schools" of thought and ideological camps who pay little heed to the facts about social stability and change.[130]

Future research on dynamic social systems cannot be accomplished by the empiricist alone. It demands a merging between theory and method.[131] It can add to knowledge only as it utilizes logic, technical skill, and imagination in diachronic analyses that deal simultaneously with interdependent parts at several system levels. In this fashion theory and empiricism can be fruitfully combined to produce a better understanding of how social systems work, thus fulfilling the promise of sociology as the purveyor of knowledge about society.

[130] See, for example, the polemical articles reproduced in the reader on *Systems, Change, and Conflict,* ed. N. J. Demerath, III, and Richard A. Peterson (New York: The Free Press, 1967).

[131] Among the incipient moves to heal the breach, the present volume is one important contribution. Another is Smelser's effort toward a general theoretical framework for studying social change, which would combine logical analysis with a synthesis of several existing studies. At present, as Smelser says, it is still "doubtful that the scholarly research on historical change, which has been conducted under . . . a multiplicity of different frameworks, would yield clearly established propositions," *Essays in Sociological Explanation,* p. 261.

THE CONTRIBUTORS

Bernard Barber is Professor of Sociology, Barnard College and the Graduate Faculties, Columbia University.

Robert N. Bellah is Professor of Sociology, University of California, Berkeley.

Albert K. Cohen is Professor of Sociology, University of Connecticut.

Robert Dreeben is Professor of Education, University of Chicago.

S. N. Eisenstadt is Professor of Sociology, Hebrew University, Jerusalem.

Mark G. Field is Professor of Sociology, Boston University and Research Associate, Russian Research Center, Harvard University.

Clifford Geertz is Professor, Institute for Advanced Study, Princeton, New Jersey.

Alex Inkeles is Professor of Sociology and Education, Stanford University.

Harry M. Johnson is Professor of Sociology, University of Illinois.

Leon H. Mayhew is Professor of Sociology, University of California, Davis.

Edward E. Nelson is Professor of Sociology, Rutgers — The State University, New Brunswick, New Jersey.

Thomas F. O'Dea is Professor of Sociology, University of California, Santa Barbara.

Matilda White Riley is Professor of Sociology, Rutgers — The State University, New Brunswick, New Jersey.

Edward Shils is Professor of Sociology, University of Chicago and Fellow, King's College, Cambridge.

Neil J. Smelser is Professor of Sociology, University of California, Berkeley.

Robin M. Williams, Jr. is Professor of Sociology, Cornell University.